Developing e-Commerce Systems

Jim A. Carter

Department of Computer Science
University of Saskatchewan

Prentice
Hall

Upper Saddle River, New Jersey 07458

Library of Congress Cataloging-in-Publication Data

Carter, Jim A.
  Developing e-commerce systems / Jim A. Carter.
    p. cm.
  Includes bibliographical references and index.
  ISBN 0-13-091112-7
    1. Electronic commerce. I. Title.

HF5548.32.C3635 2002
658.8'4--dc21   2001035986

Vice President and Editorial Director, ECS: *Marcia J. Horton*
Senior Acquisitions Editor: *Petra J. Recter*
Editorial Assistant: *Karen Schultz*
Vice President and Director of Production and Manufacturing, ESM: *David W. Riccardi*
Executive Managing Editor: *Vince O'Brien*
Managing Editor: *David A. George*
Production Editor: *Lynn Steines*
Director of Creative Services: *Paul Belfanti*
Creative Director: *Carole Anson*
Art Director: *Jayne Conte*
Art Editor: *Adam Velthaus*
Manufacturing Manager: *Trudy Pisciotti*
Manufacturing Buyer: *Lynda Castillo*
Senior Marketing Manager: *Jennie Burger*

© 2002 by Prentice-Hall, Inc.
Pearson Education, Inc.
Upper Saddle River, New Jersey 07458

The author and publisher of this book have used their best efforts in preparing this
book. These efforts include the development, research, and testing of the theories to
determine their effectiveness. The author and publisher make no warranty of any kind,
expressed or implied, with regard to the documentation contained in this book.

10 9 8 7 6 5 4 3 2 1

ISBN 0-13-091112-7

Pearson Education Ltd., *London*
Pearson Education Australia PTY, Limited, *Sydney*
Pearson Education Singapore, Pte. Ltd.
Pearson Education North Asia Ltd., *Hong Kong*
Pearson Education Canada, Ltd., *Toronto*
Pearson Educacíon de Mexico, S.A. de C.V.
Pearson Education—Japan, *Tokyo*
Pearson Education Malaysia, Pte. Ltd.

To my family, Nancy, Mary, Elizabeth, and Peter.
May this book help make our world a little better place for us all.

Brief Contents

Contents

Preface

e-Commerce is the largest growth area of today's economy and is likely to remain so for many years to come. In just a few years it has grown to handle significant portions of both business-to-business (B2B) and business-to-consumer (B2C) transactions. Each year, and in fact each day, both its volume and percentage of all business transactions keeps increasing.

As the use of e-Commerce grows, so also grow the demands of those who use it. People and organizations can readily shop around the Web to find the products, prices, and services that suit them best. Any e-Commerce system must meet its users' needs better than its competition in order to survive. All e-Commerce systems need to be constantly evolving and improving in order to remain competitive.

Developing successful e-Commerce systems requires a unique set of computer and business development skills. This book provides the reader with a start at acquiring these skills by:

- Describing the context of e-Commerce systems development
- Discussing the major issues involved in e-Commerce development
- Explaining the processes required for successful e-Commerce development
- Describing how organizations can apply this development information
- Suggesting how students can apply selected development processes and techniques in a series of interrelated assignments

- Providing examples of applying these processes to an e-Commerce application
- Discussing challenges and opportunities that students and/or professionals have in developing real e-Commerce systems

This book is intended for a wide range of users, including both students and professionals, who are interested in developing e-Commerce systems. This text is intended for aspiring systems developers, business students, developers of traditional information systems, and organizational professionals.

However, it is impossible for a single text to be all things to all people. It is even impossible for one text to deal with all the important aspects of e-Commerce. This book focuses on those concepts that are at the core of developing effective e-Commerce systems, as illustrated in Figure p-1. It is intended as a starting point for the study of how effective e-Commerce systems are developed. It can be used early in either an academic program that is interested in e-Commerce systems development or early in the explorations of business or computing professionals who are interested in moving into e-Commerce. The development processes described in this book provide a foundation for both further investigation into particular issues and actual development of successful e-Commerce in the real world.

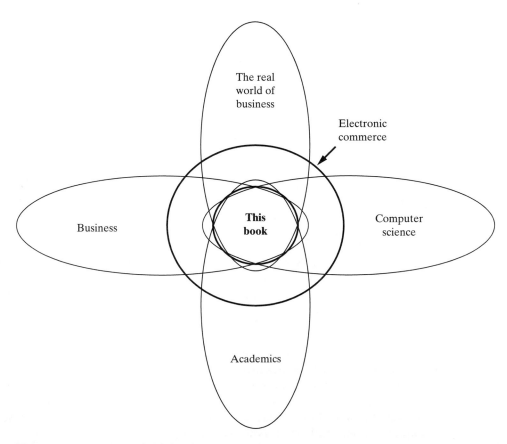

Figure p-1   The focus of this book

Successful e-Commerce uses a smooth combination of computing and commerce techniques to provide an inviting environment for users to conduct their business. This book identifies commerce-related issues and techniques within the framework of describing the computing processes required for the development of e-Commerce systems.

- It provides computer scientists with guidance in identifying and dealing with e-Commerce related issues within a set of software engineering processes.
- It also provides computer science students with an introduction to the set of software engineering processes identified by the Organization for International Standardization.
- It provides business professionals with an understanding of how software engineering processes are applied to developing e-Commerce systems and their role in this development.
- It also provides business students with an introduction to some of the unique issues that come from e-Commerce systems operating on the World Wide Web.

Successful e-Commerce goes beyond meeting the basic needs of their users. Developing such systems requires a high level of understanding and cooperation between developers and users who are involved in the development process. This book identifies the roles of various participants in development and the various issues that they must resolve together.

This text does not require any particular programming or other systems development skills as a prerequisite. Common sense, wide experience with the world, and a sense of adventure are the best possible prerequisites. However, because many people, including the author, are still developing these skills, this text will try to provide all the background that a typical person would need to be able to learn some valuable lessons about developing e-Commerce systems.

Issues described in this book can be used as a basis for discussion in classes, small groups, or even in organizations. Readers are encouraged to consider and discuss this material before trying to apply it. Because many of these topics are constantly evolving, readers are encouraged to check the associated Web site for supplementary information.

An overview of the contents and organization of the book is described in Section 1.5.

The Associated Web Site

Since e-Commerce is evolving daily, there are many aspects that need constant updating, including links to exemplary Web sites. This text focuses on an approach to developing e-Commerce systems that can be used for many years to come. Rather than including information that is subject to frequent change, the author has developed a Web site containing Cyber Supplements for each of the chapters in this book. This Web site includes:

- New information to supplement each chapter
- Comments on and links to numerous e-Commerce sites that illustrate the concepts being discussed
- Links to other Web sites with (and to other sources of) further information related to the concepts being discussed

A unique Web Reference Icon is located throughout the chapters to highlight topics that are covered by the Web site in order to provide the latest and most reliable information and links. Each chapter ends with a summary of what to look for in its Cyber Supplement.

Supplementary Materials

An instructor's CD is available. It contains:

- Strategies for using this text in various types of classes (for computer science or commerce) and over various time frames (10-, 13-, or 16-week classes)
- Lecture notes (in both PowerPoint and HTML format) that include:
  - Summaries of the key concepts
  - All of the illustrations from the text
  - Additional perspectives for considering the material
  - Information on the development of an additional example application within a class
  - Suggestions for invited guest presentations
- A test item file (containing both true/false and multiple-choice answers)

Acknowledgments

To be successful in e-Commerce requires bringing together a wide variety of skills from a number of disciplines. I have been fortunate to have been given examples of these skills by a number of people, starting with my parents. The acquisition is ongoing, being assisted by my various students and colleagues.

My mother, Stephania Carter, who was the first woman of Ukrainian descent to achieve a Bachelor of Commerce in North America, showed me that it is easier to understand and to learn something if you see how it is or could be applied in the real world.

My father, Allison Carter, who was a professional manager for as long as our lives overlapped, showed me the complex interrelationships between various aspects of a business. He also showed me that information systems should serve their users rather than requiring the users to server them.

My Scoutmaster, Ben Hauchhausen, who was a professional engineer, showed me how to solve problems that were new to me with whatever tools were available rather than waiting until the problem was familiar and the usual tools were readily available.

My academic mentor, the late Dr. Henry Ziel, who was an educator, showed me how to recognize and forecast emerging trends in technology.

My students and colleagues keep showing me that there is always more room to develop these and other skills.

I wish to acknowledge and give thanks to all the above and to those below who provided more specific help that made this text possible.

The contents of this text were collected, developed, and redeveloped for my students in CMPT 275 at the University of Saskatchewan over the last 6 terms. Their questions, comments, and projects have helped to improve the contents to where they are of use to a much wider audience.

I wish to thank Phil Rivard, President of ECS Global, and Seth Shacter, of the U. of S. Computer Science Department, for their assistance with various portions of Chapter 12.

I wish to thank the various reviewers, who will remain nameless and blameless, for their many comments that helped me improve this book.

I wish to thank my family, my wife Nancy, my daughters Mary and Elizabeth, and my son Peter, for their love and encouragement and for putting up with the demands of the development of this text. I also wish to thank Nancy for her proofreading and other efforts that helped to ensure that this text was easily readable.

A Context for Developing e-Commerce Applications

Outline

1

1.1   INTRODUCTION TO DEVELOPING E-COMMERCE APPLICATIONS

e-Commerce has significantly transformed the way organizations do business. It has rapidly grown from an alternative method for reaching new customers to a full-featured way of serving the needs of many operations and people associated with an organization. This development has been aided by the highly competitive and interactive nature of the World Wide Web.

In less than a decade, the World Wide Web has grown from an experimental tool for sharing academic ideas to an established and accepted tool for communications and commerce. While unrestricted experimentation and innovation fueled its early growth, many lessons have been learned that provide an important basis for the success of future developments. The worldwide nature of the Web quickly transforms successful experiments by innovators into standard expectations by users. Without ongoing development and innovation, an application that was at the innovative forefront only recently, can quickly be surpassed and made obsolete.

The ease of accessing competitive systems has made consumers, whether individuals or organizations, more demanding in their expectations of e-Commerce systems. Although many systems may provide similar functions, the most successful systems tend to provide their users with a more complete experience that appears tailored to their unique needs.

This text takes many of the lessons learned from the development of successful e-Commerce applications and provides an approach, using widely accepted software engineering processes, to build on these lessons to create the e-Commerce applications of the future. It makes reference to a range of international reports and standards on e-Commerce, software engineering, and related topics.

This chapter provides a context for studying and applying these lessons by introducing major concepts, groups of people, and development processes relating to e-Commerce systems development. Because e-Commerce is constantly and rapidly evolving, some introductory material is best presented via the World Wide Web, where it can be kept current and complete.

 Whenever you encounter the Web Reference Icon, you can find additional material in the chapter's Cyber Supplement on our Web site: http://www.prenhall.com/carter_commerce

1.1.1   e-Commerce

e-Commerce is a generic term that means many things to many people. e-Commerce generally refers to commerce applications that are performed with the assistance of computers and (usually) the Internet. While some people would use e-Commerce to refer to specific applications, including the use of the World Wide Web to conduct business, other people use it to make existing commerce computer applications seem modern and up-to-date. According to the Organization for Economic Cooperation and Development (OECD),[1] electronic commerce "refers generally to all forms of transactions relating to commercial activities, including both organizations and individuals, that are based on the processing and transmission of digitized data, including text, sound and visual images."

Rather than try to tightly define e-Commerce as a particular application or set of applications, it is useful to consider it as a philosophy that involves the overall integration and application of computers and information to the benefit of one or more organizations. This philosophy of interconnectedness and integration often takes us beyond traditional system boundaries to better serve the needs of both organizations and individuals. According to ISO 15944-1,[2] "The underlying principles and characteristics of e-Commerce, e-Administration, and e-Business etc. include: (1) being business transaction-based (of both financial and nonfinancial nature); (2) using information technology (computers and telecommunications); and (3) interchanging electronic data involving established commitments among persons."

1.1.2 e-Business

The term *e-Business* has a variety of different meanings to a variety of different people. These meanings range from the general to the specific.

- IBM uses the term in reference to the larger concept that most other people refer to as e-Commerce and uses e-Commerce to refer to activities that involve business transactions. "e-business is the use of Internet technologies to improve and transform key business processes."[3]
- Some people use the term to refer to those e-Commerce activities that involve business transactions. Within this book, **e-Business** refers to conducting any type(s) of business (between an organization and its customers) via the Internet. This typically involves setting up "virtual businesses" or "electronic storefronts" on the World Wide Web. Although some new start-up organizations may conduct all of their business via e-Business, other more established organizations may use e-Business as just another way of reaching their customers.
- Some people use the term to refer to e-Commerce activities that are conducted exclusively between businesses, which is often referred to as business-to-business (B2B) e-Commerce.

1.2 BACKGROUND CONCEPTS FOR E-COMMERCE SYSTEMS DEVELOPMENT

1.2.1 Information Systems in Organizations

e-Commerce is the latest concept in the evolution of organizational information systems. The field of e-Commerce has evolved rapidly over the last few years. As in any field engaged in such a rapid evolution, there may be considerable controversy about the naming and classification of the topics and applications within it. There may even be some controversy about what truly belongs within its boundaries. While these controversies may be of some long-term use, for the purpose of this text, we should just accept that they exist and focus on what is most important for our immediate consideration.

There are all kinds of systems, dealing with all kinds of information, in all kinds of organizations. So this topic is a tremendously large one. However, it readily illustrates the biggest challenge in developing usable information systems of any type. Our biggest problem is determining *what we mean when we think about a specific information system for a specific organization and communicating it with others involved.* The text is devoted to clarifying this problem, so don't worry if at first it appears to be rather difficult.

1.2.2   Information and Related Concepts

The term *information* is used in common conversation to mean a lot of different things. Within computer science and related disciplines, we need to be more precise about what we're talking about. It is important to understand and to be able to apply the distinctions in the following definitions.

Data are the raw facts that are the basis for most (and probably all) systems of interest to us. Data can be stored, transmitted, and presented in an infinite variety of forms and formats, including numbers, words, pictures, sounds, electronic pulses, etc.

Information is a set of selected or summarized data that is useful for making some decision. How it is useful may be left up to the user or may be suggested by the system. The format and context of information presentation may influence its usefulness. Information (and the data it is extracted from) is a significant organizational resource. It has value whether it is used internally, sold, or even given away. It is the role of accountants and other organizational professionals to care for and make wise use of all kinds of organizational resources, including information.

Knowledge is a combination of information and rules for how to use the information. Correct knowledge provides individuals or systems the basis to make "correct" decisions.

Wisdom is something we should all strive for; however, it is as yet undefined in information processing. It can be loosely defined as the ability to apply knowledge appropriately. It allows a person or a system to adapt decisions to a particular context.

Algorithms are formal rules for processing data or its derivatives.

Procedures are verbal algorithms used by people to guide the conduct of operations within an organization.

Computer programs are formalized algorithms that control the operations of computer systems.

1.2.3   Systems

A **system** can be defined as an organized collection of objects that fulfill some purpose or set of purposes. This leads us to question what types of objects are or could be involved. Objects of concern could include:

- **People**—both directly and even indirectly involved (including users, their managers, and their customers)

- **Data**—which is input, output, stored, and/or processed
  - In some form (data, information, knowledge, wisdom—see definitions above)
  - In some combination of formats (textual or graphical or tonal; printed or electronic; audio or visual; or . . . .)
  - In some manner (by computer or manually)
- **Computer hardware and networks,** which physically perform the computation and communication
- **Computer software,** the programs that make the hardware and networks do what is wanted
- **Manual procedures,** both for interacting with a computer and for processing data without a computer
- **Government regulations,** which regulate the conduct of business (such as following accepted accounting practices, direct sales cancellation regulations, privacy regulations)
- **Goals and objectives** (which provide the purpose or purposes for developing a system). The goals of systems can include:
  - Organizational purposes (such as increasing profits, reducing costs, increasing productivity, or developing new markets)
  - Individual purposes (such as improving methods of accomplishing required tasks, getting increased financial benefits either in increased salaries or in cost savings, improving the user's experience with using the system)
  - Traditions (where no one can remember why something is done, just that "it always has been done so we'd better keep doing it")

A complete computer information system, with all its various interactions, is illustrated in Figure 1-1. Since systems can be defined to include one, some, or all of the above types of objects, considerable confusion often results if the boundaries of a system aren't well specified. Different people may consider a specific system in terms of only some of these components. There is a difference whether you consider a system composed of:

- Only computer hardware (which might better be referred to as a hardware system)
- Only computer software (which might better be referred to as a software system)
- Only computer hardware and software
- Only computer hardware and software and data
- Only computer hardware and software, data, and the immediate users that interact with the hardware
- Everything and everybody involved with accomplishing some application or group of applications

It makes a big difference where you consider the system boundaries. You may not be able to afford a software program, even if it is free, because of other associated costs. Consider the different costs of different systems composed of software at $300/package, hardware at $3,000/workstation, and a worker $30,000/year. We will look into the analysis of objects, as a basis of software development, later in this book.

Many of the largest problems occur when developers only consider computer hardware and software and data and leave people out of the boundaries of the system.

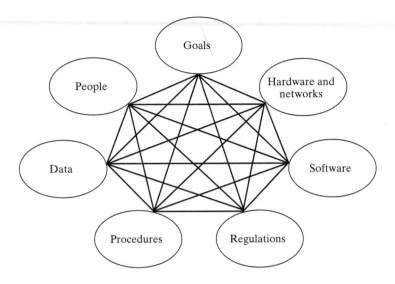

Figure 1-1 Interacting components of a complete e-Commerce system

It is much easier to only deal with computer hardware and software and data because they are inanimate and can often be dealt with via straightforward logic. However, they only become productive when they do something for people, even if only in a very indirect manner. This text will focus on developing systems that are successful in meeting the needs of their users as well as the needs of the organizations for which they are developed.

1.2.4 Organizations

An **organization** is a type of system that involves people, information, and other types of resources that work together to achieve a set of organizational goals (purposes). Organizations typically involve a number of individuals, each with their own motivations and needs. There are many types of systems that fit this description of organizations, including:

- Businesses and parts, sections, or departments of businesses
- Governments and parts, sections, or departments of governments

- Churches and other not-for-profit organizations designed for the betterment of their members and of society in general
- Clubs, special interest groups, and other informal groups designed for the betterment of their members and/or society in general
- Families

1.2.5   Users

Users include all the people and/or organizations who are involved with accomplishing part or all of an application. Users do something for a system and/or have something done for them by a system, whether they directly interact with the system or interact with it via intermediaries.

Users include all individuals who provide data for a system, use the system to accomplish some task or to process some data, and make use of the output of a system. People who create data are not necessarily users if they do not explicitly create data for the system or input it into the system; however, people who create data for a system are users of the system, even if the data is input for them by other people and they do not interact directly with the system.

1.2.6   Stakeholders

Stakeholders are people who are affected by the existence of a system, whether or not they are users of the system (i.e. they have a stake in the outcome of the system). Stakeholders are also any people that an organization cares about, or should care about, regarding how the system might affect them.

Some examples of stakeholders who are not users include:

- People who could become users, if the boundaries of the system were enlarged
- Managers of various users
- People whose interactions with users may be influenced by the user's use of the system, including:
  - Co-workers
  - Customers and suppliers
  - Family and friends

While this definition of stakeholders is somewhat broader than that used by other authors, the key concept is that negative effects on stakeholders may result in negative effects on the organization. For example, the negative effects of a system on the family of a worker may result in dissatisfied workers being less effective for the organization.

Although competitors may be affected by the existence of a system, the organization seldom cares about any negative effects that a system might have on competitors.

1.2.7   Applications

An **application** can be defined as some purpose or set of purposes that can be fulfilled by using (applying) some system (in some manner). This definition may seem rather similar to the definition of a system. However, it is purposely abstract in that it contains no objects except a reference to a system. Despite being abstract, we often talk about applications such as word processing, accounts receivable, and electronic mail.

The important thing to recognize is that an application is tied more to its purpose(s) than to any one system. There are many possible software systems (often referred to as application software packages and many other names) that can be developed and used for a given application.

It is important to distinguish between an application and various instances of application software that may be used by individuals on computers to accomplish or to assist the application. Consider how word processing is an application that can be performed by various software systems, including Microsoft Word, Write Now, Word Perfect, and many more.

Software packages generally evolve over time through many versions. You probably wouldn't recognize the original versions of Microsoft Word or WordPerfect if asked to use them today. And yet you would certainly recognize a report or letter that was developed using one of them.

If you don't understand the applications they are designed to serve, it doesn't matter how many specific software packages you "learn" today. Chances are that in a year or two they will be replaced either with new versions or new packages, but the applications will remain.

Applications, like systems, can be defined with varying degrees of precision depending on what all they involve. For example, general word processing packages (such as Microsoft Word) will work for a variety of documents, while some specialized word processing packages focus on the preparation of particular types of documents. Microsoft Power Point is specialized for presentations, Adobe Acrobat is specialized for printed publications, and Adobe PageMill is specialized for developing Web pages.

1.2.8 Major Gains in Organizational Information Systems

Each of the types of systems presented below will be discussed in greater detail in Chapter 3. This section is intended to highlight some important trends.

Data Processing Systems

Data processing systems first appeared in the 1960s.

They focused on standardized, repetitive processing of data, computerized time-consuming routine tasks, and primarily supported accounting tasks.

The most significant effects of these systems were to free people to consider the implications of the data and to fundamentally change the nature of accounting from bookkeeping to managing corporate accounting information.

Data processing systems were often directly under the control of the accounting department.

For example, these systems were used in processing accounts receivable.

Information Processing Systems

Information processing systems appeared in the 1970s and focused on providing information needed for decisions.

These systems improved flexibility in accessing and using the data, supported management, and freed people to focus on making the decisions.

These systems made information a corporate resource, managed by accounting.

They also benefited other departments with information for their needs and evolved as a separate, independent part of organizations, usually known as "Information Technology" (formerly Data Processing).

An example of the application of information processing systems is the comparison of weekly/monthly sales of a location, individual, or product to an operational forecast or budget.

Knowledge-Based Systems

These systems appeared in the 1980s and focused on providing flexibility for users.

Knowledge-based systems improved flexibility in a variety of organizational functions, supported various different people, freed the organization to respond to changing needs, and empowered individuals to focus on accomplishing tasks.

Knowledge-based systems are supported by "Information Technology," but control is distributed among individual users.

For example, these systems allow changing sales patterns to modify production schedules.

e-Commerce Systems

e-Commerce systems appeared in the 1990s. These systems focus on integrating commerce functions and users and involve multiple distinct groups of users, each with their own distinct sets of needs.

The e-Commerce system crosses organizational boundaries (both within an organization and even with other organizations) and includes information from external sources (which may be freely obtainable, may be rewarded, may be bought, or may require special efforts to obtain). Other significant characteristics of this system are that it adapts to changes (both within the competitive marketplace and in technology in general), frees the organization from traditional limitations including many geopolitical boundaries, changes the fundamental nature of business, and recognizes information as a commodity to which value can be added and from which value can be extracted.

The e-Commerce system totally integrates Information Technology with the business and often is the business; for example, completely electronic businesses that buy and sell their products via the World Wide Web.

 Find the latest information on the growth of e-Commerce in the Chapter 1 Cyber Supplement.

1.3 THE PEOPLE INVOLVED IN DEVELOPING E-COMMERCE SYSTEMS

Developing e-Commerce systems requires a team effort. While notable e-Commerce systems have originated from the imagination and efforts of an exceptional individual, they have seldom remained a one-person effort for long. The evolution of

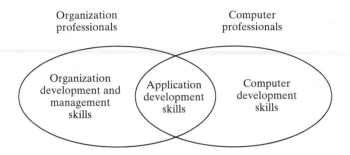

Figure 1-2   Different skill sets involved in e-Commerce systems development

e-Commerce applications and systems to support them generally requires a growing number of people with special skills in a growing number of areas.

The two main groupings of people involved with developing e-Commerce systems are:

- Organizational professionals—people who know what the organization needs and who decide what it gets
- Computer professionals—people who help the business professionals identify needs and possibilities and then turn these possibilities into realities

While each group has their own special skills, successful development of an e-Commerce system requires that they also have some shared skills that they can use together, as illustrated in Figure 1-2. The specific composition of a development team and the set of people with which it interacts is dependent both on the nature of the project and the availability of suitable people. Some people may be involved throughout a project, while others may only be involved in selected portions of a project.

1.3.1   Organizational Professionals Involved in Developing e-Commerce Systems

For e-Commerce systems to work for an organization they must be tailored to the needs of the organization—or the organization must be tailored to their needs. In either case the organizational/business professionals who run and understand the running of the organization must be involved.

While you can buy a basic accounting package at the local supermarket, you cannot expect commercially available software to provide your organization with the competitive edge that is necessary to succeed in today's evolving world of e-Commerce. Organizational professionals must take an active role in the acquisition and development of the systems they will use and/or manage the use of in their organizations. This does not mean that they have to become computer professionals and do the technical development work themselves. It does mean that they must ensure that their needs are clearly identified and met throughout the systems development life cycle. Many professional societies expect their members to learn about the development of organizational information systems so that they can ensure that the right systems are developed in the right way for their organizations.

The number of different organizational professionals involved in an e-Commerce application will vary, depending on the size and structure of both the organization and the e-Commerce application. In small organizations at the start of development of an e-Commerce application, a few well-informed individuals may fulfill a number of different roles. As the organization and/or application grows, more individuals will take on increasingly specialized roles. Regardless of the number of actual individuals, there are a number of organizational/business functions that need to be performed. The following are some of the most important organizational roles and business functions that need to be involved in e-Commerce developments.

1.3.1.1 Users/User Representatives

e-Commerce systems must meet the needs of their users if they are to be successful. Users generally come from both within and outside of the organization that develops an e-Commerce system. User-centered design principles suggest that representative users be involved in the development wherever possible.[4] However, it is seldom practical to include all types of real users of e-Commerce systems (especially those from outside the organization sponsoring the system).

- Users from within the organization can and should be included as part of the development team.
- Organizational professionals within the sponsoring organization and who regularly interact with external users may provide valuable insights into their wants and needs. Development teams should utilize these more readily available professionals to represent the needs of external users.

1.3.1.2 Management Professionals

An organization's management must be involved in ensuring that a system it is developing or obtaining, meets the needs of the organization. These needs include not only the acquisition of new capabilities but also the need to avoid causing problems to existing operations/stakeholders.

All levels of management need to be involved with the development and operation of e-Commerce applications and systems, regardless of how central these applications are to the current conduct of the organization's affairs.

- Senior management must be actively involved, because e-Commerce applications cut across boundaries both within the organization and between the organization and others. These managers will have to negotiate, approve, and champion various strategic level decisions that will have major, long-term effects on the organization.
- Other levels of management need to be actively involved, in order to ensure that the e-Commerce systems integrate within the organization and work in the interests of the organization.

The following are some of the major functions of management professionals with regards to e-Commerce applications and systems.

Overall Organization Functions

- Balancing the need for an e-Commerce application with other needs within the organization.

e-Commerce Development Functions

- Ensuring that the e-Commerce system serves the organization's objectives.
- Ensuring that all necessary organizational viewpoints are included in the development.
- Managing the organizational decisions in the development of the e-Commerce system.
- Ensuring that appropriate resources are available for the development of the e-Commerce system.

e-Commerce Operational Functions

- Ensuring that appropriate resources are available for the operation of the e-Commerce system.
- Managing the operations of the e-Commerce system once it is developed.
- Championing the further evolution of the e-Commerce application and system within the organization.

1.3.1.3 Accounting Professionals

Accounting professionals are needed to do far more than just keep the records of financial transactions relating to e-Commerce systems. They will be called upon to provide expert advice based on the needs of the organization and various analysis of financial and other management information throughout the life of the application.

The following are some of the major functions of accounting professionals with regards to e-Commerce systems.

Overall Organization Functions

- Integrating accounting for e-Commerce systems within the organization's overall accounting.
- Provide information for management activities (this often goes far beyond routine financial information to include information such as evaluations of the progress of development projects and evaluations of the effectiveness of existing systems).
- Analyze information for risk management.

e-Commerce Development Functions

- Ensure that e-Commerce systems include appropriate accounting functions and controls.
- Provide accounting and other management information support for the development of e-Commerce systems.

e-Commerce Operational Functions

- Provide ongoing accounting and auditing for active e-Commerce systems.

1.3.1.4 Marketing Professionals

Most e-Commerce applications and systems involve marketing in some form, whether marketing products and/or services of the organization or marketing the organization itself. Marketing (and related) professionals can provide expertise on how the e-Commerce system relates to external users.

The following are some of the major functions of marketing professionals with regards to e-Commerce systems.

Overall Organization Functions

- Develop and implement overall organizational marketing plans.
- Identify marketing opportunities that can be met via e-Commerce systems.

e-Commerce Development Functions

- Ensure that e-Commerce systems meet current marketing needs and are flexible to adapt to future marketing opportunities.
- Provide ongoing strategies for use in e-Commerce applications and systems.

e-Commerce Operational Functions

- Keeping product information up-to-date.
- Analyzing e-Commerce customer behavior and opinions.

1.3.1.5 Human Resource Professionals

e-Commerce applications and systems will affect many of the members of an organization. Human resource (and related) professionals can provide expertise on how the e-Commerce application relates to the various members of an organization whether or not they are the intended users of actual e-Commerce systems.

The following are some of the major functions of human resource professionals with regard to e-Commerce systems:

Overall Organization Functions

- Develop and implement overall organizational staffing plans.
- Identify challenges and opportunities that can result from e-Commerce applications.

e-Commerce Development Functions

- Identify appropriate organizational professionals to participate in the development of an e-Commerce system.
- Arrange training and staff development activities for staff affected by e-Commerce systems.
- Provide ongoing strategies for staff involvement in e-Commerce systems.

e-Commerce Operational Functions

- Keeping skills of existing staff up-to-date.
- Identifying and developing new staff as required.

1.3.1.6   Legal Professionals

e-Commerce applications cross boundaries of many different legal jurisdictions, on both a national and an international scale. Legal professionals need to continually identify and monitor legal implications of e-Commerce systems in the various jurisdictions in which they may be used.

1.3.1.7   All Organizational Members

In addition to the above-mentioned functions, and the job-specific functions of other members of the organization who may be affected, all members of an organization need to be:

- Making their needs and wants known
- Suggesting organizational strategies for growth and development
- Keeping the organization aware of the state of the competition
- Using the resulting applications, where applicable

1.3.2   Computer (and Related) Professionals Involved in Developing e-Commerce Systems

Computer professionals, whether regular employees of the organization or not, are expected to take an objective role in identifying what the users may need or want, obtaining decisions from management, and then implementing these decisions. Just as with organizational professionals, there are a number of roles for computer (and related) professionals.

1.3.2.1   Systems Analysts/Software Engineers

Systems analysts (SA)/software engineers (SE) interact with organizational professionals to analyze requirements and develop solutions. A senior systems analyst or software engineer usually acts as the project manager for a team developing a new application system.

NOTE: While some people may make distinctions between systems analysts and software engineers, there is no industry-wide consensus on a distinction in roles.

The following are some of the major functions of systems analysts/software engineers with regard to the development of e-Commerce systems:

Applying appropriate development methods (techniques) and methodologies (organized sets of techniques) throughout the development project.

NOTE: Methods and methodologies will be discussed throughout this book.

- Maintaining a knowledge of the relevant state of computing technology
- Identifying the needs and wants of the various groups of users and potential users
- Identifying features of similar applications and systems that might be applied to the system under development
- Identifying other opportunities and challenges
- Providing organizational managers with understandable information so that they can make decisions about the development in an informed manner
- Facilitating the involvement of users and stakeholders throughout the development

- Developing suitable documentation for the project
- Designing an optimal system for the application
- Supervising and optionally participating in, the construction, testing, and implementation of the system

1.3.2.2 Programmers

Programmers construct and/or modify, test, and install the software programs based on the design specifications for the system. Programming may be done by systems analysts, who are in contact with users, or programmers who are only in contact with systems analysts and other computer professionals.

When questions arise regarding a design or when alternate implementation strategies are possible, the programmer should consult with other computer professionals rather than making a decision on his or her own.

1.3.2.3 User Interface Developers/Designers

The importance of good user interfaces is increasingly leading to the need for computer professionals (or related professionals such as ergonomists, usability specialists, and graphics designers) who specialize in user interface (UE) development/human-computer interaction (HCI). User interface developers may come from a variety of backgrounds and may use a variety of approaches in fulfilling their role, which is to optimize the users' roles in the system. User interface developers combine existing design guidance with user testing to evaluate and improve the usability of systems.

1.3.2.4 Network Administrators

Network administrators (NA) are responsible for the effective operations of an organization's information infrastructure. They ensure that all users have adequate resources to perform the various applications that they require using the hardware, software, communications, and data that the organization controls. They seldom get involved in the detailed running of an individual system other than to analyze performance problems and to suggest resource changes that would improve performance. Network administrators need to be involved in development projects to identify the potential effects of new projects on existing resources and to suggest any additional resources that may be required.

1.3.2.5 Database Administrators

Database administrators (DBA) are responsible for a variety of technical aspects relating to the organization's databases, including:

- Integrity (correctness, protection, and security)
- Sharability (between users on a "need to know" basis)
- Availability (on-line, when needed)
- Evolvability (to meet changing needs)

Database administrators control the organization's data on behalf of the organization. It is still up to the organization to determine how that data is used for the benefit of the organization. Given a potential use, database administrators can suggest what data is already available and how additionally required data could be incorporated within the organization's database.

1.3.2.6 User Support Specialists

User support specialists provide ongoing support of systems that have been implemented. They interface between organizational professionals and computer professionals to assist with a variety of functions, including:

- Answering system-related questions
- Solving problems with the system or with using the system
- Providing training, documentation, and updated information about the use of systems
- Assisting users in performing unusual tasks, such as generating specialized, one-time reports
- Customizing users' interactions with a system, where such customization is available

1.3.3 The Overlap Between Organizational and Computer Professionals

Organizational professionals are generally the only people who understand the full implications of various organizational strategies, including the potential use of e-Commerce applications in the organization. They can evaluate and select various strategies without a thorough understanding of how to technically implement them. e-Commerce issues primarily of concern to organizational professionals are dealt with by Turban in *Electronic Commerce: A Managerial Perspective*.[5]

Computer professionals are generally the only people who understand the full details of how to technically implement computer applications. They can do this without a thorough understanding of the full implications of applications on the organization. Deitel deals with e-Commerce issues for computer programmers in *e-Business & e-Commerce: How to Program*.[6] This book introduces a number of issues in the development of e-Commerce systems for other computer professionals.

Development must bring these two sets of expertise together. To do so, both groups of professionals must be able to communicate with and to interact with each other. This book will focus on this area of overlapping involvement. Each group needs to understand the role of the other in order to provide the necessary information to the other group, ask the necessary questions of the other group, interpret the answers of the other group, and help contribute to the joint development efforts.

Development involves a series of interactions between organizational professionals and computer professionals:

- *Organizational professionals* provide inputs of their needs, wants, and opinions throughout development. These inputs may be limited or biased by personal experience and organizational traditions. Many of these inputs may be described in very imprecise terms, which cannot be directly translated into requirements of a computer system.
- *Computer professionals* gather and organize these inputs and identify various development decisions that need to be taken (including selecting which inputs to focus on at this time). Computer professionals often use formal language and

structures that are readily translated into a computer program, but which may be difficult for users to understand directly.

- *Organizational professionals* make development decisions based on the analysis and recommendations they are provided. In order to make good decisions, they must understand what they are deciding and the implications of various alternatives.
- *Computer professionals* implement the development decisions.

Management and accounting professionals especially need to understand the development of e-Commerce applications because they have to continually interact with developers throughout the entire life of these applications.

1.3.3.1   Project Managers

Each project will require a manager who understands how to combine the skills of organizational and computer people in order to achieve a successful development. Project managers may come from either an organizational or a computer background. When managing a project, it is important that they are able to mediate between competing viewpoints and help achieve the optimal outcome.

1.4   SYSTEMS DEVELOPMENT LIFE CYCLES

Applications are implemented as systems that will be used for a period of time and that may be replaced by a new or improved system at some future time. Systems seldom come close to doing everything and doing it in the best possible manner for an application. Rather, systems are typically developed to maximize the benefits of a limited set of available resources. This means that there is usually room for future improvements, even on the first day a system is put into productive use.

The **life cycle** of a system is a concept that unifies all the phases of a system's "life," from its start (the identification of a need), through the development of a system, its actual use to solve the problem, up to its end (its eventual replacement). All systems have a life cycle. Some examples of life cycles include:

Human Life Cycle
- Hatch (birth)
- Match (mating)
- Dispatch (death)

Engineering Life Cycle
- Analysis
- Design
- Construction
- Testing
- Implementation
- Repair
- Replacement

Creative Life Cycle[7]

- Explorer (investigation)
- Artist (development)
- Judge (evaluation)
- Warrior (implementation)

Although the life cycles of different systems may appear to vary considerably, the variance is often more in how the life cycle is described than in the actual activities within the life cycle. Differences occur in (1) the names and number of phases or phases identified and (2) the focus on deliverables or processes.

1.4.1   Deliverables

The various products of development that are given to the owners and/or users of the system are considered **deliverables.** The format of a deliverable is not as important as the information it contains. While most deliverables are tangible, all deliverables are clearly recognizable by both users and developers.

Deliverables are created and modified throughout the system development life cycle. Various expectations regarding deliverables should be specified at the beginning of a development life cycle. These expectations may include:

- A schedule of expected deliverables
- Formatting expectations of individual deliverables
- Acceptance criteria to be used in evaluating deliverables

Some of the main types of deliverables of application development include:

- Software programs
- Documentation
- Reports
- Presentations
- Training

Early software engineering approaches (such as structured development) focused more on producing deliverables that could reassure managers that progress was being made than on the actual processes involved in development. As a result, development was generally divided into particular phases, whose completion was announced by a series of these deliverables. Once a phase was officially complete, developers were expected to move on with the next phase. In addition, developers were often reluctant to make any revisions to previous phases, even if such revisions were essential to the success of the project.

Structured development focused on developing logically correct systems. However, systems need to be more than logically correct. They need to be usable. The development of many logically correct systems that were difficult to use, led to focusing development on those areas where changes were actually needed. Object-oriented methods have focused on understanding the existing objects within a system, and evolving this understanding throughout development. Care needs to be taken that focusing on existing objects does not unnecessarily limit change.

1.4.2   The Waterfall Approach

The simplest way of progressing through the systems development life cycle is to progress through a series of discrete phases. Each phase has to be substantially complete before the next phase can start. When diagrammed, such a life cycle takes on the appearance of a "waterfall." In waterfall development, each phase adds information to the developer's knowledge of the system to be built. The developer then transforms this knowledge into a working system that is complete enough to be given to its intended user. Each phase defines what development information is needed, and the sequencing of phases defines when it is obtained.

This strict phased approach has been found to be more useful as a means of organizing ideas about life cycles (for instructional purposes) than it has been for actually developing real systems. The unfortunate side effect of expecting that a phase is substantially complete before starting another is that it inhibits needed changes. This approach implies that development involves one pass through each successive phase. Since few of us are perfect, it isn't even likely that we will get everything right on our first try. We should expect to revise our work by iterating each phase (either before proceeding to the next phase) or when a later phase finds the need for changes. In addition to changes needed due to the development process, requirements may change or new requirements may become increasingly important throughout the life cycle because of changing external factors.

Going back to a previous phase, in a waterfall-style development, is often considered a sign of failure on the part of the developers. Developers tend to try and ignore changes that would require redoing previous work. Pressure to deliver a system makes fixing of requirements and design important in order to avoid an endless set of changes (such as often occurs in hacking). The longer needed changes are ignored, the more costly their eventual correction will be. Ignoring needed changes leads to failures in the developed system (even if major problems in completing development can be avoided).

Despite the disruptive nature of changes, some changes may be crucial to the success of a system and should not be avoided. A mechanism is needed for evaluating proposed changes and acting on those that are found to be justified.

Iteration is the revising of the results of any development process when new information makes this revision desirable. Iteration does not mean that developments should be subject to infinite revisions, which would never allow systems to be implemented and utilized. It does mean that developers must evaluate any new development information they come across to determine whether it warrants causing revisions to the existing development. Where warranted, these resulting revisions should be welcomed, rather than avoided, to ensure the success of a development project.

Iteration is especially important for e-Commerce development. e-Commerce systems must constantly evolve to meet new demands of their users and to stay ahead of the competition. Thus, iteration occurs both within the development of each version of a particular e-Commerce system and between different versions of that system.

Figure 1-3 illustrates a waterfall model of development with iteration. A waterfall is still useful in representing the main phases in the life of a system from

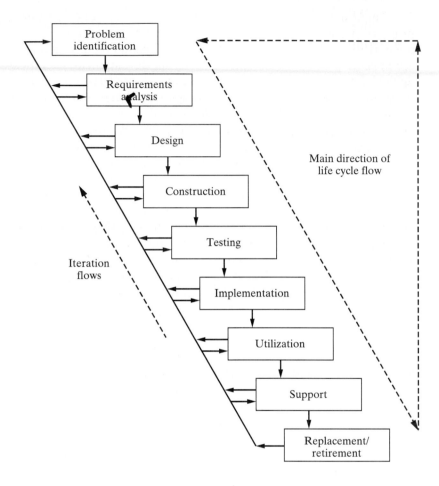

Figure 1-3   The technical systems development life cycle of an e-Commerce system

problem identification to replacement/retirement. The figure, however, recognizes both that phases often overlap with one another and that there are many times when iteration between phases is necessary. It shows that the needs of a phase may require iteration back to revise any phases that may have been performed previously.

1.4.3   Spiral Development

Various other models of development have been proposed to illustrate and to promote the importance of the following:

• Iterating various development activities

- Involving the user throughout the development
  - To provide information on what is required
  - To evaluate what has been developed
- Performing various development activities in parallel

Many of these models describe development as a spiral. Spiral models consist of a set of development processes that are applied a number of times. Each time the processes are applied, they expand the amount of development information that has been obtained and validated. Development information evolves from the center of the spiral, where it only specifies the problem identification, to the outer edge of the spiral, where it has been used to fully specify a system that can solve the problem.

Boehm[8] proposed a spiral model of development that provides a "risk-driven" approach to software development. Each level in the spiral involves planning, risk analysis, and prototyping in addition to one of the usual stages of software life cycles (requirements analysis, design, construction and testing).

A **prototype** is a model of a system that can be used to communicate the requirements and design of that part of the system between developers and their clients. Prototypes are often used in all forms of development and are not limited to use within a particular model of development. **Prototyping** involves developing a prototype and using it both to confirm what is already included within the prototype and to explore what should be added. Prototypes and prototyping will be discussed further in Chapter 5, Managing Pervasive Development Processes, and in Chapter 11, Detailed Design.

Connell and Shafer[9] proposed evolutionary rapid prototyping as an approach that applies the phases in the system development life cycle in a highly iterative manner also based on a spiral form of development. After a brief problem identification phase, a prototype is developed and used as the basis for a number of prototyping cycles. Each prototyping cycle can both modify and add to the requirements analysis, design, construction, and testing of the prototype. Although each cycle includes elements from four traditional life cycle phases, the relative proportions of these elements change throughout the series of prototyping cycles. Traditional life cycle phases can provide useful guidance for developers rather than formal points at which "completed" specifications are fixed for the duration of the life cycle. This involves selecting which activities to do immediately and which activities to defer until later in the life cycle. In both the obtaining and using of user needs information, each piece of information must be evaluated as to whether or not it pertains to the current (or to a previous) phase of the life cycle. The earlier cycles tend to be most focused on requirements analysis, with the focus of later cycles migrating through the traditional life cycle phases until the prototype evolves into a fully developed system.

Successful prototyping must be carefully managed to ensure that all aspects of development are properly completed before a prototype is transformed into the system that is then implemented.[10] Given the highly evolutionary nature of successful e-Commerce systems, they may often appear similar to prototypes. However, it is essential that each version of an e-Commerce system be fully developed and tested before being put into productive use. Users, if encouraged by easy feedback mechanisms, may help provide developers with considerable information to help improve the system.

1.4.4   Technical Development Processes

Because the phases of a development life cycle are not clearly distinct, with one phase starting only when the previous phases have been completed, it is increasingly popular to consider systems development in terms of a set of development processes, rather than in terms of a set of fixed deliverables or phases. By accepting a process-oriented view of development, developers are given greater flexibility in the selection of specific activities (often referred to as development methods) to accomplish a process, and in the scheduling of various processes, subprocesses, and/or activities to be performed in parallel or in whatever order is most convenient.

Process-oriented approaches to development focus on the right things to do rather than the right deliverables to produce. Thus, where certain activities were limited to distinct phases of development, it is now recognized that many processes may need to be conducted throughout the development life cycle.

Processes
- Are required in order to achieve some desired accomplishment.
- Tend to be thought of as more general in nature.
- Tend to occur over long and often undefined periods of time.
- Are often discussed in terms of the accomplishments they are intended to produce.
- May be accomplished by various different activities.

Activities
- Are often interchangeable in the achievement of some desired accomplishment.
- Tend to be thought of as more specific in nature.
- Tend to occur over short and often well-defined periods of time.
- Are often discussed in terms of the action they involve.
- May be combined to accomplish various processes.

This book is organized around the presentation of a general set of software engineering life cycle processes. There are many more detailed approaches to identifying the essential processes involved in the development of software systems, including:

- The ISO Standard for Software Life Cycle Processes (from a software engineering perspective)[11]
- The ISO Standard for System Life Cycle Processes (from a software engineering perspective)[12]
- The ISO Technical Report on Software Process Improvement and Capability Determination[13]

Within a process-oriented life cycle, the main analysis is still a prerequisite to design, which is a prerequisite to construction. However, all of the analysis need not be accomplished before proceeding to design, and not all of the design needs to be accomplished before proceeding to construction. A process-oriented approach recognizes the importance of iteration. For example, as design proceeds, there is often a need for further analysis.

The development of e-Commerce systems involves a number of main technical processes, which are introduced below and discussed in depth throughout this book. Most discussions of systems development life cycles focus on what has to be done, assuming that it will be done correctly. However, since we're all human, things seldom go as they are supposed to. Thus, it is important to consider the potential difficulties, as well as the objectives, of each process.

1.4.4.1 Problem Identification

Problem identification involves:

- Recognizing that there is a problem (challenge or opportunity)
- Identifying what it really is
- Deciding whether or not it is feasible to try and do something about it

Some difficulties with problem identification include:

- Limiting the problem to traditional objectives
- Limiting the problem to traditional boundaries/users
- Political influences on the problem and its boundaries

1.4.4.2 Requirements Analysis

Requirements analysis involves:

- Identifying what is currently done
- Identifying problems with what is currently done
- Identifying what isn't done but perhaps should be
- Identifying other factors related to this problem area
- Deciding how much will be done in this project

Some difficulties with requirements analysis include:

- Identifying what really is currently done
- Rushing into design prematurely

1.4.4.3 Design

Design involves:

- Selecting from alternative solutions
- Describing the selected solution in a way in which it can be implemented

Some difficulties with design include:

- Ignoring the needs, wants, and capabilities of users
- Including bells and whistles to show off design prowess

1.4.4.4 Construction

Construction involves:

- Obtaining the resources necessary for construction
- Developing the designed solution

Some difficulties with construction include:

- Faking decisions that require additional analysis and/or design before being made
- Rushing systems into use without adequate testing

1.4.4.5   Testing

Testing involves:

- Ensuring the developed solution meets the requirements
- Ensuring the developed solution functions as was intended
- Ensuring the developed solution is usable

Some difficulties with verification and validation include:

- Leaving all forms of testing until the end of development, when changes are too costly to make
- Testing that involves self-fulfilling prophesies

1.4.4.6   Implementation

Implementation involves:

- Preparing users for the new system
- Installing or upgrading any hardware required for the utilization of the new system
- Installing the software
- Converting the data
- Establishing or modifying procedures to support the other implementation activities

Some difficulties with implementation include:

- Not starting implementation activities early enough
- Rushing implementations

1.4.4.7   Utilization

Utilization involves the intended user actually using the system:

- Sometimes as it was intended to be used
- Sometimes in ways other than were intended
- Sometimes for purposes other than were intended

Some difficulties with utilization include:

- Getting users to use it as it was intended to be used (it might not be as easy to use as was intended)
- Allowing users to use it in ways other than were intended (they might find a better way but be discouraged by standard operating procedures)
- Helping users to use it for purposes other than were intended (they might find additional benefits that could be realized with just a little extra help)

1.4.4.8   Support

Support, which includes maintenance, involves:

- Providing advice/training to assist users so that they can use the system
- Fixing problems that were not caught in testing

- Enhancing the system to meet with uses beyond those initially intended (only in traditional developments)

NOTE: e-Commerce systems need to be continually evolving. This evolution needs to go beyond the fixing of problems to the creation of significant enhancements. Because of the importance of this evolution, enhancements are less likely to be considered part of support and are more likely to be the basis for further new development that involves processes from problem identification through utilization and eventual support.

Some difficulties with support include:

- Figuring out how the system actually works
- Using incorrect documentation or not having any documentation to use
- Documentation may be far from sufficient to meet the needs of maintenance (since the one thing developers like less than doing maintenance is developing documentation)
- Side effects introduced by modifications
- Developers don't generally like doing maintenance—the fun is in new development
- Projects that have been rushed into use are likely to be insufficiently documented, making maintenance very difficult to perform (sort of like a video adventure game)

1.4.4.9   Replacement/Retirement

Replacement/retirement involves:

- Accepting that repair/enhancement is no longer feasible
- Developing or acquiring an alternative system or method of doing the system's work
- Phasing out the old system

Some difficulties with replacement/retirement include:

- Accepting that repair is no longer feasible
- Starting from scratch to rebuild the same old system again

NOTE: Replacement/retirement only occurs occasionally with most types of systems, including e-Commerce systems.

1.4.4.10   Overcoming Difficulties in Systems Development

A number of general techniques can help overcome the variety of difficulties that often occur during systems development. These include:

- Significant user involvement throughout the life cycle
- "User-Centered Design" techniques as opposed to focusing on technology
- Powerful management support of the project
- Keeping options open as long as possible
- Keeping time expectations realistic
- Good project management

1.4.5   Project Processes

The need to manage projects, including managing iterative development, has led to the recognition of a number of additional project processes. While computer professionals may perform these processes, management professionals often perform them with the assistance of accounting professionals. These processes work with the set of technical processes as the basis for e-Commerce systems development as illustrated in Figure 1-4. The management of e-Commerce systems development involves a number of main project processes, introduced below, and is discussed further in Chapter 5, Managing Pervasive Development Processes.

1.4.5.1   Planning and Assessment

Planning and assessment involves:

- Identifying and scheduling project processes and activities
- Identifying criteria for assessing progress and methods for monitoring progress
- Providing suitable management accounting of the project
- Informing management of challenges and opportunities affecting the development of the system

Difficulties with planning and assessment include:

- Reporting progress: developers often have difficulty in estimating the actual amount of progress they have made toward completing some development phase or activity prior to its actual completion. Successive progress reports may claim that (50%, 75%, 88%, 94%, 97%, 98%, 99%, 99.5%, 99.75% . . . .) of a given phase is completed. When pressed to complete something, a developer may claim that it is completed and be forced to move on despite not actually having completed it.
- Monitoring progress: people monitoring development rely on formal reports and lines of code (neither of which they may actually understand) as indications of progress.
- Handling changes: developers are expected to handle unexpected changes throughout the life of the project and still complete the project on time and under budget. It doesn't happen. Are you surprised?
- Timing: software developments frequently take longer than estimated.
- Rushed delivery: where delivery is required by a certain time, incomplete or incompletely tested products are often rushed into use with various bugs and deficiencies.

1.4.5.2   Control and Decision Making

Control and decision making involves:

- Dealing with challenges and opportunities affecting the development of the system
- Taking action to correct problems in development processes
- Ensuring that required decisions are made by the appropriate people

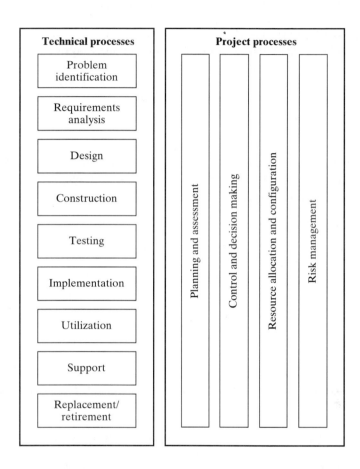

Figure 1-4   The processes involved in e-Commerce systems development

Difficulties with control and decision making include:

- Lack of understanding: organizational professionals lack the understanding of system development well enough to ensure that it is properly controlled
- Passing on decision making: it's generally easier and faster for developers to make decisions, on their own, without consulting the appropriate people

- Communication: managers and developers often don't understand each other and thus only communicate in artificially formalized ways

1.4.5.3   Resource Allocation and Configuration

Resource allocation and configuration involves:

- Identifying, obtaining, and allocating resources for developing the system
- Identifying, obtaining, and allocating resources for operating and supporting the system

Difficulties with resource allocation and configuration include:

- The treatment of costs: the development of information systems is often treated as a cost item by organizations rather than as an investment.
- Who benefits: there may be a difference between who pays for development and who benefits from it. Thus, some of the actual benefits may be discounted because of organizational or political barriers when justifying developments.

1.4.5.4   Risk Management

Risk management involves:

- Identifying and minimizing risks to successful systems development
- Identifying and minimizing risks posed by the e-Commerce system being developed

Difficulties with risk management include:

- Cost overruns: software developments frequently run considerably over budget due to poor estimates and unforeseen requirements.
- Achieving benefits: proposed benefits cannot be guaranteed and are seldom actually measured when they occur.
- Misunderstood or overlooked risks: there is a wide variety of organizational and computer-related risks that need to be considered in the development and operation of an e-Commerce system.

1.4.6   Challenges in Managing Systems Development

When I used to work for IBM they used to say, "there are no problems, only challenges and opportunities." **Challenges** exist where significant improvements should be made in a development or to a system. Since no development or system is ever perfect, there are always possible improvements. **Opportunities** exist where significant additions should be made in a development or to a system. There are always more possible improvements and additions that could be made than there are resources to make them. **Significant** improvements or additions are ones that are important to the success of the development or system.

There are definitely many challenges in developing e-Commerce systems that we will consider throughout this text. Despite the many challenges, good software is often developed (it is estimated that about 20% to 30% of major software projects are considered highly successful). Many software developments wind up shelved and ignored (estimated at about 50% to 60% of developments). What really concerns most of us is the bad software that we wind up having to use (estimated by some to be most of the software).

The difference in success is based on how successfully both developers and their clients work together. Each party to systems development must understand their role and accomplish it for success to occur. By understanding the development processes and identifying potential challenges and opportunities, we can minimize our risks and maximize our chances for success. This text will help you to meet the challenges and help ensure that systems developed for you and your organization are what you need.

1.5   THE ORGANIZATION OF THIS BOOK

The linear organization of a printed book forces the author to make a number of choices in the order in which concepts are presented. This text is organized based on the progressive discovery of information about e-Commerce systems development in a manner similar to the way in which e-Commerce systems are developed, with each chapter building on information from previous chapters. Chapters dealing with development processes are organized in the order they typically commence within the development life cycle. This does not mean that they should only be applied with a waterfall-style of development. Real developments seldom progress in a purely linear manner. Figure 1-5 provides an overview of the structure of the chapters and their contents, to allow the reader to anticipate what is ahead and/or to go directly to the material that is of most immediate interest.

In this figure, development processes are arranged in the form of a pyramid or iceberg. This is to suggest that:

- Identifying the problem is only the tip of development
- Development involves using a set of technical processes in the progressive discovery of knowledge about the application (and the system being developed to serve it)
- Pervasive development processes are needed throughout development to support the technical processes

The following chapters provide material relating to the overall understanding and development of e-Commerce systems:

- *Chapter 1—A Context for Developing e-Commerce Applications* provides a basic introduction to e-Commerce systems development and to the remainder of the book. It focuses on discussing selected background concepts, roles of people, and approaches to development.
- *Chapter 2—Some Interesting Types of e-Commerce Applications* identifies and briefly describes a number of general types of e-Commerce applications.
- *Chapter 3—Software Systems in Organizations* provides a framework for understanding how e-Commerce fits into organizations and discusses how an organization can get started in developing an e-Commerce system.
- *Chapter 5—Managing Pervasive Development Processes* identifies and discusses processes and activities that should be applied throughout the development of an e-Commerce system.
- *Chapter 15—Evolving Ahead* provides a conclusion to the book and a discussion of how to manage the development of continually evolving e-Commerce systems.

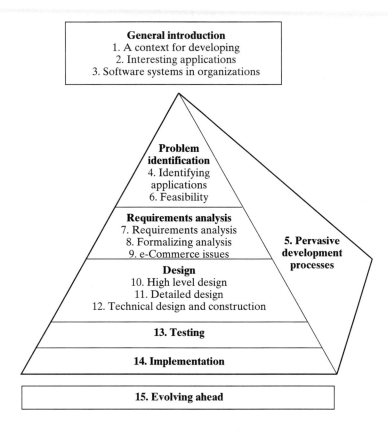

Figure 1-5 The organization of chapters in this book

The following chapters discuss specific (life cycle oriented) technical development processes:

- *Chapter 4—Identifying and Describing an e-Commerce Application* discusses identifying competitive e-Commerce applications and developing application descriptions that form the basis for their systems development.

- *Chapter 6—e-Commerce Feasibility* discusses how feasibility of potential e-Commerce systems can be evaluated.
- *Chapter 7—e-Commerce Requirements Analysis* discusses the identification of tasks, users, content, and tools to develop a detailed description of the requirements of an application.
- *Chapter 8—Formalizing Analysis* discusses translating a requirements analysis based on the users, content, and tools into a formal object-oriented analysis, including object classes, and further analyzing these classes in terms of their relations, attributes, and operations.
- *Chapter 9—Some Important e-Commerce Issues* introduces a number of specific e-Commerce issues that may have been missed in an analysis and that present important requirements that e-Commerce systems must meet.
- *Chapter 10—High-Level Design* discusses how to design a suitable Web site to meet the needs of an e-Commerce application. It focuses on the relation of pages in the site to the needs of the content, users, and tasks.
- *Chapter 11—Detailed Design* provides design guidance for individual pages within an e-Commerce Web site. It includes considerations of how the pages will look and how they will work.
- *Chapter 12—Technical Design and Construction* introduces various technical issues that need to be resolved as a basis for the technical design and construction of an e-Commerce Web site. It does not provide details of how to construct a Web site because such details require major texts totally dedicated to that subject.
- *Chapter 13—Testing* discusses the wide range of testing necessary to ensure that an e-Commerce system is able to achieve its objectives.
- *Chapter 14—Implementation* discusses the range of implementation activities necessary to ensure that an e-Commerce system actually achieves its objectives.

This book contains an ongoing set of student assignments and detailed examples that can help the reader in applying the information presented in various chapters. They both are intended to follow the development of an e-Commerce system for a specific application. Due to resource limitations (both the size of this book and the amount of time a student can spend on assignments) they do not completely develop a system. Rather, they highlight and illustrate the major processes in e-Commerce systems development.

The assignment/example in:

- *Chapter 3* deals with the identification of an e-Commerce application to be developed. The assignment deals with establishing project teams for student projects. The example provides background, which will be used in future chapters, about an established coffee shop supplier wishing to develop an e-Commerce system.
- *Chapter 4* deals with conducting an initial investigation of an e-Commerce application that can be used as the basis for future assignments and examples. Students are allowed to choose an application of interest to them as long as it has the potential to be successful both as a project and as a real e-Commerce system.
- *Chapter 5* deals with critiquing an initial investigation into a chosen e-Commerce application.

- *Chapter 6* deals with conducting a feasibility study of the chosen application.
- *Chapter 7* deals with conducting a task analysis of the chosen application.
  - The assignment is structured in a manner that provides students with an experience in identifying and analyzing select user groups, tasks, content chunks, and tools and supports further assignments.
  - The example focuses on describing how select task analysis information was obtained and structured.
- *Chapter 8* deals with transforming task analysis information into a formalized analysis. It also deals with adding additional analysis information to the resulting formalized analysis.
- *Chapter 9* deals with recognizing the impact of important e-Commerce issues on the selected application.
- *Chapter 10* deals with developing a high-level design to a selected portion of the application.
- *Chapter 11* deals with developing a detailed design for a selected Web page (or a small number of selected Web pages that work together) that can be used by a variety of different scenarios. Rather than advocating a specific design, the example explains the design decisions that should go into the creation of a design. The accompanying Web site presents various designs that could be developed.
- *Chapter 12* deals with constructing a prototype of the screen(s) and scenarios designed in Chapter 11. Because of the nature of an on-line prototype, the example for this chapter is located on the accompanying Web site.
- *Chapter 13* deals with testing the prototype developed in Chapter 12. This example is located on the accompanying Web site.
- *Chapter 14* deals with developing an implementation plan for the different groups of users and stakeholders.

Each chapter also identifies a number of challenges and opportunities related to developing e-Commerce systems and information on what to look for at the Web site that accompanies this book.

1.6   CYBER SUPPLEMENTS FOR CHAPTER 1

 Look at the Chapter 1 Cyber Supplements on the Web to find:

- The latest information about the growing use and expanding roles of e-Commerce
- Links to other Web sites with introductory information about e-Commerce
- Suggestions for further investigations into the use and roles of e-Commerce

REFERENCES

[1] Organization for Economic Cooperation and Development (OECD), *Electronic Commerce: Opportunities and Challenges for Government* (The "Sacher Report," 1997) (downloadable from *http://www.oecd.org/dsti/sti/it/ec/index.htm*).

[2] "International Organization for Standardization," ISO/IEC 2nd Committee Draft of International Standard 15944-1, Business Agreement Semantic Descriptive Techniques—Part 1: Operational Aspects of Open-edi for Implementation, 2000.

[3] *http://www-3.ibm.com/e-business/overview/28212.html,* IBM e-Business.

[4] "International Organization for Standardization," ISO International Standard 13407, Human Centered Design Processes for Interactive Systems, 1997.

[5] E. Turban, J. Lee, D. King, and H. M. Chung, *Electronic Commerce: A Managerial Perspective* (Upper Saddle River, NJ, Prentice-Hall, 2000).

[6] H. M. Deitel, P. J. Deitel, and T. R. Nieto, *e-Business & e-Commerce: How to Program* (Upper Saddle River, NJ, Prentice-Hall, 2001).

[7] R. von Oech, *A Kick in the Seat of the Pants* (New York, NY, Harper & Row Publishers, 1986).

[8] Barry W. Boehm, A Spiral Model of Software Development and Enhancement, *IEEE Computer,* May 1988, pp. 61–72.

[9] John L. Connell and Linda B. Shafer, *Structured Rapid Prototyping* (Englewood Cliffs, NJ, Yourdon Press, 1989).

[10] Jim Carter, Managing to Succeed with Rapid Prototyping, *Proceedings of the 36th Meeting of the Human Factors Society*, 1992, pp. 404–408.

[11] "International Organization for Standardization," International Electrotechnical Commission International Standard 12207, Information Technology: Software Life Cycle Processes, 1995.

[12] "International Organization for Standardization," International Electrotechnical Commission 2nd Committee Draft for International Standard 15288, Life Cycle Management—System Life Cycle Processes, 2000.

[13] "International Organization for Standardization," International Electrotechnical Commission, TR 15504-2, Information Technology: Software Process Assessment: Part 2: A Reference Model for Processes and Process Capability, 1998.

2

Some Interesting Types of e-Commerce Applications

Outline

2.1 INTRODUCTION TO DIFFERENT TYPES OF E-COMMERCE APPLICATIONS

e-Commerce applications are continually developing and evolving as people identify new uses for increasingly complex and flexible networks of computerized organizational systems. In general, e-Commerce applications tend to have the following characteristics:

- They involve multiple distinct groups of users (each with their own distinct sets of needs)
- They cross organizational boundaries (both within an organization and even with other organizations)
- They include information from external sources (which may be freely obtainable, may be rewarded, may be bought, or may require special efforts to obtain)
- They adapt to changes (both within the competitive marketplace and in technology in general)
- They recognize information as a commodity (to which value can be added and from which value can be extracted)

e-Commerce often involves enterprise-wide systems integration. **Enterprise-wide systems integration** involves developing or redeveloping of an organization's information infrastructure in a manner that optimizes the benefits to the whole organization rather than to individual parts of the organization. It is a strategy rather than a type of application. Applications analyze/control the operations of an organization. This may include redefining the applications that interact with this information infrastructure. It often includes some extent of organizational restructuring.

e-Commerce makes a variety of just-in-time activities possible within an organization. **Just-in-time** is a business strategy involving deferring acquisitions or development of resources (material, product, and people resources) until they are needed. Organizations use a variety of just-in-time strategies to delay investing in resources until the resources are assured of producing a profit for the organization.

The types of interesting e-Commerce applications, discussed in this chapter, have evolved from the results of interviews with a number of business experts and the ongoing evolution of e-Commerce systems in industry, especially those featured in various trade press articles. They are still evolving today. Visit the companion Web site for information on the latest evolutions.

The names used in this chapter for e-Commerce application types are not necessarily the only or even the best names used for them. Different people may use these names to refer to other types of applications. However, they provide a useful start to understanding the range of different e-Commerce applications.

The information in this chapter provides a general idea of some of the possibilities of these applications. The selected information also includes notes that can help developers avoid making limiting or incorrect assumptions about various possibilities of each of the applications. The rest of the text provides a method for gaining a deeper understanding of any chosen application and for developing a system to serve it.

2.2   CONSIDERING THE VARIETY OF E-COMMERCE APPLICATIONS

The most typical types of e-Commerce applications interface an organization with external individuals and/or organizations. These applications generally involve the buying, selling, trading, and/or promoting of products and/or services. They include:

- e-Businesses
- e-Brokerages
- Information utilities
- Customized marketing
- Custom manufacturing
- On-line procurement
- Supplier-customer systems integration
- Logistical management of commodity suppliers
- Human resource planning and management
- Support for non-profit organizations

Additional applications, involving enterprise-wide systems integration, are closely related to the above types of e-Commerce applications. While these types of applications are primarily internal to an organization, they:

- Generally require information external to the organization
- Cross organizational boundaries within the organization
- Contain the other attributes of a typical e-Commerce application

The internal nature of these applications leads organizations with successes in these areas to be relatively secretive about them. Thus, it may be difficult to find sufficient information about the state of the art to fully understand what other organizations are doing about them. These types of applications include:

- Advanced compensation systems
- Matrix Management Support
- Support for distributed workers
- Business modeling
- Auditing support systems

These different types of applications, which are briefly described below, are not totally distinct from one another. Rather, there is considerable overlap between them, as is illustrated in Figure 2-1. Support for non-profit organizations is not illustrated in the figure because it may involve some or all of the other application types.

The focus of each of the following descriptions is to identify the range of tasks that an application may involve for its various users. **Tasks** are specific (usually

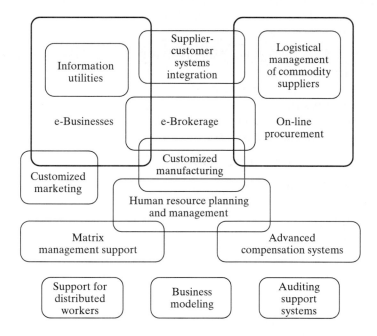

Figure 2-1   Overlapping types of e-Commerce applications

work-related) accomplishments of a person (or group of persons). Tasks accomplish work and/or personal objectives. Applications are typically composed of a number of related tasks that work toward accomplishing major organizational goals. Tasks define what has to be accomplished without dealing with how it will be accomplished. Most tasks can be accomplished in a wide number of ways, using various tools and/or procedures.

e-Commerce often involves a variety of external and internal users. **External users** are those users who are not employed by or responsible to (as with members of a non-profit group) the organization that controls the e-Commerce system, regardless of whether or not they use the system externally to the organization's facilities. **Internal users** are those users who are not employed by or responsible to (as with members of a non-profit group) the organization, that controls the e-Commerce system, regardless of whether or not they use the system externally to the organization's facilities.

2.2.1 e-Businesses

e-Businesses (also known as electronic storefronts) involve setting up Web sites that provide the main interface between an organization and its clients. e-Businesses go far beyond the average corporate home pages, which are little more than an acknowledgment that the corporation exists. Likewise, they should provide more than an online version of traditional catalog shopping. Successful e-Business sites generally:

- Provide a full range of services both to customers and to employees of the e-Business.
- Serve the whole business, including all traditional aspects of: marketing, sales, and support.
- Identify what type of products and/or services they provide and what types of clients they intend to serve.

Special types of e-Businesses include:

- e-Brokerages
- Information utilities
- Customized marketing
- Customized manufacturing
- Supplier-customer systems integration

It is important that an e-Business provide some unique competitive advantages that will entice potential customers to give it a try. Chapter 3 contains a discussion of various e-Commerce competitive advantages.

Start-up e-Business organizations are most successful if they focus on a specific type of business in a particular industry. Some examples of specific e-Business opportunities include:

- A special interest gift store
- An outfitter specializing in a particular sport
- A conference-organizing company specializing in a particular locale
- Music by a particular artist or group
- Crafts of a unique style and/or theme
- Health products focused on a particular set of diseases

Often these businesses can only exist in cyberspace because their potential customers are too spread out geographically for any physical location to achieve a high enough amount of sales. Existing businesses need to provide a reason for their customers to shop on-line rather than just go to the local shopping center and look for what they want. A possible feature could help customers get products that they want as quickly and easily as possible by identifying the closest physical location that has a desired item in stock.

NOTE: If e-Businesses are not directly involved in adding value to the products and/or services that they sell, then they may be particularly vulnerable to other e-Businesses with any type of competitive advantage. Some of the earliest successful e-Businesses were based on offering a wider variety of books or music than might be found at individual physical stores. They were able to provide this variety without excessive inventory costs by using taking orders for items that they would then acquire from various suppliers. However, this strategy is easy to copy, and e-Businesses who just resell the products and/or services of other organizations can easily lose out to direct sales by the organizations that produce the products and/or services. Currently, e-Businesses provide value by a number of techniques, including:

- Producing or modifying the product or services to suit the customer
- Lower prices than are available through local stores
- Larger selection than is typically available locally
- Fast delivery compared with ordering through a local store
- After-sales service

The main users of e-Businesses include:

- External users
  - External product sources—those who create products outside the organization
  - Customers—those who want or need the products/services
    - Current customers of the organization
    - Potential customers of the products/services
- Internal users
  - Product procurers—those who obtain any products that come from outside the organization
  - Internal product sources—those who create products inside the organization
  - Consultants—those who provide services for hire to those outside the organization
  - Product line managers—those who decide what products/services to offer to the customers
  - Marketers—those who identify needs and clients for products/services and decide how to market them
  - Support personnel—those who provide product/sales support
  - Accountants—those who provide accounting services for the e-Business

The main tasks of e-Businesses include:

- Managing product lines
- Acquiring products
- Providing service
- Marketing
- Support customers
- Purchasing
- Obtaining required support
- Providing accounting support for these tasks

Special considerations for e-Businesses include:

- e-Businesses need to create a steady stream of sales. They can only expand, if sales also expand.
- While products/services may be sold via the Web, some organizations will also maintain traditional sales methods, such as real stores.
- Delivery of products/services may be done in many ways, with Web delivery only suitable for information-based products.

Find reviews of and links to examples of e-Businesses in the Chapter 2 Cyber Supplement.

2.2.2   e-Brokerages

e-Brokerages are a specialized type of e-Business where the main business function of the organization is to bring buyers and sellers together. e-Brokerages often also include features of *on-line procurement.* Some traditional businesses that are based on brokering include:

- Travel agencies
- Stock brokers
- Real estate agencies
- Insurance agencies
- Employment services
- Auction services

NOTE: These traditional business areas are already heavily served by various e-Brokerages.

The ease of using the Web has greatly expanded the concept of brokerage to all types of products and services. There are a number of techniques that are currently being used, including:

- Gateways to selected groups of e-Businesses that have chosen to affiliate themselves, often based on their serving a similar group of customers
- Electronic shopping malls, which promise greater exposure and sometimes design consulting to the e-Businesses that pay to join them
- Electronic shopping services/agents, which will try to find desired products/services for clients at the "best" possible price
- Electronic auctions
- Reverse auctions, where customers post their wants and the prices they are willing to pay
- Barter exchanges, where members barter their products/services rather than buying/selling them

New techniques keep evolving and appearing.

Like other types of e-Businesses, it is important that an e-Brokerage have unique competitive advantages in order to gain customers (in this case, both buyers and sellers). Some of the earliest successful e-Brokerages were based on offering discount-priced airfares or insurance. They were able to provide this advantage by dealing with a number of different competing suppliers. However, the airlines and insurance companies are large organizations that can undercut prices offered by such brokers whenever they wish. Whereas most e-Businesses are actively creating or adding value to the products or services that they sell, e-Brokerages generally concentrate their servicing to arranging the sale and leave product servicing to be arranged between buyer and seller. e-Brokerages may also broker product/servicing–related insurance (such as trip cancellation insurance or extended warranties on equipment) to protect buyers and/or sellers from problems with their sale.

An e-Business with some products and/or services of its own may choose to also e-broker-related products and/or services in order to provide a larger selection to its customers without increasing its inventory or staff costs.

NOTE: Since e-Brokerages are not directly involved in adding value to the products and/or services that they broker, they are particularly vulnerable to changes in the way people choose do business and to other e-Brokerages with any type of competitive advantage. Traditional brokerages sell their services based on the expertise they can provide buyers and sellers in making good deals. When buyers and sellers do not feel the need for this expert advice, they will often find it cheaper to deal directly with one another. Where this advice is found valuable, it may lead the organization to market the advice directly either in the form of an *information utility* or a *consulting* e-Business.

The main users of e-Brokerages include:

- External users
  - Sellers, who create products and/or services outside the organization
  - Customers, who want or need the products/services
    - Current customers
    - Potential customers
- Internal users
  - Product line managers, who decide what products and/or services to handle and who manage and assist individual brokers
  - Brokers, who match customers with sellers and who may assist in the negotiations between them
  - Marketers, who decide how to market brokerage services
  - Support personnel, who provide product support
  - Accountants, who provide accounting services for the e-Brokerage

The main tasks of e-Brokerages include:

- Standardizing product identifications and descriptions
- Matching customers and sellers
- Providing advice
- Assisting negotiations
- Marketing brokerage services
- Providing accounting support for these tasks

Special considerations for e-Brokerages include:

- e-Brokerages need to create a steady stream of sales because their income is based on the commissions from these sales.
- e-Brokering can occur at considerable distances from both buyers and sellers.

 Find reviews of and links to examples of e-Brokerages in the Chapter 2 Cyber Supplement.

2.2.3   Information Utilities

Information utilities are a specialized type of e-Business whose main activities include the obtaining, trading, selling, and giving away of information (including advertising). This may include:

- Entertainment—such as on-line radio and television
- Expert opinions—such as technical or financial advice
- Facts—such as sports scores, weather reports, historical or scientific data
- Games—whether played on the Web, on the client's computer, or otherwise
- Graphics—such as clip art, photos
- News and news analysis—whether the same as provided via another medium or uniquely via the Web
- Any other forms of information that may be provided for the use of individuals and/or organizations

Many existing (print and broadcast) media have adopted the use of information utilities as an additional format for disseminating their information. In many cases their main costs of producing the information have already been covered in their original medium, and the information can be converted for reuse on the Web at very little cost. This provides these media with a new source of both advertising revenue and exposure.

The Web has made possible the relatively low-cost publishing of all kinds of information. It also makes it easier to find people interested in this information. However, just because someone wishes to publish some information and other people are interested in the information does not guarantee that there is the potential for a viable information utility. Information utilities need to make money from their efforts. It is very possible that advertisers may not be available and that people interested in the information may not be willing to pay for it.

NOTE: Despite copyright laws and other forms of intellectual property "protections," many individuals and organization may readily pirate information that is posted on the Web or that is provided to them via other media. Thus, as information gets older, the likelihood that it may be used without compensation increases. Information utilities need to be continually creating new information in order to maintain their viability.

The main users of information utilities include:

- External users
  - External information providers, who generate the information outside the organization
  - Information sponsors, who add their own advertising information
  - Information consumers, who want or need the information
    - Current consumers
    - Potential consumers
- Internal users
  - Internal information providers, who generate the information inside the organization

- Information gatherers, who gather and/or input the information
- Information editors, who decide what information to provide
- Information processors, who format, process, or otherwise modify the information to make it more useful to information consumers
- Information marketers, who identify needs and consumers for information ser-vices and who market these services
- Accountants, who provide accounting services for the information utility

The main tasks include:

- Gathering information
- Editing and processing information
- Marketing information
- Consuming information
- Providing accounting support for these tasks

Special considerations for information utilities include:

- Information utilities need to keep a steady stream of new information to maintain the interest and confidence of information consumers.
- While information is usually delivered to information consumers via the Web, it may first exist and be transformed through a number of other formats at a number of different locations.

 Find reviews of and links to examples of information utilities in the Chapter 2 Cyber Supplement.

2.2.4   Customized Marketing

Customized marketing involves using individual customer profiles in identifying opportunities for customized offers that will be of particular interest to individual consumers, communicating these opportunities to the consumers, and following up on them, as appropriate. Customized marketing is generally implemented as a part of an e-Business application. It may also be used with other e-Commerce applications, especially: e-Brokerages, and information utilities. Customized marketing may also be involved with *the electronic support of non-profit organizations.* Customized marketing is based on customer profiles that involve analyzing individual customer's interests and buying patterns (which the customer often has to be bribed into providing via "shopping club" and similar incentives) to predict the effect of an organization's changes in products or services that are offered to different customers.

NOTE: Customized marketing has to be sensitive to the customer's rights to individual privacy and should avoid pestering or otherwise irritating the customer.

The main users of customized marketing include:

- External users
  - Customers, who want or need the products/service
    - Current customers
    - Potential customers

- Suppliers, who supply products and/or services to the organization to sell to the customers and who may receive customer profiles to help them improve
- Marketing analysis consultants, who can provide profiles of various groups of potential customers
- Internal users
  - Product line managers, who decide what products and/or services to offer to the customers
  - Customer analysts, who develop profiles and buying projections of customers
  - Marketers, who decide how to market products and services
  - Product engineers, who design products and/or services for customers
  - Product procurers, who help obtain products and/or services from suppliers to sell to customers
  - Support personnel, who provide product support
  - Accountants, who provide accounting services for customized marketing

The main tasks of customized marketing include:

- Monitoring consumer trends
- Profiling customers
- Tracking customer purchases
- Managing product lines
- Advising suppliers about product requirements
- Advising on the design of new products
- Designing marketing strategies
- Designing customer rewards and incentives
- Planning required support
- Marketing
- Providing required support
- Communicating with customers
- Providing customer rewards and incentives
- Providing accounting support for these tasks

Special considerations for customized marketing include:

- Organizations need to decide whether to periodically contact customers or to contact them only when it has a new product or service in which they might be interested.
- Customer profiling should be conducted on an ongoing basis so that profile information is available when needed.
- Communications with customers about products and/or services may be done in many ways (including personalized mailings (electronic or traditional), telephone calls, and so on) with Web delivery only suitable for follow-up information on products or services.
- Customer profiling is generally a strictly-guarded, private, internal activity, but may include obtaining additional information from marketing analysis consultants and/or suppliers.

 Find reviews of and links to examples of customized marketing in the Chapter 2 Cyber Supplement.

2.2.5   Custom Manufacturing

Managing custom manufacturing (which is a type of "just-in-time" activity) involves the optimization of allocation and scheduling of various internal and external resources (including people, equipment, materials, and facilities) to efficiently meet rapidly changing needs.

Although this is often developed as a primarily internal application, there are an increasing number of organizations that recognize that customized manufacturing can provide them with a competitive advantage in their e-Business. It is useful to be able to provide prospective customers with the ability to specify what they want and to provide them estimates of when their custom orders are likely to be completed.

Custom manufacturing may interact with a variety of other applications, including *e-Business, e-Brokerage, on-line procurement, human resource planning and management, supplier-customer systems integration,* and/or *logistical management of commodity suppliers.*

NOTE: Because of the large number of other applications that custom manufacturing can include or can interact with, it is important to define clear boundaries between what is being considered as part of this application and what is being left to other applications.

The main users of custom manufacturing include:

- External users
  - Part sources, which create provide required parts and materials from outside the organization
  - Customers, who want or need the products
    - Current customers
    - Potential customers
- Internal users
  - Product procurers, who obtain any parts and materials that come from outside the organization
  - Product line managers, who decide what products to offer to the customers
  - Production managers, who manage the manufacturing process
  - Production workers, who perform the actual manufacturing
  - Marketers, who identify needs and consumers for products and/or services and decide how to market them
  - Accountants, who provide accounting services for the custom manufacturing

The main tasks of custom manufacturing include:

- Managing product lines
- Acquiring material and parts
- Scheduling manufacturing
- Manufacturing
- Marketing
- Ordering custom products
- Obtaining required assistance
- Providing accounting support for these tasks

Special considerations for custom manufacturing include:

- Custom manufacturers need to create a stream of sales that supports a steady stream of manufacturing. They can only expand if sales also expand.
- While the manufacturing of products can be arranged via the Web, some organizations will also maintain traditional sales methods, such as real offices.
- Delivery of products and/or services may be done in many ways, with Web delivery only suitable for information-based products.

 Find reviews of and links to examples of custom manufacturing in the Chapter 2 Cyber Supplement.

2.2.6 On-line Procurement

On-line procurement involves using the Internet to improve the flexibility in choosing suppliers and to reduce the financial and time costs in an organization's procurements of various materials, products, and/or services. It is especially important for organizations with frequent custom (changing) needs for materials, products and/or services. On-line procurement needs to be flexible enough to take into account a variety of differing procurement needs from within the organization it serves. It should assist people throughout the organization to post the specifications of what they require, to receive bids on these needs, and to evaluate them electronically. It should assist the purchasing and accounting departments to monitor, advise, and otherwise assist in these procurements, in an "as required" manner.

On-line procurement may be used to support various business activities, including: e-Businesses that sell products produced by other organizations; e-Brokerages; and custom manufacturing. Special cases of on-line procurement include *supplier-customer systems integration* and the *logistical management of commodity suppliers*.

Traditionally, most on-line procurement has been performed by large organizations that expect potential suppliers to keep up with their changing needs. Individuals and smaller organizations are now able to utilize on-line procurement services via the assistance of e-Brokerages. However, in such cases they make use of the brokerage's systems rather than developing systems of their own.

NOTE: On-line procurement only works if there are suppliers who are interested in providing the required products and/or services at the required price. It can seldom be fully automated, and only then where it handles existing contracts, as in supplier-customer systems integration and the logistical management of commodity suppliers. In other cases, considerable human intervention may be required to ensure obtaining all required goods and/or services.

The main users of on-line procurement are:

- External users
  - Suppliers, who sell products and/or services outside the organization and who may support those products/services
    - Current suppliers
    - Potential suppliers

- Internal users
  - Product procurers, who help obtain products and/or services from outside the organization
  - Managers, whose departments require the products and/or services and who have a budget to obtain them
  - Workers, who will use the products and/or services
  - Accountants, who provide accounting services for the on-line procurement

The main tasks of on-line procurement include:

- Identifying the need for products and/or services
- Justifying the need against the budget
- Selecting between competing products and/or services
- Ordering products and/or services
- Receiving products and/or services
- Paying for products and/or services
- Obtaining required support
- Providing additional accounting support for these tasks

Special considerations for on-line procurement include:

- Products and/or services need to be procured quickly and efficiently whenever they are needed.
- The source of the products and/or services is less important than their quality, cost, and availability to the organization when and where it requires them.

 Find reviews of and links to examples of on-line procurement in the Chapter 2 Cyber Supplement.

2.2.7   Supplier–Customer Systems Integration

Supplier-customer systems integration is a specialized combination of e-Business and on-line procurement. Supplier-customer systems integration generally involves development of complimentary systems to be used by suppliers (e-Business) and their customers (on-line procurement) to handle automatic ordering and other regular business transactions. "Suppliers" typically develop customer systems that include additional features (such as inventory control), which entice their customers to use the systems, locking them in with (or at least favoring), the particular supplier. Such systems are also developed in service industries (such as the travel industry). It is possible for both parties to enter jointly into the development of shared systems where they will each benefit. In some cases, it may be difficult to determine who is the "supplier" and who is the "customer."

Most current supplier–customer integrated systems are currently developed for use between businesses (or other organizations). However, individuals are getting increasingly integrated with organizations with which they regularly do business. The key element in supplier–customer integration is creating and supporting a dependency of one individual or organization on another via sharing systems and information.

NOTE: The customer systems need not be resident on the customer's computers. Suppliers may "generously" provide most (or all) of the hardware as well as providing the software for meeting all of the customer's needs. In this way they hope to gain a greater influence on the customer's purchasing.

The main users of supplier-customer systems integration include:

- External users
  - External product sources, which create products outside the organization
  - Customers, who want or need the products and/or services
    - Current customers
    - Potential customers
- Internal users
  - Internal product sources, which create products inside the organization
  - Product procurers, who obtain any products that come from outside the organization
  - Product line managers, who decide what products to offer to the customers
  - Marketers, who identify needs and consumers for products and supporting ser-vices and decide how to market them
  - Support personnel, who help develop product support systems
  - Accountants, who provide accounting services for the supplier–customer systems integration

The main tasks of supplier–customer systems integration include:

- Managing product lines
- Acquiring products
- Marketing
- Integrating support
- Purchasing
- Providing support for related tasks
- Providing accounting support for these tasks

Special considerations for supplier–customer systems integration include:

- This only works in industries where the ordering, handling, and/or the use of products requires a high level of support or where special tools can enhance the use of certain products.
- Typically the Internet and the Web should be involved in providing the support or in some other way linking the customer to the supplier.

 Find reviews of examples of customer-supplier integration in the Chapter 2 Cyber Supplement.

2.2.8 Logistical Management of Commodity Suppliers

Logistical management of commodity suppliers is a specialized case of on-line procurement that involves the development of systems by large consumers to manage the ongoing procurement and delivery scheduling of commodities. Initial commodity contracting can be done via either traditional or on-line procurement. However, in commodity-based industries, such as agri-food, contracts will be established between consumers (generally manufacturers who use the commodities as raw materials) and suppliers (such as farmers) without fixing the price or delivery date. Further logistical management is required to fix the dates and quantities of deliveries.

This allows the consumer to adjust the price for deliveries on a given date based on demand and allows producers to assess their options (including different prices) in fixing the date of delivery at a future time (after the initial contract is agreed upon).

NOTE: Suppliers must be convinced that the benefits they receive will outweigh their efforts in using the system. Forcing commodity suppliers to use an electronic system may decrease the number of suppliers available to the organization. Provisions may need to be made to allow important suppliers to continue doing business with a human representative.

The main users of logistical management of commodity suppliers include:

- External users
  - Commodity suppliers
    - Current suppliers
    - Potential suppliers
- Internal users
  - Commodity procurers, who help obtain and schedule commodities
  - Managers, whose departments require the commodities
  - Workers, who will use the commodities
  - Accountants, who provide accounting services for the logistical management of commodities suppliers

The main tasks of logistical management of commodity suppliers include:

- Identifying the need for commodities
- Justifying the need against the budget
- Advertising the need for commodities
- Selecting between competing suppliers
- Purchasing commodities
- Scheduling delivery of commodities
- Receiving commodities
- Paying for commodities
- Providing additional accounting support for these tasks

A special consideration for logistical management of commodity suppliers is that this application will be performed centrally by an organization that may interact with a large number of commodity suppliers.

 Find reviews of examples of logistical management of commodity suppliers in the Chapter 2 Cyber Supplement.

2.2.9   Human Resource Planning and Management

Human resource planning and management involves optimizing the placement of people within an organization. This includes:

- Identifying upcoming personnel needs
- Tracking the skills and performance of current employees

- Anticipating future training and promotion or reassignment of employees within the organization
- Recruiting both internal and external applicants to fill positions that occur

Human resource planning and management may involve matrix management techniques to optimize the allocation of human and other resources to various projects in matrix-style organizations.

NOTE: Human resource planning and management involves considerably more than just using the Web to post jobs and to obtain job applications. It needs to integrate these activities within an ongoing human resource plan for the organization.

NOTE: This application is generally performed internally by an organization that employs or that intends to employ the people it is planning and managing. It is not typically performed by an external recruiting service or placement agency, which would be a form of e-Brokerage. Human resource information is highly confidential, and allowing an outside organization to manage it could lead to various privacy problems and conflicts of interest.

Special cases of human resource planning and management are used for customized manufacturing, advanced compensation systems, and matrix management support.

The main users of human resource planning and management include:

- External users
  - Employment candidates, who are looking for a new job
  - External people, who might consider working for this organization
  - Current employees, who might want a change in jobs (and who are normally external to the selection process)
  - Employment services, which place people registered with them (for a fee)
  - Training services, which provide various types of training courses and consulting
- Internal users
  - Human resource professionals, who help manage the efficient use of employees for the organization
  - Managers, whose departments or projects require employees and who have a budget to obtain them
  - Workers, who are interested in advancing themselves
  - Trainers, who train employees within the organization
  - Accountants, who provide accounting services for human resource planning and management and who handle the accounting of the employee payroll

The main tasks of human resource planning and management include:

- Identifying upcoming personnel needs
- Tracking the skills and performance of current employees
- Anticipating future training and promotion or reassignment of employees within the organization
- Forecasting the need for future training and hiring
- Developing job descriptions
- Advertising open positions
- Identifying potential internal candidates for positions as they become available

- Selecting between competing applicants
- Reviewing applications
- Interviewing
- Conducting hiring negotiations
- Providing company orientations to new hires
- Arranging training programs for employees
- Providing additional accounting support for these tasks

Special considerations for human resource planning and management include:

- Human resource planning and management is an ongoing activity that should be performed periodically (e.g., every quarter) and that may need to be performed on demand as the needs of the organization change.
- Employees need to be hired quickly and efficiently whenever they are needed.
- Human resource planning and management is generally a strictly guarded, private, internal activity, although it may interact with externally available training programs.
- Sometimes an organization may prefer to limit employment searches to current employees, sometimes to non-employees, and sometimes it will be open.
- The current location of an employment candidate may affect both the interviewing process and the costs of hiring.

Find reviews of examples of human resource planning and management systems in the Chapter 2 Cyber Supplement.

2.2.10   Advanced Compensation Systems

Advanced compensation systems involve the use of information systems to support a variety of compensation schemes that can be customized to individual employees. This needs to involve much more than just computerizing the payroll. Errors in compensation systems can lead to high levels of employee discontent.

Users
- External users
  - Banks, which receive deposits for employee payrolls
  - Accounting consultants, who may help with compensation processing for the organization
  - Income tax collectors, who want records of compensation and amounts of the compensation, sent directly to them in anticipation of taxes on the compensation
- Internal users
  - Human resource professionals, who help manage the efficient use of employees for the organization
  - Managers, whose departments or projects require employees and who have a budget to pay them
  - Workers, who may be compensated in a variety of ways for a variety of accomplishments
  - Accountants, who provide accounting services for advanced compensation systems and who handle the accounting of the employee payroll

The main tasks of advanced compensation systems include:

- Designing specialized compensation schemes
- Communicating these schemes to the affected employees
- Evaluating employee contributions to the organization according to these schemes
- Updating employee records with appropriate information regarding their performance
- Evaluating the results of advanced compensation schemes
- Providing accounting support for these tasks

Special considerations for advanced compensation systems include:

- Employees need to be compensated (by pay and other means) appropriately within a reasonable time of when the compensation was earned.
- Some organizations will handle their entire compensation system in-house, while many smaller organizations will have their compensation processed for them by banks or accounting consultants.

 Find reviews of examples of advanced compensation systems in the Chapter 2 Cyber Supplement.

2.2.11 Matrix Management Support

Matrix management support involves managing and optimizing the allocation of human and other resources to various projects in matrix-style organizations.

The main users of matrix management support include:

- External users
  - Employees, being managed (note they are usually external to this application, because they often have little or no control over it)
  - Customers making use of the services of these employees
- Internal users
  - Project managers, who require employees and who have a budget to obtain them
  - Project schedulers, who manage the resource needs of one or more projects
  - Human resource professionals, who help hire employees for the organization
  - Inventory managers, who handle the acquisition, storage, and allocation of inventory
  - Facilities managers, who handle the scheduling and allocation of facilities
  - Accountants, who provide accounting services to deal with the allocation of salaries and other resource costs to individual projects

The main tasks of matrix management support include:

- Establishing projects
- Establishing and managing project budgets
- Establishing and managing project time lines
- Identifying and allocating, reallocating, and/or obtaining suitable resources, including:
  - People
  - Inventory

- Facilities
- Other
- Evaluating projects, including evaluating:
  - Overall project success and profitability
  - Worker contributions
  - Inventory used
  - Facilities used
- Providing additional accounting support for these tasks

Special considerations for matrix management support include:

- Projects go through their own life cycles. Organizations conducting a number of projects at a time may need to manage not only each individual project, but also the reallocation of various resources between projects, as needed, to optimize the success of all projects.
- Matrix management support is only relevant within a project-based organization or an organization with a number of projects as a part of its regular operations.

 Find reviews of examples of matrix management support systems in the Chapter 2 Cyber Supplement.

2.2.12   Support for Distributed Workers

Support for distributed workers involves helping managers and other support personnel to support workers who are located at a variety of different locations other than where the manager or support person is located. While work can be accomplished in a distributed manner, many of the traditional interactions (management–worker and worker–worker) may be inhibited by this distribution. This may include the remote support of sales and service personnel with sales and/or service packages that can be used by sales or service personnel from a customer location.

The main users of support for distributed workers include:

- External users (indirect)
  - Customers to whom the worker is selling to or supporting are indirect users, but are not likely to be allowed direct access
- Internal users
  - Managers, who manage workers who are usually or occasionally at a different location from the manager
  - Sales, support, production, and other workers and/or managers
    - Who work at home
    - Who work at a branch location away from the main location
    - Who are visiting or working at a customer's location
    - Who are away at a training course or conference
    - Whose manager is temporarily at another location
  - Administrators, who establish organizational policies and procedures that everyone is expected to follow
  - Support personnel, who may be needed to assist the worker with technical and other matters

The main tasks of support for distributed workers include:

- Communicating scheduling information
- Reporting on the status of work
- Reporting on meetings with customers
- Conducting regular, scheduled distributed meetings
- Getting advice and decisions on an "as required" basis
- Getting technical support on an "as required" basis
- Ensuring easy access to memos and other organizational news
- Ensuring easy access to organizational policies and procedures

Special considerations for support for distributed workers include:

- Support for distributed workers needs to be constantly available during regular working hours and to a limited extent also outside working hours.
- This support should be available at as many locations as possible.

 Find reviews of examples of support for distributed workers in the Chapter 2 Cyber Supplement.

2.2.13   Business Modeling

Business modeling involves developing and analyzing models of the interactions of significant parts of an organization and potentially of other entities with which parts of the organization interact. Business modeling may investigate the effect of changes in the organization on a wide range of issues, including profitability, quality of products or services, customer satisfaction, and resource utilization. Some specialized types of business modeling are described below.

2.2.13.1   Dynamic, Real-Time Business Performance Control

Dynamic, real-time business performance control involves tracking the time and costs of production from marketing through scheduling, production, and delivery to the consumer to assist in both the organizational management of these processes and the tactical evaluation and redesign of affected organizational processes and units.

The main users of dynamic, real-time business performance control include:

- External information providers (who may have limited access to the system for purposes of providing data to be used in the modeling)
  - General purpose information sources, which are available to all organizations
  - Consultants, who gather specific external information specifically for the organization
- Internal users
  - Strategic managers and planners, who want to evaluate and improve the performance of the organization
  - Tactile managers, who need to improve the performance of areas they manage and to coordinate the interaction of their areas with other areas in the organization
  - Operational managers, who must provide input data and implement control decisions

- Industry analysts, who try and determine typical performance expectations in similar organizations and industries
- Accountants, who accumulate and process relevant data

The main tasks of dynamic, real-time business performance control include:

- Obtaining information about industry performance expectations
- Obtaining performance measures within the organization
- Planning performance objectives
- Evaluating performance (including the effects of changes)
- Planning changes to meet performance objectives
- Communicating changes to all affected
- Implementing changes

Special considerations for dynamic, real-time business performance control include:

- Dynamic, real-time business performance control is an ongoing activity that leads to both minor and major changes.
  - Minor changes may occur daily or weekly.
  - Major changes may occur every few months.
- Dynamic, real-time business performance control is generally a strictly-guarded, private, internal activity, although it often makes use of information about the environment in which the organization interacts.

2.2.13.2 Multi-Dimensional Profitability Tracking and Analysis

Multi-dimensional profitability tracking and analysis involves tracking and managing the costs of production and of servicing customers to focus on the most profitable mixes of products, product lines, territories, and even individual customers. This may include evaluating the viability of companies as potential investments by comparing their performance and potential with other companies and with industry-wide expectations. This should go beyond traditional measures of past performance to include modeling various factors that may be significant to future potential.

The main users of multi-dimensional profitability tracking and analysis include:

- External information providers (who may have limited access to the system for purposes of providing data to be used in the modeling)
  - General purpose information sources, which are available to all organizations
  - Consultants, who gather specific external information specifically for the organization
  - Customers, who have purchased products and/or services
- Internal users
  - Marketers, who use this information to adjust pricing
  - Production, which uses this information to improve productivity
  - Support, which uses this information in determining levels of support to provide different customers
  - Industry analysts, who try and determine typical performance expectations in similar organizations and industries
  - Accountants, who accumulate and process relevant data

The main tasks of multi-dimensional profitability tracking and analysis include:

- Obtaining information about industry profitability expectations
- Obtaining profitability measures within the organization
- Planning profitability objectives
- Evaluating profitability (including the effects of changes)
- Planning organizational changes to meet profitability objectives
- Planning marketing changes to meet profitability objectives
- Implementing changes

Special considerations for multi-dimensional profitability tracking and analysis include:

- Multi-dimensional profitability tracking and analysis should provide input on a regular basis to help the organization adjust both its internal efficiency and its external prices.
- Multi-dimensional profitability tracking and analysis is generally a strictly-guarded, private, internal activity, although it often makes use of information about the customers and environment with which the organization interacts.

2.2.13.3 Competitive Analysis/Benchmarking

Competitive analysis/benchmarking involves obtaining corporate intelligence (which isn't necessarily readily available) about one's competitors, using this intelligence to predict their likely corporate strategies, and then determining a corporate strategy to match or beat theirs.

The main users of competitive analysis include:

- External information providers (who may have limited access to the system for purposes of providing data to be used in the modeling)
  - General purpose information sources, which are available to all organizations
  - Consultants, who gather specific external information specifically for the organization
- Internal users
  - Strategic managers and planners, who want to evaluate and improve the performance of the organization
  - Tactile managers, who need to improve the performance of areas they manage and to coordinate the interaction of their areas with other areas in the organization
  - Operational managers, who must provide input data and implement control decisions
  - Industry analysts, who identify performance measures of competitive organizations
  - Accountants, who accumulate and process relevant data

The main tasks of competitive analysis include:

- Obtaining information about the strategies, organization, and performance of competitors
- Obtaining performance measures within the organization
- Planning strategies and changes to beat the competition
- Implementing organizational changes

- Evaluating performance (including the effects of changes)
- Communicating changes to all affected

Special considerations for competitive analysis include:

- Competitive analysis needs to be an ongoing activity resulting in changes whenever they are deemed necessary.
- Competitive analysis is a strictly-guarded, private, internal activity, although it requires considerable information about the competition

2.2.13.4   Organizational Planning and Rationalization

Organizational planning and rationalization involves identifying different users of common information and people performing similar tasks and restructuring the organization (using information engineering techniques) to increase the efficiency of the organization.

The main users of organizational planning and rationalization include:

- External information providers (who may have limited access to the system for purposes of providing data to be used in the modeling)
  - General purpose information sources, which are available to all organizations
  - Consultants, who gather specific external information specifically for the organization
- Internal users
  - Strategic managers and planners, who want to improve the efficiency of the organization's particular business tactics
  - Operational managers, who must provide input data to the planning process and implement decisions based on the resulting plans
  - Organizational planners, who analyze the existing organization and suggest changes
  - Market analysts, who try to determine information about external forces on the organization
  - Accountants, who accumulate and process relevant data

The main tasks of organizational planning and rationalization include:

- Analyzing the existing organizational and informational structure
- Identifying potential changes in organizational and/or informational structure
- Evaluating the potential of structural changes to improve the efficiency of the organization
- Implementing changes:
  - To the organizational structure
  - To the informational structure
  - To the personnel in the organization
- Providing accounting support that evaluates the potential for and the results of these changes

Special considerations for organizational planning and rationalization include:

- While these processes could continually identify potential improvements, major organizational changes need to be made only infrequently due to the stresses they cause on organizational personnel.

- Organizational planning is a strictly-guarded, private, internal activity, although it often makes use of information about the environment in which the organization interacts.

2.2.14   Auditing Support Systems

Auditing support systems involve sophisticated tools for in-house and for independent auditing of organizations in a range of areas, including: finances, management, and security. The greatest challenge is to identify how to integrate auditing support into a variety of different organizational units and information systems.

The main users of auditing support systems include:

- External users
  - Consultants, who conduct various external audits of the organization
  - Income tax collectors, who want financial records of the organization and its business dealings
  - Investors, who have a financial interest in the organization
  - Partners, stockholders, and other owners
  - Banks and other organizations providing loans
  - Government granting agencies
- Internal users
  - Managers, who are responsible for the proper running of the organization
  - Accountants, who are responsible for organizational accounts
  - Auditors, who conduct internal audits
  - Information technology professionals, who conduct information audits

The main tasks of auditing support systems include:

- Accumulating data about systems to be audited
- Accumulating data about business practices to be audited
- Protecting audit data
- Analyzing the reliability and accuracy of audit data
- Analyzing the suitability of business practices
- Summarizing audit data for presentation
- Identifying situations requiring improvement

Special considerations for auditing support systems include:

- While traditional audits need to be performed at the end of an organization's financial year, many other audits may be required from time to time in an organization. Data to support audits needs to be accumulated on an ongoing basis.
- Some organizations will handle most of their auditing in-house, while many smaller organizations will have consultants perform some or all of their audits.

2.2.15   Support for Non-Profit Organizations

Electronic support for non-profit (or "not-for-profit") **organizations** involves setting up Web sites that support interfacing between a non-profit organization, its various executives, its general membership, and its potential members. These sites should provide a full range of organizational services. They must go far beyond being electronic versions of traditional newsletters. Often they involve aspects of e-Businesses and information utilities.

NOTE: Individual members can often identify a wide variety of services that could be provided by a non-profit organization's on-line system. Non-profit organizations need to make careful decisions about which services they can provide and the order in which they provide these services. Many members will not be willing to support raising membership fees or other organizational revenues to support growing bureaucracies of professional organizational staff. The alternative is the use of volunteers to support particular aspects of the organization. However, individual volunteers often are limited both in terms of the time they have to give and in their particular talents.

NOTE: Electronic support for non-profit organizations can easily grow into a very large and very useful application. It may be important to ensure that the needs of developing and supporting this application do not distract from the main purposes of the organization and thus defeat their purpose.

The main users of electronic support for non-profit organizations include:

- External users
  - Product sources, which provide supplies and/or services from outside the organization
  - Customers, who are outside the organization and who want or need the services and/or products
  - Current customers
  - Potential customers
  - Potential members, who might become members
- Internal users
  - Members, who are inside the organization who want or need the services and/or products and who, by their membership, have a say in the running of the organization
  - Product procurers, who obtain any supplies and/or services that come from outside the organization
  - Project managers, who decide what services and/or products to offer to the clients/members
  - Project workers, who develop special services for clients/members
  - Fundraisers, who raise funds to support the organization's projects
  - Support personnel, who provide support to clients/members
  - Accountants, who provide accounting services for the non-profit organization

The main tasks of electronic support for non-profit organizations include:

- Managing projects
- Acquiring supplies and/or services
- Producing and/or providing products
- Providing services
- Fundraising
- Registering membership

- Supporting members
- Purchasing memberships
- Obtaining required services and/or products
- Providing accounting support for these tasks

Special considerations for the electronic support for non-profit organizations include:

- Non-profit organizations exist to serve their members/clients. They can be evaluated by how effectively they fulfill their objectives rather than in terms of dollars of sales. However, they can only expand if income (from memberships, fundraising, and/or sales) expands.
- While services and/or products may be sold via the Web, some organizations will also maintain traditional methods of interacting with their members/customers (such as newsletters, meetings, and offices).
- Delivery of services and/or products may be done in many ways, with Web delivery only suitable for information-based services and/or products.

 Find reviews and examples of and links to non-profit organization sites in the Chapter 2 Cyber Supplement.

2.3 APPLYING KNOWLEDGE OF DIFFERENT TYPES OF E-COMMERCE APPLICATIONS

2.3.1 Migrating Legacy Electronic Data Interchange (EDI) Systems to the Internet

Prior to the emergence of the World Wide Web, various organizations had their own unique systems for conducting business using a combination of computers and telecommunications. These systems generally involved proprietary techniques for **electronic data interchange** (EDI) that were only available for use between branches of the organization and for use by other selected organizations in doing business with the organization that developed the software. Electronic data interchange is, "the automated exchange of any predefined and structured data for business purposes among information systems of two or more organizations."[1]

These pre-Web systems are often referred to as legacy systems to denote their use of older technologies. **Legacy systems** are systems that are already in use by an organization that continue to fulfill an important need within the organization but that include outdated and/or non-standard technologies that do not readily integrate with current technologies. Migrating legacy EDI systems onto the Internet involves both technical and competitive challenges and opportunities. The technical challenges and opportunities of migration will be discussed in Chapter 12.

Migrating to the Web makes it easier for traditional users to access both an organization's e-Commerce system and the systems of the organization's competitors. While this may increase the potential for increased business, it will also increase the competitive pressures on the organization. Once an e-Commerce system migrates to the Web it must be prepared to evolve, just as any other e-Commerce system would, in order to stay ahead of its competition. To prepare for this evolution, it is important for organizations to understand the various development processes discussed throughout this book.

2.3.2 New e-Commerce Applications for Existing Organizations

Existing organizations can make use of the above types of e-Commerce applications as a basis for identifying how e-Commerce could be integrated with their existing activities. It should be remembered that these types are only generalizations of common e-Commerce applications and will need to be modified to suit any organization. This modification may involve dealing with only part of a type, either on its own or in combination with parts of other types. It is important that any resulting system suit the particular needs and strengths of the organization.

Existing organizations may follow a variety of strategies in selecting the first area in which to develop an e-Commerce system. Some of these strategies include:

- A retail sales organization may build on its strengths by developing an e-Business as an on-line "branch" operation similar to opening a physical "branch" at some real location. This branch might offer a similar set of products and/or services to customers around the world, and especially to customers not close to any existing physical branch.
- Other kinds of organizations similarly may build on their strengths by developing other types of e-Commerce applications. For example, publishing organizations may wish to develop information utilities, and manufacturers may wish to develop on-line procurement.
- An organization may wish to develop an e-Commerce application that allows it to diversify its operations. For example, a retail sales organization may wish to develop an e-Brokerage to help its customers obtain items that it does not normally handle.
- An organization may wish to develop a small e-Commerce application in an area that allows it to gain experience with e-Commerce without risking major impacts on its main line of business. For example, an organization might develop some form of business modeling that can both assist with existing activities and can provide experience in the complexities of e-Commerce applications without major involvement of external users.

Whatever business strategy an organization wishes to pursue, it needs to further identify the major factors and investigate the feasibility of the application area before proceeding to authorize the expenditure of major amounts of resources on a full-scale development.

2.3.3 e-Commerce Applications for Start-up Organizations

Many people, buying into the promise and the hype of e-Commerce, consider developing their own e-Commerce businesses. While there are many good opportunities, an individual or a group of people needs to be careful that there is a sound business case for establishing such a business.

People need to recognize that an e-Commerce start-up business still has all of the organizational and financial start-up needs of a regular business, in addition to the needs to develop a suitable e-Commerce system to conduct business with its customers. Some of these start-up concerns include:

- Having a thorough knowledge of the intended products and/or services to be offered
- Establishing, registering, and optionally incorporating the business
- Obtaining sufficient start-up financing to run the business until it has an established cash flow (which is often longer than optimistically expected)
- Marketing the business and finding customers
- Hiring and managing staff
- Obtaining and furnishing a business location
- Identifying and conforming to applicable government regulations

There are three types of e-Commerce systems that are most suited for start-up businesses:

- e-Businesses selling products or services can be successful, especially where there is little likelihood of direct competition over sufficient time to get established.
  - Custom-made products, especially if custom manufactured, are generally fairly safe from direct competition. Even where there is competition, the uniqueness and quality of the particular products may help to minimize the effects of competition.
  - Products specific to a small and geographically diverse niche market are usually safe from competition by large organizations, which aim for mass markets. They are not immune from being copied by customers who think they can do better.
  - Services that need to be delivered locally may have little competition, depending on the locale, but may not have sufficient exposure to be successful.
  - Services, which can be delivered at a distance, may have to compete, but may be successful based on their quality, if this quality can be proved to potential customers.
- e-Brokerages have an advantage over other e-Businesses in that they do not have the costs associated with the inventory being sold and/or staff whose services are being sold. The brokerage activity is a service that can be performed at a distance from both customers and suppliers. e-Brokerages can be especially successful where they broker-unique products and/or services that they are knowledgeable about to an identifiable niche market. In such circumstances, the knowledge of the brokerage organization adds additional value beyond the basic service of brokering.
- Information utilities can be developed to help market a consultant's expertise on a wider and potentially mass market scale.
  - Many of the most successful information utilities provide information free to end-users. While this may involve repackaging information that has already been collected or created for other purposes, a business needs income to survive. Businesses can only afford to give things or information away if giving them away generates revenue. While many existing information utilities generate their revenues via sponsorship or advertising, there is only so much money that can be obtained from sponsors or advertisers. Much of the advertising or sponsorship revenue that might be obtained is already committed.

- The alternative to giving away all information is to sell part or all of it. This is most successful where giving away some information acts as advertising that convinces its readers to buy other services or information from the information utility.

In either case, an information utility has to convince someone to pay, either as a sponsor or as a buyer, for its information products.

2.3.4   Student Assignment—Identifying an Interesting e-Commerce Application

2.3.4.1   Preparing Yourself for the Project

It is recommended that project work be posted onto the World Wide Web where your instructor, your marker, and other students can read them.

Developing Web pages can be done easily in the current versions of a variety of word processing software packages (such as Microsoft Word and WordPerfect). It can also be done in special Web page creation tools (such as Page Mill) and in special features of major Web browsers (such as Netscape Communicator). Students can choose the Web page development tool of their choice. The Web pages to be developed for student assignments in this book require very few features. The main features to learn include:

- Paragraph text
- Headings
- Lists
- Links (to pages, sections within pages, and "mailto")

Advanced features that are desirable to learn include:

- Including pictures within pages
- Creating tables
- Creating forms
- Using custom background colors or designs

Students may wish to learn additional features. However, there is no requirement for students to do so.

2.3.4.2   Building a Personal Home Page

If you have not already done so, you should build a personal home page for yourself. The page should contain, as a minimum, your name, department, year, and a "mailto" link to allow people to send you e-mail. It is recommended that you include something about your skills, interests, and the courses you are currently taking. If you like, it could even contain your on-line resume. It could contain links to sites you are interested in and/or sites of the courses that you are currently taking. Remember, the whole world (including potential employers) can access your Web pages, so use your personal Web page to do your credit.

It would be nice if your site contained a scanned photo of your face so that other people involved with the class can put a name to your face. However, this is not essential. Some people prefer to remain anonymous and they should have their right to privacy respected.

2.3.4.3   Researching an e-Commerce Application

Each student should identify a potential application of interest. It is recommended that later assignments be done in teams so that students can help each other to learn. However, it is best for each of the students to first do a little research on their own. You should select and research an e-Commerce application that you would be interested in using as the basis of your team project.

You should start your consideration of your chosen application by identifying challenges with the current state of the application (that could lead to improvements) and opportunities for new features—both of which could provide a competitive advantage until the competition copies them. You should identify a minimum of five potential competitive advantages that could be added to go beyond the best combination of features in current (state of the practice) application systems. If you cannot find five good potential competitive advantages, then you should choose a different application.

Despite the rapidity of evolution of e-Commerce applications, users around the world have come to expect the latest features in any systems they use. The ease of accessing competitive Web sites makes it increasingly difficult to maintain the loyalty of those individuals and organizations with which your organization does business. To do so requires not only keeping up with the competition but also generally keeping ahead of them by evolving new competitive advantages before they do. You may wish to continue researching your chosen application area throughout the assignments in this book. To ensure that you can do so, you should identify sources of information that will not only help you for this assignment, but also provide additional help on future assignments as you gain a deeper understanding of the application.

You should include selected references both to some Web sites and to some other sources of information about what the application involves or could involve. Other sources of information may include:

- Professional journals, magazines, newspapers, and newsletters in your library
- Faculty members
- Professionals in various organizations

For each reference you should provide:

- Basic information about the reference (name, author, and location of the information referenced)
- A brief summary of what you learned about the application area from the reference
- Why the reference source may be useful in the future

You should identify a minimum of five references that provide a breadth of information about the application area and that you can consult for further information to help you to further understand the application. If you cannot find five good references, then you should choose a different application.

You should post the results of your investigation into your chosen e-Commerce application in a Web page that is located in your own directory and linked to by your personal home page.

2.4 SOME EXAMPLES OF E-COMMERCE APPLICATIONS

The following are just a few examples of some innovative e-Commerce applications that currently have potential. They range all the way from food, clothing, and shelter to luxury items and services. When considering them, it is important to remember that on the World Wide Web there is little need of redundancy. Once one system serves an application, there is limited need for others, especially within the same country.

2.4.1   e-Groceries

The idea of on-line grocery stores was one of the first discussed when e-Commerce was just emerging. However, in general, it hasn't happened. Here are some of the reasons:

- The provision of general groceries would require a large inventory or buying the items from other stores (who would have no incentive to give you a discount) and just being a shopping service that specializes in groceries.
- It would be hard to satisfy a sufficient number of customers.
- Catering to busy working people would mean a very small window of potential delivery times. Also, many busy working people eat out rather than taking time to prepare regular meals.
- Shut-ins, who could make use of such a service, are often on a limited budget and would not be able to afford high delivery fees.
- Often, when people want particular groceries, they want them sooner than a delivery could be guaranteed to arrive.
- Delivery costs would greatly increase the cost of groceries, which could lead more people to eat out.
- Some products could pose extra difficulties.
  - Many people like to choose their own produce and meats. Problems could arise from lack of customer satisfaction.
  - Delivery of frozen foods, produce, and meats requires refrigeration, which raises the costs of delivery.

This does not mean that on-line grocery sales are infeasible. It does suggest that an on-line grocery store might wish to do business differently than a traditional one.

- Limiting items to packaged ones, that require no special handling or refrigeration, could greatly increase product satisfaction and reduce the inventory costs of spoilage and special storage.
- Focusing on hard-to-get items, sizes of items, and specialty items not normally carried by traditional grocery stores could shift the emphasis from expectations

of immediate delivery to acceptance of time required to satisfy special orders. It should be noted that thanks to the sales analysis performed in modern grocery stores, many good products are discontinued every year in favor of others that sell faster.

- By focusing on unique products that people would be willing to wait to receive, lower-cost delivery methods could be used while expanding the market to a regional or national scale.

2.4.2   e-Clothing

After food comes clothing in our list of personal needs. As with food stores, most larger communities are well served by clothing stores. However, unlike food stores, clothing stores do not carry a relatively stable set of products. Fashion dictates changing inventories. Store size dictates carrying only a limited number of any item in any size and relatively few versions (colors or patterns) of any item.

- It is possible for a large clothing chain to have the exact item a customer would like, but not have it in a store handy to that customer. An e-Commerce system could allow stores and customers to order the size and color of an item from anywhere within the chain.
- Customized manufacturing, which is referred to in the clothing industry as custom designs or as made-to-measure, has always existed as an option for clothing customers. However, the recent trend to mass production and mass marketing has limited this option and made it very expensive. Customized manufacturing would be attractive to customers if the cost and delivery times could be limited by the use of e-Commerce systems.
- Manufacturers are increasingly opening their own stores to market directly to their customers. An e-Business would be a logical extension of this trend and could have the additional advantage of offering a greater variety of sizes and colors than a single physical outlet store could carry.

2.4.3   e-Builders

While the real estate industry has been quick to adopt e-Commerce, builders have not generally gotten involved yet. This may be due to the geographical bounds in which individual builders typically operate. However, the Web could be useful to the building industry in various ways, including:

- People wanting a custom house or other building often have a limited exposure to different designs and may have a hard time visualizing what they haven't seen. The visual nature of the Web makes it a perfect medium for displaying different designs, which could be customized and sold to builders or their clients.
- Building firms making pre-fabricated buildings could get greater exposure to potential customers.
- Local builders could use the Web to display their work and their workmanship. This would allow potential clients to see more projects than are typically ever on display at a single time.

2.4.4 Services for Individuals

Custom shopping, as discussed above as related to e-Groceries, can also serve a number of other specialized needs, including:

- Specialized gift shopping, wrapping, and delivery
- Handling personal reservations, like a concierge in a hotel
- Arranging other purchases or services

These services go beyond brokering, because they often involve a considerable amount of effort in finding and obtaining the desired items or services and then ensuring their delivery. While many of these services are location-specific, some could be conducted on a larger geographical basis.

2.4.5 Services for Businesses or Professionals

In addition to standard professional services, such as accounting and engineering, there are various other areas of services intended for businesses or professionals that could be conducted via e-Businesses.

- Currently small business owners either have to develop their business all on their own, arranging for consulting assistance on a case-by-case basis, or they have to buy into a franchise and follow its dictates exactly. e-Commerce makes possible a third alternative. e-Businesses could be established that would provide industry-specific support, without the requirements of being franchises, and that would sell a range of high-quality, industry-specific products to independent businesses. The independent businesses would be free to choose how much to rely on the support business.
- Artists, writers, and other creative professionals often rely on agents to sell their products. Agents generally focus their time and effort on works they believe will sell the best, yielding them the largest commissions. Beginning creative professionals may have difficulties in finding a suitable agent. What help is available to unknown or beginning creative artists is often very expensive to obtain. There are opportunities for organizations that can help to develop creative artists while helping market their works.

2.4.6 Niche Market Sales and Services

There are many areas in which niche markets are not currently served as well as e-Commerce could make possible. Some of these areas include:

- People may be interested in books, art, music, giftware, and other cultural artifacts specific to particular ethnic groups. However, stores serving a particular group only exist where large concentrations of the group's members can be found. There are currently many opportunities for culturally-specific e-Businesses and e-Brokers.
- People may be interested in particular pets, but often have to make do with whatever breed is available locally. A wider variety could be made available by an e-Brokerage that represented a large variety of pet breeders.

- People may be interested in various specialty luxury items, such as wines, beers, or art that are not readily available in all locations. e-Brokerages dedicated to specific luxury items could make them available to much wider markets.

2.5   CYBER SUPPLEMENTS FOR CHAPTER 2

Look at the Chapter 2 Cyber Supplements on the Web to find:

- Information about the latest types of e-Commerce applications
- Reviews of and links to examples of each type of e-Commerce application
- Suggestions for further investigations into identifying interesting e-Commerce systems

REFERENCES

[1] ISO/IEC International Standard 14662, Information Technologies—Open-EDI Reference Model, 1997.

Software Systems in Organizations

3.1 INTRODUCTION TO SOFTWARE SYSTEMS IN ORGANIZATIONS

This chapter considers the variety of applications and software systems that can serve an organization. It focuses on a number of major characteristics, features, and functions of different types of applications and especially highlights how these characteristics apply to e-Commerce applications.

The concepts discussed in this chapter are important for understanding how e-Commerce goes beyond traditional organizational information systems and why traditional approaches to information systems are not sufficient. This chapter also provides a basis for recognizing that e-Commerce systems need to be uniquely developed and/or modified for an organization.

3.2 UNDERSTANDING E-COMMERCE AS A NEW TYPE OF APPLICATION

3.2.1 Traditional Software Applications

Most people have experienced only a few of the many types of software packages that are currently available. Rather than focusing on one or two packages, it is important to understand the great variety of ways computer software can help individuals and organizations. This broader understanding is important in realistically determining relative priorities for acquiring different systems for an organization. It is also important to realize how these application systems may be integrated for the corporate good (as opposed to being optimized for the good of a given department). It is especially important to understand traditional business applications in order to recognize how e-Commerce systems are changing the way organizations operate.

Traditional business applications and systems are often categorized in terms of what level of an organization they served and what type of data they used. Table 3-1 identifies some of the characteristics that are used to distinguish between different types of traditional business systems.

3.2.1.1 Data Processing Systems

Data processing systems were the first type of computerized information system for businesses. **Data processing systems** (DPS) process various accounting transactions for an organization. They are designed for operational level workers and concentrate more on the processing of raw data than the production of information. Other types of organizational information systems may include data processing directly or may input the results of data processing systems. Since basic accounting applications (such as accounts payable, accounts receivable, general ledger, sales recording, and inventory recording) are among the oldest major computer applications, there are many excellent accounting software packages available. Most have advanced beyond the data processing level to include a variety of management information functions.

Current accounting packages facilitate user customization of headings and other descriptive details to a given organization without compromising the accounting integrity of the information processed by the package. Some accounting software packages, such as Quick Books, are designed for use by people with little or no formal accounting expertise. Other accounting packages are designed for use by professional accountants. It is useful to select a complete set of accounting software packages from a single vendor to ensure that data can be easily transferred between application programs.

Table 3-2 presents a description of the main characteristics of data processing systems. (It makes use of a format for describing applications that will be discussed further in Chapter 4.)

Table 3-1 Organizational and data characteristics of traditional information systems

Information Characteristics	Operational Level	Tactical Level	Strategic Level
Time frame	Past and present	Short-term (past–future)	Future
Source	Largely internal	Both internal and external	Largely external
Scope	Detailed	Exceptions and summaries	Highly summarized
Frequency	Ongoing daily	Weekly or as needed	Occasional
Form	Specified by formal structures	Specified by management needs	Generally unstructured
Accuracy	High level required	Desirable, but not always essential	Impossible, but desirable to limit uncertainties
General System Type	Data Processing System (DPS)	Management Information System (MIS)	Decision Support System (DSS) or Strategic Information System (SIS)
Examples	Accounts Payable (AP) Accounts Receivable (AR) General Ledger (GL)	Inventory Control (IC) Sales Analysis (SA)	Budgeting Planning

Table 3-2 A description of data processing systems

Application Type	Data Processing Systems
Who:	Operational workers in an organization
What:	Input, edit, and store business transactions and related data
Where & When:	Ideally transactions are captured as close as possible to where they are generated (e.g., point of sale)
	Usually within or under the control of accounting departments
	With on-line systems, transactions are captured and processed as they occur
Why:	Can create savings both by automating manual accounting procedures and by optimizing the use of resources (including money in accounts payable and accounts receivable)
How:	(see description and examples in Tables 1 & 2 above)
How Much:	Depends on frequency of transaction within the organization
With Which:	Content limited to particular types of transactions

3.2.1.2   Management Information Systems

Management information systems analyze data (largely gathered from data processing activities or systems) to provide information that can be used in the ongoing management of an organization. Management information software systems (such as sales analysis, inventory control) assist tactile managers by providing analysis of trends and exceptions in the data that can be useful for management decisions. Where sales recording, accounts receivable, and/or inventory recording systems record what is happening, sales analysis and inventory control systems can help managers by identifying business challenges (such as poor sales of a product) and opportunities (such as the need to reorder a product to maintain sufficient inventory levels). Over time many of these activities have become routine (either by automation or by developing corporate procedures for how to use the information) and have been passed on to non-management workers within the organizational structure.

Additional management information can be produced by the use of query packages and report generators that work with organizational databases to allow users to get specific information they need on demand. Obtaining information often involves sophisticated knowledge of both where to obtain the required data and how to process it in order to obtain the desired information. In most cases involving non-routine information, managers will have experienced knowledge workers obtain the desired information from the databases. The main characteristics of management information systems are described in Table 3-3, in a manner similar to that used for data processing systems.

3.2.1.3 Strategic Information Systems

Strategic information systems analyze combinations of internal and external information in an attempt to forecast the success of potential future operations of an organization. Strategic information systems (other than general budgeting and planning systems) often need to be custom-built to meet the needs of a specific organization. They depend upon the types of information the strategic managers want to analyze and upon the availability of this information that is typically obtained from a variety of external sources.

The main characteristics of strategic information systems are described in Table 3-4.

 Find information on a variety of software systems that organizations may already be using prior to developing e-Commerce systems in the Chapter 3 Cyber Supplement.

3.2.2   Basic Functions Performed by Information Systems

There are four basic functions that all types of information systems perform: inputting data, processing data, outputting data, and storing data. These functions are not just limited to computer systems—people also act as information systems. The following discussion refers to information systems as objects without specifying whether the objects are computer programs or human users.

Objects are real things or concepts that we deal with in our everyday life. Most people should recognize and agree upon the recognition of most objects.

Developing systems based on objects from the real world (**object-oriented** systems) makes it easier to validate that the system corresponds appropriately to the real world. The use of objects also helps in the development and testing of future modifications and additions to the system.

Some examples of objects involved in e-Commerce include:

- Users
- Software systems and their major components

Table 3-3   A description of management information systems

Application Type	Management Information Systems
Who:	Tactile management and their staff of information/knowledge workers
What:	Provide managers with summaries and listings of exceptions
Where & When:	Reports may be produced at regular intervals (e.g., month end), on demand, or when exceptional circumstances occur that should be brought to the attention of the users
Why:	Their information can increase profits and reduce losses in a timely manner
How:	Analyze stored data in order to alert management to current challenges and opportunities
How Much:	Depends on the type of management information involved
With Which:	Uses data accumulated by data processing system

Table 3-4   A description of strategic information systems

Application Type	Strategic Information Systems
Who:	Strategic management and their staff of knowledge workers
What:	Processing combined internal and external data in order to produce predictions and plans for the future
Where & When:	On demand
Why:	Supporting the planning process so that the organization can prosper in the future
How:	By predicting the results of alternate scenarios
How Much:	Depends largely on the interests of the strategic managers
With Which:	Make use of stored internal data and input additional external data

- Computer hardware
- Documents and other media that are readable/writeable by users
- Data files that are readable/writeable by computer hardware

Objects may be able to input, process, and output data in a number of different ways. The **interface** to an object is defined in terms of its valid inputs and outputs. The processing of an object can be hidden, as can any of the data that an object possesses/stores. Object-oriented analysis will be discussed in Chapter 8. Object-oriented design will be discussed in Chapter 10.

Inputs are defined in terms of the object that receives them, and can exist regardless of the object that generates them. Data that an object receives can be considered to be **input,** if the object is capable of recognizing and acting upon receiving it. Data that an object does not recognize are not considered to be input. Data that an object recognizes and refuses may be considered invalid input. Both users and computer systems receive and process a large variety of inputs. Inputs may contain data and/or requests for the object to take some action. Inputs take the form of information and/or business transactions. Inputs to computer systems can come from users or from data storage files. Data processing inputs usually focus on business transactions. e-Commerce inputs can involve business transactions and/or information transactions.

Many objects (including people, computer systems, and a variety of other machines) are capable of processing information. **Processing** can involve the analysis, manipulation, transformation, use, and/or storage of information. Processing includes validating the contents of inputs, making decisions based on input data and program logic, and taking actions based on these decisions. Processing is related to, and interacts with, the inputting and outputting information. Data processing systems are generally limited to the processing required by a limited set of business transactions. e-Commerce systems often process a wide range of information and business transactions.

Outputs are outputs just because an object produces them, whether or not they are useful to (or input by) any other object. Both users and computer systems produce a large variety of outputs. Communication between users and computers is successful only where the output of one object is a valid input of the other object. Outputs from users become inputs to computers, and outputs from computers become inputs to users. Outputs from data processing systems may take the form of: reports recording inputs or processing, new business documents, and/or updates to data storage files. Outputs from e-Commerce systems cover a wide range of business and information transactions.

An object may store information that it has produced in its own internal **data storage.** It can then recall this information at a later time for use in a similar manner to using information that might be input from some external source. Financial transactions have rigid requirements for storing data that can be properly audited. Computer systems can store data on a variety of media (including magnetic and optical disks) in formats that they can reuse. People may choose to store data by remembering it or to store it in some external format (such as printed or on a personal computer file).

There are specialized versions of each of these four basic computing functions that are used to manage the operations of an information system: feedback, control, adjustments, and learning. **Feedback** is a specialized type of output that is used as an input to determine how the object producing it is operating.

Feedback can relate to any of the operations of a system, including validity checking of inputs and performance monitoring of the operation of the system. Feedback on input errors generally requires the attention of the user who inputted the questionable data. It is important that such feedback be as helpful as possible to the user to aid in deciding what control function to exercise. Feedback on the operation of computerized information systems can be output as reports, files, or real-time displays that describe selected operating details. This feedback can be analyzed and acted on by people and/or automatically by the computerized information system.

While feedback generated by people provides information on how they are operating, it is often an important indicator of difficulties that they are experiencing that may be created by a system that they are using. Feedback generated by people takes a variety of forms, many of which may not be input to or recognized by the computer. People are constantly generating feedback through their unconscious or semiconscious actions (such as their body language, tone of voice, and speed and accuracy of acting) as well as via more conscious forms of feedback (such as specific comments or requests for changes). However, only feedback that is recognized by the computer can be acted upon by it. It is important that e-Commerce systems provide ample opportunities for users to enter their feedback.

Control involves processing, which is intended to analyze feedback and to produce adjustments that will influence the operations of an object. Feedback should always be processed by a control, whether immediately or at some predetermined or dynamically determined time in the future. The user generally exercises control of data processing systems. Control by a user (which acts as additional processing) involves analyzing the feedback, consulting memory, and determining any adjustments to make to a system. In e-Commerce systems, only selected users may have the authorization to perform control functions. Automated control of a system may be used for a variety of purposes, including auditing the performance of the system.

Adjustments are the outputs of an object that are intended to influence the operations of some object. The object to be influenced can be the same object or a different object from that outputting the adjustment. Adjustments, decided by control, can include:

- Doing nothing, if changes are not appropriate
- Modifying inputs and resuming processing
- Rejecting individual inputs for manual correction and later re-input
- Halting processing until corrections are made to individual inputs
- Modifying the processing

Learning takes place when an object stores knowledge that it can use to improve its future processing (including its future controlling). This knowledge may have resulted from processing/control done by the object or from inputs/adjustments into the object. Learning may involve remembering what worked and what didn't as well as what happened and why it happened. Learning is the most complicated of the basic functions. While it readily is performed by many users, it is only included within advanced information systems. Learning is of little use for data processing. e-Commerce systems often use learning techniques to profile users in order to better adapt to the individual needs of these users. Table 3-5 illustrates how basic functions are performed similarly for various data processing systems.

 Find a discussion of the use of the major functions on an example e-Commerce site in the Chapter 3 Cyber Supplement.

3.2.3 Transaction Processing by Information Systems

In the simplest of terms, information systems process transactions. A **transaction** is any agreed-upon exchange of data between two or more objects that accomplishes some recognized purpose. This exchange may involve one or more communications between the objects involved in the transaction. Data processing systems basically record completed financial transactions. A **financial transaction** is a transaction that involves data relating to some exchange of money and/or products and/or services with some monetary value. e-Commerce systems create business transactions which may include financial transactions.

According to ISO 14662,[1] a **business transaction** is, "a predefined set of activities and/or processes of organizations which is initiated by an organization to accomplish

Table 3-5 Examples of the functions of major data processing systems

	Accounts Receivable	**Accounts Payable**	**Inventory Recording**
Inputs	Sales slips	Receiving slips	Receiving slips
	Return slips	Vendor invoices	Sales slips
	Payments received	Vendor credit notes	Return slips
	Customer account changes	(Purchase orders)	(Purchase orders)
		Vedor Account	Adjustments
	Adjustments	Payment Instructions Changes	
		Adjustments	
Data Stores	Receivables file	Payables file	Inventory file
	Customer file	Vendor file	Backup / history files
	Backup / history files	(Purchase order file)	
		Backup / history files	
Processing	Input transactions	Input transactions	Input transactions
	Edit transactions	Edit transactions	Edit transactions
	Update receivables file	Update payables file	Update inventory file
	Update customer file	Update vendor file	Produce requisitions
	Produce invoices / refunds	Produce payments	Produce reports
		Produce reports	
	Produce reports		
Outputs	Error listings	Error listings	Error listings
	Invoices / refunds	Payments	Requistions
	Reports	Reports	Reports
Feedback Control	Error listings	Error listings	Error listings
	Check error listings	Check error listings	Check error listings
	Produce adjustments	Produce adjustments	Produce adjustments
	Nothing or reject transactions or halt processing	Nothing or reject transactions or halt processing	Nothing or reject transactions or halt processing

an explicitly shared business goal and terminated upon one of the agreed conclusions by all the involved organizations although some of the recognition may be implicit."

Business transactions involve legal persons (whether individuals or organizations or systems representing them), business processes (which are a series of interactions that lead to the accomplishment of tasks), and data. All business transactions involve the exchange of data, while only some business transactions actually result in binding financial transactions (of the type that would be recorded by a data processing system). Chapter 4 presents a framework for describing applications and systems and Chapter 7 presents a method for analyzing requirements that involves persons, business processes, and data.

ISO 15944-1[2] provides "a methodology for specifying common business practices as parts of common business transactions." It recognizes that a business transaction may involve one or more of the following five types of fundamental business activities:

- **Business transaction planning** is a situation in which the buyer and seller exchange information to help them decide on what actions to take to acquire or sell a good or service. A major focus of this activity is bringing buyers and sellers together. This may involve a range of specific activities from market research to producing or reviewing advertising.
- **Business transaction identification** is a situation in which information is exchanged about the goods, services, and/or participants in the transaction. e-Commerce systems involve a wide variety of this type of activities, including activities in which employees of an organization update the information that the system presents to various users, and activities in which various users obtain or exchange various types of specific types information.
- **Business transaction negotiation** is a situation in which information is exchanged in order to achieve an explicit, mutually understood and agreed-upon realization of a financial transaction along with any applicable terms and conditions. Negotiations may involve a variety of issues, including price, availability, delivery method, and associated services.
- **Business transaction actualization** is a situation in which information is exchanged to formally commit to a financial transaction. Business transaction actualization includes the exchange of payments for goods and/or services. Data processing systems are usually limited to recording the results of business transaction actualization. While the main goal of most e-Commerce systems is business transaction actualization, they typically achieve this goal by providing considerable support for the other types of fundamental business activities.
- **Business transaction post-actualization,** more commonly known as servicing, is a situation in which information is exchanged relating to follow-up activities that take place after a good or service is delivered.

 Find a discussion of and links to examples of different types of fundamental business activities at various e-Commerce sites in the Chapter 3 Cyber Supplement.

The use of this business transaction model within requirements analysis (as discussed in Chapter 7) can lead to a number of important requirements for e-Commerce systems. Each activity should be of benefit to its users and to the system, whether or not it is accompanied by other activities. Activities should also promote the benefits of performing related activities. It needs to be recognized that there are many possible conclusions of a business transaction, including termination of any activity. The consequences of termination (such as failure to save the results of a negotiation that has not been actualized) and any actions that may lead to termination of an activity (including failure to respond within an agreed time period) should be clearly understood by the user.

Implementing this model in the technical design and construction of a system (as discussed in Chapter 12) can facilitate interaction between an organization's e-Commerce system and a wide range of other systems including those on the Web, those utilizing mobile computing, and specially developed automated EDI systems.

3.2.4   The Evolution of Software Applications

The rate at which advances in information systems are adopted has accelerated to the point that if something new comes along, you can easily be left behind. It is no longer good enough to join the pack; you must work constantly to be the leader (and even then you'll often just be keeping pace with others who are also trying to lead).

Data processing systems took a while to catch on. They were made possible by advances in computing technologies, including the decreasing cost of computation.

- In the 1950s only very large organizations (5000+ employees) had them
- In the 1960s many large organizations (500+ employees) got them
- In the 1970s medium organizations (50+ employees) got them
- In the 1980s even small organizations needed and got them
- In the 1990s anyone who wanted them could get them cheaply

Management information systems caught on more quickly. They were made possible by advances in database technology.

- In the early 1970s large organizations got them
- In the mid 1970s medium organizations got them along with DPS
- In the early 1980s small organizations got them too

Strategic information systems didn't really catch on. Their objectives were too vague and too grandiose and were not readily tied with any particular technological advances. Instead, a limited amount of strategic information processing was done using spreadsheets. Organizational size had less to do with adoption than the attitudes of the organization.

- In the early 1980s progressive organizations started to use them
- In the mid 1980s average organizations recognized their usefulness
- In the early 1990s everyone accepted their usefulness

e-Commerce use is growing exponentially. While only a few years old, e-Commerce continues to evolve, with an increasing number of both leaders and followers. e-Commerce can now be ignored only by small, local organizations with very secure and traditional connections to the people they serve; and there's getting to be fewer of those every day.

The world is constantly changing, and information systems are under exceptional pressures to continually evolve in order to adapt to the changing world. Few systems remain the same over long periods of time.

- If they are bad, they are replaced (with something better)
- If they are just adequate, they are improved (to make them better)
- If they are good, they are enhanced (to add more functionality)

The actual length of long periods of time depends upon the systems involved.

- Geological systems change over millions of years
- Political systems change over decades and centuries
- Tax systems change over years
- Computer systems change over months
- e-Commerce systems change over weeks and even over days

Toffler[3] provides a variety of insights into the evolution of modern information systems. Couger[4] provides research and advice on how to help make system evolution happen.

Rather than try to describe or proscribe the evolution of systems before presenting a basic understanding of systems development, this section will present four examples of the evolution of particular systems. In order to get a glimpse at systems evolution in computing, we will look at these examples of evolution, in a similar manner to James Burke's various *Connections*[5] television series and books. The examples are full of connections involving improvements and enhancements that go off in many directions (and sometimes cross paths with themselves). These examples are presented to illustrate systems evolution, not as formal histories, and may not be 100% historically accurate. However, they are accurate enough for our purposes.

3.2.4.1 Magnetic Media

The first magnetic media used for computers involved magnetic tape (which evolved from magnetic tape recorders for voice and sound, which evolved from records for voice and sound). Magnetic tape is limited by its serial nature. To get to a particular piece of data, you have to keep looking for it all the way from the start, potentially looking at a lot of stuff you aren't interested in before you get to it. Then, if you're not sure that the next piece you want follows it, you have to rewind and start all over.

To get around the limitation of serial reading, computer disks were developed, where the read-write head can easily go to any location on the spinning disk. Originally computer disks were large (14″ in diameter) and permanently attached to the disk drive. That limited the amount of data that could be stored.

Removable disks were developed (just as big, but now removable) to allow more data to be used on the system. After all, tapes were already removable and exchangeable. The big removable disks were heavy and a nuisance to store. They were also made of hard plastic and broke if dropped (which wasn't good, because of the loss of data and the high cost of the removable disks).

Smaller, cheaper, and more durable removable disks first appeared as 8″ floppy disks. However, they were still a little too big. You can't properly fit an 8″ item into a pocket designed to go into a loose leaf binder, because the pages are normally only 8 1/2″ wide and take about 1″ on the side for the rings to go through the pages. However, nothing was done until desktop microcomputers came onto the scene.

Desktop microcomputers started out using cassette tape players, but they weren't very reliable and were a throwback to magnetic tape.

Eight-inch floppy disks were too large compared with the rest of a desktop computer, so 5 1/4″ floppies were developed. You can stack two 5 1/4″ floppies on an 8 1/2 × 11 page. So why go any further in miniaturizing? The floppy nature of these disks limited the amount of data that could be stored reliably.

Reducing the size further to 3 1/2″ and adding a hard case allowed further improvements to be made. They are still with us. You may ask why, and I'll suggest that it's because they fit into a typical shirt pocket!

There have been various attempts to introduce 2 1/2″ and other smaller diskettes for laptop computers, but they haven't caught on in a big way! There was no need, since 3 1/2″ diskettes fit in a shirt pocket! Recent high-capacity ZIP and similar disks have retained the 3 1/2″ size.

I suppose this is a story of try, try, and try again until you get it right. In this case, keep trying until it fits in your shirt pocket! Who would have thought that the shirt pocket would present a major requirement for the development of computer disks?

3.2.4.2   The Cash Register

Where clerks have to type in the prices of each item there is a risk that clerks will make typing errors. The stores don't like errors that cost them money, and the customers don't like errors that cost them money. The more items, the greater the chance of errors. Grocery stores were especially susceptible to errors.

The universal product code (UPC) was developed by a group of grocery stores, computer companies, and other interested parties in order to reduce errors and speed up checkout processing. Scanners were developed that could read the UPCs. Initially, stores even went to the trouble of making their own UPC stickers for products, until they could get enough buying clout to force manufactures to include it on their packaging.

Things were good. In order to use UPCs the computerized cash registers had to be connected to a product database to be able to look up the prices. While they were connected, they could also record that the item was sold and thus no longer in inventory. Inventory control was a bonus that could easily be added.

Things were good for the stores. Computerized cash registers allowed stores to limit the quantities of an item that a customer could get at a special "loss leader price" and charge a higher price for additional quantities of the item. Customers wishing more items at the bargain price were inconvenienced by having to go through the checkout more than once.

Things were good. As well as keeping track of when items needed to be reordered, the database could keep track of how many items were on the shelf and how many were in the back of the store waiting to be put out. It could therefore schedule which items should be restocked on the shelves next. All this was a further bonus.

Things were good. If the contents of shelves were tracked, then the productivity of the shelves could also be analyzed to determine how many dollars each square inch of shelf space was generating. Low profitability products could be discontinued in favor of other products that might make more money. And they were, and still are, in the thousands of dollars per year. The bonuses of the UPC keep mounting.

Things were good for the stores. But what about the customers? Scanners could scan more than UPCs. So reward schemes were introduced to entice customer loyalty, and they made use of the scanners already in place. The cash register became even more useful.

Things were good. If customers were willing to use personal identifications in return for rewards, the stores could go even further in analyzing the available information if they had their own "clubs" and information on their customers. Scanned club cards could give customers selected rewards for their letting the stores monitor their buying habits.

Things were good for the stores. By keeping a record of customer purchases associated with a Club card, the stores can now limit the quantity of an item sold at a special price over a given time period. After all, if you don't identify yourself with your Club card, then you won't get the discount; but if you do identify yourself, you still won't get the discount if the store limits the quantity at the bargain price.

Things are good! What's next?

3.2.4.3   The World Wide Web

The World Wide Web began as a way of exchanging technical reports between scientists without having to e-mail them to individuals. Instead, people could access them on a want-to-know basis. It was one of many similar attempts. It succeeded because it was the most adaptable, and many people got involved in adapting it. While a consortium was formed to guide and encourage its evolution, commercial interests jumped in, and evolution has occurred at an unprecedented rate. Some of the major technical evolutions of the Web are identified in Table 3-6. Likewise, the use of the Web for business has evolved rapidly, as Table 3-7 briefly summarizes. And the evolution keeps going on and on and on.

Table 3-6   Some technical evolutions of the Web

Evolutionary Phase	Challenges and Opportunities
First there was text	Scientific reports need illustrations, so picture formats were added
Plain text isn't attractive, especially next to pictures	Formatting text makes more attractive and allows easier use of resulting documents
One information format leads to another, and more people start using the Web	Some control on document distribution was wanted
Data input was added for passwords	Visual modalities can be enhanced by sound and animation, which lead to the need for further controls
Various input controls	Allowed a range of interaction to be added, suggested that databases be added to handle larger volumes of data
Linking databases	Allowed complicated interactions, including the use of the Web to conduct business
e-Commerce	Increasing the sophistication and expectations of users

Table 3-7   Major developments in organizational use of the Web

Challenges and Opportunities	Organizational Applications
Home pages started as merely (individual) advertisements, with links to other pages	Corporate home pages
Customers wanted more information	Corporate sites included information about products and services
Once products were described, customers wanted to interact	Adding interactions allowed sites to sell items and services
The possibilities grew	Virtual branches and businesses were created
Development also moved inward	Internal corporate sites (intranets) were developed

3.2.4.4 The Evolution of Recruiting in Organizations

Recruiting has evolved from a rather simple task to a major application composed of a number of different tasks. As tasks evolve they are often formalized and may even be considered as parts of a system or as systems themselves. Thus, the following scenarios illustrate the evolution of both the recruiting task and an organizational system to support recruiting. They also illustrate how analyzing the evolution of an application can suggest the opportunity for making further improvements, which can provide an organization with significant competitive advantages until other organizations copy these improvements.

1. Owner directly hires employees. Many organizations start with a single individual. That person "owns" the organization and controls all business decisions for it (within the bounds of the law and any agreements with financial backers). Expansion involves hiring additional individuals whose hiring and employment will be controlled by the owner.

- The owner of an organization identifies the need for a new employee and allocates money for hiring the employee
- The owner advertises his need for an employee
- Individuals apply for the position
- The owner selects an individual and makes an offer
- The individual decides whether or not to accept the offer
- If the individual accepts the offer, the recruiting process is complete; otherwise, the owner repeats some or all of the above steps

2. Owner promotes employees. As the organization becomes more established, the owner promotes some employees, giving them more responsibilities. However, instead of promoting an employee, the owner may choose to hire someone new for the responsibilities and leave the old employees with their existing responsibilities.

- The owner of an organization identifies the need for new responsibilities to be performed by an employee and allocates money for paying for this work
- The owner decides whether or not to promote an existing worker or to hire a new person for these responsibilities (if the latter decision is taken, go to previous scenario of the owner directly hiring employees)
- The owner identifies an employee to promote and makes an offer
- The individual decides whether or not to accept the offer
- If the individual accepts the offer, the process is complete; otherwise, the owner repeats some or all of the above steps.

3. Manager hires employees with owner's approval. One of the responsibilities controlled by the owner that may be given to an employee is the responsibility of hiring additional individuals.

- A manager in an organization identifies the need for a new employee and requests permission and funds to hire an employee
- The owner decides whether or not to allow the hiring of an employee and allocates money for hiring the employee
- The manager advertises his need for an employee
- Individuals apply for the position

- The manager selects an individual and recommends hiring the individual to the owner
- The owner decides whether or not to allow the hiring of that individual
- The manager makes an offer
- The individual decides whether or not to accept the offer
- If the individual accepts the offer, the recruiting process is complete; otherwise, the owner repeats some or all of the above steps

4. Manager promotes employees with owner's approval. Likewise, a manager may be given the responsibility for promoting employees.

- A manager in an organization identifies the need for new responsibilities to be performed by an employee, identifies an employee to promote, and requests permission and funds to promote an employee
- The owner decides whether or not to allow the promoting of employee and allocates money for paying for this work
- The manager makes an offer
- The individual decides whether or not to accept the offer
- If the individual accepts the offer, the process is complete; otherwise, the owner repeats some or all of the above steps

5. Managers may be given authority to act within budgets without needing direct approval of owners. This would involve simpler versions of scenarios 3 and 4.

6. Human Resource Departments may take the place of owners. As organizations grow, many organizations evolve extensive control mechanisms to standardize and manage functions that occur throughout the organization. Personnel/Human Resource Departments (HRD) have grown from the role of centralizing hiring and payroll to many other personnel-related functions within modern organizations. However, for purposes of this example, we will focus only on their role in recruiting.

The simplest role for an HRD is to take on at least some of the role of approving hiring and promoting. It may share this role with senior managers who will be responsible for the individual to be hired or promoted. This would involve similar scenarios to 3 and 4.

7. Human Resource Departments take on additional responsibilities. Because of their greater expertise in the hiring process, HRDs often take over other parts of the recruiting process that might traditionally have been done by a manager or owner.

- A manager in an organization identifies the need for a new employee and requests permission and funds to hire an employee
- The manager's manager and/or the HRD decide whether or not to allow the hiring of an employee and allocate money for hiring the employee
- The HRD advertises the need for an employee and specifies how to apply
- Individuals apply for the position
- The HRD receives applications, helps the manager to identify potential candidates to interview, and sets up interviews
- The manager interviews the candidates and selects an individual and recommends hiring the individual to the manager's manager and/or the HRD

- The appropriate organization's authorities decide whether or not to allow the hiring of that individual
- The HRD makes an offer
- The individual decides whether or not to accept the offer
- If the individual accepts the offer, the recruiting process is complete; otherwise the owner repeats some or all of the above steps

Identifying Further Challenges and Opportunities

Scenario 7 introduces a number of new tasks:

- Specifying how to apply
- Identifying potential candidates
- Selecting potential candidates
- Setting up interviews
- Interviewing

They all result from the increasing complexity of trying to find the right individual to hire. Similar complexity is involved with deciding who to promote.

In the future, recruiting will be required to do more than electronically advertising and receiving applications. It needs to increasingly assist organizations to get the best individuals in the best positions for the best of the organization. At the same time, as it meets the needs of the organization it must meet the needs of the individuals, who must be satisfied with their roles in the organization in order to motivate them to be productive. Here are just some of the many possibilities for improvements that could come from e-Recruiting:

Finding the Best Fit for the Organization

Recruiting generally focuses on finding the best fit for a predefined position. However, this significantly reduces the likelihood of finding what you want. It may be possible to get good results by choosing a very good candidate with slightly different capabilities and rearranging the existing set of other employees to get a better overall fit for the organization than would have been possible if there was no flexibility in the hiring process. Such flexibility:

- Readily exists in scenarios 1 and 2
- Often exists in scenarios 3 and 4
- Is often lost where recruiting is increasingly the responsibility of persons (whether inside the organization or external to it) who are not directly involved with the work that needs to be done by the person to be hired

Involving Workers to Help Define Needs

Defining the recruiting needs of an organization has traditionally been done by owners, managers, and others who need not ever have done the work that a person is being hired to do. Non-management workers familiar with the real work to be done may have valuable insights that could result in better recruiting. Furthermore, the aspirations of existing workers could be better accommodated if they were free to suggest that they could (and/or would like to) move laterally into the available position. This could lead to greater flexibility in recruiting the best person for the organization rather than just focusing on recruiting for a particular predefined position.

Going Beyond Traditional Recruiting Documents

In simpler recruiting situations, applicants often have the opportunity to talk to the person doing the hiring before being discounted. In more complex situations, they often have to rely on documents they supply and/or that are supplied on their behalf to get them the opportunity to speak for themselves. Typical documents may include:

- A resume
- A letter of application
- Filling out an application form that generally takes the place of a resume and/or a letter of application
- A set of references

These documents have generally been limited to factual/historical data. Potential candidates for further consideration are generally selected based on matching this relatively brief data with a predefined set of "requirements" for the position. The most important information in actually selecting a candidate is often left to be collected in an interview. This is partially an artifact of the traditional methods of obtaining data and information from applicants. Applicants won't know what you really want to know about them if you don't ask them. When organizations ask candidates for anything other than a resume, it is often to fill out a standard employment application form that does little more than standardize the format of data that would typically be on a resume.

However, it is readily possible to have applicants answer a number of interview-like questions via an e-Recruiting system, which would allow a more informed consideration of applicants before deciding on those to interview. While the answers to these questions could be subject to applicants being coached or being dishonest, such situations would be easily detected in the other employment screening tasks (such as actual interviews and reference checks). The e-Recruiting system would offer the advantage of providing a potentially better picture of applicants before rejecting their chances for further consideration.

Ideally, the questions used should be customized to the position involved and not just be another set of general application form–type questions. It should be recognized that once questions are used, they may become public knowledge and may easily be copied by competitors. However, a competitive advantage can be maintained by skill in the analysis and use of the answers received.

3.2.5 The Increasing Complexity of Information Systems

Toffler's[6] concept of three waves of development applies to information systems as well as to general economic activity.

In first-wave economies and information systems, activities happen in a simple sequential manner. Agriculture, for example, follows the growing cycle from planting to harvesting, year after year. Data processing systems, such as accounts receivable, follow a similar cycle from entering sales slips and account changes through updating master files to producing invoices and reports.

First-wave information systems are characterized by the linear structure of their components. A **linear structure** organizes a set of objects or activities in a sequence in which each component (object or activity) is associated (at most) with one previous

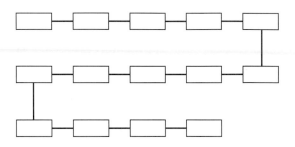

Figure 3-1   A linear structure

component and one following component. Figure 3-1 illustrates a typical linear structure. A single linear path is the only way of moving between components. Because of the large number of components, they are arranged over three rows in this illustration.

People tend to perform various tasks in first-wave systems on their own with little interaction with other people or tasks. Growth or evolution of first-wave systems, if they are to remain linear, is primarily limited to improving individual components within the existing system. As further growth is desired, first-wave systems are often transformed into second-wave systems.

In second-wave economies and information systems, specialization occurs. Management activities are added to coordinate the various specialized production activities. Manufacturing, for example, utilizes supervisors to manage the activities of various factory workers. Management information systems, such as sales analysis, provide the capability of generating a number of different reports to analyze sales from a number of different perspectives.

Second-wave information systems are characterized by the hierarchical structure of their components. A **hierarchical structure** organizes a set of objects or activities in a tree-like manner in which each component (object or activity) is associated (at most) with one higher-level component but may be associated with multiple lower-level components. Figure 3-2 illustrates a typical hierarchical structure. Movement is only allowed between components at different levels. To move between components at the same level requires moving first up a level in the hierarchy and then moving back down again.

While a number of people may be involved with a hierarchical system, the involvement of each is often specialized and limited to certain parts of the hierarchy. People tend to perform specialized tasks in first-wave systems with limited interactions with selected other people or tasks. Growth or evolution of second-wave systems, if they are to remain hierarchical, is primarily limited to adding additional layers to the hierarchy and improving individual components within the existing system. As further growth is desired, second-wave systems are often transformed into third-wave systems.

In third-wave economies and information systems, activities make use of a variety of available resources in various ways to maximize the number of possible results. Various types of customized production, from restaurants to construction, allow the customer to combine a number of choices in order to receive a unique result. Infor-

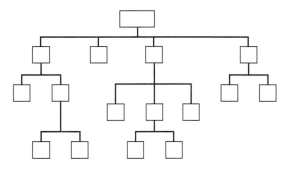

Figure 3-2   A hierarchical structure

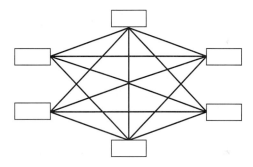

Figure 3-3   A network structure

mation processing is especially well suited to obtaining extra value from existing data by reusing it in various manners because data are a unique commodity that does not get "used up" when used. It is often possible to add value to data by combining the data in new ways with other data. Successful e-Commerce systems often maximize opportunities for value-added processing of the information that they handle. **Value-added** is a phrase used to describe the synergistic effect of a system being of greater value than the sum of the individual values of its components.

Third-wave information systems are characterized by the network structure of their components. A **network structure** organizes a set of objects or activities in an interconnected manner, where each component (object or activity) may be associated with multiple other components. Figure 3-3 illustrates a typical network structure. Movement is allowed between any two components either directly, if a path exists, or indirectly, via other components that are part of the network.

Third-wave systems allow all people to perform any available tasks in any valid order unless they have been purposely limited in what they can perform. Individual

Table 3-8 Some important characteristics of different organizational applications

Traditional Information Applications	e-Commerce Applications
Improve the current way of doing business	Improve the current way of doing business and evolve new ways of doing business
Generally involve only one or two distinct groups of users	Tend to involve multiple distinct groups of users— each with their own distinct sets of needs
Are narrowly focused to serve a single part of the organization	Are broadly focused involving much of the organization and even some external organizations
Strengthen existing organizational divisions	Tend to cross organizational boundaries—both within an organization and even outside the organization to interact with other organizations
Entrench existing organizational relationships	Create new organizational relationships
Rely primarily on internal data	Include information from and about external sources
Extend the life of supporting systems by entrenching existing operations	Tend to adapt to changes—both within the competitive marketplace and in technology in general
Treat data processing as a cost of doing business	Recognize information as a commodity—to which value can be added and from which value can be extracted

users may still specialize perform a limited selection of tasks, if they wish, but they are not limited in what they do by the structure of the system. The use of networked structures facilitates the growth and evolution of third-wave systems.

3.2.6   A Comparison of e-Commerce with Traditional Applications

A preliminary comparison of traditional information applications and e-Commerce applications is presented in Table 3-8. By using a set of questions (such as the traditional reporter's set of "who, what, where, when, why, and how") we can better structure our comparison between types of applications and identify additional important information, which is added in italics, in Table 3-9.

The characteristics of e-Commerce applications, identified in Table 3-9, can be used for evaluating whether or not a proposed application actually involves e-Commerce. Wherever characteristics do not seem to apply, further investigation should be done to see if they really don't apply or if they were just overlooked. This investigation may identify additional challenges and opportunities, which were originally overlooked, that should be considered when developing a new system for an organization.

3.3   PREPARING FOR E-COMMERCE SYSTEMS DEVELOPMENT

3.3.1   Determining the Organizational Environment

The development of e-Commerce goes far beyond just changing which functions are performed by computers and which are performed by people. e-Commerce

Table 3-9 Characteristics of different organizational applications identified within a structured description

	Traditional Information Applications	**e-Commerce Applications**
Who:	*Limited involvement to select users* One or two groups of specific users *within the organization*	*Including everyone who should be involved* Many groups of users *both within and external to the organization*
What:	Improve the current way of doing things	Improve the current way of doing business and evolve new ways of doing business
Where:	Within a single part *or a very limited number of specific parts* of an organization	Across all parts of the organization *that might benefit from or contribute to the application* Also often involves external *individuals* / organizations
When:	*In large organizations since the 1960s* *In medium organizations since the 1970s* *In small organizations since the 1980s*	*Most organizations have started in the last two years or will start in the next two*
Why:	*To serve a single part of the organization that paid for the system out of its budget* *DPSs save time and money by optimizing resource use and improving accuracy* *MISs increase profits and reduce losses* *SISs support planning* *Even so, this processing is generally considered a cost of doing business*	*To server the whole organization that owns the system* To help the organization to evolve *to meet changing times and to capitalize on new opportunities* This recognizes information as a commodity—to which value can be added and from which value can be extracted
How:	Major developments are succeeded by long periods of use before new major developments replace existing ones Efforts are made to extend the life of existing systems which, in turn, entrench existing operations *past their usefulness and ignore new opportunities*	To be successful, e-Commerce systems *must be able to be adapted quickly* to a variety of changes, including: • Competition • New technologies • *New opportunities*
How Much:	*Used on a "when needed (to support particular operations)" basis*	*Use of e-Commerce systems is central to operating the organization*
With Which:	Rely primarily on internal data	Include information from and about external sources

often not only changes the structure of organizations but also reinvents the whole concept of an organization. Some ways in which e-Commerce changes organizations include:

- Boundaries
  - e-Commerce organizations are all worldwide
  - Only a small number of major organizations actually operate worldwide
- Physical facilities needs
  - e-Commerce organizations operate primarily in a virtual location and may exist with a minimum of physical facilities to support them
  - Traditional organizations, with ongoing daily operations, usually must acquire and manage significant physical locations
- Resources
  - Information is often the main resource in e-Commerce organizations
  - Traditional organizations often consider information a cost rather than a resource. Even when they consider it a resource, it seldom is the main resource to be managed and exploited.
- Automation
  - e-Commerce often places a greater reliance on computers providing operational level control of organizational interactions
  - Traditional organizations place a greater emphasis on people rather than computers providing operational level control

For e-Commerce to be successful, the organization has to be able to accommodate these and other changes. Some organizations may be able to adapt smoothly to conduct some or all of their operations via e-Commerce systems. However, some organizations may have severe difficulties in adapting to utilize e-Commerce for a number of reasons:

- Because of rigidities of their structures, procedures, and/or people
- Because they lack people with the skills to help them adapt
- Because they don't understand what's needed and/or what's possible

Before assuming that e-Commerce can be implemented within an organization, it is important to evaluate the strengths and weaknesses of the organization. Evaluations of existing organizations should consider:

- The organization's goals, mission, vision, etc.
- The organization's current structure and operations
- The strengths and weaknesses of its staff
- Its ability to change and to adapt
- Its strengths and weaknesses compared to its competition

Evaluations of startup organizations should consider:

- The strengths, weaknesses, and interests of the founding members
- How the organization can differentiate itself from existing competition
- How the organization might be vulnerable to new competition

Evaluations of student project teams should consider: the strengths, weaknesses, and interests of the members.

Determining an organization's strengths and weaknesses and its organizational environment:

- Should be performed as a basis for identifying potential e-Commerce systems within a real organization
- Can be left until after a team is established and an application is chosen in a series of student assignments

3.3.2   Identifying Team Roles and Establishing a Project Team

A project development team should take into account a number of roles that would be involved in the development of an actual system, including:

- Organizational management—are responsible for approving the development project and changes to the organization that may result from it. It is important that at least one senior manager is chosen to act as a sponsor and actively promote this development effort at the organizational level in order to enlist and/or enforce organizational-wide cooperation. The sponsor(s) should be kept informed of the progress of the development team, but might not be a regular participant in its activities.
- Project management—are responsible for the progress and eventual successful completion of the project. Project management is also responsible for resolving conflicts within the development team. Project management may have to go to the sponsor(s) to resolve conflicts between the team and other members of the organization. Project management can be provided by organizational and/or development professionals.
- User representatives—are responsible for advocating the needs of each of the groups of users. However, they should not be the only users consulted throughout the development of a system. In fact, as a project progresses, user representatives tend to become increasingly more associated with the development team than the users. It is important to get good user representation on a development team, at least on a part-time basis. Care needs to be taken to avoid delegating this duty to workers who are considered "expendable" or "unfit to do the real work" by the groups that they are chosen to represent.
  - Internal users—from various groups within the organization, can be directly represented. A member of each of the major groups of users should be part of the development team.
  - External users—are usually represented by a member of the organization team, with a considerable understanding of their needs and with a range of contacts among real external users.
- Developers—are part of the development team because they have the skills to perform the technical aspects of development.

Teamwork often is split, based on the skills and interests of the team members.

- If everyone always works together on all of the teamwork, teams will likely spend an excessive amount of time
- If everyone does their own part in total isolation, the parts will likely not fit and the systems will likely be a disaster

- Thus, teams need to operate in between these two extremes:
  - Planning of long-term goals and short-term assignments needs to be done by the whole team
  - Specific development work should be delegated to individuals or to small groups
  - The delegated work, including testing or evaluating its suitability, should be completed by the individuals or to small groups
  - The delegated work should be combined and evaluated by the whole team
  - Further planning, including planning improvements to completed work, should be done by the whole team

Each team member is responsible for the successful completion of the project. If problems occur for any reason, they need immediate correction. If the person identifying them cannot correct them immediately, that person should notify the person with the authority to do so.

- In a real organization, problems should to be brought to the attention of the project manager
- In a class situation, problems should be reported to the instructor as soon as they arise to avoid unnecessary complications and/or penalties

In most cases, teams will work well together and help each other to succeed. However, in some cases, problems may occur in a team. Some frequent team problems include:

- People not pulling their weight and not doing their share of the work (whether by ignoring the team, doing a real quick and dirty job, or using an endless series of excuses)
- The team breaking into factions whose differences lead to a lack of cooperation, and even open feuding
- A lack of sufficient team-level planning and control of the project

Establishing a project development team:

- Can be left until after a project is identified within a real organization
- Should be performed at the start of a series of student assignments, such as at this point in this book

3.3.3 Student Assignment—Establishing a Project Team

3.3.3.1 Establishing a Project Team

Individual students need to join together, either on their own or with the assistance of their instructor, into teams that will work together for the remainder of the course. These teams will complete a series of development assignments focusing on a particular e-Commerce system that will be chosen by their team in the next assignment.

NOTE: The development assignments in this book do not include programming the actual application.

Once formed, the team should meet and determine how it intends to operate. Some operational decisions may include:

- The preferred times and places for regular team meetings
- The methods of communicating between members
- The roles to be played by individual members

While individuals can be assigned to perform particular roles, as discussed above, rotating duties so that all team members learn each role may be desirable.

 Find advice on successful student project teamwork in the Chapter 3 Cyber Supplement.

3.3.3.2   Creating a Team Home Page

Each team should create a home page named for their team in their team's Web directory. The home page should:

- Identify the team
- Identify the members of the team and contain links to the home pages of each team member
- Contain links to the different applications researched by team members, including the student assignments from Chapter 2
- Contain links to each of the team's weekly assignments as they are completed
- Provide a means to contact the team members (which can be implemented as a "mailto" the e-mail addresses of the team members or to a team e-mail address)

3.4   BACKGROUND FOR A SET OF FUTURE EXAMPLES

NOTE: The following example, which will be followed throughout this book, is based on the class project of Kelsey Bartel, Amy Grant, Marc Hoffort, and Lian Ruetz in CMPT 275 at the University of Saskatchewan developed during the Winter term in 2000. It is adapted and used with their permission.

The name of the organization "Savor the Cup" is my own invention and is intended as a fictitious company. It is hoped and intended that it does not conflict with any existing businesses.

The following discussion of the *Savor the Cup* organization provides a basis for the examples in future chapters. *Savor the Cup,* an existing organization selling custom-roasted coffee beans to specialty coffee shops and restaurants, is considering using e-Commerce to broaden its range of products and services within its field of business.

Savor the Cup's goals include:

- Providing the highest-quality coffee and related products
- Increasing the company's market share annually
- Focusing on the company's strengths in the market

- Being responsive to customer needs
- Keeping up with changes in the industry

Savor the Cup is currently structured into four divisions. The Administration division manages worldwide operations and handles all accounting and legal matters. There are three operating divisions:

- Purchasing, which buys coffee and related products
- Manufacturing, which roasts and packages coffee and manufactures or contracts for the manufacturing of related products. It decides whether related products should be:
  - Products that are sold as *Savor the Cup* products, which are manufactured by or for *Savor the Cup* and which involve the manufacturing division at least in their design
  - Products that are just purchased and sold with their own brand names, which do not involve the manufacturing division
- Manufacturing also controls warehousing and shipping of coffee and related products
- Sales, which sells coffee and related products to specialty coffee shops and restaurants. Sales also identifies customer needs, changes in the industry, and related products that the organization should sell.

Savor the Cup is headquartered in Vancouver, Canada, with branches in major countries around the world. Each branch has its own administration that reports to the central administration at headquarters. Different branches may include sections of one or more of the operating divisions, depending on local needs. The current structure provides complications for the sections of operating divisions in the various branches, since they have to report both to their local administration and to their division at the headquarters.

Despite the difficulties created by double reporting paths, *Savor the Cup* has been very successful due to the high quality of its employees. These employees are highly knowledgeable in their field and are quick to make suggestions for improvements both to *Savor the Cup* and to those doing business with *Savor the Cup*. Although this helpfulness of employees to customers and others is encouraged by *Savor the Cup*, it has been recently noted that:

- The extent to which customers and others are asking for assistance has been steadily increasing
- The overall productivity of benefit to the organization of many employees is being reduced by the increased time they spend being helpful
- An increasing number of requests for assistance cannot be accommodated by the existing employees

The information technology section of *Savor the Cup's* administration has satisfactorily met most of the previously identified needs. However, it has no expertise in e-Commerce systems. Although *Savor the Cup* has not made any major organizational changes recently, it has kept up with changes in its industry and general changes in technology. By supplying various independent coffee shops and restaurants it has distinguished itself from coffee organizations that focus on franchising. However, given the range of advice it provides and the demands for its products and help, *Savor the Cup* has increasingly been dealing with customers who might otherwise become franchisees of one of its competitors.

In summary, *Savor the Cup* has a number of strengths that it can use to turn its current weaknesses into challenges that may be met via developing an e-Commerce system. What it now needs is a senior manager to take the initiative to sponsor an e-Commerce project.

3.5   CHALLENGES AND OPPORTUNITIES IN PREPARING FOR E-COMMERCE SYSTEMS DEVELOPMENT

One of the biggest challenges in preparing for e-Commerce systems development is ensuring that all the project team roles are fulfilled throughout the life of the project. Often developments start off with a few, key people, each performing multiple roles. As development progresses, many people tend to focus their efforts in increasingly specialized efforts. Additionally, provision needs to be made to replace people who leave a development project. Some examples include:

- A senior executive who starts off sponsoring a development may become separated from the development effort to the point of not being interested in or able to help the development team keep the necessary support of senior management.
- An internal user who identifies a need and starts developing an application may get so involved in the role of being a developer that there becomes a need for other people to represent the internal users.
- An individual who starts as a representative of a number of user groups may over time focus more on the needs of a particular group and less on the needs of other equally important groups.

Another major challenge is dealing with the concerns of people who feel threatened by the changes taking place. People do not have to be actually threatened to feel threatened. Thus, the threat may be more widespread than would be expected. Often this challenge can be minimized by good communications within an organization about the true effects of the change and by describing how individuals, as well as the organization, will benefit from the proposed changes. Including representatives of each user group can help to minimize this challenge.

e-Commerce systems can be developed to run on their own, along with existing operations. By developing them as separate operations, an organization can try out different organizational strategies before implementing them in the existing portion of the organization.

3.6   CYBER SUPPLEMENTS FOR CHAPTER 3

Look at the Chapter 3 Cyber Supplements on the Web to find:

- Information about DPS, MIS, and DSS systems that are used by various organizations

- A discussion of how an example e-Commerce site uses the major functions discussed above
- A discussion of and links to examples of different types of fundamental business activities at various e-Commerce sites
- Advice on successful student project teamwork
- Suggestions for further investigations into the evolution of organizational information systems

REFERENCES

[1] ISO/IEC International Standard 14662, Information Technologies—Open-EDI Reference Model, 1997.

[2] "International Organization for Standardization," ISO/IEC 2nd Committee Draft of International Standard 15944-1, Business Agreement Semantic Descriptive Techniques—Part 1: Operational Aspects of Open-EDI for Implementation, 2000.

[3] Alvin Toffler, *Power Shift: Knowledge, Wealth, and Violence at the Edge of the 21st Century* (New York, NY, Bantam Books, 1990).

[4] J. Daniel Couger, *Creativity & Innovation: In Information Systems Organizations* (Danvers, MA, Boyd & Fraser, 1996).

[5] James Burke, *Connections* (Boston, MA, Little Brown, 1978).

[6] Alvin Toffler, *The Third Wave* (New York, NY, Bantam Books, 1981).

Identifying and Describing an e-Commerce Application

Outline

4.1 INTRODUCTION TO IDENTIFYING E-COMMERCE APPLICATIONS

This chapter focuses on the initial e-Commerce development process of identifying a potential application. It provides guidance on identifying and initially describing potential e-Commerce applications, as part of what is often referred to as an initial investigation.

Development projects start from suggestions that have passed the scrutiny of an initial investigation. Anyone in an organization may make a suggestion. For a major suggestion, such as developing a system, to be acted upon generally requires the support of someone in management. Because e-Commerce systems affect most or all of an organization, suggestions to develop e-Commerce systems generally require the approval and support of someone in senior management.

In order to get support, a proposed application needs to be described with more than just a name. However, there may be few resources available initially to go much further than providing a good application description prior to getting this needed support. Once such a description is developed, the proposed application often will have to compete with other proposed investments before being funded. The working of such competitions varies from organization to organization and is beyond the scope of this book.

Initial investigations are used to quickly, and with little expenditure of resources, determine whether or not a proposal is worth investigating further. In some organizations, initial investigations occur as mere conversations between a person with a suggestion and a manager who could authorize further investigation, while in other organizations initial investigations follow a formal, well-documented procedure. Regardless of how an initial investigation is conducted, it should consider the issues discussed in this chapter.

A decision to proceed with consideration of an application may involve developing a formal business case or conducting a feasibility study. Business case development is beyond the scope of this book, and feasibility studies are discussed in Chapter 6.

4.2   UNDERSTANDING E-COMMERCE APPLICATION OPPORTUNITIES

4.2.1   e-Commerce Systems Serve Individuals and Organizations

e-Commerce is evolving so fast that new theories about it are often superceded in short order by yet newer theories. Recently, many authors have taken to trying to categorize e-Commerce systems as being either:

- Business to Business (B2B) e-Commerce, which usually refers to e-Commerce between a limited number of organizations with significant and regular business transactions that are well-defined
- Business to Consumer (B2C)

While B2C applications are far more likely to be publicized, all the research shows that the dollar volume of B2B transactions far exceeds that of B2C transactions. However, it's not any wonder that B2B dollar volume surpasses B2C, because B2B has the following characteristics:

- It is a natural outgrowth of distributed processing which occurred within organizations prior to the Web
- It involves an application of relatively limited scope namely customer–supplier integration, which often consists of only providing a catalog and an order-processing capability

- It is often based on an established stable customer–supplier relationship, avoiding the need of finding new customers on-line
- It is often supported by both purchasing agents (at the customer side) and sales support staff (at the supplier side) who handle aspects other than ordering
- It generally has customers who know what they want or will talk to a sales support person if they need specific details
- It generally involves more dollars per transaction
- Customers typically make their choice based on fixed criteria:
  - Their relationship with the supplier
  - The price
  - The availability of the product
  - Some combination of the above

This does not mean that B2C cannot be profitable. It's just that B2C hasn't developed as quickly. There's lots of potential. However, before it catches up, it might be surpassed by a new hybrid: B2B2C (business to business to consumer) systems.

Increasingly, e-Commerce will need to integrate multiple branches of an organization and even multiple organizations in order to serve the needs of individual customers. This will evolve the model of basic e-Commerce systems from being based on either B2C (business to consumer) systems or B2B (business to business) systems to being a model of B2B2C systems. Many of the e-Broker applications popular on the Web today involve B2B2C.

In selecting an application to pursue, organizations should look toward the future and feel free to invent an application that can be the next success story in the field of e-Commerce. Once they identify different potential applications, they can evaluate whether or not each application makes business sense.

Rather than using B2B and B2C to describe whole applications, it is more useful to use these concepts to describe activities within applications. Many systems contain both types of activities, and potentially even others.

> "Electronic commerce can be broadly categorized into:
> - Business to business,
> - Business to public administration,
> - Individual to business,
> - Individual to public administration,
> - Public administration to public administration,
> with the understanding that each scenario holds in both directions."[1]

Individual to individual is another important category of e-Commerce[2] that has been gaining importance.

We can simplify the set of different activities somewhat by considering that both businesses and public administrations (and even occasionally some individuals) are all instances of organizations. For purposes of our consideration we should recognize that there are three main types of activities that may occur within an e-Commerce application:

- Individual to individual activities
- Organization to individual (or individual to organization) activities
- Organization to organization activities

Each activity:

- May be initiated by one or either of the parties to the activity
- May involve third-party mediation or other support services

The main differences (in general, with some exceptions) between individuals and organizations include their typical:

- Scale of operations—organizations being composed of a number of individuals can generally accomplish a greater range of major projects at a given time
- Amount of resources—organizations usually have greater resources, including greater financial power and greater inventories and greater amounts of support
- Amount of flexibility—individuals are usually more flexible than organizations, which tend to have their flexibility limited by their structures
- Number of instances—organizations tend to deal with many more individuals than the number of organizations an individual will deal with personally
- Duration of relationships—business relationships with organizations tend to be longer than business relationships with individuals
- Treatment—more resources may be extended in developing a system to deal with an organization than would be expended in developing a system for an individual. The grouping of large numbers of individuals may be used to achieve economies of scale. These economies of scale can only be realized if the individuals are grouped appropriately.

It is important to recognize the general characteristics of an application early in the development because the greater the involvement of individual users, the greater the complexity needed to deal with them. Each of the differences, discussed above, may have a number of effects on the specific requirements for an e-Commerce application, which are discussed in Chapter 7.

 Find reviews of and links to examples of individual to individual, organization to individual, and organization to organization e-Commerce activities in the Chapter 4 Cyber Supplement.

4.2.2   e-commerce Competitive Advantages and Disadvantages

The evolution of the Web, in general, and e-Commerce, in particular, keeps changing what is and is not a competitive advantage. However, the basics remain the same. To have a competitive advantage, an organization must have relatively exclusive possession of something that people want and for which people are willing to reward the organization (via their business or via other forms of rewards).

It's hard to keep exclusive possession of a competitive advantage on the Web where millions of people will be exposed to it. This wide exposure is both: good—in convincing people that they want it and are willing to reward the organization; and bad—in that the Web makes it very easy for the competition to copy or imitate the advantage.

Techniques and features that impress people today, giving their developers a competitive advantage for now, become expected and commonplace tomorrow, only producing competitive disadvantages to those who haven't yet caught up. Already there have been a number of competitive advantages and disadvantages that have been widely-used and imitated to help expand the role of e-Commerce on the Web and in the world. Over time, some techniques and features cease to be competitive advantages and become part of the basic set of expectations of any serious system.

Both e-Commerce, in particular, and the Web, in general, are evolving so quickly that what was a significant competitive advantage just recently, becomes expected today and passé tomorrow. To remain relevant, an organization must keep evolving both to match the competition and to stay ahead or at least to stay unique.

This section will deal with a number of features that have at one time or other been considered to be competitive advantages. Although many of these advantages are tied to e-Businesses, similar advantages are being tried across e-Commerce applications.

NOTE: It is not enough just to consider the following set of potential competitive advantages, either for student assignments or for an organization to remain competitive. Organizations must be constantly on the look out for new ideas that you can turn into new competitive advantages.

Some competitive advantages include:

- A Web presence
- Discussion groups, chat rooms, and the like
- Giveaways
- Detailed product information
- Low prices
- Rewards for customer loyalty
- Large selection of products
- Unique products
- Unique methods of doing business
- Customizing the site for individual users
- A local presence
- Customer service
- Focusing on services rather than products

It should be noted that few of these "advantages" are unique to the Web, although many of them are readily facilitated via Web and other electronic technology. Most are just good marketing and business sense.

 Find reviews of and links to examples of the use of various types of competitive advantages in use at e-Commerce sites in the Chapter 4 Cyber Supplement.

It should also be noted that while most of these "advantages" were introduced as major steps forward in e-Commerce, their quick adoption by competitive organizations generally led to very short-term advantages for their pioneers. However, in some cases these pioneers were able to generate sufficient interest to quickly establish their foothold and to gain a respectability that has weathered many additional challengers. The key is being able to quickly capitalize on a competitive advantage during the brief period when you hold it. Some organizations, such as *Amazon.com,* keep following one innovation with another in order to keep the competitive advantage.

It must be remembered that in any industry there tends to evolve industry leaders who often can gain an almost monopoly status. Likewise, in most industries, large organizations with sufficient resources can buy into a position of leadership, taking it away from smaller players. One of the secrets to success is to identify new industries or new niches and to hold on to them long enough to prosper and grow.

4.2.2.1   A Web Presence

In the early days of the Web, merely having a home page was considered good. It was even better if it had a "mailto;" that would accept comments and questions from prospective customers. Many organizations thought of such sites as ongoing advertising that, once paid for, could be left to reap its rewards. Some people even thought that all you had to do was set up a home page and it would bring you enough business to set up a new company based on it (without considering the other aspects of a business that are necessary to operate, let alone to succeed).

Few potential customers were as enthusiastic about the various home pages they visited as were either their creators or the media. Rather than considering home pages as at least the equivalent of "Yellow Pages advertisements," which could be consulted whenever a product was desired, many home pages were little better than newspaper advertisements, which, if they are ever read a first time, are seldom ever read again. The world eventually learned that the Web was no "Field of Dreams" where, "If you build it, they will come"—even if they came, they might leave quickly, never to return.

Early home pages were plagued by a number of design problems that often aggravated their visitors. These included:

- Pages with an organization's name and/or logo with no information about the organization, including:
  - Information about what the organization did
  - Information about where the organization was located
  - Information about how to contact the organization
- Pages that didn't work, weren't there, or that disappeared or moved locations frequently
- Pages that contained too many "bells and whistles," especially ones that required many obscure "plug-ins" or other technology that the user might not have readily available
- e-mail addresses or "mailto" features that had users sending mail that was not responded to in a timely manner, if at all

While once having a Web presence was unique, it is now expected. But these Web presences must not be passive, merely flaunting the ego of their owners and designers. They must be active, engaging the interests of the users.

4.2.2.2   Discussion Groups, Chat Rooms, and the Like

An early form of engagement of users was to provide, support, or link to some mechanism, allowing users to interact with the organization and or other users. In many cases, these mechanisms were considered similar to organizational meetings and special interest groups. However, unlike their more formal predecessors, they often were difficult for the organization to control and manipulate in a favorable manner (if the organization was willing to commit the resources to try to do so). It was possible for discussions to lead to negative consequences for the organization, including:

- Groups of users ganging up on the organization and demanding changes to its products or policies
- Disgruntled individuals using it as a forum to try to discredit the organization
- Well-meaning individuals spreading informed or uninformed information that might lead potential customers to the competition

Although discussion groups and the like could provide useful support in many cases, the proliferation of such forums quickly eclipsed their uniqueness. Individuals have only so much time to spend in such activities (and many individuals spend far too much for their own good). As chat rooms and other discussion mechanisms multiplied, individuals have had to choose their preferred ones, and often ignore the creation of new forums, even where they might be more in line with the individual's interests.

The success of any such mechanism depends more on the individuals involved than on the organization that sponsors it. Likewise, the benefits accrue more to the individual. This is not to say that there is not room for selected new endeavors of this type, just that most topics and groups of individuals are already served and that where they exist, there is increasingly less and less likelihood of using such a feature as a competitive advantage.

4.2.2.3 Giveaways

Most people like getting something for free. However, as many people have found out the hard way, there is little that is truly free. Someone generally has to pay for it. Likewise, just because you gave something to someone, doesn't mean that they will be grateful, let alone that they will repay you with kindness. The most common giveaways tend to be:

- Various information products (such as e-magazines)
- Information services (such as indexes and comparison services)
- Other entertainment services (music, videos, and games)
- Service vouchers (discount coupons and phone card numbers), where the giveaway can be easily and cheaply delivered via the Web to their recipients

Giveaways, at best, get attention for those giving them away. Once the initial attention is past, they may have little or no lasting effect on most of their recipients. Giveaways tend to be tied to advertising schemes, where they can do quite well. For example, various Internet indexes such as *Yahoo.com* are able to give away their services thanks to a number of sponsors. In return for their sponsorship, organizations get a small portion of screen in which to try to interest the user of the service in visiting the organization's site. Currently this often involves promising further giveaways to entice the user.

Where attention is not enough, "givers" try to extract some immediate benefit from the intended recipients, making the giveaway no longer truly free. Again, the easiest medium for achieving this benefit is electronic. Often a user is asked for "just a few pieces of information" in order to qualify for the giveaway. These pieces of information are then used to evaluate the user and potentially to initiate follow-ups to entice the user to establish a long-term business relationship.

In either case, giveaways tend to be one-shot opportunities (contests are a specific type of giveaway that are typically one-shot opportunities for influencing a user). To get the user to return to a business or e-Commerce site, something further must be given away the next time. While there is an ongoing market for information products and services, other giveaways may lose their repeat appeal. In any case, there will be ongoing expenses for an organization to continue to provide new giveaways to entice users back time and again. To pay for these ongoing expenses, the organization must receive ongoing benefits, which are usually received in terms of sponsorship, direct sales, or useful information. In the case of the latter, once an organization has gotten its "just a few pieces of information" it may not gain anything by getting the same information again. However, limiting giveaways to one per customer can be costly and may lose its usefulness over time.

Finally, one has to consider the large number of giveaways available on the Web. Even the greediest of users does not have the time to try to get them all. Users are becoming more and more selective about which giveaways they spend time acquiring. This requires organizations to compete with each other to give away more attractive products and services. And that leads to very expensive advertising, if it cannot be made to reach a large audience efficiently.

4.2.2.4   Detailed Product Information

Customers and potential customers often want detailed product information. It can help them to decide on which product to purchase. Making a decision to purchase a product does not, however, guarantee that the product will be purchased from the organization providing the information. Some people may use the Web to research products and then purchase them directly (without the Web) from local vendors. Additionally, when an organization is selling products produced by another organization, potential customers may bypass the selling organization and deal directly with the manufacturer if they can readily identify it.

Competitors can use this same information to copy or surpass the competitive advantage of any of the features described, including low prices, and thus take away business. Product comparison services use this information to make positive or negative recommendations about one product versus another. When detailed information is not available, various product/price comparison services may ignore its availability.

Thus, although providing detailed product information can have its benefits, it also has a number of potential disadvantages. Marketing people generally attempt to provide only that information that supports their product and to provide it in a manner that also supports their organization.

There is little interorganizational consistency in what detailed information is given about products, although competitive pressures may accelerate the demands for disclosure. Detailed product information can include a number of items, such as:

- General product description
- A list of product features
- Detailed product technical specifications

- Product cost
- Product source/manufacturer
- Delivery time and cost estimates
- Comparison with similar products

It may also include providing a sample of various information products and a picture of various physical products. Additional information may include:

- Tutorial information about the use of the product
- Demonstrations of the product being used
- References to satisfied customers
- Safety information relating to the product

Although marketing personnel seldom wish to talk about the failings of a product, some organizations may also choose to link product support information (including product cautions and fixes) to the other detailed information about a product.

4.2.2.5 Low Prices

It is important to consider what low prices really involve. A customer has to be certain of what is being bought, even if it essentially involves buying the same product.

The only addition to the price of most products in a local store is generally the tax. Even on large items requiring special delivery, local stores will often negotiate or completely waive delivery charges. Where they don't they are clearly stated and fixed at the time of sale. Many Web-based businesses advertise low product prices, which they then supplement with high "shipping and handling prices." In many cases, while e-Businesses provide fixed prices for products, they only provide estimates for shipping and handling. Additional costs may accrue in terms of exchange rates, customs, and taxes on items purchased from other countries, regardless of whether or not the customer is made aware of the international nature of the transaction. Although an organization can often hide these additional costs from a new customer until after the sale is transacted, unwelcome hidden costs can discourage customers from giving it repeat business.

With a local sales staff, a customer may go to them to have problems resolved. The level of after-sale customer service of many, but not all, e-Businesses is currently very poor. Providing good customer service costs money. Many organizations often lower their prices by eliminating or separating service from product costs. Product returns (for repair, refund, or exchange) to distant e-Businesses often cost the customer additional shipping and may involve additional charges.

Another technique used to lower prices is to act as a "box mover" or e-Broker by ordering products (from manufacturing or from one's suppliers) only when they have been sold to a customer. However, this technique has the disadvantage of increasing delivery times and exposing an organization to direct competition from its suppliers.

If people are only concerned with low prices, they will likely be very careful to get the truly lowest price. Keeping an organization's price the lowest price requires continual vigilance and considerable abilities to survive price wars. If this is the only competitive advantage of an organization, it can be readily overcome by a rich competitor who temporarily cuts prices further to drive out its competition.

4.2.2.6 Rewards for Customer Loyalty

Rather than give up low prices on each individual sale, many organizations choose to provide differential rewards to customers with large aggregate purchases. Rewards are like getting a giveaway that is tied to one, and it is hoped more, purchases. They appeal to people's desire to get something for nothing, even if it isn't really for nothing. Reward programs very considerably:

- Often, this involves convincing the customer to give up immediate advantages for deferred benefits. These deferred benefits must be substantially more attractive than current savings to be a competitive advantage.
- The range of benefits vary from free gifts, to cash rebates, to increasing levels of future or immediate discount.
- Some organizations (such as airlines) use "reward" schemes to "earn" the "loyalty" of individuals who would not receive the benefits of immediate savings to their organizations.
- Organizations often concoct unique reward programs that they market based on their best possible outcome and that are difficult to completely compare with competitive programs. Despite intentional complexities, knowledgeable customers may be a member of competing reward programs and may make their decisions based on a combination of factors, including both low prices and loyalty rewards.

Customer loyalty programs have another advantage (potentially both for the customers and the organization). They make it desirable for customers to allow the organization to gather information about their buying habits, which the organization may then use to better "serve"/market to the customer. Reward programs often give an organization an excuse to send "special offers" to "select customers." Reward programs may also provide customers with other special privileges, such as increased access to customer support.

Because of the costs and complexities of reward programs, it is important that an organization understand the motivations of the customers it is trying to reward. Otherwise a program may offend current customers and fail to attract any new ones. One example of where care is needed is the provision of special rewards for new customers without recognizing the importance of long-time customers.

4.2.2.7 Large Selection of Products

There are various ways an organization can provide a large selection of products. The organization can:

- Manufacture them itself or purchase them from other organizations
- Warehouse them to have on hand or manufacture/purchase them on demand
- Deal with lots of different product lines (like a department store) or deal with lots of items within a limited product line (like a specialty store)
- Deal with existing products or deal with custom (made-to-order) products

e-Businesses can gain a competitive advantage over traditional businesses by providing a larger selection of products than would be feasible to inventory in most physical stores. Over the last decade, traditional businesses have been increasingly analyzing their sales to optimize their product offerings, focusing on offering the products with the highest turnover and eliminating products with low sales. This reduces inventory, handling, and storage costs and directs the application of these resources to more profitable products. By reaching larger markets, by having lower (if any) inventory and storage costs, and by making a profit on handling costs that are charged to the customer, an e-Business can offer many products whose low volume of sales would lead traditional businesses to discontinue carrying them.

Organizations use large selections of products to try to meet more needs of more customers and thus to increase sales. However, having a large product selection may not be sufficient to accomplish these organizational goals.

Having a large selection will appeal to some people, but the effort required to deal with this selection may repel others. The larger the selection, the more work the customer may have to go through to find a product that meets the user's current interests, which may be:

- A specific product that is currently desired
- The product that best meets the current set of needs
- Just browsing through interesting or new products

Where an organization's Web site focuses on only one of these types of user accessing, the complexities of a large selection of products may actively inhibit meeting the others. In any case, having a large selection may not guarantee sales if other organizations carry the same products and have other competitive advantages more desirable to the users. The more products an organization has, the greater the likelihood that users will wish to compare between similar products. Once this comparison starts, there is not necessarily any reason for them not to compare also the products offered by various competitors.

4.2.2.8   Unique Products

Even businesses with large selections of products may miss or ignore certain specialty products. While there is likely to be considerable competition between major e-Businesses that leads to considerable consolidations and failures, there is a tremendous opportunity for e-Businesses that cater to niche markets. The challenge if for these e-Businesses to be able to clearly identify themselves in such a way that their intended customers can easily find them.

Having a unique product does not, however, ensure consistent success. The market for some products may reach saturation or may disappear with changing consumer interest. As other products become more popular, regardless of the reason, they may move from being niche products into the mainstream where established, large e-Businesses may be able to take over some or all of their markets. It is important for organizations focusing on unique products to continue to identify new unique products to adopt as they loose others, either due to loss of consumer interest or due to increased competition.

Another danger in using unique products as a competitive advantage is the desire to expand a business by taking on an increasing amount of not-so-unique products. While such a strategy may work for a short time, especially with established customers, it may bring a business into direct competition with larger, more established e-Businesses. It should be remembered that competition can come from other similarly focused e-Businesses and from suppliers deciding to market their products directly, as well as from larger, more general e-Businesses.

Maintaining a focus on unique products can be assisted by research into the interests and lifestyles of the consumers of these products. By focusing product lines on particular lifestyles, a Web site can work on gaining credibility with a particular group of potential customers. It may be better to set up separate complimentary e-Business sites, each catering to distinct groups, rather than losing the uniqueness that may have led to initial successes.

Having unique products is often just a part of what distinguishes specialty businesses from others. Many customers expect and/or require specialized sales and service to go along with the availability of unique products. While this specialized sales and servicing can increase costs, it also provides extra value to the customers of specialty businesses.

4.2.2.9 Unique Methods of Doing Business

Many recent advances in e-Commerce are related to "new" ways of doing business that information technology and communications have made feasible. This is most apparent in the expansion in various forms of e-Brokers (and similar services) from the traditional domains of finances, real estate, and travel to all fields of business. Buyers and sellers or producers and consumers can now do business in a variety of ways, including:

- Electronic stores (e-Businesses) such as *Amazon.com*
- Electronic auctions such as *eBay.com*
- Electronic tendering such as *Priceline.com*
- Electronic brokers (who primarily represent various sellers)
- Electronic agents (who primarily represent buyers)
- Electronic barter exchanges
- Electronic cooperatives such as *Naptster.com*

This list keeps expanding as creative individuals find different ways of serving the needs of e-Commerce. While each of the above methods of doing business has analogs in the traditional world, there is no need that new ones do also. What is important is that each of these methods fills a need so that people will be willing to use it and is easy to understand and to use so that people can and will use it.

Each method relies on attracting a sufficient number of users to make it viable. While profits from or commissions on each sale may be sufficient to finance most methods, various sites using these methods may attempt to obtain additional benefits from advertising and/or from customer profiling.

While each of the above methods of doing business works for the sale or exchange of tangible products, they also work with the sale or exchange of less-tangible products such as personal or professional services. Because the same products can be bought or sold via any of these methods, there is no need to restrict one's business to using only one of the methods. However, since using multiple methods could lead to confusion and/or resentment with an organization's intended customers/suppliers, it may be preferable to use separate methods in parallel in separate Web sites.

Developing new methods of doing business, including new e-Commerce approaches, will involve a certain amount of cross-elasticity, in which customers may shift from one product to another or from one way of interacting with an organization to another. **Cross-elasticity** results from increases in the demand for one product or service, causing a corresponding decrease in the demand for other products and/or services. Competing with oneself need not be bad if it increases the net benefits to the organization!

Care should be taken that internal competition does not lead to different business methods becoming the domain of different parts of the organization, which then undercut one another and decrease the overall benefit to the parent organization. Rather than allow destructive competition, an organization should consciously plan for the migration of business from one method to another.

4.2.2.10 Customizing the Site for Individual Users

Customizing a site for individual users, while offered by some sites for a relatively long time, has received mixed levels of acceptance among various users. It reaches its highest level in customer–supplier (so called business to business) systems integration. It has also become popular with many users/customers of information and entertainment sites.

The basic intent of customizing sites for individual users is to improve the relationship between them. While this improved relationship can have benefits for both parties, many external individuals or organizations who are offered this relationship may be wary of becoming increasingly dependent on the organization that offers the relationship.

Generally, customization is based on the external individual or organization providing a variety of information that can be used not only for customizing access to the Web site but also for various types of customer profiling and direct marketing. There can be a variety of concerns about these other uses and the potential for misuses of customization information. It is becoming increasingly expected that organizations post privacy policies as part of any sites that collect large amounts of potentially sensitive or private information. Privacy considerations are discussed in Chapter 9.

4.2.2.11 A Local Presence

There are an increasing number of agreements being negotiated between major retailers (with lots of convenient locations) and major Internet organizations. These agreements involve working together to promote and support each other. The traditional retailers hope to easily jump into e-Commerce with the help and expertise of their new associates, while the Internet organizations hope to gain the local presence and support that their on-line nature has lacked.

Some examples of relationships include:

- Kmart with Yahoo!
- Wal-Mart, Barnes & Noble, and Blockbuster with America Online
- Best Buy and Radio Shack with Microsoft

Having a local presence will both increase the marketing scope of the Internet organizations and provide potential customers with live human beings to locally turn to for support. Additionally, specially developed (and limited capability) Internet stations available at local facilities will increase the accessibility to these Internet organizations for many people who do not have their own Internet access.

Currently, many people are not interested in purchasing items from e-Businesses in other countries due to potential hassles with local duty, customs, and taxes and with concerns over the e-Business not needing to be accountable to local business practices and legislation. Many of these concerns could be reduced or eliminated if the e-Business had even a minimal presence in each country where it did a significant amount of business. (For example, I might be more likely to buy from *Amazon.com* and other American companies if I didn't have to deal with all the duties and fees involved with importing goods into Canada from the United States.)

Only the largest and most powerful of Internet organizations may be able to arrange a high-profile and ubiquitous local presence. However, some form of local presence can help most e-Businesses and many other e-Commerce applications. Smaller organizations, without widespread branches, may choose to enter into alliances and cooperative arrangements with similar organizations in other locations. Organizations, which start such alliances, can be expected to get more benefits than organizations, which join them at a later time.

4.2.2.12   Customer Service

The main reasons most people with Internet access give for not using e-Commerce involve either security concerns or the poor state of customer service provided by most e-Businesses. While technology has come a long way in securing transactions, many organizations have a long way to go in providing satisfactory service. It is important to recognize that different groups of users often have different servicing needs and that one servicing solution seldom fits all those who need service.

It is interesting to note that when surveyed, many organizations cite providing better customer service as one of their chief motivations for and their perceived successes with going to e-Commerce. This disparity in opinions shows that many organizations have a long way to go to providing good service because they first have to realize that they have a severe problem.

While some of the above points touched on some customer service issues, there are many others that should also be considered.

4.2.2.13   Changing the Focus from Products to Services

It is difficult to be successful if you compete directly against big organizations. And yet, every day some small, local businesses flourish in the shadow of "big box" competitors. It's useful to consider how they manage, especially considering that their prices may be higher than their competition. The answer involves more than their customers are willing to support local businesses.

Big box organizations focus on selling products. They have to sell lots of products to survive. By selling lots of products they compete based on:

- Low prices (or at least the perception of low prices)
- High visibility (including lots of advertising)
- Expected availability of popular products

Selling products based on these factors is like having a series of one-night stands:

- A relationship of convenience is established
- The relationship (sale) is consummated
- The relationship automatically ends

Each new sale is dependent on establishing a new relationship of convenience. Where customers are conditioned to maximize their convenience in terms of price, they can be easily attracted by a better price. Big box outlets, with high volumes, can undercut the price of specialty shops. However, manufactures, selling directly to customers, can win in a price war whenever they wish, if enough customers are just searching for low prices.

Specialty shops, which realize they are selling more than products, tend to be the most successful local businesses. Successful specialty shops provide (sell) services, which just happen to include products. In selling services, they are establishing and maintaining long-term relationships, which may lead to the sale of various products over time.

The sale of products focuses on the present, based on information from the past. Selling products relies primarily on information about current sales and possible future industry trends. Where any information is obtained regarding customer wants or needs it only comes from a small and often unrepresentative sample.

The sale of services combines a focus on the present with one on the future. Selling services often involves inputting information about what each individual customer wants and needs. This information is used both to satisfy the customer's wants/needs with your products and to determine the future directions of your organization.

Focusing on services does not mean that services are necessarily priced separately from products. Often customers would be unwilling to pay extra for these services, but may be willing to pay more for products related to these services. Focusing on services can add value to the products in a number of ways, including:

- Assisting customers in finding the types of products that meet their needs, rather than just presenting your products based on traditional product categories
- Providing after-sale assistance in using products that have been purchased
- Checking on customer satisfaction with products that have been purchased
- Finding additional products that could meet the needs of current customers
- Informing customers of new products that meet their specific needs, while avoiding pestering them about other products

Each of these ways of adding value involves communications and information, making them good potential candidates for being included in e-Commerce systems. Identifying and understanding them comes from shifting our emphasis from "how can we sell stuff to customers?" to "what do customers need to help them with what they want?"

It is important that the provision of services not be separated too far from the sale of products, which finances those services.

- If an e-Commerce site gives away information that leads customers to choose products that readily can be purchased much cheaper from another e-Commerce site, it may provide services without receiving any return benefits.

- If an e-Commerce site has a number of interrelated products reasonably priced that a customer needs, customers may chose to pay a little more to avoid trying to find the best price on each individual item. Where shipping and handling charges are added, it is often more economical to buy a number of items from a single source at a single time, even if individual items are not the cheapest.
- If an e-Commerce site has some unique products that go with other, more common, products to fill unique customer needs, then it may have an easier time selling its more common products.

4.2.2.14 Further Competitive Advantages

New competitive advantages and new applications of these competitive advantages are being developed all the time. Some organizations mimic the latest trends without fully understanding how they can best be incorporated into the way they do business. It is often easy to recognize the difference between changes that are made as opportunistic gimmicks and will last only as long as they seem fashionable and changes that involve true commitments to better serving the users. Getting the most out of a competitive advantage often requires organizations to make fundamental changes to their business practices.

Find reviews of and links to examples of some of the best and worst of current e-Commerce business practices on the Chapter 4 Cyber Supplement.

4.2.3 The Major Components of e-Commerce Applications

According to ISO 15944-1, e-Commerce systems are built around sets of business transactions that involve legal persons, business processes, and data.[3]

When analyzing the e-Commerce applications they are intended to serve, it is useful to distinguish between the tasks that business processes accomplish and the tools that are used to accomplish them. **Tools** are any of the many things (computerized or non-computerized) that help a user accomplish some task (or set of tasks). The main goal of most e-Commerce development projects is to develop a system that will serve as a multifunctional tool for a variety of users. Parts/subsystems of an e-Commerce system may each be treated as separate identifiable tools, in that they may each help accomplish different tasks. Because an e-Commerce system will be just one of the many different tools used by each of these users, it will need to integrate with and/or be compatible with other tools that they may use. Developers also use tools. The particular development tools available to a developer may help and/or limit them in developing e-Commerce tools for users.

In defining the needs of different business transactions it is useful to separate consideration of the content of the data from its presentation. Different tools may utilize different formats of the same data content. Within this book, **content** includes all the material that is processed and presented by an e-Commerce system regardless of how it is processed or presented. Although most content should be relevant to the accomplishment of application-specific tasks, some content may be added to systems merely to make them more appealing (which is an example of a more general task, namely "engaging the user").[4]

While content may often be referred to as the information contained by an application, it may actually consist of:

- Data
- Information
- Knowledge
- Wisdom

The content of e-Commerce applications can exist in and may be transformed between a variety of media formats or combinations of media formats. e-Commerce content may utilize various media formats, which can be:

- Textual (using words and numbers) and/or graphical (including pictures or tunes)
- Audio (sound, including speech) and/or video (visual, including displayed or printed)
- Fixed and/or changing over time (temporal)

e-Commerce applications bring people (*users*) together using computer systems (*tools*) that manipulate data, information, knowledge, and wisdom (*content*) in order to accomplish a set of purposes (*tasks*), as illustrated in Figure 4-1. Each of these components can influence the success of an e-Commerce system.

Traditional software application systems often have a single set of tools used for a single set of tasks and used by a single (expected) type of user. e-Commerce systems tend to combine different sets of tools that can be used for different sets of tasks by different groups of users. This greatly increases the complexity that needs to be handled in order for the system to be successful.

A description of an e-Commerce application should identify each of the different components that may be significant in its success. Practicing iterative development recognizes that additional components may be identified later and added to this initial set. Analyzing important details of these components will form the basis for requirements analysis as described in Chapter 7.

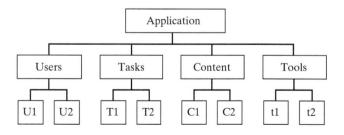

Figure 4-1   The major components of an e-Commerce application

4.3 DESCRIBING E-COMMERCE APPLICATIONS

Each organization needs to identify what applications they need. Often they may do this with reference to applications others have already identified. Some long understood and established and relatively simple applications (such as accounts receivable) may appear to have a widely accepted definition. However, there may be a number of differences between organizations in the details and even in the overall way the application is defined. One major difference in accounts receivable is the choice of method (balance forward, open item, or hybrid). A number of interesting types of e-Commerce applications were suggested in Chapter 2. However, some people might argue with each of the definitions and even with many of the names used for them.

What is important is that applications help people accomplish some purpose or set of purposes in some way. You should remember that an application can be defined as some purpose or set of purposes that can be fulfilled by using (applying) some system (in some manner).

It is one thing to identify an application with a commonly used name, and another to truly understand what it involves for those people who will use it for a given organization. Different people will often have very different expectations of what an application is really supposed to accomplish and who it might involve.

A common approach (and format) can be used for describing both applications and the software packages developed to serve them. The development of new application packages can start from consideration of the needs of applications, add the needs of users and content, and then add an appropriate look and feel based on existing software packages and appropriate design guidance to come up with a new design.

This format can be used to describe applications and application software packages and can be used to identify how they relate to their environment. Initial application descriptions are far from complete. Rather, they should provide a starting point for further analysis of what is really involved in the application for a given organization. They identify a number of components of the application, which will each require their own description and further analysis before we can claim to understand enough of the application to properly design a system to serve it.

The format, presented in Table 4-1, is based on the traditional reporter's set of questions (who, what, where, when, why, how, and how much). It can be used to describe both applications and software packages to serve them. This format was already demonstrated in Chapter 3 as a basis for comparing traditional information applications with e-Commerce applications. A detailed example of using this format in describing *Savor the Cup's* application is provided later in this chapter.

The **name,** used to identify an application or software package, is very important in ensuring successful communication between people. Names should be distinctive from one another to avoid communications difficulties such as mistaking applications for packages, packages for other packages, etc. Unfortunately, in the real world people are often very sloppy about naming both.

Where an application has an existing name that is commonly understood by the various users, developers should use that name. Where an application is known by a variety of existing names, the most common is not necessarily the best for all user groups. Problems may result for one or more user groups. The various names should

Table 4-1   A Format for Describing Applications and Systems

Application or Package:	*Insert* name *here*
Who:	*Insert* names of user groups *here*
What:	*Insert* a general description of what tasks the application or software package accomplishes *here*
Where & When:	*Insert* special circumstances that apply to application or software package use *here*
Why:	*Insert* the benefits for the organization and users *here*
How:	*Insert* how the software packages are used for the application *here*
How Much:	*Insert* general estimate of frequency and quantity of usage *here*
With Which:	*Insert* names of major pieces of content used *here*

be investigated to see if one could achieve a high level of recognition without causing difficulties for any particular group. If none of the existing names can be used without significant difficulties, then a new name may be needed.

Names of application packages should not be confused with names for the application. Using such generalized names for the task will blur the distinction between the task and the tool and can cause problems by placing unnecessary restrictions on the task. For our purposes, this name should include either "application" or "package" to distinguish which we are talking about.

"Who" should describe the various stakeholders involved with the application and with software packages used for the application. This includes (but is not limited to):

- Different groups of users who need the application performed
- Different groups of user(s) who will actually use the application package directly
- Other people that supply or receive data or information to/from the application
- Various managers involved with each of these groups

NOTE: Lumping all users into a single group can lead to developing for the lowest common denominator and satisfying no one.

When the development of software for the application is financed (not just developed) by some outside organization, it also has a stake in the application. It is important to include the type of involvement of different groups of stakeholders in the descriptions of software packages. It also may be useful to briefly describe other characteristics of these user groups that may influence the design requirements of any software packages being developed.

Each user/stakeholder group should be identified both with a distinctive name and with a description that briefly describes the distinguishing characteristics of the group of users or stakeholders. These distinguishing characteristics should include both differences in their need for or use of the application and personal differences that help distinguish which group an individual is likely to belong to.

"What" should identify the general purpose of the application and describe what set of tasks (specific work objectives) or activities the application or software package is to accomplish or achieve. Answers to "what" provide a means of generalizing from specific work tasks to the organizational objective(s) that they meet.

It is important to avoid confusing applications with software packages. The description of an application should encompass a wider understanding of "what" the application can and does involve than would typically be dealt with by any single application software package. It should include the identification of the main activities (work tasks) that are part of the application, along with a brief description of each, regardless of how these tasks are to be accomplished (e.g., manually or via some computer application package). This discussion of main application tasks should be sufficient to distinguish the application from other applications and from particular application software packages that are intended to assist in performance of the application.

The description of application software packages will focus on the features of the package that may be used to accomplish the tasks of the application. Well-known software packages need only brief descriptions of their major features. Obscure or otherwise relatively unknown application packages may require either further description or a reference to some source of such further description. When describing an application package, note should be made of major differences between the package and the application, especially noting tasks normally associated with an application that are not performed by the package.

"When" and **"where"** should identify and briefly describe the conditions in which the application is to be performed. It should include a discussion of where (organizationally) the application is performed, both within the organization and in related organizations.

Special consideration should be noted of where these conditions may be at variance with those already noted for application packages intended to serve the application. Where conditions are more limiting for application packages, additional tools may be required, or the application package may need a major redesign. Where conditions are less limiting, this may indicate the potential to be used for additional tasks.

An increasingly important consideration is the potential for e-Commerce to be used via mobile computing as well as via traditional computers that are attached to the Web.

"Why" should describe the benefits to both the organization and its potential users. This can start with a consideration of why the application or package is needed and the major competitive advantages that it can provide. For particular software packages it should also include a brief comparison between the use of this package and other packages that might optionally be used instead of this package.

It need not involve a detailed cost-benefit analysis (which will be added later), but rather should focus on the importance of the application or software package to the users and to their organization. Where these benefits differ between users or between groups of users and the organization, these differences should be noted.

"How" needs to propose a general strategy for meeting some or all the needs of the users (the Who) and the tasks (the What) as identified above. It should start by identifying the boundaries of the application that would distinguish it from other related applications. It should describe the general manner in which the application is currently accomplished and/or manners in which a software system could be used to accomplish the application. However, it should avoid making any commitments to a particular design. Much more analysis is needed before particular designs should be considered. It should also include identifying any major current difficulties with the current operation that should be improved upon.

"How much" should identify measures relevant to the accomplishment of the application or the use of the application package. These measures may include:

- An estimate of the frequency and quantity of use
- Criteria for evaluating the success of the application or the software package

"With which" should describe the information content that the application or software package uses and/or provides and the major (organizational) sources of this content. It can also briefly identify the nature(s) of this use, especially where different pieces of content are used differently.

4.4 IDENTIFYING E-COMMERCE APPLICATIONS

4.4.1 Identifying e-Commerce Applications in Organizations

Organizations need a method of identifying and evaluating potential applications and selecting the ones to investigate further.

Many initial suggestions need further work before they are ready to be evaluated and acted upon. People often don't really understand what they really need. As a result, they propose things that they think would help them. It is better to first identify needs and then to consider the range of things/systems/solutions that might meet these needs. Often there is a better solution possible than the one first suggested. This does not mean that we should discourage suggestions, however they are worded. It does mean that we need to work on them before we are ready to properly evaluate them. An initial investigation is how we work on suggestions once we have them.

First, we need to have the suggestions. There are more sources of suggestions than there are people in any organization.

- Of course, the suggestions of people in the organization should be considered and even encouraged. People in an organization can develop suggestions based on needs they experience in the organization and based on ideas they observe outside the organization. Reward schemes can increase the number of suggestions but can also increase the amount of work required to consider them all.
- Senior management, regardless of their particular responsibilities, are usually in charge of overall planning for an organization. They often get ideas from external sources, including industry news services and analyses of competitors. Suggestions from senior management have the advantage of already having a sponsor.
- If an organization has formalized organizational planning, the people performing that function should be especially on the lookout for possible applications. However:
  - Sometimes the planning function is carried out by someone who is too busy to constantly be planning
  - Sometimes the planning function is carried out by someone who doesn't understand the possibilities of technology in general and of e-Commerce in particular
- If an organization has a Chief Information Officer, that person should be especially involved in identifying potential information related developments, including the potential for e-Commerce systems.

- Books and other publications may suggest applications that might work in some organizations, but people have to consider how they might be adapted to work in a particular organization.

Once potential applications have been identified, an application description should be developed. This description:

- Provides a basis for communicating between individuals about the proposed application
- Provides a basis for evaluating the merits of the proposal
- If accepted, provides the basis for further analysis
- Regardless of whether accepted or not, provides documentation of the proposal for later reference

Developing an initial application description has the additional purpose of triggering an organizational evaluation of the proposal. Often informal, verbal suggestions can be easily made and easily forgotten. Formalized and documented proposals expect and deserve some level of formal consideration and response. Most organizations have their own, often unique, method for dealing with such formal proposals. Regardless of the method, the important thing is that a proposal may identify an important challenge or opportunity and should be evaluated.

4.4.2 Proceeding Beyond the Initial Investigation

Once a decision has been made to develop an e-Commerce system for an organization, a whole range of development activities need to be initiated. Project processes are discussed in Chapter 5, and the discussion of further development processes continues in Chapter 6.

The organization also needs to decide whether to manage and perform these processes on its own or with the help of outside consultants or to totally contract the development to outside sources. Regardless of who manages and performs the development, it is essential that the organization for which the system is being developed remain involved throughout the development to ensure that the right system is being developed. Remaining involved requires understanding of the processes in this book and ensuring that they are being satisfactorily performed. Chapter 12 discusses particular issues relating to making use of consultants in the construction of a system.

4.4.3 Student Assignment—Identifying e-Commerce Applications

Each team should choose an e-Commerce application as a project topic and should create a Web page describing their choice. The application will be developed for an organization (which you will specify next chapter) to use for itself and not for resale as package software to other organizations.

NOTE: While it is useful to investigate the needs of real organizations, it is suggested that you not customize your application to meet the needs of any particular existing organization. Often, existing organizations have various constraints on their operations that may interfere with or complicate the learning objectives in the following assignments. It is generally easier to develop an application in your assignments that could be used by various similar organizations. Thus, *Savor the Cup,* which is used in the examples in this book, is a hypothetical, rather than a real, organization.

4.4.3.1   Choosing a Project Topic

Prior to the team choosing a project topic, each team member should have researched one e-Commerce application area. The results of this research should be linked to the team's home page. The members of a team should research at least three different e-Commerce applications, in order to select one that has the best promise for them to use.

Teams should choose a topic that they believe is relevant to their studies. It is through your choice of topic that you will learn how to apply the course material to your area of study. Teams should identify the choice of topic on the team home page, which was created in the student assignment in the previous chapter.

NOTE: It is essential that your project be unique in terms of having unique competitive advantages that you can develop. It is not acceptable to do a project that duplicates existing versions of systems being used for the application if the project does not involve significant additions or modifications that could go beyond what is currently available.

4.4.3.2   Developing an Initial Application Description

The main portion of this assignment is creating an initial description of your application, posting it in your project's Web directory, and creating a link to it from your team's home page. Your project description should use the format discussed in sections 4.2 and 4.3, Identifying and Describing an e-Commerce Application.

The discussion of interesting types of e-Commerce applications in Chapter 2 can provide a starting point for you. Your application does not have to fit neatly into only one of the types described. In fact, the most innovative applications tend to invent their own unique types, which may cross boundaries of what already exists and which may include additional users and tasks not yet envisioned. It is suggested that you identify all the general types of e-Commerce applications that your application might involve.

The discussion of application types can provide a starting point, but you need to go beyond what is there to identify and describe a specific application that has specific unique advantages beyond what is already being done on the Web. It is important that you go beyond Chapter 2 by:

- Doing further research, beyond that done in your assignment for Chapter 2, to determine the current state of the art of similar applications
- Developing a more detailed and specific description of your application than is provided in the brief and partial information provided on general application types in Chapter 2

Your description should demonstrate:

- Your understanding of the application area
- The potential for the specific application you are proposing
- The potential for you to use this application successfully as the basis for future assignments, which will go into further depth and uncover further complexities of the application

The emphasis should be on identifying the needs and components of an application rather than designing particular application software packages to serve the application. In your project you are expected to go beyond what currently exists and to identify new opportunities within an application area.

4.5   AN EXAMPLE OF IDENTIFYING E-COMMERCE APPLICATIONS

Note how an understanding of the organization, as produced in the Chapter 3 student assignment, helps to customize the description of this application. However, this description goes beyond what currently exists and identifies what might exist.

Name:

On-line Coffee Supplier Application
This application currently involves: *e-Business* and *Custom Manufacturing* and can involve *Supplier–Customer Systems Integration*.

Who:

External Users
- External Product Sources:
  - Coffee equipment/supplies manufacturers—supply the equipment and other supplies to be used by the organization and to be sold to the customers.
  - Coffee bean growers—supply a wide variety of coffee beans. These suppliers are from many different regions around the world.
- Customers:
  - Potential customers—individuals interested in setting up a coffee shop. Will offer them consulting/training and product and equipment supply. May also include individuals purchasing for home use.
  - Current customers—who may require continual support for product and equipment supply and upgrading training. May also include individuals purchasing for home use.
  - Expanding customers—existing businesses that want to expand into new areas of the industry. Will provide consulting services.

Internal Users
- Purchasing—buys coffee and related products.
  - Grower contacts—will interact with the coffee bean growers to secure contracts. They will also be concerned with the quality and variety of the beans.
  - Equipment and supplies procurers—ensure timely delivery and receipt of durable, high-quality products.
- Manufacturing—roasts and packages coffee and manufactures or contracts for the manufacturing of related products. It decides whether related products should be *Savor the Cup* products that are manufactured by or for *Savor the Cup* or should be products, with their own brand names, that are just purchased

and sold without involving the manufacturing division. Manufacturing also controls warehousing and shipping of coffee and related products.

- Coffee roasting—roasts, blends, and packages the coffee to customer specifications. Will be concerned with the quality and timing of the coffee product.
- Product manufacturing—manufactures or contracts for *Savor the Cup* brand products.
- Logistics—coordinates all aspects of product storage and the shipping of products to customers, ensuring timeliness and reliability of delivery.

- Sales—sells coffee and related products to specialty coffee shops and restaurants. Sales also identifies customer needs, changes in the industry, and related products that the organization should sell.
  - Sales representatives—sales representatives will be in contact with customers by providing blend samples and expert advice on coffee blends and mixes. Also, they will be responsible for the continuing contact for initiating customer support.
  - Marketers—interact with potential customers, sales representatives, and current customers to determine the needs in the coffee industry. Will also maintain the marketing aspects of the site.
  - Consultants—consultants will provide in-person and on-line services in the areas of:
    - General business operations and start-up
    - Employee training in equipment use
    - Expanding customer consulting
    - Updating training
    - After-sales service—provide support to existing customers with product and equipment concerns.

- Administration
  - Management at all levels
    - High-level management sets the boundaries for all levels
    - Lower-level management would ensure that everything is running smoothly
  - Accounting—handles all accounting and auditing for all applications
  - Information technology (IT)—develops and maintains systems for the organization (While IT is not a user, it was identified here, because IT people will be involved in the development of the proposed system.)

- All employees—news bulletins for idea and industry happenings. (While most of these employees already fit into one of the above categories, it was thought to be important to recognize this general role of employees within the organization.)

What:

The objective of this application is to provide a means to get information to the customers, allow the customers to order the products efficiently, and to get the product to the customer. There should be several different ways through which they can select unique blends that will be offered exclusively to that business. It will also formalize the provision of special services to help independent coffee shops and restaurants get established.

The main tasks include:

- Managing product lines—involves coordination of information obtained by sales representatives and management regarding demand in the market. It also involves coordination of and communication with purchasing and manufacturing.
- Product acquisition—communicating with sales representatives to determine customer needs. It also involves communicating with suppliers to determine availability of coffee beans and machinery.
- Marketing—interacts directly and indirectly with customers by:
  - Creating an excellent reputation for our bean products
  - Marketing the company and its products and services directly to business customers.
- External customer support—initiates contact with customers to ensure that their needs have been met and that they are satisfied with the entire purchase experience. They also respond to customers' questions and concerns after sales have been made.
- Order taking—dealing with customers to take their orders on-line or in-person.
- Order filling—involves coordination between sales, manufacturing, and sometimes with purchasing. It can involve:
  - Purchasing supplies and/or products
  - Scheduling manufacturing activities
  - Conducting manufacturing activities
  - Warehousing the supplies and/or products
  - Shipping the coffee and/or products
- Service providing—provides in-person and on-line consulting services in the areas of:
  - General business operations and start-up
  - Employee training in equipment use
  - Expanding customer consulting
  - Updating training
- Providing internal support—connecting employees with those who can solve their problems or address their concerns.
- Accounting support for these tasks includes:
  - Budget development and analysis to provide feedback to managers to ensure budgets are being met and cost and profit issues are discussed.
  - Accounts receivable handling to ensure payments are received from customer orders. This will go beyond billing and receiving payments if on-line sales are involved.
  - Accounts payable handling to ensure that suppliers are paid. This can involve monitoring ordering to ensure that the organization will have an appropriate cash flow to handle the orders it places.
  - Auditing both the conduct of business and the corporate accounts.

When:

- By going on-line, the organization makes its products and services available whenever they are needed.

- There will be significantly different demands from each of the three sets of customers.
  - Potential customers may require a considerable amount of time to be spent on them, at their convenience, in order to transform them into current customers.
  - Current customers will require a basic level of maintenance and will need to be responded to quickly when they have special needs.
  - Expanding customers will require considerable amounts of time, but their needs can often be scheduled in advance.
- Products must be delivered very quickly following order placement, which means that the production and ordering processes must be reliable.

Where:

- Customer support will be provided both on-line and in-person, as requested by the customer.
- Involves a virtual business, as well as physical locations.
- Ensures accessibility for users speaking various languages around the world and maintains cultural sensitivity. Specific employees, at all organizational locations, will have access to post information onto the site.
- Maintain steady supply of product from suppliers in all environmental conditions.

Why:

Competitive advantages include:
- There is currently a lack of custom coffee businesses on the Web. However, this cannot necessarily be expected to last for long.
- There are no organizations that provide the type of specialized advice that *Savor the Cup* has been providing to help independent coffee shops and restaurants get established. This requires the specialized knowledge that only *Savor the Cup* and certain coffee shop franchising organizations currently possess. It is unlikely that the franchising organizations will move into this field because it would be in direct competition with their franchising efforts. However, there is a significant demand for help in establishing independent coffee shops that are not bound by a franchise agreement.
- *Savor the Cup* already has a well-established international presence to build on, which also includes local support in a number of countries.

Benefits to the organization and to individuals include:
- Increasingly quick access to the information that could be contained in the proposed system is required, even to maintain business as it currently operates.
- The organization needs to improve coordination of all its activities if it is to be able to further expand.
- There is a need for personal services for small businesses to assist them in their start-up and continuing operations. Currently, *Savor the Cup* is giving these services away as a cost of doing its business. However, the demand is such that it could sell these services for a profit.

- There is an increasing demand for specialty coffees. Entrepreneurs also desire to set up their own unique businesses, but need assistance in some areas. They do not want to have the obligations and restrictions involved in a franchise agreement.
- With the increase in custom coffee shops, there is in increasing demand for unique blends that allow coffee shops to distinguish themselves in the market. *Savor the Cup* already meets some of this market and could meet more of it with the wider exposure that is possible via the Web.
- There are a growing number of individuals with particular tastes for specialty blends of coffee and related products. Currently an individual's choices of coffees are primarily limited to those available from local coffee shops. Currently, *Savor the Cup* only deals with businesses. These individuals could provide a major new market if e-Business can keep the cost of selling to these relatively small customers to a minimum.

How:

- The current system:
  - Does not involve the use of e-Commerce
  - Is limited to serving major customers in person via sales representatives in branches around the world
  - Provides special services for free to its customers
  - Sometimes suffers due to delays in communications between various employees within *Savor the Cup*
- The proposed system would largely deal with the interactions between *Savor the Cup* and its customers. *Savor the Cup* employees would still be available to customers when personal sales and servicing are required.
  - The system would provide communication between different *Savor the Cup* employees to support these interactions but would not attempt to fully integrate all aspects of the organization.
  - It would provide information for prospective suppliers but would not involve on-line procurement at this time.
- The organization, although it has physical locations, would expand to use e-Commerce on the Web as well as these physical locations.
- A current customer would decide if they wanted to order services, products, or equipment via the Web or personally from a sales representative.
  - The customer or the sales representative could use an access code to place the order quickly and efficiently so that the information was immediately transferred to *Savor the Cup*. This information would then be available to the appropriate staff so that the physical aspect of the order may be completed.
- A new customer could use the Web to:
  - Get industry information and find out more about the products and services offered by *Savor the Cup*
  - Purchase special sample packs to get acquainted with the quality of coffee available
  - Contact *Savor the Cup* to get a sales representative to deal with directly

- Expanding customers may use the Web to:
  - Evaluate their needs and place an order
  - Request a sales representative contact them with the information they need

How Much:

- The application would be used frequently, estimated at 1000 to 5000 hits per day, by organizational staff who would be accessing all aspects of it, as it is central to daily operations.
- Current customers would access the application about 100 to 500 times per day to order, check new research, chat with others in the industry, and so on.
- Potential customers and those wanting to expand would be accessing the application to determine why this business should be chosen over others on the market. They would access it approximately 10 to 100 times per day.
- Easy accessibility and quick service provision with minimal waiting time during uploading must be available without sacrificing information quality.
- The site should include suitable graphics that are visually appealing but not overstimulating.

With Which:

- The main content of the application will describe the products and services available from *Savor the Cup*.
- Customers require additional content that:
  - Assists them in ordering products and services
  - Provides the status of outstanding orders and invoices
  - Assists them in contacting a sales representative
  - Informs them about industry trends of interest
- Sales people require content that:
  - Provides an analysis of sales trends
  - Provides a history of individual customers
  - Provides confidential information for establishing custom pricing
  - Provides information on product availability, including the availability of manufacturing custom products
  - Reminds them to contact major customers on a regular basis
  - Helps them track progress with potential customers
- Manufacturing needs content that:
  - Provides information on current inventories
  - Provides information on the status and details of outstanding orders
  - Schedules manufacturing activities
  - Provides recipes for custom roasting and blending
- Purchasing needs content that:
  - Provides information on current inventories
  - Provides information on the status and details of outstanding orders
  - Provides information on suppliers including their prices, reliability, and quality
- Administration needs content that:
  - Analyzes the success of *Savor the Cup's* operations
  - Analyzes *Savor the Cup's* accounts and finances

4.6   CHALLENGES AND OPPORTUNITIES IN IDENTIFYING E-COMMERCE APPLICATIONS

The following are the most frequent problems encountered with developing e-Commerce application descriptions. They only apply to some developments. They are listed here to help you avoid them.

Challenges with uniqueness.

- Some developers do not describe the application to be unique in any way from those already available.
- Some applications described are just not unique from other versions of the application currently available.
- Developers need to explicitly state what makes their application different.

Challenges with understanding the application's possibilities.

- Some developers do not sufficiently research examples of what is already available on the Web.
- Some developers do not describe a specific application; they describe a general topic area involving their application.
- Some developers describe a particular application package that already exists.

Challenges with naming the application.

- Some application names are too generic and do not explain what the application specifically accomplishes.
- Some developers name their application after the organization without any suggestion of what is being accomplished.
- Some developers do not distinguish between applications and systems intended to serve the applications.

Challenges with level of detail in application descriptions.

- Some developers miss describing parts of the application description.
- Some developers miss the point of the parts of the application description.
- Some parts of an application description lack sufficient detail and do not provide sufficient grounds to determine whether or not an application is worth investigating further. If further investigations occur, there may be little basis for understanding what should be involved in these areas.
- Some parts of an application description may involve too much detail for an initial investigation, making it hard to get a good picture about what the overall application involves.
- Some parts of an application description may be copied from a general description of a type of application without any evaluation about whether they apply or not.
- Some information is placed under an inappropriate heading, making it difficult to find later in the development.

Specific challenges with parts of application descriptions.

- Developers may not consider the needs of both internal and external users of the system (who were listed in "Who" in the preceding example) throughout the rest of the application description. They may especially fail to consider the internal users.

- Developers need to recognize that the tasks (identified in "What" in the preceding example) are tasks because some users want or need to use them and not because systems developers or anyone else wants or expects the users to do them.
- Developers need to clearly distinguish between **what** needs to be done and **how** it currently is done or **how** it might be done. "What" deals with desired accomplishments regardless of how they are accomplished.
- The justification may be lacking if the benefits identified in "Why" do not differ from those already available from similar applications and do not include unique benefits.
- "Where" and "When" are often not considered specific enough, both within and outside the organization.
- The "How" might not relate back to the tasks identified in the "What" section or the users in the "Who" section.

4.7   CYBER SUPPLEMENTS FOR CHAPTER 4

 Look at the Chapter 4 Cyber Supplements on the Web to find:

- Reviews of and links to examples of individual to individual, organization to individual, and organization to organization e-Commerce activities
- Reviews of and links to examples of the use of various types of competitive advantages in use at e-Commerce sites
- Reviews of and links to examples of some of the best and worst of current e-Commerce business practices
- Suggestions for further investigations into identifying opportunities for developing unique, competitive e-Commerce applications

REFERENCES

[1] The Business Team on Electronic Commerce and Cultural Adaptability of ISO/IEC's Joint Technical Committee (JTC1), 1998.

[2] "International Organization for Standardization," ISO/IEC 2nd Committee Draft of International Standard 15944-1, Business Agreement Semantic Descriptive Techniques—Part 1: Operational Aspects of Open-EDI for Implementation, 2000.

[3] "International Organization for Standardization," ISO/IEC 2nd Committee Draft of International Standard 15944-1, Business Agreement Semantic Descriptive Techniques—Part 1: Operational Aspects of Open-EDI for Implementation, 2000.

[4] "International Organization for Standardization," ISO Draft International Standard 14915-1, Software Ergonomics for Multimedia User Interfaces: Design Principles and Framework, 2000.

5

Managing Pervasive Development Processes

Outline

5.1 INTRODUCTION TO PERVASIVE DEVELOPMENT PROCESSES

Before considering processes associated with particular stages in the development life cycle, it is useful to get an appreciation of those processes that need to be performed throughout the life cycle. While these processes are not unique to the development of e-Commerce systems, they are essential to this development.

Pervasive development processes are those processes that need to be performed throughout the systems development life cycle. There are two types of pervasive development processes that should be considered at this time:

- **Project processes** are those processes necessary to manage a development project. Project processes were first introduced in Chapter 1 and will be elaborated in this chapter.
- **Pervasive technical processes** are those processes that are used in the development of a system at various points throughout the systems development life cycle. Pervasive technical processes are introduced and discussed in this chapter.

5.2 UNDERSTANDING PROJECT PROCESSES

Project processes can be performed by computer professionals, by organizational professionals, or by a combination of both. Because various people might perform these processes, there is sometimes confusion about who should perform them. This confusion may even lead to some important project processes being neglected, which in turn can lead to project failures.

Project processes are a major topic of their own that requires a more thorough consideration than is available here. There are many books, courses, and standards that provide more detailed information about various project management processes. The purpose of this section is to provide an introduction to the main project processes that are essential to support and manage e-Commerce system development. This set is based on consolidating a variety of sets of project management processes from various software development standards, including ISO 15288,[1] ISO 12207,[2] and ISO 15504-2.[3]

 Find references to further information about project processes in the Chapter 5 Cyber Supplement.

It is vital to the success of an e-Commerce development that skilled project managers ensure that each of the project processes discussed below are properly performed. The people performing these processes need to be able to balance the needs of the organization for controlling the project with the needs of the developers for the freedom to develop the project in the best way they can, given the constraints placed upon them. Glass[4] provides a number of insights about balancing the need for control with the need for creativity.

5.2.1 Planning and Assessment

Planning and assessment activities provide a basis for overall project coordination and control.

5.2.1.1 Scheduling Project Processes and Activities

There's an old proverb, "If you don't know where you're going, how will you ever get there?" While an initial application description can provide a general idea of where a development project could be going, there is a need for a detailed plan of how the development will proceed to ensure that it succeeds.

Each project needs to apply the systems development life cycle, introduced in Chapter 1, and the various development activities, discussed throughout this book, in a unique way to succeed in developing a particular system to meet a particular organization's needs.

A project schedule provides a detailed plan of activities that need to be completed in order to develop a particular system and the resources that will be allocated to complete them. Project schedules can be developed by:

- The systems development life cycle, which provides an initial framework for starting the development of a project schedule. Each of the technical processes in the life cycle up to, and including, implementation and each of the project processes need to be completed.
- The schedule should be elaborated by including detailed activities required for each of the life cycle processes.
- The schedule should be further elaborated by determining how each of these activities applies to the particular application.
- Time estimates need to be added for each of these particular activities.
- Prerequisite relationships need to be identified between activities. It may be useful to analyze the requirements of certain user groups before other groups. It also may be possible to analyze the requirements of some user groups in any order and/or at the same time.
- The time estimates for activities, the availability of resources (including developers, managers, and users) and the set of prerequisite relationships can be used to create a schedule that assigns particular resources to particular activities during particular times in the future. A project may be limited either by trying to meet a particular deadline or by having limited resources available. Either of these limitations will affect how an actual schedule is developed. Where resources may not be available, either due to their allocation to a higher priority activity or due to delays in obtaining them, the schedule will need to be adjusted accordingly.

For example:

- The life cycle includes requirements analysis.
- Requirements analysis includes analyzing user groups.
- Each user group requires analysis.
- The requirements of each user group will have their own time requirements, which are not necessarily the same as the time requirements for analyzing other user groups.
- Requirements analysis could proceed for a number of these user groups at the same time, if developers are available.
- A limited number of developers may require the scheduling of the requirements analysis of a number of different user groups, which could occur simultaneously, to be spread out over a longer time than would be required if more developers were available.

NOTE: Trying to meet a too-tight deadline with an insufficient amount of resources (such as developers) will result in a poor-quality system that may not be worth developing at all. However, adding large numbers of resources may not meet all of the needs of a tight schedule. If individual activities are not carefully planned to make use of them, adding resources may not help meet the requirements of a schedule and may even cause increased problems.[5]

It is important that the developers, whose work is being scheduled, are involved in developing the schedules that they are expected to meet. Glass[6] discusses various studies in which productivity was found to be higher when developers were allowed to schedule their own work.

A project schedule is an ideal plan for completing a development. However, various unforeseen circumstances can be expected to disrupt any plan. For example, delays may occur if representatives of a particular user group are unavailable during the time originally scheduled to analyze their requirements.

For a schedule to be of any use it needs to be regularly revised. The revision of schedules is related to the assessing and monitoring of progress of a project. While initial estimates used for planning may be educated guesses, as the project progresses it should be possible to make increasingly accurate predictions about the time and resources required for future activities.

- Many people underestimate the time and/or resources required to complete future activities. This is because developments are seldom as simple and straightforward as they initially appear. Experienced estimators have generally learned how much they tend to underestimate and will use this knowledge to adjust their estimates before they put them into a schedule. Information about completed parts of a project can be analyzed to identify where actual resource usage is consistently under- or over-estimated amounts. The result of this analysis can be used to adjust future estimates.
- At the start of a project, few of the detailed requirements can be foreseen, thus, schedules tend to consider general development activities rather than specific ones. As a project progresses, the specific development needs become clearer. Individual activities dealing with specific development requirements can replace single general activities, making the schedule both more detailed and more accurate.

Scheduling and rescheduling of e-Commerce developments is complicated by a number of factors, including:

- e-Commerce systems need to keep evolving. Thus, schedules for their development need to include not only the development of the current system, but also considerations of the development of future evolutions of this system.
- e-Commerce systems need to have one or more competitive advantages. Other systems will be evolving their own new advantages during the development of this system, which could place new demands of catching up and/or finding new advantages of its own. Meeting these new demands will usually affect the current development schedule.

5.2.1.2 Assessing and Monitoring Progress

There's a major difference between having a schedule and using it to manage a project. Project failures often occur where progress is not actively monitored. The monitoring of progress involves: accurately assessing progress as it relates to the project schedule and comparing this progress to the schedule and identifying any major discrepancies.

Assessing project progress is generally conducted by developers and/or their managers and reported to the person(s) in charge of monitoring progress. The assessing of progress should not be optional or done carelessly just to satisfy project managers. It needs to be done on time and accurately.

In order to assess progress properly, readily agreed-upon and applied project measures are needed. These measures should be identified when the project schedule is created and/or modified. The easiest measure to use is the time until the completion of a scheduled project activity. Where reporting periods are shorter than the time allotted to activities in the schedule, developers often have difficulties in estimating progress. Developers often are very enthusiastic about their early progress and overestimate it. As a project continues, many will keep splitting the difference between the original estimate and 100% until an activity is deemed complete. Thus, it is not unusual to see a series of project reports that claim progress of 50%, 75%, 87%, 94%, 97%, 98%, 99%, 99.5%, 99.75%. To avoid this problem, it is useful that the schedule is detailed enough to identify a number of activities per reporting period and that regular audits are conducted to ensure the accuracy of progress reports. It also is useful to establish a number of checkpoints in a project where the actual progress, to date, is carefully assessed and adjustments are made to the remaining schedule.

Not all discrepancies between the assessed and scheduled progress are of major concern.

- Activities may have been performed in a different order than originally scheduled in order to avoid delays or to take advantage of opportunities.
- Regardless of whether activities have been completed ahead of schedule, on time, or late, what is important is their effect on the overall project.

Care needs to be taken that creative processes are not over-managed. Developers need to have sufficient autonomy to optimize their activities for the good of the development. This may include restructuring, combining, adding, and at times, eliminating specific activities. Rather than forcing developers to report progress according to an inappropriate schedule, which they may not even be following, it is important to allow the developers to provide progress reports that update the development activities being performed as well as the level of completion of these activities.

The **critical path method** (CPM) (also referred to as PERT/CPM) is a common technique for monitoring progress based on analyzing a networked schedule of activities, linked to their prerequisites. Where a number of activities can occur in any order, they are represented as a number of parallel links to a common prerequisite. Likewise, an activity can be linked to a number of prerequisites. Table 5-1 lists an example set of 10 activities that are part of a particular development. The units used for all activity durations need to be the same, whether hours, days, weeks, months, or some other convenient unit. CPM analyzes the network to identify the critical path. The critical path is that set of linked activities that will take the longest time to progress through in the network. Any change in timing of any of these activities will change the time of completion of the overall project (for better or worse). Noncritical path activities will not affect the overall project schedule unless they are not completed in time for any critical path activities for which they are prerequisites.

Table 5-1   An example set of activities within a development

Activity	Duration (weeks)	Prerequisites (activity #)
1	5	—
2	3	1
3	6	2
4	8	2
5	2	3,4
6	9	—
7	4	3,6
8	3	4,7
9	2	5,6
10	1	8,9

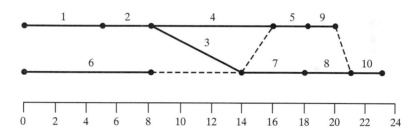

Figure 5-1   An example critical path diagram

Figure 5-1 illustrates the critical path diagram constructed from these ten activities in the above example and identifies the critical path through the set of activities (which is illustrated using the darker lines).

The critical path can be analyzed to identify opportunities for optimizing development activities, including:

- Speeding up development
- Minimizing the number of staff required for the project
- Optimizing the use of project development resources
- Sharing of project development resources with other projects or organizational duties

Whenever progress is assessed, CPM can be used to analyze changes to the critical path and any resulting changes to the project schedule. These changes can occur even where the overall time to complete the project has not changed, such as:

- Where a noncritical activity that has been delayed becomes critical
- Where a critical activity that is ahead of schedule becomes noncritical, but the critical path does not change because it includes another critical activity in parallel with this activity

Project assessments should be reported regularly to project management and be used to revise the project schedule. It is generally useful to communicate the revised project schedule to all participants in the project so that they can follow the progress and prepare for future activities.

5.2.1.3 Management Accounting

While assessing and monitoring progress concentrates on timing and resource scheduling, management accounting is needed to deal with resource utilization. Management accounting of a project may include:

- Providing information on previous projects to be used in the scheduling and budgeting of a new project
- Developing and updating the project budget
- Identifying major discrepancies between actual costs and the project budget
- Ensuring suppliers and contractors are paid on time
- Various other project-related accounting activities

5.2.1.4 Identifying Challenges and Opportunities Affecting the Development

Challenges and opportunities affecting the development can be identified by a number of sources, including:

- Developers and their managers identifying better ways of developing the system
- Users wishing changes in the scope or function of the system
- People monitoring the progress of the project
- Management accountants evaluating the utilization of resources on the project

Because there are so many potential sources, it is important that a specific project process be responsible for gathering and identifying these challenges and opportunities and ensuring that they are dealt with by the control and decision making project process.

With e-Commerce developments it is also important to monitor the evolving competitive environment and to reassess how the system being developed will fit within this environment. There is little value in continuing on schedule to develop a system that will be competitively disadvantaged when it is finally implemented.

5.2.2 Control and Decision Making

Each project needs an established structure of authorities and responsibilities.

5.2.2.1 Dealing with Challenges and Opportunities Affecting the Development

There are usually more challenges and opportunities than are possible to satisfy. Dealing with challenges and opportunities generally requires both resources and time. Both may be limited, even where their investment could return a significant profit.

An analysis of the effects of identified challenges and opportunities and the potential effects of various ways of dealing with them is necessary before deciding what to do about each of them. These analyses should consider the goals of the organization as well as any opportunities for profit or other, more specific impacts. The extent of analysis of challenges and opportunities will depend on the magnitude of their potential effects. Where minor effects are involved, there may be little formal analysis. Where major effects are involved, a challenge or opportunity may lead to major changes to an existing development or even to the initial investigation of a separate development project. This analysis can then be used to provide a ranked list of challenges and opportunities for the consideration of organizational or project management decision-makers.

With traditional systems, a single analysis of a challenge or opportunity is generally sufficient for making a final decision about it. However, with e-Commerce, some decisions may need to be reevaluated in the future as the state of the art and the state of the competition change. Part of the initial evaluation of any e-Commerce challenge or opportunity should include identifying factors that should trigger a reevaluation, such as changes in certain types of competition and/or some period of time over which changes may be expected to occur.

Once challenges and opportunities have been evaluated, a decision needs to be made by the person or group of people with the appropriate authority. While it is common to document what happens with decisions to act on a challenge or opportunity, it can be useful to document the reasons for a decision not to act. Changes in reasons of decisions not to act can be used to trigger reevaluations of the potential of various challenges and opportunities.

One particular challenge that is often overlooked is the burnout that can occur to developers when they are pressured into performing extended hours of work close to deadlines and especially close to the planned date of implementation. While most developers are used to working under a certain level of stress, if they exceed that stress they may make an increasing number of errors even before they burn out. These errors may not be identified prior to implementation and may lead to various difficulties. It is usually better to delay the schedule than to implement an inadequately developed product. Project managers should monitor developers and limit related development pressures to avoid problems related to burnout.

5.2.2.2 Taking Action to Correct Problems in Development Processes

A good understanding of the existing development processes is essential to making decisions to correct problems with these processes. Changes need to be considered in terms of their desired effects and their chances for success. General changes to established processes are preferred to ad hoc changes that are made to work around individual problems. It is desirable that these changes be recognized and reused in future development activities and projects to help avoid similar problems.

Once decisions are taken, it is essential that they be communicated to all people who need to implement them immediately and to all people who may need to implement them in the future. Where decisions involve major changes, it may be appropriate to conduct a seminar or training meeting to ensure that all developers understand and can implement them. The decisions also should be incorporated into the organization's development policies and procedures, where appropriate, for long-term reference.

All decisions having a major impact on development should be collected, communicated, and recorded for future reference, regardless of their source. In some instances, important development decisions may be made in a decentralized manner. It should be required of people with distributed authority to communicate decisions to their managers as well as their subordinates, to ensure that they are recorded appropriately.

5.2.2.3 Ensuring That Required Decisions Are Made Appropriately

It is important that the many decisions made during a development project be made by the people best able to make them and in time to be of use to the development. It is important that the potential effects of different actions (including their effect on quality and costs of a system) be understood before deciding on a particular action affecting the development.

Major development activities may require formalized decision tracking to ensure that decisions move from the challenges and opportunities that identify them, through analysis, to being made by the appropriate authority, and finally to being implemented in the project. Each step involves identifying people to be involved and allocating a time frame for their involvement. The timing of each of these steps needs to fit within the overall project development schedule, although individual decisions may not be given the status of project activities.

Decisions need to be tracked, whether they are recorded in the overall project development schedule or they are tracked by some other means. Since steps in decision making may appear smaller than other development activities, there may be a tendency to put them off in favor of others. Follow-ups may be required when a person does not complete a decision-making step on schedule.

5.2.3 Resource Allocation and Configuration

Resources need to be allocated and configured both for the development and for the operation and support of a system. Resource allocation often involves dealing with a variety of resource managers within an organization to obtain the necessary resources, including:

- Senior managers to approve the acquisitions
- Managers responsible for existing employees (both development and organizational professionals)
- Human resource professionals responsible for recruiting new employees
- Accounting/financial managers responsible for ensuring funds are available to pay project costs and that payments are made in a timely manner
- Facilities managers responsible for the facilities used by the project/operational system
- Procurers responsible for any acquisitions required by the project/operational system

In many instances, especially with people and computing resources, resources may need to be shared with other projects/organizational activities. Previous commitments may constrain their availability to a new project both in terms of amount of time available and in terms of particular times available.

Since e-Commerce systems usually cut across departmental boundaries within an organization, it can be expected that resources may be drawn from many departments. If departments are allowed to choose the resources they contribute, some departments may contribute their weakest resources and keep the best resources for themselves. It is important that the needs of the organization come before the needs of individual departments in this allocation. It also is important that, once human resources are allocated, their primary responsibility is directed toward the system being developed for the duration of their allocation.

Once resources are allocated, they need to be configured to the current and future needs of the project/operational system. Changing needs may require frequent reconfigurations. Reconfiguration planning needs to consider the amount of non-productive time involved in making changes, such as the amount of time required for a worker to get acclimatized to or trained into a new job.

It is important to communicate anticipated allocations and reconfigurations well in advance, wherever possible, to all the people affected. This can help prepare everyone for necessary changes. Where the allocation or reconfiguration of people is concerned, there may need to be more than just communication. Team building and/or maintenance activities may be necessary to ensure the success of the resulting changes in the various groups affected.

In general, the main difference between resource allocation and configuration for projects and that for operating and supporting the system is that

- With projects, the resources typically are managed by the managers of the development project who are responsible for obtaining and configuring them.
- In the implementation of systems, the resources are typically going to be managed by users who might not be involved in allocating and configuring them.

Further information about the identifying, obtaining, and allocating of resources for operating and supporting the system is discussed in Chapter 14.

5.2.4 Risk Management

The development of an e-Commerce system is subject to a wide variety of risks, both accidental and purposeful in their nature. The consequences of these risks can vary considerably. It is not necessary to manage all risks, but it is necessary to identify and evaluate them all. Risks should be managed if the cost of managing them is less than the benefit of managing them. The benefit of managing a risk can be calculated as the sum of the costs of individual exposures. One category of risks can involve many exposures. Exposures are occasions of loss to an organization. The cost of an exposure is equal to the loss (that an organization may incur if the risk occurs) multiplied by the probability that the loss will occur.

Risk management involves:

- Identifying risks and exposures
- Evaluating the costs of exposures
- Where feasible, avoiding the risks/exposures by utilizing appropriate management techniques ahead of time is preferable
- If the exposure cannot be avoided:
  - Establishing techniques to identify the occurrence of exposures
  - Utilizing feasible management techniques to stop or to limit losses as soon as exposures are identified
  - If possible, utilizing additional feasible techniques (such as legal actions or applying to insurers) to recover losses

The major categories of risks involved with the development of an e-Commerce system include: poor quality of development, errors and omissions in the development, security breaches, fraudulent activities, and lost development work.

5.2.4.1 Poor Quality of Development

The causes of poor quality of development include:

- Not performing one or more development activities/processes in a suitable manner
- Rushing development or developing on schedule without having adequate resources to handle schedule demands
- Using poor-quality development resources, including staff who do not have proper training and/or experience

Exposures include:

- Delays and increased costs in redoing development activities/processes
- Failure in meeting the objectives of the system
- The occurrence of various problems when the system is put in operation
- The need for excessive amounts of maintenance

Management techniques include:

- Using a proper development life cycle, with suitable processes and activities
- Following the guidance of this book and further guidance from other sources, especially in areas not covered in depth in this book
- Obtaining training, where necessary
- Involving a quality development staff

5.2.4.2 Errors and Omissions in the Development

The likely causes of errors and omissions in development include:

- Rushing development based on insufficient analysis
- Not investigating all possible sources of information
- Biases in the information provided by individuals
- Limiting the scope of development based on historical boundaries and/or organizational politics
- Failing to foresee future possibilities

Exposures include:

- Failure to meet the objectives of the system
- The occurrence of various problems when the system is put in operation
- Missing opportunities that the system could have met
- The need for excessive amounts of maintenance

Management techniques include:

- Using a proper development life cycle, with suitable processes and activities
- Using an iterative development approach
- Involving the users and stakeholders throughout development
- Involving a quality development staff

5.2.4.3 Development Security Breaches

Causes of development security breaches include:

- Dissatisfied employees, who give or sell information about the development to competitors
- Employees who are hired by competitors to work on similar developments
- Competitors actively conducting industrial intelligence or espionage
- Accidental leaks in casual social conversations of organizational employees away from the organizational environment
- Accidental leaks from customers/suppliers involved in development efforts with the organization
- Accidental leaks via newsletters or other formal communications that discuss how advanced the organization is
- Accidental browsing of sites under development not properly equipped with user authentication processing

Exposures include:

- Competitors copying innovative features, removing competitive advantages
- Other organizations recognizing the potential and becoming competitors
- Various people getting unrealistic expectations of your system before it is even available:
  - Expectations can be too high to be met realistically
  - Expectations can be so low that people will never try it

Management techniques include:

- Keeping employees satisfied
- Limiting access to development information and test systems
- Informing all people involved with the project of the need for security with regard to sensitive information
- Having select individuals sign confidentiality agreements

5.2.4.4 Fraudulent Activities

Potential causes of fraudulent activities include:

- Employees or other individuals purposely sabotaging development activities or the system being developed
- Employees or other individuals inserting code into the system being developed to enable them to embezzle once it is utilized
- Suppliers providing defective information or products to be used in the development

Exposures include:

- Delays and increased costs in redoing development activities/processes
- Failure in meeting the objectives of the system
- Financial losses (including embezzlements) when the system is put in operation
- The occurrence of various problems when the system is put in operation
- Missing opportunities that the system could have met
- The need for excessive amounts of maintenance

Management techniques include:

- Keeping employees satisfied
- Limiting access to development information and test systems
- Using a proper development life cycle, with suitable processes and activities
- Keeping track of all development activities and the people involved with them

5.2.4.5   Lost Development Work

The causes of lost development work typically include:

- Computer system failures
- Accidental erasure or overwriting of documentation or programming
- Fire or other natural disasters
- Illness of key employees (who haven't properly documented their recent work)

Exposures include:

- The cost of redoing the work
- The costs of any delays, including:
  - Delays in earning income with an operational system
  - The loss of competitive advantages to competitors who are developing similar systems

Management techniques include:

- Off-site backups of documentation and software programs
- Insisting on regular documentation of work in progress and of completed work
- The use of teamwork to limit the reliance on individuals

The above discussion focuses only on management techniques to avoid risks and exposures. Additional management techniques will be needed to deal with exposures that have occurred, in order to limit the losses involved. Major developments may require the assistance of a risk management professional to ensure that all risks are properly identified, evaluated, and managed. Identifying and minimizing the risks posed by using e-Commerce systems once they are developed will be discussed throughout the rest of this book and especially in the chapter dealing with implementation.

5.3   UNDERSTANDING PERVASIVE TECHNICAL PROCESSES

There are a number of pervasive technical processes that are led by developers and that involve users to a considerable extent.

- Development information is gathered throughout the life cycle, not just during requirements analysis.
- Alternatives are identified throughout the life cycle, not just during design.
- Usability testing needs to be performed throughout the life cycle, not just after construction is complete.
- Prototyping can be used throughout the life cycle, not just during design.
- Documentation needs to be created and maintained throughout the development life cycle, not just during implementation.

5.3.1 Gathering Development Information

There are a number of techniques that can help an individual to creatively explore ideas, such as those suggested by von Oech.[7] However, systems development requires that developers first and foremost meet the needs of their users and the stakeholders. If you don't meet the needs of the users and the stakeholders, then you are a failure, no matter how creative you have been. Developing systems is about meeting needs. Successful development combines:

- Recognizing the needs and wants of users and stakeholders
- Recognizing additional challenges and opportunities that they may have missed

A successful developer has to be a good detective to find out what's really important. As many people who enjoy a good mystery know, good detective work can often result in new understandings about an organization and its possibilities.

There are a number of methods for gathering development information. A **method** is a particular way of accomplishing a process. People may be able to choose between various methods that all could be used for a process. The choice of method often involves consideration of:

- The individual's experience and confidence with each of the methods
- The available tools and support for each of the methods
- The particular advantages and disadvantages of the methods
- The various circumstances in which the method will be used
- Constraints (including time, money, and other resources) on the selection and use of the methods

Each method has its own strengths and weaknesses. Developers need to choose wisely to get the most and the best possible development information in the most efficient manner. This generally involves using a mix of methods, with each method used to gather certain types of information from particular potential sources.

The choice of methods may also involve consideration of which methods the developer is skilled in and comfortable in using. Each method has its own subtleties that need to be learned and practiced before a developer can be expected to be proficient with it.

 Find further information about various information-gathering methods, including discussions of how they apply to different types of users and information, in the Chapter 5 Cyber Supplement.

5.3.1.1   A Requirements-Gathering Life Cycle

Information gathering, like most other activities, has its own life cycle of processes, which must be accomplished in order to meet success. While these processes should start in the order in which they are described, each of the processes tends to continue being performed until all requirements have been gathered and specified.

Analysis of What to Gather

Information gathering involves:

- Elaborating on aspects and requirements of the system already identified in previous development activities

- Identifying changes that should be made to the boundaries of the application which may include some additional requirements and may preclude some existing requirements. These cannot be anticipated, but should be actively looked for throughout the information gathering activity.

This analysis must do the following:

- Establish criteria for how far to go in gathering development information
- Establish criteria for evaluating potential changes to the boundaries of the application under development

Design of How to Gather

There are many approaches to, and methods for, gathering development information. Each may work well in some circumstances and may pose problems in other circumstances. It is important to be aware of a variety of them and to choose the most appropriate. A variety of common methods that can be used to gather development information are discussed below.

e-Commerce information gathering involves special challenges, especially in gathering information about the needs and wants of external users. Techniques that can readily work with an organization's internal users may not be appropriate for users outside an organization. Also, information gathering should not be made so public that it alerts an organization's competitors to its intentions.

Construction of Support for Gathering Development Information

Some approaches or methods may require the analyst to develop tools and/or make arrangements prior to being able to actually gather information leading to requirements.

Testing of Gathering Tools and Methods

Just because a method has been selected or a tool has been developed to gather development information, does not mean that it will work. Developers must evaluate how well a method or tool works, while they are using it, and be prepared to change or replace it if necessary.

Implementation of Requirements Gathering

Various methods are used to gather information and potential requirements for the application. While this information is being gathered, it is important for the analyst to reserve judgment about the validity of this information. Failure to do so may result in the analyst being caught up in an organizational power struggle.

The actual gathering of development information may lead to the identification of the need to gather further information for several reasons:

- Because the desired information could not be gathered via the method used
- Because of the identification of further relevant information that needs to be gathered
- Because of contradictions in the information gathered

Requirements Specification and Evaluation (prior to Utilization
of Requirements in the Development)

It should not be up to the developer to determine the importance or the validity of individual requirements. The users and stakeholders, especially those responsible for funding the development, should make the decision as to which requirements are to be met by a new system. The role of the developer is to compile the list of proposed requirements, along with suitable feasibility information on each, in a manner that these users can clearly evaluate and decide which are to be met.

5.3.1.2   User-Oriented Information Gathering Methods

There are various methods for gathering user-oriented information, including:

Individual Interviews

Individual interviews are best conducted at or near the user's or stakeholder's usual place of work. This helps connect them with the application that they will be discussing and provides them ready access to any materials or examples they may wish to use as illustrations. Advantages of interviews include:

- Being flexible and adaptive
- Producing high-quality information
- Having an ability to elaborate where desirable

  Disadvantages of interviews include:

- Being time consuming
- Being expensive
- Presenting difficulties in comparing results of different interviews
- Introducing biases by inexperienced interviewers
- Obtaining only a limited amount of information per interview

Group Meetings

Various techniques can be used in meetings to gather and to evaluate various development information. Different techniques may be more appropriate for use with different groups to gather different types of development information. Advantages of meetings include:

- Getting input from a number of users at once
- Being flexible and adaptive
- Obtaining generally high-quality information
- Being able to elaborate where desirable
- Being less expensive than individual interviews

  Disadvantages of meetings include:

- Being time consuming
- Being difficult to schedule
- Having individuals be shy about discussing their true feelings in front of their co-workers, managers, and/or subordinates

- Requiring greater preparation and skill to use than individual interviews
- Obtaining a limited amount of information per meeting (before burnout)

Questionnaires

Questionnaires can be used to communicate with large numbers of people on relatively standardized topics in a relatively short period of time. However, questionnaires are generally of limited value in gathering anything other than general requirements.

Advantages of questionnaires include:

- Allowing individuals to be anonymous in their responses
- Being relatively inexpensive
- Being able to reach large groups quickly

Disadvantages of questionnaires include:

- Being very difficult to construct in order to obtain useful results
- Not allowing much opportunity for elaboration
- Resulting in lots of data but little information
- Having trouble getting users to respond

5.3.1.3   Task-Oriented Information Gathering Methods

There are various methods for gathering task-oriented information, including:

Observations

The developer either is open about observing (risking the Hawthorne effect) or tries to be secretive (risking even greater user resentment) and tries to observe how work is actually accomplished. Decisions have to be made about what to observe and how long to observe it.

Advantages of observations include:

- Observing actual performance
- Observing performance as it is happening
- Having high validity if users are comfortable with analyst

Disadvantages of observations include:

- Focusing on pre-e-Commerce systems
- Missing some important events
- Being influenced by Hawthorne or other adverse effects
- Being expensive and time consuming to do thoroughly

The Hawthorne effect occurs when workers, who know they are being observed, temporarily change how they are working in response to being observed. Often, this change involves working according to the rules established by management (also known as "working to rule") even if that is far less efficient than the usual method of work.

Examining Documented Procedures

Developers can determine what is, or is supposed to be, done by examining procedure manuals, training materials, and related business document formats.

Advantages of examining documented procedures include:

- Being easily done without disturbing users
- Providing a good background at the start of the investigation

Disadvantages of examining documented procedures include:

- Focusing on pre-e-Commerce systems
- Being mislead by out-of-date documents
- Identifying only what ideally happens, and missing what really happens

Sampling Business Transactions

Developers can examine a sample of business documents/transactions, which record information passing through the system.

Advantages of sampling business transactions include:

- Seeing the results of actual processing
- Reducing large amounts of similar data quickly
- Providing a historical perspective

Disadvantages of sampling business transactions include:

- Focusing on pre-e-Commerce systems
- Missing infrequent exceptions
- In some cases, requiring statistical analysis to reduce large amounts of data
- Being limited to types of information available via documents

5.3.1.4 Tool-Oriented Information Gathering Methods

There are various methods for gathering tool-oriented information, including:

Examining Existing Systems

Developers can inspect existing systems (where available) and/or reviews of existing systems to determine what they are intended to do and how they do it.

Advantages of examining existing systems include:

- Providing a starting point for identifying what can already be expected to be done
- Providing insight into what isn't done or what is currently done poorly
- Easily finding a number of examples and/or reviews on the Web

Disadvantages of examining existing systems include:

- Many competitive systems may not be easily available for inspection
- In addition to copyright concerns, some features of existing systems might not be appropriate for this organization, even if they could be easily copied

Prototyping

Developers can use incomplete models of a system to gather and to evaluate various development information in an iterative manner. Prototyping is discussed further in a later section of this chapter.

Advantages of prototyping include using realism for:

- Assisting users and developers to communicate about the same concepts
- Investigating possibilities of how a system could evolve

Disadvantages of prototyping include:

- Requiring considerable time and effort to use
- Giving a false sense of completion to the prototyped system

5.3.2   Identifying Alternatives

Wherever information is gathered, there is always the question of how much to gather. Since e-Commerce systems are constantly evolving, whatever was good enough yesterday is no longer good enough today and will be sadly inadequate tomorrow. Developers often want specific guidance that the users and other stakeholders cannot give them in terms of how much information to gather and how many alternatives to consider.

The following is an approach that I personally find useful:

- Given some understanding of the boundaries for gathering information or identifying alternatives, developers start their work.
- Often external pressures to finish an activity and move to the next activity artificially limit this gathering or identification.
- Where the activity is not limited by time, developers often gather or identify until they believe they have "enough." This amount varies between developers, largely related to their level of experience. Inexperienced developers tend to rush gathering and identification more so than truly experienced developers. However, "enough" is seldom really good enough and is often inadequate when dealing with e-Commerce systems.
- Another invalid stopping point is the claim that there is nothing more available to gather or identify. It is always possible to gather or identify more information or alternatives.
- The best condition to use in determining when to end is:
  - Stop when all of the information and/or alternatives you continue to gather turns out, on further consideration, to be a minor variation of information and/or alternatives already gathered.

 Find references to further information about identifying alternatives in the Chapter 5 Cyber Supplement.

5.3.3   Usability Testing

Unlike testing of programs, usability testing doesn't have to wait until the final system has been constructed. Rather, usability testing should occur throughout the development life cycle.

ISO 9241-11[8] defines usability as a combination of:

- Effectiveness—the accuracy and completeness with which users achieve specified goals
- Efficiency—the resources expended in relation to the accuracy and completeness with which users achieve goals
- Satisfaction—positive attitudes to the use of the product and freedom from discomfort in using it

It also provides a framework for specifying software usability involving:

- Context of use (users, equipment, environments, goals, tasks)
- Usability measures (effectiveness, efficiency, satisfaction)
- Specification and evaluation of usability during design

Even if we can specify the usability of software, the question remains how to design for it. Often products are designed and constructed first, and then subjected to token usability testing just before delivery. At this late stage in the development cycle, little can easily be done to improve usability. Changes to the product are often only made when testing uncovers a catastrophic flaw. It is far easier to identify factors that contribute to a lack of usability than those that will ensure the presence of usability. ISO 9241 Part 10 Design Principles[9] identifies seven general design principles intended to improve the usability of the software dialogues by directing the developer to concentrate on the needs of the user. A **dialogue** is a set of interactions "between a user and a system to achieve a particular goal." These principles are:

- **Suitability for the task.** "A dialogue is suitable for a task when it supports the user in the effective and efficient completion of the task."
- **Self-descriptiveness.** "A dialogue is self-descriptive when each dialogue step is immediately comprehensible through feedback from the system or is explained to the user on request."
- **Controllability.** "A dialogue is controllable when the user is able to initiate and control the direction and pace of the interaction until the point at which the goal has been met."
- **Conformity with user expectations.** "A dialogue conforms with user expectations when it is consistent and corresponds to the user characteristics, such as task knowledge, education and experience, and to commonly accepted conventions."
- **Error tolerance.** "A dialogue is error-tolerant if, despite evident errors in input, the intended result may be achieved with either no, or minimal, corrective action by the user."
- **Suitability for individualization.** "A dialogue is capable of individualization when the interface software can be modified to suit the task needs, individual preferences and skills of the user."
- **Suitability for learning.** "A dialogue is suitable for learning when it supports and guides the user in learning to use the system."

Such guidance may be too general to be readily applied at a high level by developers who are not intimately familiar with the application. It also may be too difficult to ensure that it is applied to each possible dialogue within a system. Usability testing can be vital in helping developers to focus on usability issues throughout the development process.

A thorough consideration of usability issues belongs at the start of each stage of the development life cycle, even the initial analysis stage.

- If a system lacks usability, then the user won't use it, or at least won't use it well.
- If a design method lacks usability, then the developer won't use it, or at least won't use it well.

Development decisions should be based on usability evaluations. These usability evaluations provide qualitative and quantitative information that can guide the development process. Continual evaluations throughout the life cycle should include:

- Evaluating the usability of methods and methodologies for developers
- Evaluating the usability of applications, designs, and developed systems for users

Usability concerns can be balanced for users and developers by:

- Identifying opportunities for improving usability for users
- Identifying the most usable development guidelines and methods for making these improvements
- Evaluating the resulting usability for both users and for developers before going forward
- Iterating the process

In requirements analysis we should determine not only the requirements of the application but also the usability requirements that must be met by the system being developed. We are all users we just sometimes forget to be demanding users. If we think like users, we can uncover many secrets to improving usability. We can use the Web both to learn about usability, and to set our expectations realistically. While no design can be expected to be perfect, any design wanting to be taken seriously should be as good as, or better, than the competition. The Web is a window on the competition that allows us to see the good, the bad, and the really ugly in action. We can learn about usability and in doing so, identify basic usability requirements by becoming users of:

- Competitive sites
- Similar sites
- "Hot" or "new and interesting" sites
- "Worst of the Web" sites

Usability requirements should lead usability evaluations:

- Quantitative data can indicate that something is wrong but seldom identifies what is wrong or how to fix it.
- Qualitative data can help find what is wrong or what can use improvement.
- All designs and redesigns should be evaluated, even ones resulting from changes based on previous evaluations.

Usability tests involve:

1. Identifying what you want to test:
    - Completeness
    - Individual tasks
    - Content
    - Presentation
2. Developing an experiment for the test:
    - Developing test tasks and scenarios
    - Selecting test subjects to participate

- Developing testing protocols (specifying how each part of the test is to be accomplished in detail, including what the testers are to tell the test subjects)
- Pilot testing the test
- Evaluating the results of the pilot testing and, if necessary, making modifications and retesting
3. Conducting the test with a suitable number of test subjects by:
   - Introducing the test subjects to the testing environment
   - Advising the test subjects about the testing and their rights as test subjects
   - Having the test subjects focus on trying to accomplish scenarios
   - Observing the test subjects performing scenarios and "thinking aloud"
   - Asking the test subjects questions after they perform the scenarios
4. Evaluating the test:
   - Identifying what was learned
   - Developing recommendations

NOTE:

- Recommendations are different from conclusions
- Recommendations are different from designs
- Recommendations should suggest what the developer should do next

Reasons for usability tests include:

- Testing to ensure you have the analysis right
- Testing prototypes before investing lots of hours in further development
- Testing after completing significant development portions
- Testing the complete system
- Testing a variety of systems to get the comments of real users about them

There are various ways of finding users to test systems, including:

- Real users are the best
- People who could be real users are next best
- Some of your friends are better than just you
- Then, and only then, there's you

Usability testing can be conducted in varying degrees of formality, depending on its intended uses and the amount of resources available for conducting it. For many development efforts, informal usability tests are sufficient and a major improvement over the alternative of not testing. Formal usability testing, which is generally required for "scientific" studies:

- Generally involves more work and more cost
- May be important in comparing alternatives
- May not be needed or justified for all developments

 Find further information about usability testing in the Chapter 5 Cyber Supplement.

5.3.4 Prototyping

Prototyping is a method of using a prototype to identify challenges and opportunities where users evaluate and speculate on a prototype. A **prototype** is a mock-up of a system that can be used to identify requirements for a system and to design specific details of a system. Prototypes are intentionally incomplete models of a proposed or an existing system. Prototypes are demonstration vehicles intended to elicit comments from those who look at and/or interact with them. A prototype provides a realistic representation of some properties of a system, without the cost (in time or other resources) required to completely construct the system. The level of complexity of a prototype should suit the purpose for which it is intended:

- Simple prototypes can be created by a series of one or more pictures to give a viewer the general impression of the main components or features of a system. For example, painted backdrops are often used in theatres to give the impression of real surroundings for the staging of a play or other performance.
- Very advanced prototypes can range all the way to being fully functional systems that have not yet been put into general production. For example, concept cars are developed by major auto manufacturers to evaluate the potential for various new features being introduced into their regular product lines.

Prototyping is a type of user testing that can be used throughout most of the development life cycle. In prototyping;

- The developer and user actively communicate throughout the prototyping session
- The developer actively guides the user through a preplanned set of activities that include:
  - Using the prototype to identify scenarios, tasks, content, and even other user groups
  - Using the prototype to try out scenarios and to evaluate the presentation, functioning, and content of tools

Evolutionary rapid prototyping[10] is a method that can be used throughout the system development life cycle, from initial problem identification to the delivery of a first-generation production system. Rapid prototyping is a powerful tool both for analyzing user requirements and for involving the users in the design of suitable user interfaces. The developer builds an initial prototype to demonstrate the initial requirements and then uses it, as illustrated in Figure 5-2.

The developer conducts one or more prototyping sessions with users who try to accomplish scenarios with the prototype and are asked for suggestions about what should be added to the prototype. This is done to:

- Evaluate existing requirements that have been incorporated into and that are demonstrated by the prototype
- Identify and/or evaluate additional requirements that correspond to the current development activity (requirements analysis, design, testing) for which the prototype is being used and that should be incorporated in the next version of the prototype

The developer then incorporates any new development information and/or requirements obtained from the prototyping sessions into a new version of the prototype. A number of cycles of using and revising the prototype are conducted in order to evolve the prototype to fully represent the desired specification of the system.

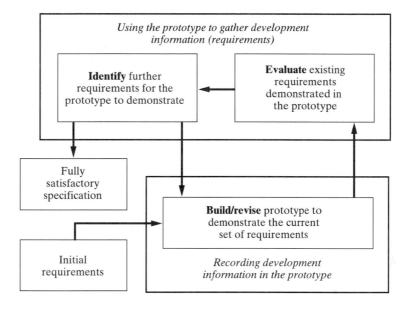

Figure 5-2 Using prototyping to develop specifications

Rapid prototyping uses a number of small, focused prototyping sessions to help avoid expending costly resources on developments before they are necessary and agreed upon. Developers have users focus on frequent presentations of incomplete prototypes in order to get realistic expressions of the users' needs and wants. If not properly managed, these presentations may miss their objectives and either become high-pressure sales pitches for designs or endless cycles of minor changes. The successful use of prototyping requires careful planning and use.

Prototyping sessions should last less than an hour, so that the users and the developers don't burn out. However this doesn't mean that there is one full hour to devote to new information acquisition. A typical prototyping session might take:

- Five minutes for getting started. This should include greeting each other and introductory pleasantries. While many technical types dislike wasting time on such small talk, the users need to be made to feel welcome and comfortable if they are to perform as required.
- Ten minutes for reviewing reports of results from the previous prototyping session and for going over the agenda for today's session. If these reports are too long or get ahead of the prototype, valuable prototyping time may be lost to this activity.
- Fifteen minutes for going over improvements to the prototype made to correct problems noted at the last prototyping session. This does not mean going over

the entire prototype. Rather it should focus only on those areas where problems were identified that require changes.

- Twenty minutes for using the prototype to identify further opportunities. This time may be eroded by previous steps taking longer than planned. This time should focus on identifying what needs to be done and should strongly avoid trying to speculate how it can or should be done. That should be left up to the developers. When used in the design phase, what needs to be done includes how the system should interact with the users but should avoid how the developers get it to do so.
- Ten minutes for getting agreement on where to go next, based on:
  - Whether the current objectives have been completely satisfied or if further prototyping of them is necessary
  - What changes/additions the developers should make for the next prototyping session
  - When the next prototyping session should occur for this user or group of users

Prototyping sessions should have a clear plan, which includes:

- Identifying the current phase of the systems development life cycle, which should be used to limit what is and is not relevant to be considered during the prototyping session
- All information from previous life cycle phases that the user brings up must be considered
- The developer should limit the consideration of new material (not from previous phases) to the current phase. For example, a discussion of the user's preference for colors to be used on a screen belongs in detailed design rather than in analysis.
  - To help avoid such issues coming up, the prototype should not use special colors until they are discussed in the design phase.
  - Where the user brings up matters that belong later, the developer should note them but politely return to the current objectives.
- Identifying the specific objectives of the current prototyping session, which can be used to focus the user and to help avoid discussion of other matters that are not suited at the current time. The developer can also use these objectives to return focus that may have wandered away. Example objectives could include:
  - Identifying additional tasks, beyond those already identified
  - Identifying specific content required by particular tasks
  - Evaluating how certain scenarios could be accomplished by a particular design
  - Identifying other scenarios that the design could be used for (evaluating how they could be accomplished may be deferred to a later session, especially if it is not straightforward)
- Identifying the specific way these objectives are to be accomplished, which can provide suggestions to developers. Examples could include:
  - Brainstorming what could be added to the prototype
  - Using the prototype to consider current tasks or content and to think how each could be generalized to accomplish more

- Using the prototype to initiate discussions of how the user typically accomplishes tasks or uses content in order to identify scenarios
- Using scenarios to evaluate the design of a prototype
- Identifying who should be involved in the session, in order to limit each prototyping session to the investigation of the needs of a particular group of users.
  - A single version of a prototype may be subjected to a variety of similar prototyping sessions if a number of different user groups are involved.
  - Each session should focus on the needs of the particular user group and avoid being sidetracked into speculating about those of other groups.
- Providing a brief report to the user for verification and approval. The report should contain:
  - An agenda for this meeting that identifies the general (phase of development) objective, the specific objective, and the proposed method of accomplishing it
  - A brief report of the decisions from the previous session and a report on the progress towards meeting them

Prototyping sessions should fit into a larger plan that is flexible enough to allow inserting new sessions or modifying the objectives of existing ones in the plan. This larger plan should identify and tentatively schedule all the prototyping sessions necessary for completing the current phase of development.

In conducting prototyping sessions:

- Attention should be focused on the prototype, rather than on any associated documentation, during a prototyping session
- Attention should be focused on participants keeping to their particular roles. Multiple people may be involved, including:
  - The developer(s) who typically leads the session
  - The user(s) who responds by focusing on their needs
  - A person or machine to record the main points in the prototyping session, including the user's observations and the agreed-upon decisions
  - An (optional) independent moderator to avoid tensions by making sure that both the user(s) and the developer(s) keep to their roles and to the agenda and maintain a polite discussion
  - Attention should be focused on the agenda. When other ideas come up that distract from the agenda, they should be recorded for exploration at a future prototyping session. However, it is preferable to try to keep to the current agenda for this prototyping session. In that manner, the new matter can be dealt with, and this session can still succeed. The alternative is a failure to succeed in the current session and often a failure of management to recognize why the session has to be held again.

Suitable management methods[11] are required to ensure that the use of prototyping provides its expected benefits. There are many strong advocates both for and against the use of rapid prototyping in systems development. The advocates for it often talk about their personal successes, while the advocates against it talk about specific examples of failures. What is needed is a proper management approach to ensure that developers succeed with rapid prototyping.

Despite a familiarity with the principles of prototyping (to the point of being able to rotely state them) developers often manage to violate each of them during the development of their projects. The following briefly summarizes some of these problems that need to be managed.

Developers may have limited familiarity with the prototyping software before using it on a project and thus have to learn as they go. This limited knowledge either encourages them to expend a minimal amount of effort in building the initial prototypes or causes massive frustrations as they try to learn all they might need to know before starting. In the latter case, this may lead to trying to build a more complete prototype than is necessary.

Modifiability requires more than just a suitable prototyping tool. Modifiability is largely assisted or inhibited by the limitations encapsulated in the design of the prototypes. Conscious efforts have to be made to plan and to design for flexibility. This often requires making the minimum number of design decisions and deferring the others. Potential problems occur whenever the developers treat their decisions as final and don't evaluate them via prototypes with the users, such as where:

- Developers have major disagreements among themselves that they attempt to solve on their own
- Developers discover a wonderful way of designing a requirement that is instantly agreed upon by all development team members

The ultimate goal of extensibility is the development of a fully working system. Thus, by the end of the process the prototype must reach total fidelity. However, because the process is one of extension, this can include extensions in fidelity as well as in the prototype. This can be accomplished by using a single prototyping tool in different ways, depending upon the circumstances. Developers tend to violate both of these types of extensibility by making limiting design decisions prematurely, thus requiring the replacement of prototypes rather than their extension. For example:

- Where early, low-fidelity prototypes are created with a paint program rather than as printouts of screens created using the prototyping tool, they require replacement at a later time.
- Developers often attempt to fully implement functionality while they are gathering requirements. Screen painting with limited additional functionality is generally sufficient for prototypes being used for requirements gathering. Later, high-level changes may often necessitate re-implementation of new versions of any functionality that is developed prematurely.

Probably the hardest principle to accept is that prototypes should be partially specified. Developers usually want to include everything they know or think they know, and may even include what they are only speculating on within the prototypes. It is very difficult to limit the contents of the prototype to only what was agreed upon in the previous prototyping session. However, this is necessary to limit the amount of time spent in corrections and to provide a good basis for exploring the next phase of the project (regardless of whether it is further analysis or design details).

The idea of a working model may mistakenly be equated with a high-fidelity model. However, the criteria for working can be interpreted as what works for the current prototyping needs. Thus, early in the projects, when basic requirements are being gathered, a low-fidelity model is often superior in focusing the prototyping sessions on these basic requirements and away from design details. Likewise, later in the projects, much higher fidelity of both design and interaction is required to provide the aspect of working. Developers often attempt to achieve higher-than-required fidelity and then are constrained by what they get working in time for the next presentation, which often may be less than the required fidelity.

Because prototypes are implicit designs, developers often allow design issues to overshadow the need for requirements gathering early in the life of a project. This leads to making decisions that may limit the modifiability of the prototype and make difficult the inclusion of the missed requirements.

It is important to appreciate the potential need for additional iterations, especially after prototyping sessions with the users that do not accomplish all of their goals. Iteration needs to continue at any phase of the life cycle until that phase is sufficiently completed.

While prototyping sessions need to focus on the prototype, it is still important for developers to use other, more technical forms of development documentation, such as task analyses and object models. Many developers would prefer to just focus on programming the prototype. However, traditional documentation is important in both ensuring completeness and consistency and in providing sufficient understanding of what really was determined via prototyping to support later developments.

The rapidity of iterations is often limited by the availability of the users involved in the prototyping sessions, who generally have other major obligations. The rapidity of accomplishments is limited to the capability of the developers to manage the prototyping sessions. This involves their ability both to focus the users on the objectives of the session and to limit discussion once requirements have been recognized.

The above challenges can be overcome, if properly managed. The following recommendations can help in this management.

Following a Definite Life Cycle

Prototyping, like all other forms of development, needs to follow a logical life cycle from problem recognition through product acceptance and delivery. Like all forms of development, it is foolhardy to expect that design can precede requirements. However, in prototyping, some design can be based on some requirements before other requirements are established. Great care must be taken to ensure that this design does not preclude this establishment. Thus, design must proceed on a "need-to-design" basis respecting the overall life cycle of systems development.

Planning Life Cycle Accomplishments

Managing the prototyping life cycle requires a shift of emphasis from producing artifacts to scheduling activities designed to achieve specific accomplishments. Life cycle phases can provide useful guidance for developers rather than formal points at which "completed" specifications are fixed for the duration of the life cycle. This involves selecting which activities to do immediately and which to defer until later in the life cycle. Development follows a cycle of obtaining information about user needs, using the information to build (once) and on later cycles modify (add to and change) a prototype, which is then used in the next cycle to obtain more information. In both the obtaining and using of user needs information, each piece of information must be evaluated as to whether or not it pertains to the current (or a previous) phase of the life cycle.

Avoiding Premature Design

Developers should avoid premature design decisions while not losing information obtained in prototyping sessions. The quantity and quality of information identified in a prototyping session can provide both developers and managers with a good indication of both the success of a prototyping session in meeting its objectives and progress through the life cycle. (The obtaining of a number of trivial analysis issues is often a better indicator of the time to start the design phase than the obtaining of a number of design issues, which may be obtained prematurely.) The users should be informed of the disposition of issues so that they are assured that they will be dealt with appropriately.

Carefully Planning Prototyping Sessions

Prototyping sessions require planning to ensure that prototyping (as opposed to waterfall development or hacking) is actually being done. Each type of development obtains information on user needs and then uses it to (it is hoped) move forward. The difference in methods can be characterized in terms of the mix of new and old information used.

- With waterfall development, sessions are focused on obtaining new information to add to existing information incorporated in documents. Changes are considered problems to be avoided, and developers exert considerable efforts to avoid making them.
- Prototyping is based on a combination of validating changes and obtaining new information to add or change the existing information as incorporated in the prototype. The process is based on managed change.
- In hacking, new information is only obtained once, and then the information incorporated in a program is changed a number of times without adding any substantially new information.

Care must be exercised so that prototyping does not degenerate into either waterfall development or hacking. This can involve the identifying and evaluating of alternative implementations of each issue to be investigated during a prototyping session and structuring of the issues to suit the prototyping process. Prototyping issues should be managed to ensure that a suitable range of alternatives are identified for each issue and that repeating their discussion and evaluation is minimized.

Agendas for prototyping sessions should be developed around the user tasks and their related issues that need further user inputs at the current phase of the development life cycle. This agenda should then be used to manage the prototyping session to ensure that it achieves its objectives.

Prototypes Should be Prototypes

According to Connell and Shafer[12] prototypes are supposed to be a specification (a living specification, in fact) of the users' requirements, not a proposed solution to these needs. The prototype only becomes a solution when the fully specified requirements become equal to a fully specified solution. Despite this philosophy, developers tend to treat prototypes as their solution. Because the management of attitudes is beyond my expertise, I cannot recommend a way to manage this problem.

The content of the prototypes, however, can and should be managed in keeping with the objectives of partial specification, keeping the prototype readily modifiable and ultimately extensible and emphasizing iteration.

The main focus should be to manage what is currently prototyped. The prototype should be limited to specifying those issues that have already been established that pertain to the current or a previous life cycle phase and to suggesting those issues that are next to be explored. In keeping with this, early prototypes should necessarily be of low fidelity, and the fidelity should increase throughout the life cycle.

Additional management can be assisted or provided implicitly through the selection of suitable development tools and techniques. Achieving these objectives can be aided by utilizing a prototyping (development) tool that can be used throughout the life cycle and at various levels of fidelity. Object-oriented design methods can support considerable modifiability and extensibility whether or not they are fully supported by the prototyping tool.

Documentation

Prototyping is an active process that requires a management method that focuses on the process of prototyping more than on the development of documentation-oriented artifacts. This does not mean that no documentation is required for its project management. Rather, it requires that documentation development is included in the development process. As already discussed, prototyping should focus on the process of obtaining information as a supplement to standard development methods, which include traditional forms of development documentation.

User-oriented documentation should support the prototyping process rather than detract from it, or even supplant it, as often happens. Users need to be informed of the progress in the prototyping developments and to be focused on their immediate role within the process. This may be best managed by giving the users summaries of the results of completed prototyping sessions and agendas of the next prototyping sessions. These user documents should focus on the issues that were dealt with in the prototyping sessions and minimize discussion of suggested resolutions of unresolved issues (which should be left to the prototyping sessions themselves).

Although screen diagrams may be helpful inclusions within the documentation to be given users during prototyping, additional documentation may be best limited to those phases of the prototyping life cycle where it is most needed. Thus, user manuals may be best reserved to the later phases of the life cycle where they should be prototyped once the system is substantially designed. Although this goes against the wisdom of some design philosophies, it may be essential to avoid shifting the users' focus from the prototype to the manual. Care must be taken to ensure that the development of a user manual receives due attention at this later time, when there is likely to be considerable pressure to deliver the now-designed system.

The minimization of documentation given to the user should not be confused with a minimization of all documentation. The developers should maintain well-structured documentation of all the issues, alternatives, analyses, and outcomes.

Various types of more traditional documentation (as discussed below) may be helpful for the developers and, where helpful, should be encouraged. Additionally, developers may be encouraged to maintain their own internal draft of the future user manual to accompany the prototype.

 Find references to further sources of information about prototyping in the Chapter 5 Cyber Supplement.

5.3.5   Documenting

Documentation is developed throughout the system development life cycle. All documentation needs to be designed to best serve its intended uses.

NOTE: Documentation is only useful if its intended users can readily use it. In most cases, this includes the end users of the system, the developers, and managers.

While different types of documentation will be begun at different stages of development and are nominally tied to those stages, each type of documentation needs to be kept up-to-date throughout the life of a system. The following describe some of the concerns for uses of different types of documentation, based on where they are originated in the development life cycle:

Analysis documentation gathers what is known about requirements.

- The analysis documentation needs to be verified for correctness and completeness by both the users and the developers.
- Despite verification, errors and omissions are likely to result. When discovered, they should be inserted into the analysis documentation and their effect carried forward in any further types of documentation that is developed, based on this analysis documentation.
- The requirements identified in analysis documentation should be used:
  - As the basis for design and construction
  - To evaluate how well a design or a developed system assists with what's needed
- Requirements, identified in analysis documentation, don't go away regardless of whether or not a system is developed to serve them. Analysis documentation should be retained for future use.

Design documentation transforms requirements into a detailed plan for constructing a system to assist in meeting the requirements of the application.

- Because many alternate designs might be developed, it is important for the design process to include user input before a final design is arrived at. Design documentation should be developed and verified iteratively.
- Once a design has been determined, it forms the basis of the rest of development. Some people believe that if design documentation is appropriately developed, it can be transformed into user documentation with a minimum of effort.
- Actual systems that are constructed should be evaluated against both the requirements in analysis documentation and the plans in the design documentation.
- Design documentation should be retained for future use, as a basis for verification, validation, usability testing, future system maintenance and modifications, and as an explanation of the current system.

- As changes are made to a system, the design documentation should be revised to correspond to these changes.

Construction documentation adds further details to designs that record how the system was constructed.

- It is important for these details to be captured, especially to support verification, validation, usability testing, and future maintenance and modifications.
- As changes are made to a system the construction documentation needs be revised to correspond to these changes.
- Construction documentation need not be a separate type of documentation. It can be incorporated within design documentation.

Testing documentation needs to ensure that all relevant tests are performed and that their results are incorporated into the system before its delivery to users. These tests include internal tests performed by the system developers and acceptance tests performed by users. Testing should be based on comparing operations of the constructed system to requirements in the analysis and design documentation. It should not be based on construction documentation because then it might lead to a self-fulfilling prophesy of the goodness of the system. The purpose of testing is to ensure that the system works as is required and as it was designed.

Testing documentation should be developed in a manner that facilitates its reuse in the verification, validation, and usability testing of any future modifications to the system. This documentation should include:

- The procedures used for the different tests
- Test data and any testing tools used, in a form suitable for reuse
- The results of test activities
- Acceptance certificates based on the test results. Acceptance certificates can be issued either by outside testing agencies or by the intended users. Developers should not issue these certificates for themselves.

Implementation documentation should include both an implementation plan and any documentation that is necessary for utilization, including:

- User documentation
- Procedures for utilization
- Procedures for support, including documentation for:
  - The reporting and analysis of problems
  - The handling of change requests
  - The controlling of various versions of the system

User documentation is important as a source of training for new users and as a source of further details for experienced users. Often these two different purposes cause user documentation to be separated into tutorial and reference materials.

- Tutorials typically take the user through the most common scenarios. (Since this type of documentation is also needed for testing and can be used even in making designs clear to users, it should be carefully developed by the time it is given to new users. However, the tendency may be for developers just to give users testing or design documentation, as is, without taking into account that new users

will likely know less about the system than users involved in the original design and/or testing.)
- Reference materials are generally provided to describe each of the functions of the system. However, users generally use reference materials to help in accomplishing infrequently performed tasks. Users may have considerable difficulty in identifying which functions are useful in assisting with which tasks.

Management documentation is needed to assess and manage the development process. When managers do not sufficiently understand the development process they may rely on the development of the other forms of documentation, discussed above, as a basis for assessing project progress. However, this can lead to significant difficulties, where developers are pressured into "completing" these other types of documentation on schedule regardless of whether they are finished or not.

 Find references to further sources of information about documentation in the Chapter 5 Cyber Supplement.

5.4 APPLYING PERVASIVE PROCESSES

5.4.1 Applying Pervasive Processes in Organizations

Organizations often can make use of their experience with other types of projects in applying the project processes, discussed above, to the development of an e-Commerce system. These processes can be performed by organizational professionals, by computer professionals, or by a combination of professionals, but they must be performed to ensure the success of the project.

Computer professionals who are part of the development project typically perform the pervasive technical processes. Often different computer professionals will have different strengths in different pervasive technical processes. Individual developers should be assigned to processes that best utilize their individual skills. When sufficient skills are not already available within an organization to perform these processes, the organization will have to consider whether to have an existing employee develop these skills or to hire a new person with these skills.

5.4.2 Student Assignment—Identifying Challenges and Opportunities

Good communication and documentation is central to the success of a major development project. Throughout the development, developers create documentation that must be reviewed by the users and that is often additionally reviewed by one or more developers outside the development project. This assignment focuses on providing and receiving suitable feedback on development documentation.

When there are a number of project teams in a course, it is valuable for each team to be assigned another team to critique on an ongoing basis. Thus, while this assignment is particularly aimed at developing a critique of another team's assignment from Chapter 4, the assignment should be repeated for each of the following assignments, starting with Chapter 6.

The critiques are intended to be positive experiences both for the team preparing them and for the team receiving them. Critiques are an opportunity for a team to get positive suggestions for improving their project that identify both where and how improvements could be made. Critiques are an opportunity for a team to get experience in providing helpful management support to developers.

Each team will have another team assigned to critique their development work. This will be done in a manner that ensures that no team critiques a team that critiques it. This will ensure that there is a clear management–developer relationship between teams and that critiques do not devolve into a mutual admiration society. Any perceived problems with the relationship between teams should be reported immediately to the instructor.

Format of Critiques

Each critique shall identify and discuss at least five major challenges and/or opportunities related to the development assignment that it is critiquing.

- Challenges identify portions of a development assignment where significant improvements should be made.
- Opportunities identify omissions from a development assignment where significant additions should be made.

Each discussion should:

- Identify what's missing or could use improvement
- Explain the significance of the proposed addition or improvement
- Suggest how the addition or improvement could be incorporated into the development assignment

Critiques can go beyond the basic requirement of discussing five challenges and/or opportunities by either adding additional discussions or by adding additional helpful suggestions or references that need not be fully discussed. It is important that critiques focus on making helpful improvements and avoid creating tensions between teams.

5.5   AN EXAMPLE CRITIQUE OF AN INITIAL INVESTIGATION

NOTE: This critique focuses on the ideas contained within the sample initial investigation (described in Chapter 4 and established in Chapter 3) and not on how the initial investigation was conducted. It demonstrates that an independent consideration of a development report may identify a number of potential improvements that could greatly improve the system being developed.

Opportunity:

Reallocate sales representatives

Identification: Because products and services are offered on-line, the need for sales representatives may be reduced because customers can order directly from your on-line service.

Significance: This may affect a number of employees. Once they hear about moves to develop an e-Commerce system, some of the better sales representatives may start looking for a job with a competitor unless they are reassured of good future opportunities with *Savor the Cup*. Reallocation can save costs and retain key people.

Suggestion: Some of these people can refocus their efforts at providing consulting services for a fee to customers.

Challenge:

Limited number of exclusive blends

Identification: It is unclear how exclusive blends can be provided to each business without limiting product variation.

Significance: This may be appealing to the client but may limit business by reducing the blends available to other clients.

Suggestion: Blends can be exclusive in that their exact recipes are kept confidential between *Savor the Cup* and the customers. *Savor the Cup* can allow customers to develop their own unique blends, which they can then claim to be exclusive in that no one else knows exactly what they are. There is an opportunity to add custom-blend development as a particular service that *Savor the Cup* can offer to customers.

Challenge:

Long-term customer retention

Identification: Charging for consulting for services previously given for free may decrease customer loyalty.

Significance: Without long-term contractual relationships, like those involved in franchises, clients could easily change to doing business with other suppliers.

Suggestion: Customer loyalty can be enhanced by continued support from sales representatives and by long-term contracts to supply coffee and associated products. It can further be enhanced by the development of supplier–customer integration.

Challenge:

Changes to existing customers

Identification: Existing customers are used to getting free consulting assistance.

Significance: If traditionally free services are now charged for, customer loyalty may decrease.

Suggestion: There will be a need to clearly delineate between services provided for a fee and services that should remain free. Free services can be gradually moved to the Web, so as not to disturb existing customer relationships.

Opportunity:

Paralleling the system to serve tea houses

Identification: There are many tea houses, similar to coffee shops, who have similar needs.

Significance: Currently there are no major franchises in the tea house market.

Suggestion: Remember that *Savor the Cup's* goals include:
- Providing the highest quality coffee and related products
- Focusing on the company's strengths in the market
- Keeping up with changes in the industry

These goals do not preclude diversifying into the tea shop market. In fact, it may be prudent to protect this market because it could pose major competition to coffee shops if customer taste trends should suddenly change. It may be possible to expand into tea via e-Commerce with much less effort than would be required via traditional marketing methods.

5.6   CHALLENGES AND OPPORTUNITIES IN APPLYING PERVASIVE PROCESSES

The following are some of the most common challenges and opportunities with applying pervasive processes in the development of e-Commerce systems. They are listed here to help you avoid them.

Challenges with Who Is Responsible for the Process

Because the project processes can be done either by organizational professionals or by computer professionals, both groups may expect the other group to perform them. It is important to establish responsibilities at the start of the project and to ensure that all project processes are performed properly on an ongoing basis.

Challenges with People Having the Right Skills

e-Commerce systems are new, and few people have significant experience with them. Many people do not recognize that the development of e-Commerce systems, while unique in many ways, involves many processes that are performed similarly in other developments. Where skills are totally lacking, people should be trained before expecting them to participate effectively in a development.

Challenges with Responsible People Having the Authority they Need

Pervasive processes generally involve multiple groups of people with specific lines of communication and responsibilities. While it is important to encourage free cooperation, individuals might retain various loyalties and responsibilities that may inhibit cooperation at times in the development. People who are responsible for a certain process must have the authority to gain cooperation or must be able to enlist the authority of someone who does.

Opportunity for Non-computer Professionals to Participate in e-Commerce Development

Organizational professionals can get involved with e-Commerce systems development by starting with performing one or more project processes. As they gain experience with the overall development life cycle, some of these people may develop skills in gathering development information, identifying alternatives, and other technical processes that rely on a good understanding of the needs of organizations and individuals.

5.7 CYBER SUPPLEMENTS FOR CHAPTER 5

 Look at the Chapter 5 Cyber Supplements on the Web to find:

- References to further information about project processes
- How various information gathering methods apply to different types of users and information
- References to further information about identifying alternatives
- Further information about usability testing
- References to further information about prototyping
- References to further information about documentation
- Suggestions for practice activities for various pervasive development processes

REFERENCES

[1] "International Organization for Standardization," International Electrotechnical Commission 2nd Committee Draft for International Standard 15288, Life Cycle Management—System Life Cycle Processes, 2000.

[2] "International Organization for Standardization," International Electrotechnical Commission International Standard 12207, Information Technology: Software Life Cycle Processes, 1995.

[3] "International Organization for Standardization," International Electrotechnical Commission, TR 15504-2, Information technology: Software process assessment: Part 2: A Reference Model for Processes and Process Capability, 1998.

[4] Robert L. Glass, *Software Creativity* (Englewood Cliffs, NJ, Prentice Hall, 1995).

[5] Frederick P. Brooks, Jr., *The Mythical Man-Month: Essays on Software Engineering* (Reading, MA, Addison-Wesley, 1975).

[6] Ibid.

[7] R. von Oech, *A Kick in the Seat of the Pants* (New York, Harper & Row, 1986).

[8] "International Organization for Standardization," ISO International Standard 9241-11, Guidance on Usability, 1998.

[9] "International Organization for Standardization," ISO International Standard 9241-10, Ergonomic Requirements for Office Work with Visual Display Terminals (VDTs): Dialogue Principles, 1996.

[10] J. L. Connell and L.B Shafer, *Structured Rapid Prototyping* (Englewood Cliffs, NJ, Yourdon Press, 1989).

[11] J. A. Carter, Managing to Succeed with Rapid Prototyping, *Proc. 1992 Annual Meeting of the Human Factors Society,* pp. 404–408.

[12] Ibid.

6

e-Commerce Feasibility

Outline

6.1 INTRODUCTION TO E-COMMERCE FEASIBILITY

It is important to evaluate the potential for success of a project before expending large amounts of resources on it. While the "true" potential cannot be evaluated until after these resources have been expended and the project is complete, it is important to ensure that a proposed project is at least feasible. **Feasibility** deals with the possibility that a system can be acquired or developed and used for some set of purposes within some environment or set of environments. Feasibility studies are designed to identify situations that if uncorrected will lead to failures. If there are no catastrophic situations that can be foreseen, then the project may be deemed to be feasible.

NOTE: Feasible is not necessarily equivalent to profitable (this will be discussed further under the heading of economic feasibility).

Being feasible does not mean that any project, including a systems development project, is the most desirable project for an organization to pursue. Often the more difficult a project is, the lower the likelihood it will be pursued, even if it passes a basic feasibility study. Individual projects that pass a feasibility study usually have to be evaluated against other feasible projects before an organizational decision is made to commit to their development. The exact criteria for deciding to go ahead with a project varies from organization to organization and may make use of some or all of the information that should be gathered in a feasibility study. Many organizations will develop formal business cases before funding major developments such as those involved with e-Commerce systems.

A feasibility study may be conducted on its own or as part of the development of a business case supporting establishing a development project. This chapter focuses on determining the feasibility of individual e-Commerce systems. However, the techniques discussed in this chapter can be used within the context of developing business cases and making comparisons between proposed alternatives.

 Find further information regarding developing business cases for e-Commerce alternatives in the Chapter 6 Cyber Supplement.

Revisions to a feasibility study should be conducted regularly throughout the life of a development project. In the development of traditional systems, feasibility is often (and incorrectly) expected to remain constant and thus is often evaluated only once, at or near the start of the project. Software developers often conduct such an initial feasibility study. As long as a project is feasible, it doesn't matter how feasible it is. Once a feasibility study has been conducted and accepted, the only elements likely to negatively affect feasibility are changes to the costs involved and the anticipated completion date. However, because costs and time already expended are not included in determining the feasibility of further development, these changes are seldom significant enough to result in a decision to scrap a project because it is now found to be infeasible.

In the development of e-Commerce systems, it must be recognized that feasibility will seldom remain constant. Competitive developments may raise the expectations of users and significantly impair the feasibility of a particular system during its development. Ongoing competitive analysis is required to ensure that the system being developed, with any modifications necessary due to competitive pressures, remains feasible.

6.2 UNDERSTANDING E-COMMERCE FEASIBILITY

6.2.1 Considering Alternatives for an e-Commerce Application

Before the feasibility of a proposed solution can be evaluated, that solution must first have been identified. However, it is important to be careful not to jump to design conclusions that are not based on sound analysis. Thus, rather than identifying specific solutions, developers should first consider a range of alternative approaches, including:

- Doing nothing
- Improving the existing system
- Buying or copying an existing system
- Developing a substantially new system

This list is ordered in terms of increasing impact on the organization in terms of change and cost to implement this change. Because e-Commerce is radically changing many of our concepts about which systems are important, we will consider this range of alternatives both for traditional systems and for e-Commerce systems.

6.2.1.1 The Range of Alternatives with Traditional Systems

With most traditional applications, there is always an existing system, regardless of whether or not it has been computerized. Even most new, start-up organizations have existing systems, if only in their minds, because they generally expect to use systems similar to those of already existing organizations. Existing traditional systems provide a ready base for comparison.

Doing nothing about the problems currently encountered with the application does not necessarily mean actually doing nothing about the application; rather it means doing nothing new or different from what's already being done. With this option, the organization's systems do not change. However, because the world is constantly changing, this does not guarantee that the organization will remain at equilibrium. Account has to be taken for changes in the relationship between the organization and other organizations and individuals with which it does business. Doing nothing is generally appropriate if all other possibilities prove infeasible.

Improving the existing system can be done in a variety of ways, including:

- *Modifying the existing system* to improve specific parts while leaving other parts unchanged. This may be appropriate if the needed modifications are localized to particular parts and if the existing system can be modified relatively easily. Modifications typically improve what is being done without adding any new features or users. Likewise, modifications typically make minor changes to an existing system without replacing major parts. Useful modifications are often put off because they do not seem as urgent or do not seem as significant as other more major improvements. However, successively putting off useful modifications can allow a system to gradually become obsolete without its owners recognizing the true significance of the lack of these modifications. It is important for organizations to keep open to the benefits of making ongoing modifications.

- *Adding to the existing system* to add specific functions and/or data. This may be appropriate if these additions can be easily added without the need for major changes to the existing system. Additions typically involve more development work than modifications and may lead to the use of an existing system to achieve a number of new organizational purposes. Additions may also involve expanding the number of users of the application.

- *Replacing part or all of the existing system.* This may be appropriate when major changes need to be made. It may be easier to replace significant parts of a system (by developing completely new parts) than to modify existing parts when large numbers of significant modifications are required. These major changes can include not only changes in functions and/or data but also major changes in the technologies used to implement the system.

Buying or copying an existing system when an existing system is available. The relative low cost of many software packages makes them a bargain, if and only if they meet the needs of the organization or can be easily and economically customized to meet these needs. This generally works well for application areas that are common to many different types of organizations.

Developing a substantially new system is often undertaken where no formal system currently exists to meet the needs of the application. However, the development of a "new" system should not be confused with developing a new implementation of an existing system using new technologies. There may be a big difference between the effects of a replacement system using new technology and a truly new system that can provide entirely new benefits.

There is a wide range of options in the acquisition of software. Widely accepted application packages often define the basic level of information processing expected in an application area. Thus, an early investigation of what's currently available can be useful whether a package is bought or built. However, the decision to buy or to build should not be rushed by discovering the availability of a potential package. The following factors can help recognize some of the indicators that can be used later (at design time) to determine whether to buy or to build a software package.

Considerations Related to Buying Packages

- Traditional, well-understood and well-established applications typically have various software packages available to purchase.
- Widely accepted application packages often have other packages that are designed to work with or to expand them.
- Popular software packages are often revised and expanded from time to time.
- Good software packages should support user customization.
- Good software packages often support multiple distributed users.
- Available support of software packages varies considerably, but seldom includes the developers making specific customer-requested modifications for individual customers.
- Most support of software packages focuses on helping people to use the packages.

- If a package fits well enough, it is usually less expensive than developing a custom-built package.
- If packages are available, your competition also has access to them.
- However, software packages are only part of a complete application system.
- If you have data that the competition doesn't, then you still have an advantage.

Considerations Related to Building Packages

- State of the art, developing, and specialized applications seldom have available software packages that can easily be applied to them (whether or not the packages were designed for their use).
- Internally developed software can go beyond the features in currently available software packages and thus go beyond what your competition may have.
- Internal software developments should make provisions for future enhancements.
- Enhancements may be built to work with available packages, focusing on unique features for a given organization.
- Building packages requires a considerable expenditure of resources before the promised benefits are realized (if they are realized). However, packages that get the jump on competition can be very profitable.

There's a Wide Range of Options for Acquiring Software

Many people consider that they only have two options: to buy a package (if one is available) or to develop a package (if one is capable of doing so). However, there really are a wide range, including:

- Purchase
  - Use as is
    - Use with default preferences
    - Change available parameters as needed
  - Modify purchased package
    - With additional purchased package
    - With externally contracted custom development
    - With in-house development
- Develop
  - In-house
    - For internal use only
    - For internal use and resale
    - For resale only
  - With externally contracted custom development
    - For internal use only
    - For internal use and resale
    - For resale only
- Modify previously developed
  - In-house
  - With externally contracted custom development

Unfortunately, people often try to decide whether or not to purchase a package before they even know what they need. A premature decision to purchase can lead to a wide variety of problems, even if they are lucky enough to choose the best package for their needs (because they may not recognize what their true needs are and thus may not utilize the package to their best advantage).

An initial consideration of major alternatives for software development or acquisition should yield a short list of potential candidates. The short list should have at least the option of doing nothing plus one of the others on our short list.

There are always a number of different possibilities for each of the alternatives.

- Replacements or new systems may be obtained through any of the acquisition options discussed above.
- Replacements or new systems may be developed using significantly different technologies or technical approaches.

Likewise, there isn't only one set of improvements that can be made. There are likely many different variations of the proposed set of organizational improvements, each with their own feasibility for success.

Rather than just comparing the feasibility of a single alternative with that of the status quo, it is preferable to identify, consider, and compare the feasibility of 3 to 7 significantly different realistic options. By considering at least three systems, there are at least two choices beyond maintaining the status quo. However, considering large numbers of systems may take more resources (including time, people, and other resources) than an initial feasibility consideration justifies.

6.2.1.2   Considering a Range of e-Commerce Alternatives

With e-Commerce systems the range of alternatives may seem overwhelming. Likewise, it might seem difficult to determine a proper basis for comparison. However, it is important to fully recognize the range of alternatives before rushing to select one to pursue. There are always lots of alternatives. Unfortunately, sometimes people stop looking at all the alternatives as soon as one that *might* work is found. By choosing the first possible solution, people often miss finding the best one.

An initial consideration of e-Commerce alternatives can involve variations of the alternatives discussed for traditional systems.

Doing nothing isn't always the same. When developing a new organization around an e-Commerce application, then doing nothing, truly means doing nothing. With it there may be nothing to lose as well as nothing to gain. When considering adding e-Commerce to an already existing organization, doing nothing means continuing to do business as usual, despite the possibility or the actuality of your competition adopting the e-Commerce application. In this case, doing nothing may cause the loss of business to the competition. This option risks the possibility of losses without providing any potential gains.

Improving the existing system may involve trying to fit a Web interface to existing systems. However, existing systems were seldom designed in a manner that adequately supports a Web-based interaction and/or security. Trying to make the necessary modifications to evolve an existing system to work as the basis for an e-Commerce system may be much more difficult than buying or developing a system designed for e-Commerce. Adding further functionality to the resulting hybrid system is often even more difficult.

The fact that modifying an existing system for use as the base for e-Commerce is seldom feasible does not mean that no systems will be modified as part of the development of a new e-Commerce system. If the e-Commerce system is to be integrated within an existing organization, it is likely that existing systems will need to be involved and may need to be modified. While improvements to an existing system are secondary to an e-Commerce system being considered, it must be feasible to make these improvements or to replace these systems in addition to being feasible to acquire or develop the e-Commerce system.

Adding e-Commerce to the existing system takes an evolutionary, rather than a revolutionary, approach to the development of the organization's information systems. Buying or developing a new e-Commerce system does not necessarily mean totally replacing the existing organizational and information system(s). This recognizes the importance of legacy systems to most organizations. Often organizations have large investments in legacy systems, especially traditional organizational information systems that have been developed using old technologies. The complexity and cost of many legacy systems makes it far more feasible to evolve these legacy systems than to replace them.

e-Commerce systems are often implemented within existing organizational structures. Thus, an e-Business is often treated as an additional branch of an organization. e-Commerce systems may require/help facilitate greater cooperation between smaller organizational units within a large organization. This may even result in changes to the boundaries of these smaller organizations, without replacing them entirely. Where an e-Commerce system includes a better means of processing information that is currently handled by an existing information system, it may replace that existing system for all users. For example, existing branches could use the order processing functions of an e-Business to replace their existing order processing system and to integrate all order processing into a single system.

e-Commerce can be added to legacy systems either by buying or copying an existing e-Commerce system or by developing a substantially new e-Commerce system.

Buying/copying an existing e-Commerce system is an option to developing a unique system. There are many software developers willing to sell you a turnkey e-Commerce application and many more who are willing to develop a "custom" application for you that looks like samples that they or someone else has already developed. While this option provides an organization with a competitive advantage that may be readily available to its competitors, it may provide some protection from being placed at a competitive disadvantage by doing nothing while the competition develops e-Commerce capabilities. Organizations need to be constantly updating their system to stay competitive and may have difficulties in ensuring that a purchased system will be updated in a timely manner in the future.

NOTE: The choice of custom developing an e-Commerce application does not mean that no new software will need to be purchased. There are an increasing number of software tools available to help develop and maintain custom e-Commerce applications and Web sites. Buying such software, however, would be considered as part of the development of such new systems.

Developing a substantially new e-Commerce system should include features that provide a competitive advantage. While some organizations may have the resources to jump right to the development of a relatively deluxe system, others will need to take a more cautious development approach by first developing a basic system and then planning to expand upon it.

Developing a basic system involves developing a version of a substantially new system that can be a starting point for further developments but that is sufficiently useful to be considered on its own. It should contain features that will give it a competitive advantage and that will encourage users to keep returning to it.

Developing a deluxe system involves the developing of a version of a substantially new system that is significantly better than any existing system. Rather than just trying to find a competitive niche in which to initially excel, this approach tries to outdo all of an organization's competitors and to jump to preeminence with an application system that contains a wide range of features that serve a wide range of users. Because e-Commerce systems must be competitive in a constantly evolving environment, it is often better to quickly build a basic system and then start evolving it toward a more deluxe one, rather than to spend the time trying to build a deluxe system all at once.

 Find further information regarding e-Commerce alternatives in the Chapter 6 Cyber Supplement.

6.2.2   Evaluating the Elements of Feasibility

Each alternative needs to be evaluated to determine its overall feasibility. **Overall feasibility** is determined by considering the combined operational, technical, and economic feasibilities. It is based on the most pessimistic evaluation from any of its constituents.

- If a system is infeasible in any manner, then it is overall infeasible.
- A system is only feasible if it is feasible operationally, technically, and economically.

Both the overall feasibility and any specific feasibilities can range from:

- Infeasible—where implementation will result in catastrophic consequences
- Feasible but with notable difficulties—where implementation is possible, but these difficulties will have to be overcome to achieve the full set of expected benefits
- Readily feasible—where implementation is both possible and desirable

Any specific finding of being infeasible, if substantiated, is sufficient to remove a potential system from consideration. However, it is often possible to revise the concept of a system to avoid (or at least to reduce into an acceptable range) the situation that led to the finding of infeasibility. Additionally, alternatives may be infeasible if too many difficulties are identified that must be overcome in order to make the alternative feasible.

An alternative can be pronounced feasible if it is not found to be not feasible in any manner. Being feasible neither ensures that the application will be profitable nor that it can be easily developed. Few systems, and especially few e-Commerce systems, are feasible without any difficulties.

A finding of "feasible with difficulties" is a warning that there are potential difficulties (and/or their remediation) which need to be controlled in order to ensure the success of the system. The controlling of these difficulties often involves costs in terms of time and resources, which must be added to the development plan and budget and should be included in the analysis of economic feasibility of a potential system. Potential difficulties may lead to the revision of the boundaries and/or functions of the system in order to avoid some costs. Information about potential difficulties should be maintained throughout systems development so that they may be eliminated or minimized whenever possible.

A finding of "readily feasible" is a recommendation for continuing analysis of a proposed system. It is not a guarantee that the system as currently proposed is the best possible. Where an alternative is considered readily feasible, the identification of further improvements can be left to the analysis and design phases.

Since many alternatives may prove feasible (even with some notable difficulties) a finding of feasible does not ensure that an alternative is the best or the most desirable. However, information obtained in a feasibility study can provide a good basis for selecting between alternatives.

6.2.3   Operational Feasibility

Operational feasibility deals with whether or not the proposed system will meet the needs of its various users and other stakeholders, be accepted by them, and be used. Operational feasibility goes beyond the traditional bounds of usability to consider the whole range of aspects necessary for the successful use of a system from containing the right set of tasks and tools to providing the right enticements to use the system.

Operational feasibility sometimes is overlooked because it is harder to quantify than economic feasibility. However, feasibility does not have to be quantified. As just discussed above, what is important is that feasibility identify situations that are infeasible and situations with difficulties.

Operational feasibility encompasses a number of related issues, any of which could result in disaster for a system. The feasibility of these issues should be evaluated separately and then the results of these separate evaluations combined into an overall evaluation of organizational feasibility.

Find references to further sources of information about various operational feasibility issues in the Chapter 6 Cyber Supplement.

6.2.3.1   Stakeholders

There are many different people who have a stake in the development of most systems, including (but not limited to):

- Users who need the application performed but have it done for them by other users
- Users who will actually use the application package directly
- Other people who supply or receive data or information to/from the application
- Various managers involved with each of these groups
- Owners of organization(s) performing or using the application

From a feasibility standpoint it is important to consider whether or not the proposed system will meet their needs:

- For accomplishing their objectives for the application—Will they get what they essentially require out of it?
- And in terms of its usability—Will they be able to use the application (if direct users) and/or the information products of the application?

A proposed system will be "infeasible" only if one or more groups of stakeholders cannot make use of the system and/or its products to perform essential tasks that they are intended to do and that cannot be accomplished in some other manner that still will be available.

While most difficulties do not make a system infeasible, consideration must be given to those that (although not apparently major or insurmountable) might become grounds for declaring a system infeasible due to their violating labor contracts or other binding regulations on the work place.

A proposed system will be "feasible with difficulties" if it is inconvenient to use or does less than expected for one or more groups of stakeholders. Due to a legacy of poorly designed systems, people may not recognize how often systems are feasible with difficulties from the start of their consideration. Early identification of these difficulties should lead to the correction or elimination of a large amount of them. It should be recognized that the remaining difficulties could result in lower productivity and a corresponding decrease in the benefits that may be realized.

A proposed system will be more likely to be readily feasible if it is a replacement system that is being developed to improve upon an existing system than if it is a new system. Revised systems can use existing systems as their base line to ensure that changes are for the better. This does not mean that this is necessarily done by the developers of revised systems—just that it could be done. New systems generally cause changes in the jobs of a variety of their stakeholders. The main anticipated changes should be analyzed to determine if the positives will outweigh the negatives for each group of stakeholders. Even where a proposed system is readily feasible, consideration of its impact on stakeholders may identify points of concern that should be noted for later consideration.

6.2.3.2   Organizations and Their Relations to One Another (Including Competitive and Complementary Organizations)

e-Commerce systems cross a variety of traditional organizational boundaries. These boundaries exist:

- Between small organizations (departments, divisions, and so on) within a larger organization
- Between organizations
- Between organizations and individuals

In most cases these boundaries are readily identified by the names given to the individual organizations involved. In many cases, they can also be located by examining relevant organizational charts. What is often less clear is the actual relationship that exists between organizations. This relationship may be other than what is expected or even desirable. For example: different units in a profit center–based company may be as competitive with each other as they are with external competitors. This competition may lead to the withholding of vital information, by a given unit, that should be shared for the corporate good.

Different organizations may have a symbiotic relationship that encourages them to help one another. This relationship may even exist between apparent competitors that are actually focused on slightly different markets (e.g., retailers and wholesalers).

For an information system to be feasible, it must be able to be accepted and supported by all of the different organizations involved with its use. (These organizations may be considered organizational stakeholders to distinguish them from individuals who have different stakes in the system.)

A proposed system will be "infeasible" if one or more organizations involved will not support the system and cannot be made to do so. This may often be based on political or economic differences that preclude the necessary level of cooperation.

A proposed system will be "feasible with difficulties" if it will take significant pressure to get one or more organizations to cooperate sufficiently to ensure the success of the system. This may require executive clout within a large organization to get different units within the organization to cooperate or may require formal contractual obligations to get independent organizations to cooperate.

A proposed system will be more likely to be readily feasible if it provides significant benefits to each organizational stakeholder that would not be available if all organizations didn't cooperate.

6.2.3.3   Operational Reliability

Once a system is implemented, it needs to be able to operate reliably without serious interruptions. **Operational reliability** is the ability to continue operating satisfactorily under changing conditions, including conditions that may have not been anticipated. The operational reliability of e-Commerce systems is based on meeting a number of needs, including:

- Ensuring that content is kept up-to-date
- Evolving to meet changing needs and/or expectations of users
- Handling varying numbers of transactions within a given time period
- Protecting the system from accidental or malicious damages

While full operational reliability can never be ensured, there will be some level at which the inability to maintain reliability constitutes an insurmountable obstacle to the success of the system. Both feasibility and operational reliability can be considered in terms of risk management. However, formal risk management may expect greater detail than is typically available during an initial feasibility study.

A proposed system will be "infeasible" only if a required level of operational reliability cannot be maintained.

A proposed system will be "feasible with difficulties" if there may be serious problems in meeting the desired level of operational reliability. Prior experience with information systems, suitable operating budgets, and the ability to quickly respond to changing operational needs can improve the level of operational reliability.

A proposed system will be readily feasible only if there are no identifiable problems in meeting the desired level of operational reliability.

6.2.3.4   The Organization's External Environment

The environments in which an organization exists and in which a system is implemented can have a number of effects on the success of the system. e-Commerce systems may be used in many different cultural, political, and social environments. Many of these environmental effects are subtle and may not be readily identified. They can include:

- Past: traditons, expectations, attitudes, and taboos
- Present: directions and strengths of power/influence relationships
- Future: openness to innovation and change

As the distance increases from stakeholders, through organizations, to their environment, the emphasis moves:

- From a need to identify positive benefits to declare the system feasible
- To a need to identify strong negatives to declare a system infeasible

A proposed system will be "infeasible" only if an environment, important to the system, is likely to strongly react against it for some identifiable reason.

A proposed system will be "feasible with difficulties" if significant problems, which are posed by an environment, can be minimized or eliminated via careful development.

A proposed system will be more likely to be readily feasible if it exists within a limited or controllable environment. A proposed system may be feasible in a number of different environments and infeasible or feasible with difficulties in others. In some instances, it may be more feasible to develop different systems for different environments rather than trying to develop one system that is feasible in all environments.

6.2.3.5 The Competitive Environment

e-Commerce systems need to do more than just provide users with needed functionality. Efforts need to be made to attract and retain users. The easy access of competitive systems on the Web can increase the difficulties of maintaining a competitive advantage. While an organization's employees can be forced to use a system, external users need to be attracted and enticed to use the e-Commerce system over and over.

It is important to avoid the "Field of Dreams syndrome" that assumes "If you build it, they will come." Even if they come, an e-Commerce system needs to consider a number of questions, including:

- Will they stay?
- Will they come back?
- Will they conduct any commerce?

As already discussed, e-Commerce exists in a global market where there is little need for organizations that don't have some form of competitive advantage. The more competitive advantages and the stronger the competitive advantages, the better. While competitive advantages should already have been identified in the initial investigation, it is important to ensure that achieving these competitive advantages is feasible. These competitive advantages need to be marketed in a manner that will attract users and need to be implemented in a manner that will retain them once they have been attracted.

The feasibility of each proposed competitive advantage should be evaluated. These individual considerations should include an evaluation of how easy it would be for competitors to copy and thus eliminate the competitive advantage.

The combination of individual competitive advantage feasibilities is different from the combination of other feasibilities.

A finding that a single competitive advantage is infeasible or only feasible with more difficulties than it appears to be worth is not sufficient cause to determine that an alternative is infeasible.

An alternative should be considered "infeasible" if there are no significant competitive advantages that are either readily feasible or feasible with manageable difficulties and if additional feasible competitive advantages cannot be identified.

An alternative will be "feasible with difficulties" if it only has competitive advantages that may be difficult to achieve or that may be easy to copy.

An alternative will be "readily feasible" only if it has significant competitive advantages that are easy to achieve and that may be difficult for competitors to easily copy.

6.2.3.6   Government Regulations

Government regulations may:

- Require a system—e.g., Workplace Hazardous Materials Information Systems (WHMIS)
- Require and regulate a system—e.g., acceptable accounting practices for income tax purposes
- Regulate a system if it exists—e.g., regulations regarding the use of Social Security/Insurance Numbers.

e-Commerce systems need to obey the government regulations of each location in which they expect to do business. Many e-Commerce sites include a statement that all business transacted with them is governed exclusively by the jurisdiction in which the organization is situated. However, it is unclear if such a disclaimer would be accepted by all other jurisdictions.

Ignorance of the law is no excuse, even if the law itself is ignorant, intrusive, or obtuse. If you don't know of any relevant government regulations, you should investigate to see if there might be some. However, attempting to determine whether there are any government regulations that might impact the system is easier to say than to do. (There are few experts who pretend to know all the government laws and regulations.)

A feasibility study is only a quick attempt to identify the obvious. Thus, while there may be need for further investigation of government regulations later during development, it is sufficient to use expert opinions from people informed about the application area to identify whether or not a proposed system might be affected by government regulations. People doing a particular job usually are aware of the main regulations that affect them.

There are almost always regulations that might affect a proposed e-Commerce system. If no applicable regulations can be found, it is likely that the investigation has not been conducted thoroughly enough. Traditional organizational and business regulations also apply to e-Commerce systems.

If regulations are found, then the application's feasibility may be:

- Infeasible, if the application is precluded from operating for some reason by a regulation

- Feasible with difficulties, if the application will need to make special provisions to meet the regulations
- Readily feasible, if there does not appear to be any major problems in accommodating the regulations
- Mandated (a new feasibility category that will overrule other categories and types of feasibility, including categories found infeasible) if the application is required by the regulation

6.2.4   Technical Feasibility

Technical feasibility deals with whether or not an e-Commerce application can be constructed in a suitable manner. Determining technical feasibility can only truly be done once a design has been developed. However, initial technical feasibility can be evaluated by examining:

- What is being done in an application area
- What else is done in other similar application areas
- What else is done to similar types of information
- The availability of data and information that may be required as inputs

Technical people often need to be restrained from turning an exploration of technical feasibility into a fixing of their preconceived design ideas. At this early stage in development it is important to keep our options open and remember that a feasibility study is most important in the potential problems that it uncovers.

As with the different components of operational feasibility, it may be useful for us to try to get a general idea of how technically feasible a proposed system is. This can range from:

- Infeasible—implementation will result in catastrophic consequences
- Feasible but with notable difficulties—implementation is possible, but these difficulties will have to be overcome to achieve the full set of expected benefits
- Readily feasible—implementation is both possible and desirable

To expedite evaluation of technical feasibility, it is useful to refer to existing systems, of which there are numerous examples on the Web. If they can do what's needed or something close to it, then it's probably technically feasible to do. (Whether such technology is also economically feasible is a separate issue). Initial technical feasibility can be determined by examining:

- The processing feasibility
- The data feasibility
- The development feasibility

Find references to further sources of information about various technical feasibility issues in the Chapter 6 Cyber Supplement.

6.2.4.1   Processing Feasibility

Processing feasibility can be determined by considering:

- What is being done in an application area? It's not only feasible to do this, it may be infeasible not to do at least this much.

- What else is done in other similar application areas? Most innovations are just borrowings of existing technologies from other application areas. Thomas Edison was a master at adapting and refining other ideas.
- What else is done to similar types of information? By considering information abstractly, we can often go beyond a limited set of immediately similar applications and identify many similar situations in which similar information is processed in a similar manner. This was noticed many years ago in comparing the operations of accounts payable and accounts receivable systems and is useful in much wider circles today.

A proposed system may be "infeasible" only if examples of one or more of its technical features cannot be found in any other system. However, just because a feature hasn't been found doesn't mean that it is truly infeasible. Rather, the expert opinion of a skilled developer should be consulted to determine whether the feature might be feasible, even if no one else has done so yet.

A proposed system will be "feasible with difficulties" if one or more proposed technical features is found to exist only in very state-of-the-art, high-priced systems, leading to the possibility that average developers might not readily have the skills to implement them. Again, this may lead to the need for an expert opinion to clarify the actual level of difficulty that might be involved.

A proposed system will be more likely to be readily feasible if each of the proposed technical features is readily found in a number of other existing systems.

6.2.4.2 Data Feasibility

Data feasibility can be determined by evaluating the availability of data and information that may be required as inputs.

A proposed system may be "infeasible" only if one or more major inputs it requires cannot be obtained in a timely manner (due to technical difficulties or restrictions on the availability of the information). However, it should be recognized that in some cases, informed approximations of the data may be available and sufficient to make the availability of data feasible.

A proposed system will be "feasible with difficulties" if a major difficulty can be identified in obtaining one or more major inputs.

A proposed system will be more likely to be readily feasible if each of the major data inputs is readily available.

6.2.4.3 Development Feasibility

Development feasibility should consider the ability of the organization to successfully develop the proposed alternative. It should review the resources (including the developers, the processes, the activities, and the development tools) that are to be used in developing the application.

An alternative will be "infeasible" if suitable resources are not available and cannot be obtained.

An alternative will be "feasible with difficulties" if problems are identified in the anticipated development processes or activities.

NOTE: It is not expected that a complete project plan be developed prior to conducting an initial feasibility study of possible alternatives. However, if the alternative is chosen, any identified problems with anticipated processes and activities should be corrected before continuing.

An alternative will be "readily feasible" if resources are available and suitable development processes and activities are anticipated.

6.2.5 Economic Feasibility

Economic feasibility considers whether or not an organization should expend the resources necessary to develop a system. Economic feasibility is different from profitability in that some systems might be economically feasible without being profitable (such as systems required by government regulations). While the organizational and technical feasibilities can be meaningful for evaluating a single alternative (do nothing, improve existing, develop, and so on) on its own, it is customary to compare the economic feasibilities of a number of alternatives together. To be able to compare alternatives, each economic feasibility evaluation should consider the same categories of costs and benefits. Where costs or benefits do not apply to a particular alternative, they should be recorded with a value of zero rather than ignored. This will assure decision makers that they have been considered in the evaluation.

Economic feasibility often goes beyond conducting a cost-benefit analysis of the development of a system. It should consider the complete range of effects that the development might have on an organization. These include both:

- The potential for profit that would be achieved by developing the application
- The potential for loss if the application is not developed

Economic feasibility should consider the complete range of effects that the development decision might have on an organization. Focusing on a single unit or a small group of units in an organization may give a misleading picture of the actual economic feasibility of an application to a given organization. Organization-wide systems need organization-wide cost-benefit analyses.

Some information systems may redefine the financial relations between an organization and others with which it interacts. Many information systems may affect other entities outside the organization. In some cases, costs (such as providing input data) may be off-loaded to suppliers or benefits charged (as value-added services) to customers.

Determining economic feasibility involves forecasting what might be and should not be limited to what currently exists. At the same time it has to be realistic. Economic feasibility involves identifying and evaluating the proposed costs and benefits of a given system and deciding whether the benefits are likely to be worth the associated costs. It is impossible to accurately determine actual future costs and benefits, especially early in a development project. Thus, it is impossible to guarantee that benefits will actually outweigh costs. Because of the uncertainty with future costs and benefits, it is better to use cost-benefit analyses to identify ranges of possible results rather than to try to rely on a single expected value.

NOTE: The following discussion is not meant to contradict or supersede any more advanced finance, economic, or accounting discussions of whether or not an investment is economically justified. Rather, this discussion provides a brief introduction to economic feasibility as it is usually applied to information systems development.

Find references to further sources of information about various economic feasibility issues in the Chapter 6 Cyber Supplement.

6.2.5.1 Determining Economic Feasibility

There is a difference between determining economic feasibility and determining profitability. Cost-benefit analysis focuses on profitability. A single cost-benefit analysis by itself can be misleading. It is important to compare the cost-benefit analyses of different alternatives (including the alternative of doing nothing).

To be economically feasible, a system has to:

- Cost less than the maximum amount available for expenditure—if it costs too much, then you probably can't consider it even if it might provide excellent profitability
- Exceed the minimum desired benefits—if it doesn't meet these basic expectations, then it's probably unacceptable no matter how cheap it is
- Meet any (optional) profitability expectations—which may not be relevant for systems that are required by law or by senior management, regardless of their profitability

As with the different components of operational feasibility it may be useful for us to try to get a general idea of how feasible a proposed system is. This can range from:

- Infeasible—implementation will result in catastrophic consequences
- Feasible but with notable difficulties—implementation is possible, but these difficulties will have to be overcome to achieve the full set of expected benefits
- Readily feasible—implementation is both possible and desirable

6.2.5.2 A Quick Evaluation of Feasibility

The following procedure can be used as a quick method for identifying projects that are very obviously not feasible. It is not sufficient, however, to determine that a project is truly feasible.

A rough evaluation of economic feasibility can be done by:

- Identifying major categories of costs and benefits
- Evaluating each category in terms of its potential magnitude (using the same relative scale of magnitude for both costs and benefits)
- Comparing the magnitude of costs and benefits

Significant costs and benefits can directly affect the viability of an overall organization.

- If significant costs or benefits are involved:
  - If significant benefits can be achieved without significant costs, then the system is readily feasible
  - If significant costs are not fully matched by significant benefits, then the proposed system is infeasible

- Wherever significant costs are involved even where they are matched by significant benefits, the best that can be expected is that the system is feasible with notable difficulties
  - Where a number of significant costs and benefits are involved, further investigation may be warranted to determine their relative magnitude

Major costs and benefits directly affect the profitability of an organization but are not expected to determine its viability. They may, however, have a major impact on particular organizational units within the organization or on the fulfillment of goals and objectives of the organization.

- If major costs are not matched by major or significant benefits, then the system will either be infeasible or feasible with notable difficulties.
- If major benefits can be achieved without major or significant costs, then the system is readily feasible.

Minor costs and benefits do not have a major effect on the profitability of an organization but may effect the profitability of a unit within the organization.

- If minor costs are matched by minor benefits, then the system will probably be feasible with notable difficulties.

NOTE: Feasibility studies are often expected to do more than determine financial feasibility and expected profitability. Thus, the following discussion will go beyond just identifying costs and benefits to some general approaches to formal cost-benefit analysis.

6.2.5.3 Costs and Benefits

Cost-benefit analysis (CBA) is a widely used method for "objectively" evaluating financial feasibility/profitability. However, it's "objectivity" is limited to the accuracy of the estimates it uses. While the accuracy of these estimates varies widely, individual costs and benefits are often classified as either tangible or intangible, depending on whether their accuracy is expected to be high or low.

Tangible Costs and Benefits

Tangible costs and benefits are those costs and benefits which have a readily identifiable price. Tangible costs and benefits often occur at a single location within an organization.

Typical tangible costs include:

- Development costs (company personnel; consultants; development systems; computer processing; supplies; overhead; start-up costs)
- Operating costs (personnel; hardware; software support and maintenance; supplies; communications; overhead)

Typical tangible benefits include:

- Cost savings (reduction in operating costs)
- Improved profitability (increased sales; increased profit/sale; improved cash flow)

Intangible Costs and Benefits

Intangible costs and benefits are those costs and benefits that are difficult to measure or estimate in monetary terms. Intangible costs and benefits often are spread across an organization. The value of intangibles depends on company goals and objectives.

Typical intangible costs include:

- Disruptions in, or lack of, information flow
- Decreases in employee/customer satisfaction

Typical intangible benefits include:

- Increases in information flow
- Increases in employee/customer satisfaction
- Improved decision making
- Improved organizational future

Despite the difficulty in evaluating intangibles, it is important to consider their impact in any determination of financial feasibility. Thus, monetary estimates are often made of intangible costs and benefits and treated as tangibles despite the uncertainty of their actual value.

Determining Costs and Benefits

Either a computer professional or a management accountant may conduct a cost-benefit analysis. In either case this person is acting as a developer rather than a user.

- Developers should, with input from the stakeholders, determine the categories of potential costs and benefits to be considered.
- Developers may provide "expert estimates" of the development and operating costs involved in various alternatives.
- Developers should not provide the estimates of benefits or "lost opportunity costs" used in the analysis, which should be provided by the users.

Considering "Doing Nothing"

It is always important to consider doing nothing as a base case for comparison with other alternatives. The option of doing nothing often should not be considered as having zero costs and benefits.

There is often an existing system with its own operating costs and its own benefits. These costs and benefits need to be "objectively" evaluated to consider the impact if the system didn't exist at all (if it were removed or turned off or if use was forbidden).

Existing systems may have problems that result in a number of negative benefits (costs). These may include:

- The costs of errors incurred by the existing system
- The costs of disruptions in other activities caused by the existing system
- The costs of working around the existing system
- The costs of ongoing maintenance and support (if not openly added to the budgeted operating costs)

Where there is no existing e-Commerce system, as with many proposed e-Commerce systems, an organization may still face a number of potential costs with related systems and/or operations. Rather than claiming "savings" as a benefit of proposed alternatives, it is useful to recognize the actual costs and benefits associated with each system. For example, where the proposed *Savor the Cup* system will reduce the cost of sales representatives directly servicing customers, it is appropriate:

- To record the current cost of sales representatives directly servicing customers in the cost-benefit analysis of the existing system
- To record the anticipated costs of sales representatives continuing to directly service customers in the cost-benefit analysis of the proposed e-Commerce alternative

Surplus Value

In many cases when a new system is considered, it is credited with the surplus value of the system it replaces as a one-time benefit. However, with information systems there seldom is any surplus value because:

- No one will buy old software, data, etc.
- There may be no one to buy old hardware
- The existing hardware/software may still be needed for some other application and so cannot be eliminated

Surplus value is not necessarily (and seldom is) equal to the depreciated book value. Depending on the actual age of a system, it might still be eligible for some amount of depreciation, where taxes are payable by an organization. In either case the values are not likely to be significant in an initial feasibility study.

The Value-Cost Relationship (Also known as the Law of Diminishing Returns)
- As you increase quality, the values (benefits) reach a maximum.
- As you increase cost, the quality reaches a maximum.
- The maximum increase in value per unit cost is reached at some point below the maximum cost or value.
- The 80/20 rule states that "you get 80% of the benefits for the first 20% of the investment."

In other words, it's seldom financially feasible to go for the most "super-duper" deluxe system with all the bells and whistles. The understanding of this relationship encourages the development of a relatively basic system that focuses on achieving the most significant benefits and/or competitive advantages, and that provides a basis for future developments to achieve additional benefits and/or competitive advantages. Where a relatively complex alternative is found financially infeasible, further consideration should be given to potentially feasible subsets of that alternative.

Uncertainty

How can you be sure about the accuracy of the dollar values in an analysis?
    You can be more certain about:

- Purchase prices of hardware and software (they usually go down if anywhere)
- Purchase prices of fixed contracts over the life of the contract
- Current salaries and costs of capital (interest rates)

You can be less certain about:

- Project development costs
- Future salaries and costs of capital
- Any anticipated surplus values
- Almost all benefits

Typically, estimated values exist in a range, not as fixed values. Accuracy in financial estimates can be improved by developing more detailed estimates and by basing estimates on documented costs and benefits. However, estimates are still estimates until they have been proved right or wrong and become history.

6.2.5.4 Methods for Conducting Cost-Benefit Analyses

There are a number of methods that may be used to conduct cost-benefit analyses, including:

- Payback period, which is a simple method for tangible costs and benefits
- Net present value (NPV), which is the preferred basic method for tangible costs and benefits
- Sensitivity analysis, which involves variations of NPV calculations to allow for uncertainty
- Attribute analysis, which is a method that includes intangibles

The following briefly summarizes how these methods can be used and some of the problems with using them.

Payback Period

Payback period is also known as break-even point analysis. The formulas for calculating payback period are:

Payback period = Development costs / Annual savings
Annual savings = Annual benefits − Annual operating costs

Organizations that use payback period generally will have a standard time that they use in determining whether a development is economically feasible or not.
Problems with payback period include:

- It deals only with tangibles, requiring forced estimates to be made of the value of intangibles, if they are to be considered at all
- It relies on estimates of costs and benefits
- It assumes uniform operating costs and benefits
- It ignores the time value of money (interest) even though most costs come early and most benefits come late
- It assumes that the system will last long enough to break even
- It doesn't provide a common basis for comparing alternative systems

Net Present Value (NPV)

NPV is also known as discounted cash flow. Formulas for calculating NPV include:

Net present value = Sum over years $i = 1$ to N of the [(Costs year i −
    Benefits year i) * Discount rate for year i]
Discount rate for year $i = 1 / ((1 +$ annual interest rate) $**i$)

NOTES:

- i is the number of years from the start of the project; thus i starts at zero.
- All costs and benefits in a given year (time period) are treated as if they are incurred at the start of that year (time period).
- Annual costs and benefits should consider expected inflation.

Organizations that use NPV may set particular criteria for determining whether or not a development is economically feasible. This criterion might require that:

- A positive NPV be at least some fraction of the total cost of development
- A positive NPV occurs when using an annual interest rate that includes both the expected cost of money and some expected amount of profit

Problems with NPV include:

- It deals only with tangibles, requiring forced estimates must be made of the value of intangibles, if they are to be considered at all
- It relies on estimates of costs and benefits
- It assumes uniform, or at least predictable, interest rates
- It assumes that the system will last long enough to break even
- It doesn't consider what would happen if estimates aren't accurate

Sensitivity Analysis

Sensitivity analysis is a variation on NPV that determines a range of NPV's rather than just a single one. Formulas for sensitivity analysis include:

Calculate three NPVs instead of just one
- for Optimistic use (lowest costs and highest benefits) then dream on
- for Expected use (expected costs and expected benefits)
- for Pessimistic use (highest costs and lowest benefits)
where
lowest is a value that will be exceeded 95% of the time
expected is a value that will be exceeded 50% of the time
highest is a value that will be exceeded 5% of the time

To perform sensitivity analysis:

- Identify factors that are significant in their impact and uncertain in their costs
- Establish the range of uncertainty (5% to 95%) for each factor. For less-accurate "quick and dirty" estimates, increase factors by 10% (or some other suitable percentage).
- Recalculate expected NPV using values at the extremes

Feasibility decisions can consider the range (from optimistic to pessimistic) of NPVs rather than just on expected NPV's:

- Even with sensitivity analysis it is never possible to be certain that it is readily feasible
- An alternative can be considered "feasible" only if all of the range is positive and this option outperforms other options

- An alternative can be considered "feasible with difficulties" if this option out-performs other options, especially if it's expected and optimistic NPVs are positive. When pessimistic NPVs indicate that a project that is expected to be profitable may lose money, the factors that might lead to a loss can be identified and should be carefully controlled.
- An alternative can be considered "not feasible" if the expected NPV is negative and there are other alternatives with better NPVs

Advanced sensitivity analysis can involve:

- Doing a series of (optimistic and pessimistic) NPVs varying only one factor at a time, keeping the others at their expected values
- Determining how sensitive the final outcome is to each factor
- Investigating how to limit the variance of the most sensitive factors to their more favorable possibilities
- Redoing regular sensitivity analysis based on revised sensitivity limits

Problems with sensitivity analysis (which are mostly the same as most of the problems with NPV) include:

- It deals only with tangibles, requiring forced estimates to be made of the value of intangibles, if they are to be considered at all
- It relies on estimates of costs and benefits
- It assumes uniform, or at least predictable, interest rates
- It assumes that the system will last long enough to break even
- The ranges of optimistic to pessimistic of two or more alternatives under consideration may (and often do) overlap, indicating that there is uncertainty as to which should be preferred

Attribute Analysis

Attribute analysis combines NPV of Costs (only) with a "points" rating of Benefits. It is most useful in situations where all alternatives will result in almost similar net profits (or all will result in similar net costs).

Steps and Formulas:

1. Calculate NPV of expected costs (the imprecision of attribute analysis doesn't justify three-figure sensitivity analysis, although sensitivity of individual costs may be done for planning project controls).
2. Select major benefit attributes (both tangible and intangible) to be considered.

NOTE: Essential attributes of a system are not included because they must be provided by any potential system that is considered as feasible.

3. Assign weights (ranking the relative importance) for each attribute based on the needs and priorities of the user. The higher the weight, the more important the attribute.
4. Rate each proposed system in terms of how well it provides the attribute from 0 (very poor or nonexistent) to 10 (excellent).

5. Calculate the weighted ratings for the attributes of each proposal by multiplying the weighting of the attribute by the rating for the given proposal.
6. Calculate the sum of the weighted ratings for each proposal.
7. Calculate the Benefit/NPV Cost for each proposal (using the results from steps 1 to 6).
8. Rank proposals on the basis of this ratio.

Example:

Consider two people, Terry and Tom, each wanting to select a mode of transportation to use over the next five years. Compare their considerations of buying a new car, a used car, or taking taxis. The expected NPV costs (calculated elsewhere) are:

New Car = 20,000   Used Car = 10,000   Taxi = 12,000

Because different people have different priorities and may perceive attributes differently, an attribute analysis may yield different recommendations for different people.

Terry, whose analysis is shown in Table 6-1, isn't as fussy about having his own new car as Tom, whose analysis is shown in Table 6-2. This shows both in their weightings of the relative importance of individual attributes and in the way they rate these attributes for each option.

Even after doing the above analysis, a taxi still seems the best for both Terry and Tom. However, a consideration of the number of significant digits in these calculations suggests that the "Benefits/1000 NPV" should not be considered to be as precise as they appear in these calculations. Both the weightings and the ratings only have one significant digit and thus this result should be rounded to one signif-

Table 6-1   Terry's Attribute Analysis of Transportation Alternatives

Terry's Analysis		New		Used		Taxi	
Attribute	weight	rating	wt. * rt.	rating	wt. * rt.	rating	wt. * rt.
reliability	2	9	18	7	14	9	18
ease of use	2	8	16	7	14	10	20
newness	1	10	10	0	0	4	4
initial cost	2	2	4	6	12	10	20
certainty of operating cost	2	7	14	2	4	6	12
speediness	1	10	10	9	9	7	7
	Sum of benefits		72		53		81
	NPV costs		20,000		10,000		12,000
	Benefits/ 1000 NPV		3.6		5.3		6.75
	Ranking		3		2		1

Table 6-2 Tom's Attribute Analysis of Transportation Alternatives

Tom's Analysis		New		Used		Taxi	
Attribute	weight	rating	wt. * rt.	rating	wt. * rt.	rating	wt. * rt.
reliability	5	9	45	5	25	7	35
ease of use	3	10	30	7	21	5	15
newness	5	10	50	0	0	3	15
initial cost	3	3	9	6	18	10	30
certainty of operating cost	5	9	45	2	10	4	20
speediness	1	10	10	9	9	5	5
	Sum of benefits		193		83		120
	NPV costs		20,000		10,000		12,000
	Benefits/ 1000 NPV		9.7		8.3		10.0
	Ranking		2*		3		1

icant digit as well. When that is done there may not be any significant difference between a new car and a taxi for Tom, leaving the final decision up to his preference, which will likely favor the new car option. Problems with this approach include:

- It suffers from a lack of precision and thus may not produce significant differences (as in Tom's case)
- Very different results can arise from different opinions as to the weights and ratings
- People have to be willing to accept the results of such an analysis

6.3 CONDUCTING FEASIBILITY STUDIES

6.3.1 Conducting Feasibility Studies in Organizations

There is a considerable variance in the extent to which different organizations make use of feasibility studies.

- Some organizations consider feasibility studies as expensive cost items that are only required if there is significant doubt about a number of competing alternatives. In these organizations, managers tend to make decisions, including the establishment of development projects, without using feasibility studies very often. Feasibility studies may only be used where major disagreements arise between managers. Once a project is started, it is assumed in the organization to be feasible.
- Some organizations rely heavily on feasibility studies to decide between alternatives as well as to evaluate individual alternatives. They use feasibility studies to provide "objective" justifications for major decisions, including the establishment of development projects. They may even use updated feasibility studies at

points within a development project to reevaluate whether or not the project is leading toward a system that will be successful.

- Some organizations may use feasibility studies to evaluate potential development difficulties that require particular attention. They use feasibility studies to help focus development efforts on those areas that:
  - Have the greatest impact on a project's success
  - Can be improved the most easily

If properly utilized, an initial feasibility study can follow an initial investigation and provide significant guidance to the further phases of development. If properly maintained, an ongoing feasibility study can provide a useful project assessment.

6.3.2   Student Assignment—Conducting a Feasibility Study

If you have done the previous assignments, you should have a good general idea of what your application involves. However, you will need to develop a better understanding as the project progresses. Developing a feasibility study will help you to:

- Confirm that you understand the basics of your application
- Confirm that you can obtain additional information about it when required
- Confirm that you have an application that will work for your project in this course
- Confirm that you can work effectively and efficiently as a team

6.3.2.1   Executive Summary

Your assignment should start with an executive summary that highlights the main points in your feasibility study and links to particular pages with detailed answers.

A good executive summary has the following attributes:

- May include a very brief introduction to what a report is about (if the title isn't sufficient)
- Presents a brief summary (that is understandable and complete in and of itself, not just a list of stuff) of the important information contained in the main report
- Presents a brief set of recommendations based on this report
- Invites the readers to consult the report for further details

A good executive summary should not have the following attributes:

- Brag or complain about the work involved in producing the report
- Contain excessive details from the main report
- Provide just a list of names of topics discussed in the report (like a table of contents)
- Be longer than a printed page (for busy executives who don't have the time to look at all the details)

6.3.2.2   Identify Your Organization

Provide a basic set of assumptions about a realistic organization that might use the application you chose in your Chapter 4 assignment. These assumptions should include but need not be limited to:

- The general industry of which the organization is part
- The type of products and/or services the organization provides

- Whether or not the organization develops or only sells these products and/or services
- The size of the organization (e.g., 1 to 10, 10 to 100, 100 to 1,000, 1,000 to 10,000, 10,000+ employees)
- Where the organization is located (e.g., single location, province wide, nation wide, continent wide, intercontinental)
- Where the organization's customers/suppliers/members are located
- What competition your organization has

NOTE: You should not use an organization, existing or start-up, in the software industry. Your organization must provide products and/or services from some other industry.

6.3.2.3 Identifying Realistic Alternatives

Consider each of the following alternatives that could be followed with regard to your chosen application and your chosen organization:

- **Doing nothing** (different from what is currently done)—to be used as a base case.
- **Acquiring an existing system**—that is also available to your competition (be sure to provide a reference to where you found out about such a system).

NOTE: You don't need to find a commercially available package, but you do need to know what the state of the practice is for systems typically used for your application. (You need to consider this even though it would not result in a good basis for future assignments.)

- **Developing a basic system**—involving the developing of a basic version of a substantially new system that might be a starting point for further developments but is sufficiently useful to be considered on its own. This basic system should include sufficient competitive advantages to differentiate it from other existing systems.
- **Developing a deluxe system**—involving the developing of a deluxe version of a substantially new system that is significantly better than any existing system.

Describe briefly what would be involved for each of these alternatives for your chosen e-Commerce application for your organization. These descriptions should be sufficiently detailed to illustrate the significant differences between each of your alternatives. Make sure that each of your alternatives is realistic for the organization you assumed.

The expectation that your application go beyond existing systems does not provide justification for "cooking" the following feasibility study. The results of your feasibility study have to be realistic. If you find that your feasibility study makes the alternative of doing nothing or of acquiring an existing system look preferable to both of the other alternatives, then it means that you have not found sufficiently important and realistic competitive advantages to be included in these other alternatives. It may also indicate that the application you have chosen may be a difficult one to continue with and that you may wish to consider choosing a different application to use for the remainder of the assignments.

6.3.2.4 Considering Their Feasibilities

Analyze the feasibilities of each of the four alternatives identified above in terms of:

- Stakeholders
- Organizations and their relations to one another
- The organization's external environment
- The competitive environment
- Government regulations
- Processing feasibility
- Data feasibility

6.3.2.5 Rank Ordering the Feasible Alternatives

Evaluate the results of your feasibility analysis, discarding the infeasible alternatives and rank ordering the remaining alternatives. Provide a brief justification of how you arrived at your ranking.

6.4 AN EXAMPLE OF A FEASIBILITY STUDY

The following is an example of a complete feasibility study for *Savor the Cup*.

- When a difference occurs between alternatives, the complete evaluation of each alternative is given, even if it involves a considerable amount of repetition, in order to ensure that each alternative has been considered fully and fairly on its own, rather than just in comparison to other alternatives.
- Where there is no significant difference between alternatives, the first alternative will be discussed completely, and other alternatives will just refer to the first discussion and repeat the similar conclusion.
- In order to help the reader recognize differences in the alternatives, the study is organized in order of type of feasibility.

Although this example is lengthy, it is relatively short compared with the amount of actual development effort that it represents. It is intended to get the reader off to a good start. Examples in future chapters will only deal with select parts of the further development efforts for the *Savor the Cup* system.

6.4.1 The Alternatives

6.4.1.1 Doing Nothing Different

Business is good for *Savor the Cup*. It has a significant share of its market and little current threat of competition. However, its growth has leveled off recently, and it recognizes that it might be vulnerable to e-Commerce based competition in the future.

6.4.1.2 Acquiring an Existing System

Various software companies produce generic e-Commerce sites that can be used to sell and service a variety of products. They often provide consulting services to modify and maintain the site for different companies. There are a number that could be used by *Savor the Cup* to get a start in e-Commerce.

6.4.1.3   Developing a Basic System

Savor the Cup could develop a basic e-Commerce system to serve the needs of customers, suppliers, and organization employees. By developing its own basic system it could:

- Better customize the system to *Savor the Cup's* style of doing business
- Provide a basis for further developments

A basic system could go beyond just selling products to helping form the basis for future e-Commerce developments.

- Customers would be able to order and pay for coffee beans and equipment on-line.
- The suppliers of the coffee beans and the equipment would be able to access the application and preview a list of the organization's product needs.
- Organization employees would be able to access customer order information and use the application to keep track of orders, suppliers, and customer-specific blends.
- This basic system will provide the traditional services of the organization on-line while also expanding to on-line supplier contacts, moving into equipment supply and exclusive blending.

6.4.1.4   Developing a Deluxe System

The deluxe system of this application would provide a wide range of services to customers, suppliers, and organization employees. Customers would use the e-Commerce system to:

- Order and pay for fresh-roasted coffee beans and equipment on-line, with the option of creating exclusive blends
- Get information about coffee, coffee shops, and many other areas related to coffee products
- Arrange for special services by *Savor the Cup* employees that would be provided for a fee

Other features of this deluxe system would include:

- The system would manage the filling of these orders for customers, including scheduling the range of interactions that involve employees of *Savor the Cup*.
- Employees would be encouraged to get as many customers as possible using the deluxe system. The range of free services to customers would be expected to decrease.
- The suppliers of the coffee beans and equipment would be expected to interact with the organization through the e-Commerce system, determining the organization's supply needs and working with the organization to ensure top-quality products.

NOTE: A deluxe system need not change the nature of an organization drastically, like the one proposed in this example. *Savor the Cup's* senior management was involved in specifying what they would expect from each of the alternatives. They specified what they would want in a deluxe system based on their limited perceptions of e-Commerce. There are many other alternatives that could and perhaps should have been considered. This example is limited, however, to the four alternatives just discussed.

6.4.2   Stakeholder Feasibility

6.4.2.1   Doing Nothing Different Stakeholder Feasibility

There are no major challenges identified with the current operations of *Savor the Cup.* It is readily feasible for *Savor the Cup* to continue meeting the needs of its stakeholders in the manner it now does.

6.4.2.2   Acquiring an Existing System Stakeholder Feasibility

- External product sources would not be directly affected, but might see an increased demand in their goods.
- New potential customers might be reached by the system. It will be important to be able to identify those potential and new customers who require personalized servicing and to allow them to deal directly with sales representatives.
- Current customers should have the option of using the system or dealing directly with sales representatives as they now do.
- Purchasing and manufacturing may be affected by an increase of small orders. Demands on the logistics staff will increase.
- Sales staff will be most affected. They may fear being replaced entirely by on-line sales. They need to be reassured that there will be a continuing role for them. Some of them may take on new on-line responsibilities. It is essential that the on-line system not be placed in competition with the existing sales organization.
- Administration will have to deal with on-line sales as it would with a new branch operating slightly differently from the other existing branches.

While a number of changes to stakeholders will need to be made, they are feasible with some difficulties.

6.4.2.3   Developing a Basic System Stakeholder Feasibility

- External product sources would be encouraged to use this system to obtain current information from *Savor the Cup* about its product needs. The suppliers will be able to determine whether their products meet the organization's needs and can contact the organization to further establish a business relationship. This application will also be useful to current suppliers, who can access the application to see what products need to be sent when and how the supplier can change its production to meet the needs of the organization.
- New potential customers might be reached by the system. It will be important to be able to identify those potential and new customers who require personalized servicing and to allow them to deal directly with sales representatives.

- Current customers should have the option of using the system or dealing directly with sales representatives as they now do. The system would also provide brief instructions for equipment and the employees using the equipment to ensure the best quality of coffee is generated for their customers. This will not be as in-depth as company-specific consulting but will be very useful to customers. In this way, the organization is going beyond the role of supplying equipment and products. By developing its own system, *Savor the Cup* can ensure that it implements *Savor the Cup's* current style of selling and servicing customers.
- Purchasing will use the system to keep track of supply requirements and post lists on the Web for supplier access.
- Manufacturing may be affected by an increase of small orders. Demands on the logistics staff will increase.
- Sales staff will be most affected. They may fear being replaced entirely by on-line sales. They need to be reassured that there will be a continuing role for them. Some of them may take on new on-line responsibilities. It is essential that the on-line system not be placed in competition with the existing sales organization.
- Administration will have to deal with on-line sales as it would with a new branch operating slightly differently from the other existing branches.

This basic system is feasible with difficulties from the stakeholder point of view. It will benefit all users who are willing to learn and to use the new system.

6.4.2.4 Developing a Deluxe System Stakeholder Feasibility

- External product sources would be expected to use this system to obtain current information from *Savor the Cup*. The suppliers will be able to determine if their products meet the organization's needs and can contact the organization to further establish a business relationship. Once a relationship is established it will be conducted primarily via e-Commerce. Many current suppliers may not be ready or willing to do business in this manner.
- New potential customers might be reached by the system. It will be important to be able to identify those potential and new customers who require personalized servicing and to inform them of the consulting services available from *Savor the Cup*. Potential customers are less likely to become customers if they have to pay for assistance right at the start.
- Current customers should have the option of using the system or dealing directly with sales representatives as they now do. However, they will be encouraged to use the system. The system would also provide a large amount of information for the customers. Further information and specialized services will be available from *Savor the Cup* consultants on a fee-for-services basis. Many current customers may not be prepared to pay for services that they have come to expect.
- Purchasing will use the system to manage interactions with suppliers. This will pose difficulties if there is a decrease in willing suppliers.
- Manufacturing and logistics will be scheduled by the system to provide just-in-time shipment of products to customers. This scheduling assistance may be welcomed if properly introduced.

- Sales staff will be most affected. Some of them may take on new on-line responsibilities. Many others will be reassigned to become consultants who are available to customers on a fee-for-services basis. A limited number of branch sales staff will be retained to deal with customers. Some staff will resist the changes or be unable to fit into the new structure.
- Administration will have to deal with major shifts in the nature of the organization. Too many changes introduced, at one time, may not be able to be managed effectively.

There are too many significant stakeholder difficulties with this proposed deluxe system. It appears to be infeasible as currently envisioned.

6.4.3   Organization Relations Feasibility

6.4.3.1   Doing Nothing Different Organization Relations Feasibility

- All of *Savor the Cup's* departments are currently cooperating to ensure an efficient flow of order taking, roasting, blending, packaging, and delivery. These changes may alienate departments, leading to a decrease in this cooperation.
- All of *Savor the Cup's* physical processing plants and offices around the world currently coordinate activities to provide customers with the most value for their money. Assistance in scheduling may help improve this coordination.
- *Savor the Cup* has good relations with its customers and suppliers which may be damaged by the major changes in relationships with this alternative.

It is readily feasible to continue with the current organizations and their relations.

6.4.3.2   Acquiring an Existing System Organization Relations Feasibility

- All of *Savor the Cup's* departments are currently cooperating to ensure an efficient flow of order taking, roasting, blending, packaging, and delivery. Information withholding is not a current problem and is not expected to become one.
- All of *Savor the Cup's* physical processing plants and offices around the world currently coordinate activities to provide customers with the most value for their money.
- *Savor the Cup* has good relations with its customers and suppliers. This alternative is not intended to change these, only to expand options for customers.
- *Savor the Cup* is used to establishing branches that each need to operate slightly differently in order to meet local cultural needs. However, it does not have multiple branches competing against one another.
  - It is important that new on-line branches complement rather than compete with local branches. This can be accomplished by crediting local branches with on-line sales, while charging them with their share of these sales. In this manner, the on-line sales will act as another sales representative in each branch.
  - Further efforts may be needed to ensure that individual sales representatives are not adversely affected by the on-line sales competing with them.

This alternative is feasible with difficulties for the current organizations and their relations.

6.4.3.3   Developing a Basic System Organization Relations Feasibility

- All of *Savor the Cup's* departments are currently cooperating to ensure an efficient flow of order taking, roasting, blending, packaging, and delivery. Information withholding is not a current problem and is not expected to become one.
- All of *Savor the Cup's* physical processing plants and offices around the world currently coordinate activities to provide customers with the most value for their money.
- *Savor the Cup* has good relations with its customers. This alternative is not intended to change these, only to expand options for customers.
- *Savor the Cup* has good relations with its suppliers. This alternative may put a strain on relations with suppliers who do not wish to use the new system. However, it may improve communications with a large number of suppliers and with additional potential suppliers.
- *Savor the Cup* is used to establishing branches that each need to operate slightly differently in order to meet local cultural needs. However, it does not have multiple branches competing against one another.
  - It is important that new on-line branches complement rather than compete with local branches. This can be accomplished by crediting local branches with on-line sales, while charging them with their share of these sales. In this manner, the on-line sales will act as another sales representative in each branch.
  - Further efforts may be needed to ensure that individual sales representatives are not adversely affected by the on-line sales competing with them.

This alternative is feasible with difficulties for the current organizations and their relations.

6.4.3.4   Developing a Deluxe System Organization Relations Feasibility

- All of *Savor the Cup's* departments are currently cooperating to ensure an efficient flow of order taking, roasting, blending, packaging, and delivery. Information withholding is not a current problem and is not expected to become one. However, this alternative could put a strain on cooperation by taking away some local autonomy that different departments currently have.
- All of *Savor the Cup's* physical processing plants and offices around the world currently coordinate activities to provide customers with the most value for their money. However, this alternative could put a strain on cooperation by taking away some local autonomy that plants and offices currently have.
- *Savor the Cup* has good relations with its customers. This alternative may change these relations (as already discussed in the consideration of stakeholder feasibility). As organizations are increasingly required to pay for services from *Savor the Cup,* they may be more willing to consider obtaining their products from its competitors.
- *Savor the Cup* has good relations with its suppliers. This alternative may put a strain on relations with suppliers who do not wish to use the new system. However, it may improve communications with a large number of suppliers and with additional potential suppliers. Supplier organizations would have to compete more actively and more often to do business with *Savor the Cup.* This will increase their cost of doing business and may lead to the end of their rela-

tionship with *Savor the Cup*. These difficulties will be most severe where a supplier has a unique product being sought by *Savor the Cup*.

- *Savor the Cup* is used to establishing branches that each need to operate slightly differently in order to meet local cultural needs. However, it does not have multiple branches competing against one another. Each branch currently works toward the same corporate-wide goals. By establishing consulting services, which are separate from sales, consultants may be torn between providing advice that is best for their customers and advice that is best for other parts of *Savor the Cup*. Such advice could include identifying cheaper sources of beans/equipment.

There are too many significant organization relations difficulties with this proposed deluxe system. It appears to be infeasible as currently envisioned.

6.4.4 Operational Reliability Feasibility

6.4.4.1 Doing Nothing Different Operational Reliability Feasibility

Savor the Cup has been operating quite successfully for some time now. There are no major problems with how the current system operates, thus it is readily feasible to continue with the current operations from a reliability perspective.

6.4.4.2 Acquiring an Existing System Operational Reliability Feasibility

One of the advantages of acquiring an existing system for *Savor the Cup* would be acquiring the necessary operational support to ensure the operational reliability of the system. It is expected that acquiring an existing system would be readily feasible in terms of operational reliability.

6.4.4.3 Developing a Basic System Operational Reliability Feasibility

Savor the Cup has both business and information systems experience that could help with the operational reliability of an e-Commerce system. However, the challenges of moving into e-Commerce can be expected to create some difficulties that will be new to the organization and its employees. The greatest challenge will be to evolve to meet changing expectations of its clients once it starts using the Web. Up to now, *Savor the Cup* and the systems it has used have remained quite stable. Thus, it is difficult to anticipate how the need for constant change will be handled. It is expected that developing a basic system will be feasible with difficulties in terms of operational reliability.

6.4.4.4 Developing a Deluxe System Operational Reliability Feasibility

Because of the nature of *Savor the Cup* and of the proposed systems, it is expected that developing a deluxe system may create more difficulties in maintaining operational reliability than developing a basic system. However, it is not believed that these difficulties are too great to overcome. Thus, it is expected that developing a deluxe system will be feasible with difficulties in terms of operational reliability.

6.4.5 External Environment Feasibility

In the past, the coffee industry has been "laid back" in terms of their attitude in demanding fresh, high-quality coffee. This applies to both consumers and vendors of coffee. The coffee industry is now more popular and profitable than it has ever been in the past. There are many small businesses whose main products are coffee and coffee-related beverages. If this current trend continues, the coffee business will be even more lucrative and more advantageous than it is now. If the current trend fades, *Savor the Cup* will need to find another opportunity for growth.

6.4.5.1   Doing Nothing Different External Environment Feasibility

Savor the Cup needs to respond to changing consumer trends. Its business has grown considerably thanks to the increase in interest in specialty coffees. While there are no signs of this interest waning, *Savor the Cup* needs to protect itself from any major switch in beverage preferences. It has made a conscious decision to avoid the bottled water and the soft drink markets because the shipping of heavy liquid products that are consumed as is (rather than custom brewed) would involve too drastic a change to its style of business. It is, however, carefully following the fortunes of the specialty tea industry, which it sees as the major potential product that might compete with coffee.

Continuing just with business as usual is feasible within its external environment as long as there is a high consumer interest in coffee.

6.4.5.2   Acquiring an Existing System External Environment Feasibility

This approach can make it easier for *Savor the Cup* to respond to changes in its external environment.

- Monitoring industry trends on the Web should be part of maintaining its e-Commerce presence.
- By establishing a format for doing e-Business, *Savor the Cup* can use this format to easily move into other complementary product lines, if and when it wishes.

It is expected that there are a number of potential customers who would be willing to make use of a *Savor the Cup* e-Commerce Web site. It is readily feasible to acquire an existing system that works within its external environment.

6.4.5.3   Developing a Basic System External Environment Feasibility

This approach can make it easier and faster for *Savor the Cup* to respond to changes in its external environment.

- Monitoring industry trends on the Web should be part of maintaining its e-Commerce presence.
- Developing a basic system will ensure that *Savor the Cup* has the technical skills to be able to quickly modify its Web site to respond to changing industry trends.
- By establishing a format for doing e-Business, *Savor the Cup* can use this format to easily move into other complementary product lines, if and when it wishes.
- By including suppliers and potential suppliers, *Savor the Cup* may be able to have a greater effect on the development of future trends in the industry.

It is expected that there are a number of potential customers who would be willing to make use of a *Savor the Cup* e-Commerce Web site. It is readily feasible to develop a basic system that works within its external environment.

6.4.5.4   Developing a Deluxe System External Environment Feasibility

There is no significant difference with regard to external environment feasibility between this option and the option of developing a basic system. It is feasible with difficulties for *Savor the Cup* to develop a deluxe system that works within its external environment.

6.4.6   Competitive Feasibility

6.4.6.1   Doing Nothing Different Competitive Feasibility

Savor the Cup has identified a market niche and has successfully remained the leader in it. Its main competitors are:

- Coffee house franchising organizations
- Coffee suppliers, who provide no additional services

To date, there has been no major competition. However, this could change quickly if a competitor established itself on the Web. Continuing just with business as usual is feasible with difficulties within the competitive environment.

6.4.6.2   Acquiring an Existing System Competitive Feasibility

Savor the Cup has identified a market niche and has successfully remained the leader in it. Its main competitors are:

- Coffee house franchising organizations
- Coffee suppliers, who provide no additional services

To date, there has been no major competition. However, this could change quickly if a competitor established itself on the Web. Adding this alternative to its existing operations is readily feasible with regards to its competitive environment.

6.4.6.3   Developing a Basic System Competitive Feasibility

Savor the Cup has identified a market niche and has successfully remained the leader in it. Its main competitors are:

- Coffee house franchising organizations
- Coffee suppliers, who provide no additional services

By developing the proposed basic system, *Savor the Cup* may work toward integrating its suppliers electronically to further strengthen its leadership in the industry.

By providing leadership in its industry, beyond merely selling its products on the Web, it will increase the cost of any potential competitors establishing themselves. To date, there has been no major competition. However, this could change quickly if a competitor established itself on the Web.

Competitive organizations would have access to most of the system (even if access controls were used to limit access to supplier-related portions) and be able to view the organization's current way of operating. The more operations that are put on the Web, the more that can be copied by existing and potential competitors. Because this is unavoidable, provisions should be made to continue expansion on the basic system to protect the competitive advantage that is developed by the use of the application.

Developing a basic system to add to its existing operations is feasible with difficulties with regards to its competitive environment.

6.4.6.4   Developing a Deluxe System Competitive Feasibility

Savor the Cup has identified a market niche and has successfully remained the leader in it. Its main competitors are:

- Coffee house franchising organizations
- Coffee suppliers, who provide no additional services

Developing the proposed deluxe system, *Savor the Cup* will be integrating its suppliers electronically to further strengthen its leadership in the industry.

Development of a complex e-Commerce system, which goes considerably beyond selling its products on the Web, will make it difficult and expensive for potential competitors to establish themselves.

Competitive organizations would have access to most of the system (even if access controls were used to limit access to supplier-related portions) and be able to view the organization's current way of operating. The more of these operations that are put on the Web, the more that can be copied by existing and potential competitors. Because this is unavoidable, provisions should be made to continue expansion on the basic system to protect the competitive advantage that is developed by the use of the application. Developing a deluxe system is feasible with difficulties with regards to its competitive environment.

6.4.7   Government Regulations Feasibility

6.4.7.1   Doing Nothing Different Government Regulations Feasibility

- *Savor the Cup* deals with the export and import regulations of the various countries in which they do business to ensure compliance with the government. Each country has its own export/import regulations, which the company follows.
- *Savor the Cup* ensures that the products of its suppliers are in compliance with local standards and continue to comply with the weights and measures acts of the different countries.
- *Savor the Cup* keeps updated with all of the tax rates and exchange rates so that its customers are charged correctly. It has to ensure that taxes are remitted to the proper government authorities.

It is readily feasible for *Savor the Cup* to continue complying with regulations.

6.4.7.2   Acquiring an Existing System Government Regulations Feasibility

- *Savor the Cup* deals with the export and import regulations of the various countries in which they do business to ensure compliance with the government. Each country has its own export/import regulations, which the company follows.
- *Savor the Cup* ensures that the products of its suppliers are in compliance with local standards and continue to comply with the weights and measures acts of the different countries.

- *Savor the Cup* keeps updated with all of the tax rates and exchange rates so that its customers are charged correctly. It has to ensure that taxes are remitted to the proper government authorities.

This alternative could expand the complexities involved in international sales.

- Currently, "local" branches handle most of the national regulations and taxes of each country that they serve. It may be easier to refer on-line sales to existing local branches for processing than to handle them centrally.
- On-line sales may grow to include countries not currently served by an existing branch. This will require gaining new expertise in national regulations.
- On-line sales would require the transmission of personal and/or corporate data across international borders, which may be subject to national regulations.

It is feasible with difficulties for *Savor the Cup* to comply with regulations in an existing system that it would acquire.

6.4.7.3 Developing a Basic System Government Regulations Feasibility

There is no significant difference with regard to government regulation feasibility between this option and the option of acquiring an existing system. It is feasible with difficulties for *Savor the Cup* to comply with regulations in a basic system that it would develop.

6.4.7.4 Developing a Deluxe System Government Regulations Feasibility

There is no significant difference with regard to government regulation feasibility between this option and the option of acquiring an existing system. It is feasible with difficulties for *Savor the Cup* to comply with regulations in a deluxe system that it would develop.

6.4.8   Processing Feasibility

6.4.8.1 Doing Nothing Different Processing Feasibility

This is readily feasible because *Savor the Cup* is already an international company with a world-renowned product.

6.4.8.2 Acquiring an Existing System Processing Feasibility

Companies in a wide range of industries are currently selling products on-line. It is readily feasible to obtain a generic e-Commerce system for use by *Savor the Cup*.

6.4.8.3 Developing a Basic System Processing Feasibility

Companies in a wide range of industries are currently having their own e-Commerce systems developed. It is readily feasible to develop a basic e-Commerce system for use by *Savor the Cup*.

6.4.8.4 Developing a Deluxe System Processing Feasibility

A few companies currently have similar e-Commerce systems developed. Each portion of the proposed deluxe system can be found being used by a number of companies. There is nothing unusual involved in the processing requirements. It is readily feasible to develop a deluxe e-Commerce system for use by *Savor the Cup.*

6.4.9 Data Feasibility

6.4.9.1 Doing Nothing Different Processing Feasibility

This is readily feasible because *Savor the Cup* is already an international company with a world-renowned product.

6.4.9.2 Acquiring an Existing System Data Feasibility

Savor the Cup already has the necessary data for order placement, order filling, and delivery from its operations in the traditional market. These data includes processing requirements, order amounts, customer locations, delivery times, and so on. Therefore it will be easy to switch to the e-Business market.

Customers will retain the option of ordering from a sales representative or ordering on-line. Thus, willingness to order electronically and submit their contact and credit card information should not be a problem.

All inputs are available, so the alternative is readily feasible with respect to data feasibility.

6.4.9.3 Developing a Basic System Data Feasibility

There is no significant difference with regard to data feasibility between this option and the option of acquiring an existing system. All inputs are available, so the alternative of developing a basic system is readily feasible with respect to data feasibility.

6.4.9.4 Developing a Deluxe System Data Feasibility

There is no significant difference with regard to data feasibility between this option and the option of acquiring an existing system. As all inputs are available, the alternative of developing a deluxe system is readily feasible with respect to data feasibility.

6.4.10 System Development Feasibility

6.4.10.1 Doing Nothing Different System Development Feasibility

This option does not involve any major development and therefore is readily feasible.

6.4.10.2 Acquiring an Existing System Development Feasibility

Savor the Cup will have to assign key staff to work with a software firm to obtain and customize a suitable e-Commerce system. Some of these staff will be required to permanently monitor the system and maintain its sales information. This should not be a problem because *Savor the Cup* has a large and well-qualified staff who are quite flexible and willing to try new things. System development involving acquiring an existing system is feasible with minor difficulties (involved in training the chosen staff).

6.4.10.3 Developing a Basic System Development Feasibility

Savor the Cup has no current experience with e-Commerce. However, it has a good information technology section of its administration, which is used to adapting to new technologies. System development of a basic system is feasible with difficulties.

6.4.10.4 Developing a Deluxe System Development Feasibility

Savor the Cup has no current experience with e-Commerce. Despite its good information technology section, the proposed deluxe system poses too great of a challenge for the current capabilities. System development of a deluxe system is infeasible.

6.4.11 Economic Feasibility

6.4.11.1 Doing Nothing Different Economic Feasibility

Categories of Costs	Significant	Major	Minor
Development/maintenance costs			X
Getting existing customers to use the system			0
Attracting new customers		X	
Disruptions to staff			0
Additional staff to handle the system			0
Legal exposures of new markets			0
Threat of competitors gaining market share by going on-line		X	

NOTE: While it hasn't occurred yet, given the increasing growth in e-Commerce in all fields, it can be expected to occur in the near future. Therefore, a cost has been assigned to this exposure.

Categories of Benefits	Significant	Major	Minor
Expanded sales and customer base			0
Revenue from consulting services			0
Expanded supplier base and increased flexibility in dealing with suppliers			0
Experience with e-Commerce to prepare to handle anticipated new competition			0
Improved handling of orders that do not require any special assistance			0
Customers are loyal to *Savor the Cup* because they are currently satisfied with its range of services to them			X

Currently doing nothing different is readily feasible, as the success of the organization demonstrates without a feasibility study. The threat of future e-Commerce competition presents difficulties to its maintained feasibility.

6.4.11.2   Acquiring an Existing System Economic Feasibility

Categories of Costs	Significant	Major	Minor
Development/maintenance costs			
• Purchasing		X	
• Customizing		X	
• Operating		X	
Getting existing customers to use the system		X	
Attracting new customers			X
Disruptions to staff			X
Additional staff to handle the new system		X	
Legal exposures of new markets			X
Threat of competitors gaining market share by going on-line		X	

Categories of Benefits	Significant	Major	Minor
Expanded sales and customer base	X		
Revenue from consulting services			0
Expanded supplier base and increased flexibility in dealing with suppliers			0
Experience with e-Commerce to prepare to handle anticipated new competition		X	
Improved handling of orders that do not require any special assistance			X
Customers are loyal to *Savor the Cup* because they are currently satisfied with its range of services to them		X	

When considering the magnitude of the costs and benefits of acquiring an existing system to go on-line with the business, the benefits outweigh the costs if the anticipated expansion of sales and the customer base is realized. As a result, this option appears readily feasible with respect to economic feasibility, provided there is money available to finance this activity.

6.4.11.3   Developing a Basic System Economic Feasibility

Categories of Costs	Significant	Major	Minor
Development/maintenance costs			
• Developing		XXX	
• Operating		X	
Getting existing customers and suppliers to use the system			X
Attracting new customers and suppliers			X
Disruptions to staff			X
Additional staff to handle the new system		X	
Legal exposures of new markets			X
Threat of competitors gaining market share by going on-line			X

Categories of Benefits	Significant	Major	Minor
Expanded sales and customer base	X		
Revenue from consulting services			X
Expanded supplier base and increased flexibility in dealing with suppliers		X	
Experience with e-Commerce to prepare to handle anticipated new competition		X	
Improved handling of orders that do not require any special assistance		X	
Customers are loyal to *Savor the Cup* because they are currently satisfied with its range of services to them	X		

It is expected that developing the proposed basic system may have a significant effect on retaining the customer loyalty that has been central to the success of *Savor the Cup*. When considering the magnitude of the costs and benefits of developing a basic system to go on-line with the business, the benefits outweigh the costs. As a result, this option appears readily feasible with respect to economic feasibility, provided there is money available to finance this activity.

6.4.11.4 Developing a Deluxe System Economic Feasibility

Categories of Costs	Significant	Major	Minor
Development/maintenance costs			
• Developing	X		
• Operating		X	
Getting existing customers and suppliers to use the system		X	
Attracting new customers and suppliers		X	
Disruptions to staff	X		
Additional staff to handle the new system		X	
Legal exposures of new markets			X
Threat of competitors gaining market share by going on-line			X

Categories of Benefits	Significant	Major	Minor
Expanded sales and customer base		X	
Revenue from consulting services		X	
Expanded supplier base and increased flexibility in dealing with suppliers		X	
Experience with e-Commerce to prepare to handle anticipated new competition		X	
Improved handling of orders that do not require any special assistance		X	
Customers are loyal to *Savor the Cup* because they are currently satisfied with its range of services to them		X	

It is uncertain whether developing a deluxe system can generate sufficient new revenues to cover the significant costs that its development will incur. It appears that it is infeasible economically.

6.4.12   Overall Analysis of Alternatives

6.4.12.1   Overall Analysis of Doing Nothing Different

It appears that doing nothing different is feasible with difficulties. It is expected that as time progresses these difficulties will increase.

6.4.12.2   Overall Analysis of Acquiring an Existing System

It appears that acquiring an existing system is feasible with difficulties. It is expected that as time progresses these difficulties will increase. Acquiring an existing system is a feasible option for *Savor the Cup* to use quickly to develop a meaningful presence in the world of e-Commerce and to be able to gain some experience with e-Commerce before attempting to develop its own system.

6.4.12.3   Overall Analysis of Developing a Basic System

It appears that developing a basic system is feasible with difficulties for starting an e-Business relatively quickly and with some additional competitive advantages.

6.4.12.4   Overall Analysis of Developing a Deluxe System

It appears that developing a deluxe system is infeasible given the current concept of what a deluxe system would involve. However, individual features proposed for the deluxe system should be individually analyzed because some of them may be not only feasible, but also highly beneficial. The major problems with the currently proposed deluxe system appear to be:

- It goes against the trends identified in other alternatives of increasing the helpfulness of *Savor the Cup* systems
- It would alienate many people by focusing on using technology rather than on serving people

6.5   CHALLENGES AND OPPORTUNITIES IN CONDUCTING FEASIBILITY STUDIES

The following are the most frequent problems encountered with feasibility studies. They are listed here to help you avoid them.

Challenges Due to a Lack of Understanding

- Some developers do not distinguish their alternatives sufficiently and/or do not consider a suitable array of alternatives.
- When some developers consider basic systems, they tend to focus on common features that do not sufficiently distinguish them from their competition. If there is nothing that would make them unique, then there is no reason to suspect that they will be used in favor over the systems of the organization's competition.
- Some developers rely on their own knowledge alone as a basis for all information in a feasibility study, without getting the appropriate guidance from users.

- Some developers treat feasibility studies as one-time activities that are only conducted between initial investigation and requirements analysis. They may fail to evaluate the effects of various changes in the project, in the organization, or in the organization's environment on the ongoing feasibility of a project.
- Some developers may consider conducting a feasibility study as all that is required to fulfill the needs for risk management of a project.

Challenges with Being Objective

- Some developers perform a feasibility study as if they had already picked out the best alternative rather than doing it in an unbiased way and then using its results to pick the best alternative.
- Some developers decide that an alternative is infeasible just because they want the alternative to be infeasible (e.g., stating that doing nothing is technically infeasible when, if they are already doing it, then it is obviously technically possible).
- Some developers go into great detail on the alternative they are choosing but lack detail in the other alternatives.
- Some developers use different methods, which are not comparable, to evaluate different alternatives.
- Some developers attribute common costs/benefits to only some of the alternatives to which they apply.
- Some developers, recognizing the need to have a feasible project, fudge the results of their feasibility analysis to support the selection of their prechosen alternative.

Specific Challenges

- Developers may focus on the environment within an organization and ignore the larger external environment in which the organization exists and does its business in the analysis of operational feasibility.
- Developers may underestimate the range of potential legal constraints on a system in their analysis of government regulation feasibility. After all, isn't the Internet an uncontrolled state of anarchy? However, all companies are bound by a range of laws regarding the conduct of business, regardless of how they conduct their business.
- Developers may make unfounded and nonreferenced claims that similar technology is used elsewhere in their analysis of technical feasibility.

6.6 CYBER SUPPLEMENTS FOR CHAPTER 6

Look at the Chapter 6 Cyber Supplements on the Web to find:
- Further information regarding developing business cases for e-Commerce alternatives
- Further information regarding e-Commerce alternatives
- References to further sources of information about various operational feasibility issues
- References to further sources of information about various technical feasibility issues
- References to further sources of information about various economic feasibility issues
- Practice activities for evaluating the feasibility of e-Commerce applications

e-Commerce Requirements Analysis

Outline

7.1 INTRODUCTION TO ANALYZING REQUIREMENTS

Establishing a business case for an e-Commerce system should not directly lead to designing or purchasing a system. Identifying a problem and/or opportunity and evaluating the feasibility of doing something about it just provides a start to finding out what is really required. A business case only establishes general agreement that something is required. If developers are allowed to rush into a premature design, there will be no basis for evaluating how useful the design really is or how well it meets the users' requirements.

Before design, it is essential to conduct a thorough analysis of requirements. Requirements analysis is discussed from different perspectives in this chapter and in Chapter 8.

- This chapter deals with identifying and analyzing the users' requirements in a manner that the user can understand, so that the user can be sure all the right ones have been considered.
- Chapter 8 describes how to transform user-oriented requirements into an object-oriented analysis that developers can use as a basis for design and for the evaluation of that design.

There is often either a shortage of requirements or an overabundance of requirements. Even with an apparent overabundance of requirements, developers may have missed some of the most important ones. They need to use a systematic approach to finding out which are the right requirements and defining them in such a manner that they can design systems to meet these requirements.

It is important to focus on real requirements as opposed to design suggestions. By focusing on what really is required, developers can better identify possibilities for significant improvements and innovations.

7.2 IDENTIFYING REQUIREMENTS

7.2.1 Getting at the Real Requirements

Requirements are specifications or descriptions of the needs and wants of users and stakeholders that are intended to be met by the system that is being developed. There are various types of requirements, including:

- Task requirements (also referred to as logical requirements)—which specify what needs to be done
- Usability requirements (also referred to as physical requirements)—which specify how it needs to be done

It is typical for most users to express their needs in terms of proposed concrete solutions (designs). They may see this approach as:

- A faster way of getting what they think they need
- An easier way of explaining their needs to someone who might not understand them
- A concrete expression (as opposed to an abstract one) of what's needed

Users may even have difficulty in trying to describe what they really need. Rather than focusing on what they need, they may identify solutions that they have heard about that they think might help them. It is also typical for developers to readily accept such "requirements" since it allows them to get through the analysis and on to the design quicker.

However, proposed designs are not real requirements. Real requirements should explain why something is needed without focusing on what that something is, since there may be many possible solutions. They need to identify a purpose, which needs to be satisfied. Unfortunately, both "purposes" and "requirements" can often be too abstract for many people to deal with properly. The following example of "hiring a person for a department" is used to provide a concrete illustration of the identification of real requirements.

Hiring a person for a department sounds like an important task that needs to be accomplished. As such it may be proposed as a requirement: The department needs to hire someone.

By asking "Why?" an analyst might find out that either the department is expanding or a person has left the department, for one of a number of reasons that could include:

- Retirement
- Moving jobs in the organization
- Going to a different organization
- Quitting (for any of a number of further reasons)
- Being fired

The analyst could also find out that the department has the funds allocated to paying for the proposed new person being hired.

However, the department doesn't want to hire just anyone; it wants to hire the right someone. This requirement needs to be elaborated on before actually doing the hiring.

- The first inclination in hiring a person, especially to replace another, is to have that new person match a particular skill set that the person being replaced had.
- Even where expansion is involved, a rigidly defined skill set is often used as the basis for hiring.
- The elaborated set of requirements is often specified in terms of the department wanting to hire someone with a particular set of skills.

Identifying a particular set of skills helps to filter out many potential applicants who will not fit into the department's needs. However, it may also filter out applicants who would be excellent, because it specifies a particular design as the"set of requirements." The more the skill set "required" is specified, the greater the limiting of potential choices.

Filtering can help reduce the number of candidates, when there are a lot of candidates from which to choose. However, it may not give the best results. If there aren't any candidates with that particular skill set required, then filtering will definitely fail. This problem is due to starting off with a design as a set of "requirements" that won't be satisfied by anything that doesn't look like the design that's expected. In this case, there is a need to back off and consider what the real requirements are:

- The Department needs to hire someone to help it to fulfill its purpose in the organization.

There are a variety of alternatives that could meet this requirement, including:

- Hiring an individual with a particular set of skills. While this is the same approach discussed above, it is only one of a number of alternatives.
- Shifting responsibilities of one or more current members (who have the skills needed) and hiring a new person to take over some of their old responsibilities. This might increase the satisfaction of current department members and/or increase the flexibility in selecting a new person.
- Training current members (in the skills required to shift responsibilities) and hiring a new person to take over some of their old responsibilities. This might also increase the satisfaction of current department members and/or increase the flexibility in selecting a new person.
- Hiring an individual who is likely to work well in the department and training that person in the necessary skills. However, the organization may not get the benefits of investing in a new and relatively unknown person if that person leaves quickly for another organization.

By looking at the more general requirement, an analyst might realize that hiring decisions should be made in light of ongoing human resource planning, rather than separate from it. The analyst can then try to optimize the results of hiring a new person along with (possibly) reorganizing the department.

7.2.2   Dealing with Individual Perspectives

While an individual investigation may have been based on the opinions of one individual, a requirements analysis should investigate the needs of all the different users from their own perspectives. Each individual will consider an application or a system in terms of those components that they are most familiar with and especially in terms of those components with which they interact. An individual's perspective of a system is illustrated in Figure 7-1. While other components may exist, the best source of information about them are other individuals who are directly involved with them. Requirements analysis involves investigating each significantly different perspective and combining the results of these investigations into a comprehensive set of requirements. Combining a number of different perspectives can also help to ensure the consistency and completeness of the resulting set of requirements.

7.2.3   A Task Analysis Approach to e-Commerce Requirements

Task analysis is a process in which developers and users (and also other stakeholders, where appropriate) work together to identify possible improvements to a set of

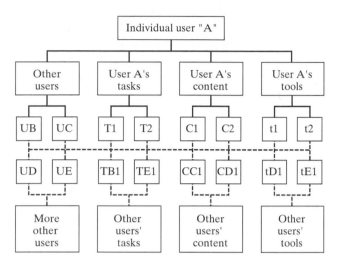

Figure 7-1   An individual user's perspective of a system

tools used by different *users* to perform *tasks* on sets of *content.* It should consider both what currently is done and what else could/should be done, by analyzing:

- The existing application
  - Understanding what's currently done in this system for this organization
- Challenges
  - Considering how to improve upon existing problem areas
- Opportunities
  - Understanding what's done in similar systems for similar organizations
  - Considering what's missing from these systems
  - Considering how to expand to new areas and/or users

A task analysis can be structured so that it:

- Is understandable and usable by both end users and developers
- Ensures that all requirements have been identified
- Helps developers translate requirements into actual designs (which may involve formalizing requirements)
- Assists in the management and evaluation of the project, including ensuring that all requirements have been met (as well as possible)
- Includes consideration of the usability of components and features of the system

- Incorporates available guidelines to help both developers and users
- Provides developers the freedom to adapt the structure to meet their needs and capabilities
- Integrates with the existing skills of the developers
- Minimizes the need for specialized modeling techniques
- Remains usable despite unforeseen circumstances and the occurrence of errors

A structured task analysis can help identify the major components of an e-Commerce application (users, tasks, content, and tools), which were identified in Chapter 4, and the requirements associated with each of them.

It is especially important that e-Commerce systems be readily usable by an organization's external users. If it is not, they may choose to use another organization's e-Commerce system. ISO Standard 13407[1] states that:

> "The context in which the system is to be used should be identified in terms of:
>   a) the characteristics of the intended users
>   b) the tasks the users are to perform
>   c) the environment in which the users are to use the system

and

> "The context of use description should:
>   a) specify the range of intended users, tasks and environments in sufficient detail to support design activity;
>   b) be derived from credible sources and adequately documented;
>   c) be confirmed by the users or those representing their interests in the process;
>   d) be made available to the design team at appropriate times and in appropriate forms to support design activities."

A structured task analysis fulfills this requirement for a context of use description. Each of the users, tasks, content chunks, and tools can pose their own usability requirements. Further usability requirements arise in the interactions between them. For example, a tool that works well for one type of user on a particular task may not work equally well for another type of user on the same task or for the same type of user on a different task. Basic usability requirements for an application can come from identifying the various potential types of users, tasks, tools, and content that it can be expected to bring together.

Task analysis can be used iteratively to build up a detailed understanding of the requirements of an application.

- The application descriptions, developed in Chapter 4, provide a high-level task analysis.
- Application descriptions identify application components that can be described individually to provide a more detailed task analysis.
- This detailed task analysis can be further refined within design to provide a task analysis of the system being designed, which is often referred to as a "use model."

While requirements analysis should begin with and focus on identifying the needs of users and tasks, additional requirements can be identified by considering the needs of:

- Exploring content chunks, which are needed by the users and tasks
- Compatibility with existing tools, which the user is familiar with, including both tools that may be replaced by the new system and those that the user will continue using along with the new system
- Limitations presented by developer tools

The complete set of requirements of e-Commerce applications are much more complicated than the hierarchically structured description of the application that was developed in the initial investigation. Requirements come from each individual component and from the relationships between components in an application. The relationship between application components and requirements for an e-Commerce system is illustrated in Figure 7-2. Although the contents of the requirements box are not explicitly illustrated in this figure, their structure should match the network of application components from which they come.

An initial set of tasks, user groups, content chunks, and tools should have been identified as part of the "what," "who," "how," and "with which" of an application's description. A subsequent feasibility study may have eliminated consideration of some of these and may have identified new possibilities requiring additional ones. Even where a feasibility study chose the alternative originally proposed in an initial investigation, it is possible that the initial investigation missed identifying some important components that should be involved with the system being developed.

Requirements analysis begins with a thorough identification of as many relevant application components as possible. It is recommended that a thorough identification of tasks and user groups be attempted before moving on to the identification of content and then to tools (where it expects that further tasks and user groups may still be added).

The name used to identify different application components is very important in ensuring successful communication between people. Names should be distinctive from one another to avoid communications difficulties.

Find further information about task analysis in the Chapter 7 Cyber Supplement.

7.2.4   Identifying Tasks

Tasks are the basis for individuals becoming users. The analysis of tasks should not be limited to only those tasks that are currently considered to be part of what an application should accomplish. The analysis of tasks should be expanded to include similar tasks and other potential tasks that may not be currently performed.

Tasks can be identified by considering:

- The various responsibilities of internal users (tasks often are listed as the basis of job descriptions)
- The various accomplishments that external users expect to result from their interacting with an organization (these interactions are often with specific parts of the organization, including specific organizational systems)

The identification of tasks (as occurs in traditional task analysis) is just the starting point for understanding what is needed. The analysis of tasks requires that we investigate the where, when, and how of these tasks in relation to their users.

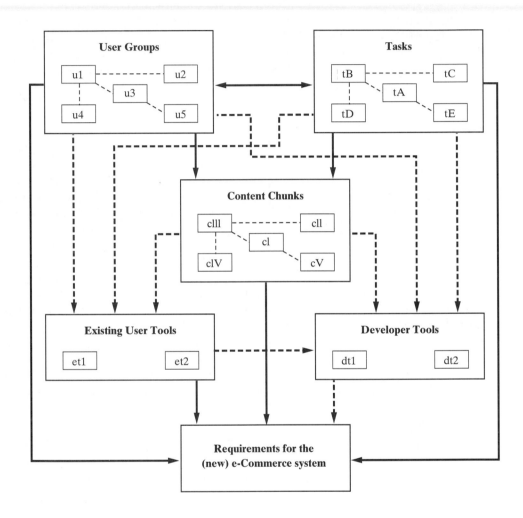

Figure 7-2 Sources of requirements for e-Commerce systems

It is important to note situations where different groups of users have different needs and/or expectations for a task or a set of related tasks.

- When comparing products, internal users may be given access to more information about the strengths and weaknesses of individual products (both of the organization and of its competitors) than external users can access.
- Because most e-Commerce tasks involve business transactions, and transactions occur between legal individuals, many tasks involved in an e-Commerce system will occur in pairs. Thus, if a customer is to access product information from a system, someone needs to be able to enter that information into the system.

e-Commerce systems need to provide value to each of their users. This value comes from helping them to accomplish various tasks. From an organizational perspective, it is important that e-Commerce systems accomplish tasks that include the actualization of various business transactions. However, actualization requires the support of four other types of fundamental business activities, identified in Chapter 3. Analyzing how user tasks relate to these types of business activities can lead to an understanding of sets of related tasks[2] that can help provide the more complete handling of various business transactions for buyers, customers and sellers, and vendors within the e-Commerce system.

7.2.4.1   Tasks Related to Business Transaction Planning

A consideration of business transaction planning can lead to the identification of tasks related to establishing the need for products and services, and strategies for obtaining or providing them. This can include the analysis of tasks that would lead external users to be interested in acquiring or selling a product or service. Recognizing these tasks can help design effective acquisition and marketing strategies that may involve a number of different media, including but not limited to those available via the Web.

Business transaction planning may involve a number of tasks for both customers and vendors. Some or all of these tasks may be suitable for inclusion within the boundaries of an e-Commerce system.

Customer tasks may include:

- Developing strategies for acquiring products and services
- Developing methods for requirements determination
- Developing methods of specifying requirements
- Identifying potential vendors of the products or services

Vendor tasks may include:

- Advertising the organization's e-Commerce Web site
- Connecting the organization's image with industries that it serves
- Connecting the organization's image with reliability and quality
- Analyzing and forecasting the market for its products and services

7.2.4.2   Tasks Related to Business Transaction Identification

A consideration of business transaction identification can lead to the identification of tasks related to marketing specific products or services via the system, including helping potential customers understand how a product or service meets their needs.

By analyzing the different uses of products and services, better information may be provided to help lead to the actualization of the transaction.

Business transaction identification may involve a number of tasks for both customers and vendors. Some or all of these tasks may be suitable for inclusion within the boundaries of an e-Commerce system.

Customer tasks may include:

- Determining their requirements for products or services
- Determining a budget for the products or services
- Obtaining approval for the expenditure on the products or services
- Determining potential vendors of the products or services
- Identifying suitable products or services
- Evaluating the reliability of a vendor
- Determining similarities between requirements and available products or services
- Selecting between competing products or services

Vendor tasks may include:

- Estimating costs of providing the products or services
- Determining a method of acquiring or creating the product or service
- Convincing a customer that the products or services will be provided reliably
- Differentiating the products or services from those offered by the competition

There are two possible outcomes of business transaction identification:

- If the product or service is significantly different from competitive products or services, the customer's selection will be based on the characteristics of the product or service.
- If the product or service is similar to competitive products or services, then the customer's selection may be influenced by the characteristics of the vendor as well as any differences in specific characteristics of the available products or services.

7.2.4.3   Tasks Related to Business Transaction Negotiation

A consideration of business transaction negotiation can lead to the identification of different terms and conditions that need to be negotiated as part the business transaction. If these terms and conditions cannot be negotiated, various transactions may be lost.

Business transaction negotiation may involve a number of tasks performed jointly by both customers and vendors. Some or all of these tasks may be suitable for inclusion within the boundaries of an e-Commerce system.

Negotiations may include:

- Product features and specifications
- Prices
- Payments
- Delivery times and methods
- Associated support
- Guarantees that the other negotiated issues will be met

7.2.4.4 Tasks Related to Business Transaction Actualization

A consideration of business transaction actualization can lead to the identification of additional related transactions. These transactions can be encouraged in conjunction with this transaction or once this transaction is completed.

Business transaction actualization may involve a number of tasks performed jointly by both customers and vendors. It also may involve a number of tasks performed by either customers or vendors. Some or all of these tasks may be suitable for inclusion within the boundaries of an e-Commerce system.

Jointly performed tasks may include:

- Concluding a formal agreement/contract
- Agreeing to the terms of the contract

Customer tasks may include:

- Receiving products or services
- Inspecting/evaluating and accepting the delivered products or services
- Paying invoices

Vendor tasks may include:

- Shipping or providing products or services
- Invoicing for the products or services
- Handling payments for products or services
- Encouraging further transactions

7.2.4.5 Tasks Related to Business Transaction Post-Actualization

A consideration of business transaction post-actualization can lead to the identification of various servicing-related tasks that may be important not only after the actualization of the transaction but also in convincing external users to do business with this organization.

Business transaction post-actualization may involve a number of tasks involving both customers and vendors. It also may involve a number of tasks performed by either customers or vendors. Some or all of these tasks may be suitable for inclusion within the boundaries of an e-Commerce system.

Jointly involved tasks may include:

- Returning products and services
- Refunding payments
- Handling questions about the use or maintenance of products
- Performing maintenance on products
- Handling complaints about the quality of products or services

Customer tasks may include:

- Making use of the products or services
  - On their own
  - Integrating the products or services with other products or services
- Reselling the products or services
- Disposing of the products when no longer required

Vendor tasks may include:

- Thanking the customer for the purchase
- Evaluating the profitability of the transaction
- Providing additional follow-up to encourage further purchases
- Reminding the customer about scheduled maintenance
- Informing the customer about product recalls

7.2.4.6 Distinguishing Between Tasks and Tools

It is very important to distinguish between tasks and tools:

- Tasks are specific accomplishments of a person (or a group of persons)
- Tools are artifacts that are used by people to help accomplish tasks

Real tasks:

- Have real users, which should be identified and further analyzed (see *users* below).
- May involve multiple users, each with their own needs and objectives. This may require flexible tools in order to meet the usability needs of each user group.
- Are different from procedures, which may be used in certain implementations of tasks and thus are actually tools (see *tools* below).
- Involve more than data plus procedures, where data is an example of content which also requires separate analysis (see *content* below).
- Do not necessarily require specific details, which may only be artifacts of current implementations of the tasks. This involves considering whether a task might be usefully applied to other similar content.
- Are specific, as opposed to applications that are more general and that usually involve a number of tasks.
- Fulfill objectives, which ties specific tasks to a more general application. Often different users may have different objectives for tasks that are shared by different user groups.
- May cross traditional application boundaries, and thus, care should be taken to identify all relevant tasks, regardless of traditional application or political boundaries.

A consideration of the purpose of the task can lead to usability concerns such as:

- Where a number of tasks can be replaced with a single generalized task; the user must be able to recognize and accept this replacement.
- Where differences in purposes exist for a single task (whether or not it is a generalized task), the user must be able to understand the effects (or lack thereof) of these differences in purposes on the task.
- Similar purposes either require similar tools or, if possible, a generalized tool. The decision to combine tools into a single tool must take into account any resulting changes in the usability of the new tool for users of the existing tools that it is to replace. Where some users may be negatively affected, there may be cause to create a separate tool (or to retain or modify an existing tool) for their use.

- If similar tools are designed, their appearance and actions should be similar. Differences in appearance and actions should be directly related to the differences in their function. These differences should be both significant and obvious to the user.
- If a single tool is designed, care needs to be taken so that the user recognizes its multiple purposes. This can be done either via the visual design of the tool, the multiple positioning of the tool within various contexts of use, or at least via training materials used to introduce the user to the tool.
- Where a tool is to operate differently in different environments/states, the state in which it is operating should be obvious to the user. Additional guidance may be required to ensure that the user operates it in the manner required by the state. The same tool (including interface objects) should not have vastly different or even contradictory purposes in different environments (states) that may be used by an individual user.

The degree of accomplishment of a task is generally more important than the method of achieving it. Thus each of the users should be allowed to select the methods and tools that are most usable for them. Although we all accomplish tasks every day, it is often difficult for people to recognize the difference between tasks and the use of tools. The following example illustrates a method of going from a description of tool use to the identification of some "real tasks":

Step 1. Identify different major activities and accomplishments that the USER does.
- One thing the USER does is "Writing a letter."

Step 2. Analyze the proposed TASK.
- Is "writing a letter" a "TASK"? that USERS perform with the TOOL?
- "Writing" is a TOOL-specific action that "prepares a communication" in a particular manner, using a "writing TOOL."
- A "letter" is a specific type of TOOL used in "communication."
- Perhaps the TASK is "communication?"
- However, "preparing a communication" is only part of "communication," which may be much more complex.
- Perhaps "communication" is an APPLICATION and "preparing a communication" is the TASK?
- However, the concept of communication is still too general to be very useful.

Step 3. Consider the real purpose.
- Communication (with letters) can be used for many different purposes, including:
  - To invite a friend to a party
  - To report to your boss
  - To order a system from a computer store
  - To complain about the quality of your cable TV service to the provider
- The purposes of these communications are:
  - To invite
  - To report
  - To order
  - To complain
- Each of these purposes is a more-specific TASK.

Step 4. Identify the real TASK.
- This may require further consultation with the USER or may have already been part of the initial identification that was previously regarded as too-specific to be a TASK.
- In this case it turned out that the user wrote letters to invite friends to parties and other occasions. Thus, the real task being accomplished was "to invite friends."
- It is easier to analyze the particular requirements of "inviting" than the more general requirements of "communicating."

 Find further information about identifying tasks in the Chapter 7 Cyber Supplement.

7.2.5 Identifying Users

Users are not all the same. Severe usability problems can occur in systems designed for a "generic" user who seldom exists. Users, while of penultimate importance, are only users if they use the system and thus are closely linked with the tasks that each group of users performs. Different users may have different needs based on the tasks they perform and their own unique characteristics. It is essential to understand the characteristics of the actual groups of users in order to develop a usable design for each of them. Developers should focus attention on user groups that:

- Can be distinguished from one another based on a unique set of common characteristics
- Are of significant enough size to justify the time and effort in serving them
- Are groups for whom the designers can create a design that meets their unique needs

It is important to consider the needs of people who provide the content to be used in a multimedia application as well as people who consume the information content from the application.[3]

Individuals may be members of one or more user groups. The user group, which most influences an individual's actions, may change based on the current goals and activities of the individual. While all individuals generally possess a number of common characteristics to some extent, the majority of individuals in certain groups may possess them to a significantly greater or lesser extent than the general population. Groups may differ significantly in terms of their:

- Demographic characteristics
- Sensing capabilities
- Performing (including movement) capabilities
- Physical capabilities
- Memory capabilities
- Cognitive capabilities
- Emotional capabilities
- Personality type
- Acquired capabilities

Consideration of each of these types of characteristics may lead to the identification of numerous specific requirements that should apply to the design of new systems for the application. For example, if a notable demographic characteristic of the group is a large proportion of middle-age males, then a relevant requirement would be to avoid using color as a sole means of coding of information because of the significant potential for color blindness in the group.

 Find further information about identifying users in the Chapter 7 Cyber Supplement.

7.2.6   Identifying Content

Content serves the users accomplishing their desired tasks and should be kept subservient to both users and tasks. Considerable usability problems may arise from structuring applications around some "ideal" organization of content rather than around how this content will be used.

The content-oriented "Field of Dreams" syndrome of "if you build it, they will come" (which is especially prevalent in the design of Web sites but also exists with many other applications) puts the ego of the developer ahead of the needs of the potential users. However, a consideration of different chunks of content related to an application may lead to discovering additional uses (tasks) that could be added to the application.

Units of content are often referred to as "chunks" because their size is less important than the meaning that they convey. Developers should focus their attention on content chunks that:

- Can be distinguished from one another both functionally and in terms of data structures
- Are significant in accomplishing one or more tasks
- Developers can provide or support in an application to meet the needs of one or more user groups

According to ISO 14915-2,[4] a **content chunk** is "a unit of content that meets the needs of some specific task. A content chunk can also meet the needs of one or more tasks for one or more users, either by itself or in combination with other content chunks."

Initial identification of content should focus on conceptual level content (regardless of its type) and its relationships with identified tasks and users. This identification should consider:

- Content needs of individual tasks (based on the identified task descriptions)
- Content needs of individual user groups (based on the identified user group descriptions)
- Common content needs of all the tasks for each user (and looking for similarities)
- Common content needs of all the users for each task (and looking for similarities)
- The content of tools used for that or similar applications

Individual chunks may be used by one or more user groups and may be used in one or more tasks. Content can exist and be presented in a variety of formats and can be processed to higher levels, such as information and knowledge. Types of content can involve:

- Data (the raw materials)
- Information (selected or summarized data useful for making decisions)

- Knowledge (information plus rules for using it to make decisions)
- Potentially, wisdom (the ability to apply knowledge appropriately)

Because applications should be as usable and helpful as possible for the user, a consideration of the type of content may suggest that the application should focus on a more useful type of content:

- Data is often the least (immediately) useful form of content because users need to process it by themselves
- Information is usually better than data, provided it has had the processing it needs.
- Knowledge may either remove the need for a user or may be useful in training a user.
- Wisdom is often the hardest to communicate. Unfortunately, no one has yet found a way to automate it.

Find further information about identifying content chunks in the Chapter 7 Cyber Supplement.

7.2.7 Identifying Tools

All artifacts that people use can be considered as tools. Tools can be used by developers to create other tools and/or used by end users for a variety of tasks (including some users the tools weren't designed for). They can be selected, modified, or built new.

Both developers and end users need and use tools. Developers use their tools to create or modify other tools (including software systems) for the end users. Different tools (or sets of tools) can be used to accomplish the same task. Tools exist at (and are designed for) various levels, from entire application systems down to individual controls within the system. Tools, like content, serve the tasks and users.

Premature focusing on tools can lead to choosing tools that are impressive to the developer but which are impractical due to various usability problems for the user. However, it is an important part of requirements analysis to determine what tools users are currently using in order to understand the environment in which any new tools (including the system being developed) will be used.

Find further information about identifying tools in the Chapter 7 Cyber Supplement.

7.2.8 An Example of Identifying Tasks, Users, Content, and Tools

Because the concepts of tasks, users, content, and tools are difficult ones, a brief example of their identification may be useful before proceeding to their further analysis. The following example describes part of the analysis of an organization that wanted to "put its newsletter on-line."

7.2.8.1 An Example of Identifying Tasks

The identification of requirements for the on-line organizational newsletter example started with a consideration of tasks. The initial problem was not stated in terms of tasks, but rather in terms of a proposed tool. By considering the definition of tasks as "specific accomplishments of a person (or group of persons)" the main "task" of a newsletter was identified as communications between members. However, this is too general to be readily of use, according to the guideline "real tasks are specific." Communications between members was therefore recognized as the basic application area that would be composed of a number of more-specific tasks.

Further task analysis guidelines, including "real tasks fulfill objectives," "real tasks may involve multiple users," and "real tasks do not necessarily require specific details," were applied. Analysis of the current role of the organization's newsletter led to identifying a number of tasks, including the following, that are part of the application communications between members:

- Communicating news of interest to the organization—while initially identified as communicating organizational news, "real tasks fulfill objectives" recognized that news from external information providers as well as internal information providers could fulfill a common objective for the members of the organization.
- Encouraging involvement in the organization—while initially identified as encouraging current members to remain as members and to get involved in organizational activities, "real tasks may involve multiple users" encouraged the recognition that encouraging involvement could go beyond current members to include all potential members.
- Encouraging participation in upcoming events—was initially identified as two separate tasks of publishing a schedule of upcoming events and advertising upcoming events. Applying "real tasks do not necessarily require specific details" recognized that the level of information about upcoming events was not as important as the objective of encouraging participation in them and thus the two different newsletter formats acted to serve a common task.

NOTE: Tasks may occur in pairs, especially where an external user's task interacts with an internal user's task. In this instance, any information presented by the newsletter must meet the needs of its potential readers or it will be ignored by them regardless of how important its authors believe it is.

Further analysis of this application in terms of business activities recognized that it currently is limited to serving specific tasks related to part of business transaction identification. Although it may be expanded in the future to handle further tasks and other fundamental business activities, an organizational decision was made to limit its scope for now.

7.2.8.2   An Example of Identifying Users

Identification continued with users. The initial set of users had been identified as organization members. The identification of tasks expanded this to include potential members. There initially seemed to be little to distinguish between these two user groups other than some individuals having paid a membership and others not. The guidelines for identifying user groups expect that the distinction between groups should be relevant to design. While nonmembership may be grounds for limiting access to some or all of the intended application, it does not necessarily have a major effect on the usability of any of the system that would be available to both groups. Further guidance regarding the use of involvement and expertise in differentiating between user groups led to splitting the group of organization members into two groups: actively involved members (whose activity would include making use of the current newsletter) and nominal members (who currently largely ignore the newsletter).

Instead of the identification of the group of nominal members leading to their being ignored, it was the basis for investigating what needs they may have in the application area of communications between members and why the current (newsletter) tool fails to meet their needs in the application area.

While the group of actively involved members may seem closer in their needs to the group of potential members, there are a number of characteristics that will likely differentiate their potential use of the application (such as experience with the tasks and tools involved with the application). However, once a sufficient differentiation is evident, further identification should be conducted before analyzing these differences in detail.

There were also two distinct groups of information providers identified: the newsletter editor and the organization's executive as important user groups involved with the application.

7.2.8.3   An Example of Identifying Content Chunks

The identification of content chunks can proceed from the identification of tasks and users. A number of different types of content can be associated with "communicating news of interest to the organization," including:

- Content that affects or may change the organization (and its relationships with various people including members and nonmembers)
- Content that affects or may place requirements on the members (including people who become members in the future)
- Content that may help the readers (and that may help both members and nonmembers)

The expectation that content should be relevant to each group of its users leads to the recognition that substantially different content may be needed for encouraging involvement in the organization by actively involved members, by nominal members, and by nonmembers. What is usable by one group may not be usable by the other groups.

- One group needs to know how to become involved in certain activities.
- One group needs to know the benefits of becoming involved.
- One group needs to know why and how to become a member.

Recognizing the differences between users encouraging participation in upcoming events leads to the need for a chunk of content that describes the requirements for participation.

Many additional chunks of potential content can and should be identified. Some of these can be identified from the analysis of tools (to be discussed next). Iterative development recognizes that it may not be possible or desirable to try to identify all content chunks before proceeding with further development activities. In this example, many attempts to identify content often led to a consideration of the content provided by current tools. So, after the identification of some additional chunks of content in a relatively tool-independent manner, attention was focused on the identification of tools before continuing to identify relevant content chunks.

7.2.8.4   An Example of Identifying Tools

While the tendency might be to consider only the current printed newsletter as the main tool, it is useful to identify other related tools, especially those already used by groups of users that can assist with the application or with tasks within the application. A number of other tools were found relevant to this application, including:

- Various forms of word-of-mouth (in personal or group) conversations conducted via a number of other tools, such as:
  - Chance meetings
  - Formal meetings
  - Telephone conversations
  - E-mail
- Advertisements in other publications or media, including:
  - Newspapers
  - Radio
  - Television
  - The World Wide Web

Given the central nature of the existing newsletter to the application and its use for multiple different tasks, it could be considered a composite tool made up of a number of other, more-specific tools. In such cases, the developer should also identify these more-specific tools. An examination of recent issues of the organization's newsletter found that it was composed of a variety of different types of content:

- A newsletter heading/logo
- A table of contents
- An editorial
- News of interest to the organization
- News about actions that may affect or may place requirements on the organization or the members
- News and commentary that may help the readers
- Schedule(s) of upcoming events
- Advertisements
- Articles encouraging involvement in the organization and its activities

Most of these (including the newly identified editorial) are just different types of content and should be treated as such (based on the distinction between tasks, content, and tools). However, two of these apparent pieces of content, a newsletter heading/logo and a table of contents, actually represent tools for the users. A further consideration of the specific tools within the newsletter led to the identification of:

- A newsletter heading/logo—used to identify the newsletter and bring it to the attention of its readers. This identifies an additional subtask, namely establishing communication that must take place before other communications will occur.
- A table of contents—used to help the readers to evaluate the newsletter quickly and to find items of interest. It does not add any new content because

it only summarizes the content contained elsewhere in the newsletter, but rather provides a tool for users of the newsletter.

- A number of sections—each containing news/opinion content chunks. These sections serve to organize, present, and highlight the various chunks of content.

The recognized effects of the identification of existing tools on the previous identification of content and tasks should guide the developer to iterate through the identification stage. This iteration should continue until further identification efforts fail to make significant additions or changes to the set of components already identified.

7.3   ANALYZING REQUIREMENTS

7.3.1   Descriptions for Application Components

Each of the identified components need to be individually analyzed and described to understand their relationships with one another and the requirements they have regarding the application.

Developing descriptions, like identifying components, starts by considering the main traditional tasks and/or user groups and spreads out from there to identify further components and relationships. The order of this description is not fixed and is often governed by the availability of information, collecting the more available information first and proceeding to gather other information as required or as it becomes available. In many cases, descriptions of individual components may evolve iteratively (rather than being produced all at once).

Descriptions should be reviewed iteratively by developers and users as part of the ongoing development process. Together they should check for:

- Correctness and completeness
- The appropriateness of including information within this emerging set of descriptions
- The identification of additional opportunities related to this information

The general template used to describe applications can also be used, with slight modifications, to describe tasks, users, content, and tools. These modifications help to capture the important aspects of each of these unique types of components.

7.3.2   Describing Tasks

Remember: an application is a collection of a number of distinct tasks. A common approach (and format) can be used for describing both applications and the tasks that compose them. In this way, task descriptions are just more detailed descriptions of some more specific purpose contained within the overall purpose of the application. Table 7-1 provides a format recommended for task descriptions.

The following descriptions are modified slightly from those previously used in Chapter 4 for application descriptions in order to better describe tasks:

It is preferable that tasks be **named** in a manner that refers more to what they accomplish than to how tools are used to accomplish the task. This can be done by

Table 7-1   A format for describing tasks

Task:	*Insert* name *here*
Who:	*Insert* names of user groups *here*
What:	*Insert* a general description of what the task accomplishes and important relationships with other tasks *here*
Where & When:	*Insert* special circumstances that apply to performing the task *here*
Why:	*Insert* the benefits for the organization and users *here*
How:	*Insert* how tools are used for the task *here*
How Much:	*Insert* general estimate of frequency and quantity of usage *here*
With Which:	*Insert* names of content chunks used *here*

referring to the accomplishment or by using a general descriptor of the activity of the task that would remain valid regardless of which different tools are used to help accomplish the task.

Where a task has an existing name that is commonly understood by the various users, developers should use that name. Where a task is known by a variety of existing names, the most common is not necessarily the best for all user groups. Problems may result for one or more user groups. The various names should be investigated to see if one of these names achieves a high level of recognition without causing difficulties for any particular group. If none of the existing names can be used without significant difficulties, then a new name may be needed.

Who should describe the various users involved with the task. This includes (but is not limited to):

- Different groups of users who need the application performed
- Different groups of user(s) who will actually use the application package directly
- Other people that supply or receive data or information to/from the application
- Various managers involved with each of these groups

NOTE: Dealing with all users as if they belong to a single group leads to developing for the lowest common denominator and satisfying no one.

It is important to include the type of involvement of different groups of users in their descriptions. It also may be useful to briefly describe other characteristics of these user groups that may influence the design requirements of any software packages being developed.

What should identify the general purpose of the task and the general activity involved in achieving this purpose. It provides a means of generalizing from specific work tasks to the organizational objective(s) that they meet. It should also identify any subtasks that may require further investigation and any other tasks that are related to this task.

When and where should describe the conditions under which the task is expected to be performed. Special consideration should be noted of where these conditions may be at variance with those conditions already noted for the application.

Why should describe the benefits of why the user would do the task. It need not involve a detailed cost/benefit analysis, but rather should focus on the importance of the task to the users and to their organization. Where these benefits differ between users or between groups of users and the organization, these differences should be noted.

How should describe the general manner in which the task is accomplished and identify the different tools that are currently or could be used to help accomplish the task. It should include identifying any major current difficulties with this operation that should be improved upon.

How much should describe what the required criteria of achievement is for the task to succeed. It also should include an estimate of the frequency and quantity of use of the task.

With which should describe the content chunks that the task uses and/or provides. It can also briefly identify the nature(s) of this use, especially where different pieces of content are used differently.

Further concerns relating to tasks are identified in the "Rules Governing the Process Component" section of ISO 15944-1.[5]

7.3.3   Describing User Groups

Remember: not all users have the same characteristics and/or needs. To be effective, a system needs to meet the particular requirements of each different group of users. Table 7-2 provides a format recommended for descriptions of user groups.

The following descriptions are modified slightly from those dealing with application and task descriptions in order to better describe user groups.

It is preferable that user groups be **named** in a manner that refers more to what characteristics their members share than to the particular tasks that the user group may be associated with (since many groups may be associated with any given task).

Where a user group has an existing name that is commonly understood by the various users, developers should use that name. Where a user group is known by a variety of existing names (or has not yet been recognized by users as a distinct group), the most common is not necessarily the best for recognition by all user groups. Problems may result for one or more user groups. The various names should be investigated to see if one can achieve a high level of recognition without causing difficulties for any particular group. If none of the existing names can be used without significant difficulties, then a new name may be needed.

Characteristics make a user group unique from other appropriate user groups. While each user group may have a number of characteristics with important design implications, the minimum needed to describe the user group consists of those characteristics that uniquely identify which user group an individual is part of at a given time. It should also identify any subgroups that may require further investigation and any other user groups that are related to this user group.

Relationships and interdependencies may exist with other user groups. The existence of relationships between groups can reinforce the distinction between the groups. An individual may be a member of various user groups, but typically acts as part of a single user group at a given time. Relationships link the user group definition with other user group definitions, which should also contain similar corresponding linkages.

Table 7-2   A format for describing user groups

User group:	*Insert* name *here*
Characteristics (who):	*Insert* unique user group characteristics and important relationships with other user groups *here*
Tasks (what):	*Insert* tasks performed by the user group *here*
Membership (where and when):	*Insert* circumstances that make an individual act as a member of this group here
Significance (why):	*Insert* the benefits of serving the group *here*
Treatment (how):	*Insert* tools currently used or proposed to serve the group *here*
Feasibility (how much):	*Insert* feasibility estimate of serving the group *here*
With Which:	*Insert* names of content chunks used *here*

Tasks link the user group definition with task definitions, just as a corresponding portion of the task definition linked it with user group (definitions). It can also consider the user's goals and objectives. Ideally, goals and objectives should be shared between the users and the tasks. However, user groups are likely to possess more goals and objectives than those associated with any one task. Where they are compatible, additional goals and objectives may suggest complimentary tasks that could be added to the set of tasks under consideration. Where incompatibilities exist, they should be examined to reduce their effect in particular tasks.

Membership should describe the conditions in which an individual will act as a member of this group. It needs to be recognized that individuals may act as members of different groups under different circumstances. Special consideration should be noted of any occasions where a user's role and group membership might change while using the application.

Significance should consider the potential benefits to the owner of the proposed system of serving the particular needs of members of the group. This is needed to justify the expenditure of resources in providing for the needs of this user group. The extent of this justification depends upon the needs of the owner. Significance may be considered in terms of size and importance of the group and its tasks to the owner of the system. Group size (which may be available from the previous identification of groups) is not necessarily the same as group importance. Both size and importance can lead to the further identification of potential benefits.

The **treatment** should specify the tools that will be available to and used by the group. It should include identifying any major current difficulties the user group experiences with these tools that should be improved upon.

Feasibility of meeting the needs of the group should consider the potential ability of meeting the unique needs of this user group and consider the potential costs and benefits to the owner of the system. The developer should determine how to deal with the group:

- Include it as an important group to design for
- Include it as a group to design for, if it can be accommodated at little or no extra cost

- Plan for future enhancements to accommodate the group
- Ignore the group by neither designing for or against it because it is not relevant to the goals and objectives of the site
- Purposely design in a manner to exclude the group (which should only be done to protect a site from potential trouble)

With which should describe the content chunks that the user group uses and/or provides. It can also briefly identify the nature(s) of this use, especially where different pieces of content are used differently.

Further concerns relating to users are identified in the "Rules Governing the Person" section of ISO 15944-1.[6]

7.3.4   Describing Content

Remember: content should serve tasks and users. Content that is presented just because it is available is just data that gets in the way of accomplishing tasks. However, if content appears to be useful on its own, then further analysis may be appropriate to identify potential tasks and users that may have been missed. Table 7-3 provides a format recommended for content descriptions.

The following descriptions are modified slightly from those previously used for application and task descriptions in order to better describe content.

It is preferable that content be **named** in a manner that refers more to the contents of the content rather than to any single task or user group. Where content has an existing name that is commonly understood by the various users, developers should use that name. Where content is known by a variety of existing names, the most common is not necessarily the best for all user groups. Problems may result for one or more user groups. The various names should be investigated to see if one could achieve a high level of recognition without causing difficulties for any particular group. If none of the existing names can be used without significant difficulties, then a new name may be needed.

Who should identify the various user groups who will interact with the content in any manner, including providing, retrieving, and/or modifying it. It should also identify user groups who are expected to know the content (and thus not be expected to need it to be provided for them). It is useful to note the type of relationships (knowing, providing, receiving, modifying, and so on) that each user group has with the content chunk.

What the content chunk is about should be described at the conceptual level by identifying the purpose of the chunk and the tasks that use the content chunk. By focusing on the conceptual level, this description will remain robust and valid despite changes in the internal content or structure of the content chunk or chunks that it describes. Many transactions require communicating the purpose of content along with the specific data contained in a particular content chunk.

When can be used to identify any particular circumstances either necessary for this content chunk to be useful or where it will not be useful.

Where can be used to identify particular sources of this content that might not obviously be part of the system being developed. This may identify special requirements that may limit the availability of the content.

Table 7-3 A format for describing content

Content:	*Insert* name *here*
Who:	*Insert* names of user groups *here*
What:	*Insert* what tasks use the content *here*
When:	*Insert* special circumstances that apply to content use and maintenance *here*
Where:	*Insert* where the content comes from *here*
Why:	*Insert* the benefits of the content for the organization and users *here*
How:	*Insert* how tools use the content *here*
How Much:	*Insert* a general estimate of the amount of actual content involved per content chunks could be involved *here*
With Which:	*Insert* details of the content chunk and important relationships with other content chunks *here*

Why should justify inclusion of the content in the proposed system by evaluating the net benefits of this content to the user groups. The consideration of costs should include the costs of obtaining, validating, maintaining, and providing the information. The consideration of benefits should be tied to the effect of the content on the users' ability to successfully accomplish tasks and the resulting benefit of accomplishing those tasks.

How should both identify the tools that use the content chunk and briefly explain how those tools use the content. This will focus on those aspects of the content chunks most important to the tools accomplishing tasks. Formatting details should be avoided, since they are more related to the needs of individual tools used for the tasks than to the actual accomplishment of tasks themselves.

How much can be used to provide a general estimate of the amount of actual content involved in a given content chunk. This can be useful in determining if the chunking has been appropriate or if some other chunking should be considered. It also can be used to estimate the number of unique (instances of) content chunks that can fit this content chunk as described. Where large numbers of similar content chunks are involved, the users may require additional help in locating the appropriate or desired content chunk to use at a given time.

With which should describe details of what the chunk actually contains. It also should identify any sub-chunks that may require further investigation and any other chunks of content that are related to this chunk. An analysis of possible content structures may lead to the identification of additional potential tasks and/or users.

Further concerns relating to content chunks are identified in the "Rules Governing the Data Component" section of ISO 15944-1.[7]

7.3.5 Describing Tools

Remember: tools help in some particular way to perform one or more tasks for one or more groups of users. Table 7-4 provides a format recommended for tool descriptions.

The following descriptions are modified slightly from those dealing with application and task descriptions in order to better describe tools.:

The **name** used to identify a tool is often chosen more for marketing purposes than to clearly identify the tool. Where tools already exist, they generally have well-established names. New tools, under development, often have a working or project

Table 7-4   A format for describing tools

Tool:	*Insert* name *here*
Who:	*Insert* names of user groups *here*
What:	*Insert* a general description of what tasks the tool is used for *here*
When & Where:	*Insert* special circumstances that apply to using the tool *here*
Why:	*Insert* the benefits for the organization and users *here*
How:	*Insert* how tools are used for the task and important relationships with other tools *here*
How Much:	*Insert* general estimate of frequency and quantity of usage *here*
With Which:	*Insert* names of content chunks used *here*

name that may be changed for marketing purposes once the system is ready to be utilized. In the case of software packages, names often include information on the version (e.g., Windows 3.1, Windows 96, Windows 98).

Who should describe the various users who will actually use the tool directly or the results of the tool. It is important to include the type of involvement of different groups of users in tool descriptions. It also may be useful to briefly describe characteristics that are important for a user group to be well-suited to the tool.

What for tool descriptions should identify the tasks for which the tool can be used to accomplish or to assist with accomplishing. This need not be limited to tasks identified within this application. Existing tools may already be used for applications other than the one currently being developed. The developer should consider whether tasks accomplished by a tool in these other applications might also apply to the present one being developed.

When and where for tasks identifies "the conditions under which the task is to be performed." These conditions involve the same basic information for tools and can help to define the particulars of the relationship between tasks and tools. Special note should be made of where these conditions may be at variance with those already noted for tasks that the tool is intended to serve. Where conditions are more limiting for tools, additional tools may be required, or the tool may need redesign. Where conditions are less limiting, this may indicate the potential to be used for additional tasks.

Why for tasks identifies "the benefits of why the user would do the task." Similarly, the "why" of tools can identify how the tool benefits the task(s) and user(s). This should also include a brief comparison between the use of this tool and other tools that might optionally be used instead of this tool.

How for tools should elaborate on how the tool is used to accomplish these tasks. It should also identify any major parts of the tools that may require further investigation and any other tools that are related to this tool.

How much for tasks identifies "what the criteria of achievement is for the task to succeed." For tool descriptions, "how much" is more appropriate to provide a general estimate of tools usage. Such an estimate is very important in determining how entrenched a particular tool is with the various users of an application.

- Where tools are used frequently, there will be a greater need that new tools be consistent, wherever possible and desirable, with user expectations that have been established by the current tool. All changes should be directly related to significant improvements for the users and should be made with consideration for the changes in user behaviors that they will necessitate.

- Where tools are used infrequently, the developer should determine what special need they are currently filling that has justified their use, even though it is infrequent. New developments often overlook infrequently used tools, leading to unforeseen problems when the old tool is eliminated without being adequately replaced.

With which should describe the content that the tool uses and/or provides. It can also briefly identify the nature(s) of this use, especially where different pieces of content are used differently.

Further concerns relating to tools are identified in the "Rules Governing the Process Component" section of ISO 15944-1.[8]

7.3.6   An Example of Developing a Component Description

The following annotated example is the result of the first attempt at (iteration of) identifying information to develop a description of the task *"encouraging participation in upcoming events."* It illustrates how structured descriptions can help guide developers in building a thorough understanding of the existing system and in identifying opportunities for making design improvements. Developing the description clarifies the task and its relationships with other components and identifies a number of further components that should be considered for inclusion in the application. These further components can lead to a more detailed understanding of what is actually required. While it provides a start for understanding the task, further iterative analysis is necessary to fully understand the task and to refine the description. Italics have been used in this example to identify various application components mentioned within the description.

Who: This usually involves the *newsletter editor* and *the people responsible for the events* (who may be considered members of an extended *organization executive* even if they are not officially considered as such) and is designed to affect *members* and *potential members* (who are currently nonmembers).

NOTE: This identifies that the task serves the organization's executive and is expected to affect others (members and nonmembers). This task is likely to fail unless there is a corresponding task for the members and nonmembers that it fulfills. Just because a tool (such as a newsletter) is usable, doesn't mean that its intended users will use it. Its success may depend on whether or not it also accomplishes important tasks for all its intended users. Where communication is involved, this may involve different tasks for different users. In this example, this can lead to the identification of different motivations (based on different tasks) of the intended users, which may encourage them to participate in upcoming events.

What: This involves *publicizing specific events* (as opposed to *encouraging membership,* which is a related task) the *registration* for these events, and *encouraging people to participate* in them as *participants* or perhaps as *volunteer staff.*

NOTE: This identifies two more specific user groups for consideration: participants and volunteer staff.

When and where: This will be done over a given period of time preceding the start of the *event*. It may be combined with *membership recruiting* in some instances.

NOTE: This identifies a relationship between this and other tasks.

Why: This is done to ensure that all *members* and *potential members know* about the *events* and that as many as possible of them *participate*. The ease of *registration* may affect achievement of the desired level of *participation*.

NOTE: This introduces three general criteria (which also happen to be related tasks) for success, which can be used in evaluating the trade-offs posed by possible designs:

- Knowing about events
- Registering for events
- Participating in events

How: This is done primarily via *printed materials* such as *newsletters* and event-specific *flyers*. These materials may include *schedules, advertisements,* and *articles* encouraging involvement in the *organization* and its *activities*. The task may also be done via *informal person-to-person communications*.

NOTE: This identifies another tool, previously overlooked, for consideration: flyers.

How much: This depends on the individual *events* and the *resources* available for this task. If advanced *registration* is involved, the extent of further promotion may be tied to the level of registrations received to date. Where there is a limited capacity for the event, the ideal may to be to reach full capacity. Where there is previous experience with the event, the objective may be to achieve a certain increase in *participation*.

NOTE: This introduces a yet-to-be-specified constraint involving limited resources that may affect the success. This constraint will require further analysis, in keeping with the accepted guidelines for trade-off analysis decided for this project, before being transformed into a specific design requirement.

With which: This task uses *information about upcoming events* that is obtained from *the people responsible for the events* and a variety of *other sources*.

NOTE: This recognizes that there may be sources other than the people responsible for the events.

7.4   PERFORMING REQUIREMENTS ANALYSIS

7.4.1   Analyzing Requirements in Organizations

7.4.1.1   Defining and Using System Boundaries

There will be more than enough to analyze within the scope of an alternative that has been chosen after a feasibility study. Care needs to be taken that developers do not get sidetracked from the analysis of relevant application components. To assist in maintaining a suitable focus, requirements analysis often is constrained within a reasonably well-specified set of system boundaries.

System boundaries can be defined either inclusively or exclusively.

- Inclusive definitions often read like grocery lists, specifying the features or main components of a system. The problem with this type of definition is that it seldom changes with changing needs. A better type of inclusive definition focuses on the goals or tasks that a system is to perform.
- Exclusive definitions focus on what the system doesn't do, with the implication that the system should do everything else within reason. Exclusive definitions can focus on the interface between a system and other systems (including systems involving identifiable users and/or organizations).

Specifying a set of system boundaries for an e-Commerce application should not result in over-constraining the freedom of developers to identify potential application components that would significantly improve the resulting system. The system boundaries for an e-Commerce system can be specified in terms of:

- The goals and objectives of the system
- Relationships between the system and other systems (including users and/or organizations)

Developers should:

- Identify application components that are clearly either within or outside of the system boundaries
- Reexamine the system boundaries whenever they encounter application components that are not clearly either within or outside of the system boundaries.

 Find further information about establishing system boundaries in the Chapter 7 Cyber Supplement.

7.4.1.2   Identifying Application Components

While system boundaries can be helpful in guiding developers, people who do not understand the potential scope of an application may easily misunderstand them. Most people are more familiar with their area of an organization than with other related areas. They may be quick to spot what's missing in an analysis if given the chance.

Therefore it is important for users to be aware of and able to comment on the set of application components that developers have identified. At the same time, users should not be led to believe that everything that goes into an analysis will be dealt with either in the way they want or at least in some manner. Users should be made aware that while the developing system will be based on the identified application components, it may not deal with all of them at this time.

7.4.1.3   Describing Application Components

Developers are responsible for developing accurate descriptions of the application components that they analyze. While individual users may often color or slant their view of application components, the developer needs to identify and remove biases, wherever possible. This often involves getting various independent viewpoints. Developers need to be careful about unsubstantiated information that is presented to them as "fact."

7.4.2 Student Assignment—Analyzing Requirements

This assignment bridges the gap between what you've already discovered and a more formal analysis to be performed in the next chapter. Specifically it should be based on the application chosen and described in the Chapter 4 assignment and the alternative for developing that application found most feasible in the Chapter 6 assignment. If your Chapter 6 assignment did not find developing an application feasible, then a more suitable application should be used for this assignment.

This assignment deals with analyzing potential requirements in greater detail. You should avoid any inclinations you may have to start designing a particular solution at this time. Your feasibility study only determined that an alternative is worth considering further, leading toward a development, not the details of what should be developed.

Applications are composed of users, tasks, content, and tools. A complete analysis should fully investigate each of these components. However, that would take longer than is feasible within a typical course setting. Therefore this chapter's assignment will focus on investigating and describing a selected group of the most important components involved in your project.

Analysis should involve finding out more about what is needed. Your starting point is your initial investigation. If it was done correctly:

- The "who's" should have identified most of the important users of the application
- The "what's" should have identified most of the important tasks of the application
- The "how's" should have identified most of the important tools that may be used with the application
- The "with which's" should have identified most of the important content chunks of the application

Since you completed your initial investigation you may have identified additional groups of users, tasks, tools, and content chunks. In this assignment you are again asked to consider which of these components are important, including ones that you may have missed. You are also asked to gain a more detailed understanding of each of these components.

7.4.2.1 Identifying User Groups and Tasks

Develop a list of user groups and a list of tasks involved with your application.

NOTE: Not all stakeholders are users.

- Start with those in your initial application description
- Identify and include at least two additional significant user groups for your application (beyond the number of who's in your initial application description)
- Identify and include at least two additional significant tasks for your application (beyond the number of what's in your initial application description)
- Rank each of the lists in order of the potential importance of the user groups/ tasks to the success of the application. Describe the criteria you chose for doing this ranking along with your rank ordered lists.

NOTE:

- If you choose to subdivide any user groups or tasks, the total numbers of resulting user groups and tasks must be at least two greater than the original numbers.

(e.g., a single user group divided into two new groups produces a net addition of one user group).

- You may also decide that existing user groups or tasks should be combined, even though this would result in a decrease in their number. However, the total numbers of resulting user groups and tasks must still be at least two greater than the original numbers.
- Your application must include some significant competitive advantages in order to be successful. Otherwise there is no major reason why users should switch to the system you are developing.

HINT: The user groups/tasks involved in your basic system, if it was feasible, should be important.

7.4.2.2   Describing User Groups and Tasks

Develop descriptions for at least the five most important items on your list of user groups and develop descriptions for at least the five most important items on your list of tasks.

NOTE:

- You may wish to do more than five descriptions of each type of component, especially if they all logically go together to describe some version of a system that could be feasibly implemented (such as your basic system).
- You may find it easiest to start with the task descriptions because their format is closer to that of the application.
- You must consider some internal groups of users as well as some external groups of users.

7.4.2.3   Identifying Content Chunks and Tools

Develop a list of content chunks and a list of user tools involved with your application.

- Start with those in the Week 2 Development Assignment.
- Identify and include at least two additional significant content chunks for your application.
- Identify and include at least two additional significant tools that might be related to your application.
- Rank each of the lists in order of the potential importance of the content chunks/tools to the success of the application. Describe the criteria you chose for doing this ranking along with your rank-ordered lists.

NOTE:

- Your descriptions of user groups and tasks may already have identified a number of additional significant content chunks/tools.
- If you choose to subdivide any content chunks or tools, the total numbers of resulting content chunks or tools must be at least two greater than the original numbers.
- You may also decide that existing content chunks or tools should be combined, even though this would result in a decrease in their number. However, the total

numbers of resulting content chunks or tools must still be at least two greater than the original numbers.

HINT: Content chunks and tools will be important if they are required to serve important tasks for important user groups.

7.4.2.4 Describing Content Chunks and Tools

Develop descriptions for at least the three most important items on your list of content chunks and develop descriptions for at least the three most important items on your list of user tools.

NOTE: You may wish to do more than three descriptions, especially if they all logically go together to describe some version of a system that could be feasibly implemented (such as your basic system).

7.5 AN EXAMPLE OF REQUIREMENTS ANALYSIS

The criteria used to rank the users, tasks, content, and tools are in direct relationship to achieving organizational goals, the ability to coordinate various user goals, and how they affect the customers (without them we have no business).

7.5.1 Identifying and Describing *Savor the Cup* User Groups

7.5.1.1 Customers

Customers are the reason that *Savor the Cup* is in business and their satisfaction is the main determinant of the organization's success. Customers are the most important users of the system being developed according to both the initial investigation and the feasibility study. Without them, this development would not have proceeded.

The initial investigation identified three different types of customers:

- Potential customers
- Current customers
- Expanding customers

The feasibility study did not eliminate the need for serving any of these three types.

Further investigations identified that a fourth type of customer should also be considered:

- Fraudulent customers—individuals who are acting like customers while intending to do harm to *Savor the Cup*. These include:
  - Competitors—trying to analyze *Savor the Cup's* operations in order to identify ways to copy it or to get a competitive advantage over it
  - Hackers—trying to steal confidential information and/or disrupt operations

Consideration of dealing with the group of fraudulent customers led to identifying a need for protecting information from unauthorized access and tampering. Consideration of dealing with competitors led to identifying different levels of legitimate customers, who should be given different levels of access to sensitive information:

- Potential customers—who could include fraudulent customers, should be provided enough general-level information and services to encourage them to become customers.
- Regular customers—(who could include competitors) who have purchased from *Savor the Cup,* either in person or on-line, should be provided with additional helpful information and services. They should also be encouraged to deal with *Savor the Cup's* sales representatives concerning any major needs of theirs. In this way, the sales representatives can filter out fraudulent customers while encouraging the development of good relations with regular customers.
- Gold Cup customers—who are legitimate regular customers who have been given access to advanced system features by *Savor the Cup's* sales representatives. It is hoped that most regular customers can be moved to becoming Gold Cup customers who will make considerable use of the system and will only need to deal with sales representatives on special occasions.

NOTE:

- Expanding customers are no longer considered a different type of customer. They could be potential customers, regular customers, or Gold Cup customers, each of whom may have a variety of needs, including the need for assistance in expanding.
- While fraudulent customers may be potential customers or regular customers (and even possibly Gold Cup customers) it will still be important to analyze how to deal with them.

Based on the above analysis, user group descriptions should be produced for:

- Customers—as a general group
- Potential customers
- Regular customers
- Gold Cup customers
- Fraudulent customers

A description of the group **customers** could include the following. *Customer Characteristics* would include:

- Customers can include individuals, small businesses and coffee shops, and large organizations.
- Customers may be looking to meet their regular ongoing needs or wanting to expand into new areas of the coffee industry.
- Customers may be located anywhere in the world. *Savor the Cup* needs to ensure accessibility for customers speaking different languages to maintain cultural and language sensitivity.
- Potential customers include:
  - Individuals wanting quality coffee and/or coffee products
  - Businesses interested in setting up a coffee shop, or looking for a new supplier
- Regular customers require continual support for product and equipment supply and upgrading training when necessary.

- Gold cup customers are regular customers who have been given access to advanced features of the system.
- Fraudulent customers are individuals who are acting like customers while intending to do harm to *Savor the Cup.*
- Depending on the customer's needs, they may be in contact with:
  - Sales representatives
  - Consultants
  - Logistics
  - Accountants

Customer Tasks could include the following:

- Placing orders regarding custom-blended coffee beans, coffee equipment, and consulting services on-line or in-person.
- Customers may search for more information about the company and the industry.

NOTE: The tasks listed here are very general. However, they go beyond the tasks from the initial investigation, which didn't actually identify any customer tasks. Further investigation will be required, and this portion of the user description will need to be modified before this analysis is complete.

Customer Membership:

- Anyone interested in coffee or coffee products can become a customer
- See descriptions of particular types of customers for further details

Customer Significance could include:

- Serving customers via e-Commerce is considered essential for the success of *Savor the Cup* in its future

Customer Feasibility could include:

- Meeting the needs of customers has been dealt with in the previous feasibility study

Customer Treatment could include:

- See descriptions of particular types of customers for details

Customer With Which could include:

- See descriptions of particular types of customers for details

A description of the group **Potential customers** could include the following.

Potential Customer Characteristics:

- Customers may be looking to meet their regular ongoing needs or wanting to expand into new areas of the coffee industry
- Potential customers need to be convinced of the benefits to them of doing business with *Savor the Cup.* There are a variety of reasons they may consider, including:
  - Quality
  - Availability
  - Support
  - Cost

- Potential customers include:
  - Individuals wanting quality coffee and/or coffee products
  - Businesses interested in setting up a coffee shop or looking for a new supplier
- Customers may be located anywhere in the world. *Savor the Cup* needs to ensure accessibility for customers speaking different languages to maintain cultural and language sensitivity
- Depending on the customer's needs they may be in contact with:
  - Sales representatives
  - Consultants

Potential Customer Tasks:

- Placing orders regarding custom-blended coffee beans, coffee equipment, and consulting services on-line or in-person
- Customers may search for more information about the company and the industry

Potential Customer Membership:

- Anyone can become a potential customer.
- Potential customers are people who:
  - Are interested in coffee or coffee products
  - Are not regular customers (see membership for regular customers)

NOTE: Occasional customers who do not meet the criteria for being considered regular customers will be considered potential customers.

- There is no commitment or other qualifications required to become a potential customer.

Potential Customer Significance:

- Potential customers provide the largest opportunity for growth for *Savor the Cup*

Potential Customer Feasibility:

- Meeting the needs of customers has been dealt with in the previous feasibility study

Potential Customer Treatment:

- Potential customers need to be encouraged to become regular customers
- Potential customers need to be allowed to purchase products as occasional customers without being required to become regular customers
- Potential customers purchasing services from *Savor the Cup* will usually become regular customers

Potential Customer With Which:

- Potential customers require information about:
  - *Savor the Cup* products and services
  - How to order products and services
  - Why they should purchase products and services from *Savor the Cup*
  - How to use products
- Potential customers may be encouraged to return to *Savor the Cup's* Web site if it provides additional information of interest regarding coffee and coffee products

NOTE: Space limitations prevent the inclusion of further user group descriptions.

7.5.1.2 Sales

Sales people are essential for *Savor the Cup* to meet the needs of their customers. It is anticipated that the development of an e-Commerce system will create some changes in the sales structure. The initial investigation identified four different types of sales staff:

- Sales representatives
- Marketers
- Consultants
- After sales service

The feasibility study did not eliminate the need for serving any of these types. However, it did not actually consider after sales service staff as separate from sales representatives and/or consultants. Further investigations suggest that the roles of sales representatives and after-sales service will merge with the shift of consulting to become a saleable service.

Based on the above analysis, user group descriptions should be produced for:

- Sales—as a general group
- Sales representatives
- Consultants
- Marketers

7.5.1.3 Suppliers

It has been decided, in the feasibility study, that the new system should start developing some aspects of supplier–customer systems integration. It will do this by allowing suppliers to use the system to obtain current information from *Savor the Cup* about its current product needs. The initial investigation identified two different types of suppliers:

- Coffee equipment/supplies manufacturers
- Coffee bean growers

The feasibility study did not eliminate the need for serving any of these types. Further investigations identified that a third type of supplier should also be considered:

- Fraudulent suppliers—individuals who are acting like suppliers while intending to do harm to *Savor the Cup*. These include:
  - Competitors—trying to analyze *Savor the Cup's* operations in order to identify ways to copy it or to get a competitive advantage over it
  - Hackers—trying to steal confidential information and/or disrupt operations.

Based on the above analysis, user group descriptions should be produced for:

- Suppliers—as a general group
- Coffee equipment/supplies manufacturers
- Coffee bean growers
- Fraudulent suppliers

7.5.1.4 Purchasing

It has been decided, in the feasibility study, that the new system should start developing some aspects of supplier–customer systems integration. It will do this by allowing purchasing to provide suppliers with current information about *Savor the Cup's* current product needs.

The initial investigation identified two different types of purchasers:

- Grower contacts
- Equipment and supplies procurers

The feasibility study did not deal with either of these types on their own. Further investigations found that there was little difference between types, given their expected role in the system.

Based on the above analysis, a user group description should be produced for:

- Purchasing

7.5.1.5 Accounting

Accounting will be needed to ensure that all sales are properly recorded, processed, and paid for. Accounting will also need to prepare a variety of management reports analyzing changes to existing sales patterns.

7.5.1.6 Logistics

Logistics may be involved to ensure that the correct order is delivered promptly and in good condition to the customers.

7.5.2 Identifying and Describing *Savor the Cup* Tasks

The initial identification example in Chapter 4 had the following characteristics:

- Only identified tasks of the *Savor the Cup* and not tasks of either their suppliers or customers (this is further reinforced by the weak statement of the "what" in the descriptions of customers and of potential customers found in the example above)
- Identified a number of tasks that could be part of a deluxe system but have been excluded for the time being by the feasibility study example in Chapter 6

Rather than just dealing with the tasks previously identified, this example will analyze the needs of the users and the application in light of the agreed-upon basic system boundaries. Further analysis should be performed to consider how these tasks relate to the different types of business activities involved in business transactions. However, space precludes providing this further analysis as part of this example.

7.5.2.1 Customer Tasks

There were only two tasks originally identified for customers:

- Placing orders regarding custom-blended coffee beans, coffee equipment, and consulting services on-line or in person
- Customers may search for more information about the company and the industry

Both of these somewhat miss identifying the true needs of the users.

- Placing orders is just part of the task of acquiring products and/or services. Few people place orders without first determining their need for the product or service and then selecting and comparing suitable products or services.
  - Where reordering is involved, the customer may choose to give only brief consideration to these other subtasks, based on previous success
  - Where new orders are considered, these subtasks may become much more involved than the actual subtask of ordering
- Information is only sought in order to make some, as yet unidentified, decision. Besides making decisions related to acquiring products and/or services, customers may be interested in information that:
  - Helps them to use products that have been acquired
  - Helps them make other coffee industry-related decisions (such as changes to the way they run their own businesses)

A description of the task **Acquire products and services** could include:

Acquire Products and Services Who:

All types of customers, including potential customers, regular customers, and Gold Cup customers need to acquire products and services

Acquire Products and Services What:

Customers perform this task to satisfy their real and imagined needs for products and services. This task involves a number of subtasks, including:

- Determining a need for the product or service (which is generally done on one's own but which may be influenced by advertising or other information that a customer receives)
- Identifying, selecting, and comparing suitable products or services that could meet the need; this may include:
  - Sampling products—especially sampling blends of coffee
  - Selecting a reliable seller of the products/services

NOTE: Where a reorder is involved, the need for this step may be minimized.

- Placing an order, including:
  - Ordering selected specific products and/or services
  - Arranging payment
  - Arranging delivery
- Any required follow-ups, including handling problems:
  - With late deliveries
  - With product quality

Acquire Products and Services When and Where:

- Currently customers primarily perform this task and its various subtasks at their own business locations. Ordering also requires the involvement of a *Savor the Cup* sales representative.

- Provisions need to be made for delays between the time of ordering and the time of receiving products and/or services.

Acquire Products and Services Why:

- Currently customers are performing the task as a major part of operating their own businesses. Without performing the task, most of their businesses would cease to exist.
- The care they take and the flexibility available to them will have a major impact on their business's success.

Acquire Products and Services How:

- Currently customers perform part of the task on their own and part working with sales representatives from *Savor the Cup* and its competitors.
- See descriptions of particular subtasks for details.

Acquire Products and Services How Much:

- While the overall task is typically performed only once a year for most customers, individual subtasks are often performed monthly or even weekly by many customers.

Acquire Products and Services With Which:
Customers will use a range of information to perform this task, including:

- Information on trends in their industry
- Information about their customers' wants, needs, and buying habits
- Information about their competition
- Information about their own strengths and weaknesses
- Information about available products and services
- Information about companies supplying products and services
- Information about delivery times and other delivery-related options

NOTE:

- Each of the subtasks identified for "acquire products and services" needs to be analyzed and described.
- Further analysis is needed to identify and describe each of the various customer decisions that might be served by the proposed system.
- Each of the customer-related user descriptions need to have their set of tasks updated.

7.5.2.2 Sales Tasks

There are a large number of different tasks relating to sales. The initial investigation already identified a number of tasks that could be structured in terms of the sales groups responsible for performing them. This structure then formed the basis for further analysis. The following set of tasks were identified from this analysis:

- Marketing tasks include:
  - Creating an excellent reputation for our products and services
  - Marketing the company and its products and services to customers

- Identifying opportunities for gaining a larger market share via serving new customers
- Sales representative tasks
  - Helping customers

NOTE: This task comes from considering how *Savor the Cup* can assist the customer task of acquiring products and services to:

- Identify their needs
- Identify *Savor the Cup* products/services that meet these needs
- Handling customer orders, whether they are received on-line or in person, including placing orders for customers
- Initiating contact with customers to ensure that their needs have been met and that they are satisfied with the entire purchase experience
- Responding to customers' questions and concerns
- Consulting tasks
  - Providing in-person and on-line consulting services for free and/or for fee in the areas of:
    General business operations and start-up
    Employee training in equipment use
    Expanding customer consulting
    Updating training
  - Improving and developing customers' businesses. (By ensuring their success and satisfaction, their loyalty will be gained and *Savor the Cup* will be able to meet their needs efficiently and sustain its own business.)

NOTES:
- Each of these tasks and subtasks needs to be analyzed and described.
- Each of the sales related user descriptions need to have their set of tasks updated.

7.5.2.3   Supplier Tasks

Like customers, the relevant tasks of suppliers where not identified in the initial investigation. The following tasks would have been identified from developing user descriptions of suppliers and from further identification and analysis of supplier needs:

- Identifying needs of *Savor the Cup* which the supplier could fill
- Bidding on or otherwise negotiating the supplying of *Savor the Cup* with products and/or services
- Providing the agreed upon products/service to *Savor the Cup*
- Receiving payment for those products/services
- Handling problems arising from these tasks

While the feasibility study placed limitations on how far the system will go toward meeting these needs, it is within the system boundaries to provide information that could be used for each of these supplier tasks. Therefore, each of these tasks should be further analyzed and described.

7.5.2.4 Purchasing Tasks

Analysis of purchasing needs led to the following set of tasks that could be assisted by the proposed system:

- Communicating product or service needs to potential suppliers
- Advising potential suppliers how to bid on filling these needs
- Scheduling deliveries of products/services
- Handling problems from these tasks

Given the current limitations determined by the feasibility study, the list of purchasing tasks has been revised to be:

- Communicating product or service needs to potential suppliers
- Advising suppliers on how to interact with *Savor the Cup,* including how to:
  - Bid on filling needs
  - Schedule deliveries
  - Handle problems

These two tasks need to be analyzed and described.

7.5.2.5 Accounting Tasks

An analysis of accounting tasks involved in the system identified two main classes of tasks:

- Financial tasks include:
  - Handling accounts receivable
  - Handling accounts payable (refunds and payments to suppliers)
- Management accounting tasks (which will also serve the needs of management) include:
  - Analyzing sales, cost of sales, and other budget related data
  - Identifying trends
    With old and new customers
    With traditionally placed orders and with on-line orders
  - Auditing the information security of the system
  - Auditing the finances related to the system

Each of these tasks and subtasks needs to be analyzed and described.

7.5.2.6 Logistics tasks

As identified in the initial investigation, logistics involves coordination between sales, manufacturing, and purchasing. It can involve scheduling:

- Purchasing supplies and/or products
- Manufacturing activities
- Shipping the coffee and/or products

Each of these three tasks needs to be analyzed and described.

7.5.3 Identifying and Describing *Savor the Cup* Content

The original set of content needs identified in the initial investigation, like the set of tasks, should be revised to fit the boundaries established in the feasibility study and the other requirements already identified in the analysis.

Customers require content that:

- Is related to determining their needs and assist them in identifying and evaluating their own needs
- Is related to selecting and comparing products that:
  - Describes the products and services available
  - Assists them in comparing products and services
  - Assists them in developing custom blends
  - Provides them confidence in dealing with *Savor the Cup*
- Assists them in ordering products and/or services
- Provides the status of outstanding orders and invoices
- Assists them in contacting a sales representative
- Assists them in handling problems
- Assists them in using the products and services in their own business
- Informs them about industry trends that may be of interest

Sales people require content that:

- Can be used to market *Savor the Cup* and its products and services
- Identifies *Savor the Cup's* customers
- Identifies opportunities based on:
  - An analysis of sales trends
  - A history of individual customers
  - An analysis of industry trends
- Helps them identify customer needs
- Provides public information about products and/or services
- Provides confidential information to support selling products and/or services, including:
  - Information for establishing custom pricing
  - Information on product availability, including the availability of manufacturing custom products
  - Tips on selling particular products and/or services
- Assists them in ordering products and/or services for customers
- Reminds them to contact major customers on a regular basis
- Helps them track progress with potential customers
- Helps them handle consulting tasks, including:
  - Information that tells them how to provide specific consulting services
  - Information that they can give the customer during specific consulting services

Suppliers need content that:

- Describes the needs of *Savor the Cup*
- Provides them information on how to interact with *Savor the Cup*

Purchasing needs content that:

- Provides information on current inventories
- Provides information on the status and details of outstanding orders
- Provides information on suppliers, including their prices, reliability, and quality
- Can be used to get suppliers to bid on the needs of *Savor the Cup*
- Can be given to suppliers to advise them on how to interact with *Savor the Cup*

Accounting needs content that:

- Identifies *Savor the Cup's* customers
- Provides the financial details relating to the application
- Provides management information relating to the application

Administration needs content that:

- Analyzes the success of *Savor the Cup's* operations
- Analyzes *Savor the Cup's* accounts and finances

Logistics needs content that:

- Identifies *Savor the Cup's* customers
- Provides information on current inventories
- Provides information on the status and details of outstanding orders
- Provides a schedule of manufacturing activities
- Provides a schedule of required shipping dates

NOTE:

- Some of this content is used for multiple users and/or multiple tasks.
- Further analysis should be performed to consolidate content chunks that are identified multiple times in the above list.
- Clear and distinct names of content chunks need to be developed that will be used throughout all descriptions to refer to these content chunks.
- It is important to analyze and describe each of the types of content and any further types of content that this analysis might also identify.
- The content descriptions should clearly identify where content is to be restricted to select users only.

A description of the content involving **public information on products and services** could include:

Public Information on Products and Services Who:

- All types of customers
- All types of sales people

Public Information on Products and Services What:

- To suggest solutions to customer needs (and to even suggest potential wants or needs)
- To identify and describe available products and/or services
- To assist in selecting or comparing products and/or services
- To provide information on pricing and availability of products and/or services
- To provide access (links) to ordering products and/or services
- To provide reference links to how products and/or services can be used

Public Information on Products and Services When:

- This information needs to be kept current when any changes occur
- However, most of this information will remain relatively stable once it is entered
- Prices and availability are most likely to change

Public Information on Products and Services Where:

- This content is created and maintained by marketing
- Some content may include information from or references to *Savor the Cup's* suppliers; however, care needs to be taken not to have customers bypass *Savor the Cup* and go directly to these suppliers

Public Information on Products and Services Why:

- This information is central to the application

Public Information on Products and Services How:

- Currently this information is contained in sales manuals issued to each sales representative
- Portions of this information may be given to select customers, but largely this is done orally rather than in written form
- Making this information more public, via e-Commerce, can help the competition as well as legitimate customers

Public Information on Products and Services How Much:

- *Savor the Cup* has over 150 varieties of roasted coffees, which are available as beans or ground to order
- *Savor the Cup* makes over 1000 custom blends for its customers, which would remain confidential
- *Savor the Cup* has a growing selection of coffee-related appliances and other coffee-related products that currently include about 2500 individual products
- Each product or service content chunk is expected to be between one and five printed pages long with an average length of two printed pages

Public Information on Products and Services With Which:

- Product and/or service content chunks will generally contain information that:
  - Names and describes the product and/or service
  - Links the product and/or services to needs that it might satisfy
  - Shows a picture, if applicable
  - Describes quantities, prices, and availability
  - Links the product and/or service to similar or complementary products and/or services
  - Links to advice on how to use the product and/or service
  - Depending on user, links to:
    Current and past customer orders
    Confidential sales information
    Inventory levels
    Industry trends related to the product and/or service

7.5.4 Identifying and Describing *Savor the Cup* Tools

The main tool that ties this application together currently is *Savor the Cup's* customer order form. Additional tools include:

- Product samples—provided by sales to customers
- Sales manual—used by sales people
- Marketing information—provided to customers
- Industry information—provided to customers
- Meetings—in person or by telephone, between sales representatives and customers
- Telephones, mail, and faxes—for transmitting orders and other correspondence
- Supplier order forms—to record orders to *Savor the Cup* suppliers
- Inventory records—used by logistics and purchasing
- Schedules—used by various *Savor the Cup* employees

The future system would involve all these tools, but would move as much as possible to using Web-based versions to improve communications. (Obviously you cannot sample coffee on the Web, but the Web could be used to sell samples to a much larger group of customers.)

A description of a Web-based **Customer Order Form** could include:

Customer Order Form Who:

- All types of customers around the world
- Sales representatives
- Accounting
- Logistics

Customer Order Form What:

- Provides a basis for creating, tracking, and filling orders
- May involve specialty pricing for certain customers

Customer Order Form Where and When:

- Would be available on-line at all times
- Could be used by the customer on their own or via a sales representative

Customer Order Form Why:

- Greatly expands the number of potential customers
- Speeds up communications

Customer Order Form How:

- Customers decide what they want via the Web or personally from a sales representative
- Either the customer or the sales representative could use an access code to place the order quickly and efficiently so that the information was immediately transferred to *Savor the Cup*
- This information will then be available to the appropriate staff so that the physical aspect of the order may be completed

Customer Order Form How Much:

- It is expected that all of *Savor the Cup's* current orders, which average 400 orders per working day, would be placed using this system either by customers or by sales representatives

- It is expected that during the first year of operations the number of orders would grow to 1000 per day, with many of these new orders being for small quantities or sample packs

Customer Order Form With Which:

- Order forms would use content that includes:
  - Customer identification (either from an existing customer record or involving creating a new customer record)
  - Product and/or service identification (from public information on products and services)
  - Quantities of each product and/or service ordered
  - Pricing information (generated automatically by the system or specially by a sales representative)
  - Shipping information
  - Payment information

NOTE:

- The content requirements are further refined by considering the particular requirements of this tool.
- Each of the other tools need to be analyzed and defined.

7.5.5 Example Summary

Although this example is quite lengthy, it is obviously very incomplete. Not only are many components not described, but in describing components, the need to consider additional components becomes clear. It is hoped that this demonstrates the need for iterative development, since space limitations make it impossible to actually provide a complete example of iteration at work for this application.

7.6 CHALLENGES AND OPPORTUNITIES IN REQUIREMENTS ANALYSIS

The following are the most frequent problems encountered with e-Commerce requirements analysis. They only apply to some developments. They are listed here to help you avoid them.

General Challenges with Descriptions

- Descriptions are often too general. They do not exhibit a sufficient understanding of the application involved. In some cases, they demonstrate little advancement beyond the information contained in an initial investigation.
- Some descriptions may be unclear and vague; they may assume too much and don't make it obvious what they are talking about.

Challenges with Interactions between Descriptions

- A component referred to in one description may not be described separately, or its description may not refer back to the other description that referenced it.

- Names of components may not be consistent. Components may be referred to by different names.

Challenges with System Boundaries

- While it is important to consider all relevant information, care needs to be taken that each component is analyzed in terms of how it applies to the system being developed.

Challenges with User Descriptions

- For significance of user groups, some developers focus on why the application is significant for the user, not how serving this group will "benefit" the owner of the proposed system.
- Some developers deal with "treatment" from the users perspective and do not know how the company should treat the user.

Challenges with Tasks

- Some tasks are beyond the scope of the application as currently described. While it is important that projects be unique, it must be clear how unique tasks fit in with the rest of the application.
- While it is important to understand the range of tasks users perform, when considering the tasks to be analyzed by themselves, it is more important to consider those involved in the application and particularly those that automation could potentially affect.
- Some tasks are named with general phrases instead of a descriptive verb phrase that focuses on the accomplishment.

Challenges with Content Chunks

- If the detailed components of content are focused on too early in the analysis, existing content expectations may limit the analysis. It is preferable to focus on more general content chunks first and then to analyze what they might involve once the rest of the application components are better understood.

Challenges with Tools

- While it is important to understand the range of tools that users are familiar with and use, when considering the tools to be analyzed by themselves, it is more important to consider those involved in the application and particularly those that could be automated.

7.7   CYBER SUPPLEMENTS FOR CHAPTER 7

Look at the Chapter 7 Cyber Supplements on the Web to find:

- Further information regarding task analysis
- Further information regarding identifying tasks, users, content chunks, and tools
- Further information regarding establishing system boundaries
- Practice activities for conducting a task analysis-based requirements analysis

REFERENCES

[1] "International Organization for Standardization," ISO International Standard 13407, Human Centered Design Processes for Interactive Systems, 1999.

[2] "International Organization for Standardization," Annex F to ISO/IEC 1st Committee Draft of International Standard 15944-1, Business Agreement Semantic Descriptive Techniques—Part 1: Operational Aspects of Open-edi for Implementation, 1999.

[3] "International Organization for Standardization," ISO Draft International Standard 14915-1, Software Ergonomics for Multimedia User Interfaces: Design Principles and Framework, 2000.

[4] "International Organization for Standardization," ISO Committee Draft 14915-2, Software Ergonomics for Multimedia User Interfaces: Multimedia Control and Navigation, 2000.

[5] "International Organization for Standardization," ISO/IEC 2nd Committee Draft of International Standard 15944-1, Business Agreement Semantic Descriptive Techniques—Part 1: Operational Aspects of Open-edi for Implementation, 2000.

[6] Ibid.

[7] Ibid.

[8] Ibid.

Formalizing Analysis

8.1   INTRODUCTION TO FORMALIZING ANALYSIS

By this stage, a developer should have a reasonable idea of the major requirements of the application. In real life this would only be a starting point for a thorough, detailed analysis that might take any person months to do properly.

So far analysis has been considered in terms that should be most meaningful to users and stakeholders of applications. This chapter describes the transition to a more formal (structured and regulated) statement of analysis that is most meaningful to computer professionals.

Claiming that either type of analysis is stated in terms that are more meaningful to one group does not mean either that it is more important in terms of development or that the other group should not be able to understand. However, it is important to recognize that each group tends to think about and focus on aspects of analysis that are most directly relevant to their work. This difference in thinking can create considerable communication difficulties (which may lead to difficulties in the resulting system) if both groups don't make a good effort to understand each other.

8.2   UNDERSTANDING OBJECT-ORIENTED ANALYSIS

8.2.1   Modeling the Real World and e-Worlds

So far our analysis has been based on analysis of tasks and other components related to accomplishing tasks (users, content, and tools). However, tasks are a relatively abstract concept and may be a subject of considerable debate among well-informed persons.

If we want to deal with the real world, we are likely to focus on the concrete objects that interact within it. You can see, touch, and even hire people (users), documents (content), and equipment (tools). You can see them interact in real life. You can draw pictures or develop models to illustrate their interactions, even if you don't realize what their intentions are or what they might be accomplishing. And you can program systems to mimic them. (Of course, these models won't be much use if the collection of objects being modeled doesn't accomplish anything useful.)

Objects are real things or concepts that we deal with in our everyday life. Most people should recognize and agree on the recognition of most objects.

Norman[1] states, "An object is a person, place, or thing such as student, faculty, sales clerk, city hall, famous park, ATM machine, and video tape."

Smith[2] states, "An object represents an individual, identifiable item, unit, or entity, either real or abstract, with a well-defined role in the problem domain."

Rumbaugh[3] states, "We define an object as a concept, abstraction, or thing with crisp boundaries and meaning for the problem at hand. Objects serve two purposes: they promote understanding of the real world and provide a practical basis for computer implementation. Decomposition of a problem into objects depends on judgment and the nature of the problem. There is no one correct representation."

Jacobson[4] states, "An object is characterized by a number of operations and a state which remembers the effect of these operations. An object-oriented model consists of a number of objects; these are clearly delimited parts of the modeled system.

Objects usually correspond to a real-life entity object, such as an invoice, a car, or a mobile telephone. Each object contains individual information (e.g., a car has its registration number)."

Booch[5] states, "From the perspective of human cognition, an object is any of the following:

- A tangible and/or visible thing
- Something that may be apprehended intellectually
- Something toward which thought or action is directed

"An object models some part of reality and is therefore something that exists in time and space.... Some objects may have crisp conceptual boundaries, yet represent intangible events or processes.... Some objects may be tangible, yet have fuzzy physical boundaries. Objects such as rivers, fog, and crowds of people fit this definition."

Computer professionals have gone from modeling computer programs with algorithms and data structures (which they did prior to the mid-1980s) to modeling the interaction of real-world objects within computer programs (which an increasing number of them have done since then).

The result is that both the real world and an e-World can be modeled in terms of a set of interacting objects. This does not mean that e-World modeling is just a bunch of descriptions of users, content, and tools, nor does it mean that tasks can be ignored.

Modeling of e-Commerce applications:

- Starts with the descriptions we have accumulated from a thorough task analysis
- Structures some of the information we have accumulated
- Identifies additional information that is needed to transform our requirements into a formal model

This can lead to designing and developing a software system to become part of the real world and to help other objects in the real world to accomplish their tasks.

Object analyses, by themselves, tend to be difficult to accomplish, because they provide little specific guidance about what objects are important to analyze. While a task analysis (by itself) often identifies more components than an object analysis (by itself) would, it may still have missed some components. By shifting from a task analysis to an object-oriented viewpoint we may discover some additional components that were missed.

Object analyses start with looking at existing objects in the real world and tries to identify classes to which these objects belong. It then proceeds to analyze the properties and relationships of each class of objects.

8.2.1.1 Properties of Objects

Objects are defined in terms of their:

- Attributes—**Attributes** store the data (or other content) that describes an object. The value of some attributes may change from time to time reflecting the current state of the object.
- Operations—**Operations** are actions conducted by an object that cause some change to its attributes or to its environment.
- Relationships—**Relationships** specify meaningful connections between objects.

There are a number of important properties of objects that are generally considered by all object-oriented approaches. These properties include:

- **Object models**—All objects can be modeled in terms of their attributes, operations, and relationships (each of which will be discussed in detail in the following sections).
- **Classification**—Objects can be grouped into classes that act in similar manners.
- **Abstraction**—It is suitable to limit consideration of objects to those attributes, operations, and relationships relevant to the current problem/task/application.
- **Identity**—It is should be possible to identify and to distinguish between objects. Although a name can be readily used to distinguish between objects with unique names, it will not be sufficient where many objects exist that are referred to by the same name (e.g., to identify one from among a number of identical chairs). In some cases a number of attributes may need to be used together to uniquely identify an object (e.g., the third chair from the right side in the second row of room 201).
- **Inheritance**—Features (attributes and operations) defined for one class are inherited by all other classes that are instances of that more general class.
- **Encapsulation**—Each object is independent from other objects. Information about an object is only available if that object wishes to make it available to other objects. An object controls its internal operations, including changes to its attributes.
- **Message passing**—Objects interact with other objects via messages that they send requesting that the objects take some action. However, the receiving object can decide whether or not to honor the request.
- **Polymorphism**—Objects can adapt their actions to specific sets of circumstances.

 Find further information about objects and their properties in the Chapter 8 Cyber Supplement.

8.2.2   Objects and Classes

Classes are an abstract means of organizing similar objects in order to treat them in a consistent, predetermined manner. Because classes are abstractions of the real world, there is often no readily-agreed-upon, textbook-like solution to identifying the best set of classes to use.

Booch[6] states, "Whereas an object is a concrete entity that exists in time and space, a class represents only an abstraction, the 'essence' of an object, as it were."

Norman[7] states, "A class is a set or collection of abstracted objects that share common characteristics."

Rumbaugh[8] states, "An object class describes a group of objects with similar properties (attributes), common behavior (operations), common relationships to other objects, and common semantics. Person, company, animal, and window are all object classes. Each person has an age, IQ, and may work at a job."

Jacobson[9] states, "A class defines the operations that can be performed on an instance. It also defines the variables of the instance."

Most object-oriented methodologies assume that developers can identify the appropriate or "best" possible set of classes of objects and skip over this difficulty. This assumption may lead to major disagreements between developers (or between students and their instructors) as to which is the best set of classes to use in a given situation.

What methodologies often fail to say, is that most good sets of classes are probably as good as one another and that we need not spend excess time trying to find the "best" set as long as we have spent sufficient time and care in finding a "good" set. We should be able to use that set until we find some real need that it cannot meet and that thus suggests a needed modification. We will focus our efforts at correctly identifying the important objects to an application and then developing a good set of classes to use in our further development.

Objects exist in the real world. Classes and instances are used to represent objects in object-oriented development. However, the relationship between these three concepts varies slightly, depending on the author you consult. There are at least three ways of considering the relationship of these concepts:

- Some authors identify objects with classes and deal with instances separately
- Some authors identify objects with instances, and deal with classes separately
- Some authors consider both classes and instances as partial representations of objects

By taking the approach of objects being represented by classes and instances, we can further consider what classes and instances involve.

Classes are like templates for objects. They describe all possible:

- **Attributes**—Attributes are passive features of an object. Defining the set of attributes of a class of objects is similar to designing a set of forms, where each form has the same set of spaces to insert data into it.
- **Operations**—Operations are active features of an object. Defining a set of operations is similar to defining how common instincts, procedures, rules, and laws dictate how we all should act.
- **Relationships**—Relationships exist where objects share features or interactions with each other. Defining a set of relationships is similar to defining the roles and interactions of different components in a system.

Instances are particular examples of objects that belong to some class.

- You and I are instances of objects that belong to the class of "people."
  - You may be (an instance of) an object that belongs to the class of "students." However, the associated definition of you as an instance of the class of "people" encompasses a number of attributes and operations that are not needed in just considering you as a student.
  - I am an instance of class "author." Likewise I am an instance of class "people" and share with you all the attributes and operations of that class.
  - When dealing with objects we must be sure to place them in the appropriate context (instance-class relationship) so that we know what attributes and operations are important to consider.
- Attributes have their own values for each instance. Thus, we each have our own name.

- Operations are common for all instances of an object. They may be modified by particular attributes. Thus, we all eat, sleep, and walk, but we may each eat at a different speed or eat a different amount of food.
- Relationships are similar but need not be identical for all instances of an object. Thus, while we all have parents, we do not necessarily share the same parents.

8.2.3   Relationships

Relationships help us to specify how a set of objects work together to accomplish an application. Each relationship is implemented differently. There are three main types of relationships that need to be considered in object-oriented development:

- Generalization-specialization relationships are used to group common attributes and operations so that they are handled in a consistent manner.
- Whole-part relationships are used to identify different objects that need to be considered on their own.
- Association relationships are used to identify objects that need to interact with each other.

8.2.3.1   Generalization-Specialization Relationships

This is often referred to just as the generalization, or the "IS-A" relationship. **Generalizations** exist where one class of objects also IS-A complete example of another class of objects. For example, a square IS-A rectangle.

This relationship is indicated by saying that the specialized class is of the TYPE (of the) generalized class. This means that the specialized class will automatically contain all the attributes and operations defined for the generalized class. Each object that IS-A (instance of some class of objects) will have its own values for each attribute.

Rumbaugh[10] states, "Generalization is the relationship between a class and one or more refined versions of it. The class being refined is called the superclass and each refined version is called a subclass. . . . Attributes and operations common to a group of subclasses are attached to the superclass and shared by each subclass. Each subclass is said to inherit the features of its superclass. . . . Generalization is sometimes called the 'IS-A' relationship because each instance of a subclass is an instance of the superclass as well."

8.2.3.2   Association Relationships

An **association** connects two objects based on some linkage between them. It may be referred to by the name of the characteristic that provides the basis for the association (e.g., "parent–child" relation).

Associations often involve potential interactions. Objects interact with each other by each having one or more operations that interact with the other object. Objects can interact with other objects from the same class and/or with objects from different classes.

Rumbaugh[11] states, "An association describes a group of links with common structure and common semantics. For example, a person 'works-for' a company. All the links in an association connect objects from the same classes. Associations and links often appear as verbs in a problem statement. An association describes a set of potential links in the same way that a class describes a set of potential objects.

8.2.3.3 Whole-Part Relationships

A **whole-part relationship** is a special type of association that connects parts of an object with the whole object. Parts are complete objects on their own as well as parts of larger objects. As separate objects they have their own attributes and operations. Parts are included as attributes of the class that represents the whole.

There are two types of whole-part relationships:

- **Aggregations** are systems that involve a number of parts of similar and/or different types of objects. Individual objects may belong to multiple different aggregations. For example: A person may be part of many different organizations, including: families, businesses, clubs, etc.
- **Compositions** are aggregations where the parts, once created, exist only because they are part of the whole. Compositions are often used to model "roles" that a more permanent object may have. For example: A member is only a member as long as there is a club to which the member belongs. In this case a member is an instance of a person, which is created once the person joins a club. While being a member may cease upon the dissolution of the club, the individual will not cease to exist as an object.

8.2.3.4 An Example of Different Relationships in a System

Consider two classes of people:

- One class has kitchens and can invite other people to dinner
- The other class doesn't have kitchens and cannot invite people to dinner
- Both classes of people can come to dinner if invited

We actually have three classes:

- People (a generalized class)
- People with kitchens (of TYPE people)
- People without kitchens (also of TYPE people)

Consider further that people have names (they have lots more but this will do for our example). We can now describe the classes as follows:

Class: People
Attributes: Name
Operations: Come to dinner if invited (Note: Since all people can do this, it is defined here)
Class: People with kitchens
Type: (People)
Attributes: Kitchen
Operations: Invite other people to dinner

NOTE:

- People with kitchens automatically have names and automatically can come to dinner if invited because they are of type people.

- We don't need to define people without kitchens since their description would not be distinct from our description of people. We should only define them if they had some unique attribute or operation that is not shared by all people.
- We need to define kitchen as a separate object, since it exists separately, even though it is also a part of people with kitchens.

Class: Kitchens
Attributes: Stove, counter, sink
Operations: Prepare dinner

NOTE:

- This leads to identifying further objects (stove, counter, sink, and so on) that might need defining.
- We need to recognize that it is really the person with the kitchen who prepares dinner by including this operation in our description of the class "people with kitchens." The kitchen is just a tool that helps. To avoid confusion between two operations with the same name, we could rename the kitchen's operation to be help prepare dinner. In any case we will have to be sure we are clear about what exact operation each object performs.

In summary:

- We have one generalization
  - Between people with kitchens and people
- We have multiple aggregations
  - Kitchens are part of people with kitchens
  - Stoves, counters, and sinks might be parts of a kitchen
- We have one association (based on invitations and based on preparing dinner)
  - People with kitchens may invite people to dinner

8.2.4   An Example of Identifying Object Classes and Their Relationships

As an example of identifying a group of related objects, consider a bank account.

8.2.4.1   Identifying Object Classes

We can start from considering that:

- A BANK is an organization
- That provides ACCOUNTS
- For its CUSTOMERS

So far there are at least three objects related in some manner that we should consider in any analysis of a bank account:

- The BANK—an organization and thus an object
- The ACCOUNT—a business information object
- The CUSTOMER—an individual person as an object

Each of these three objects actually identifies a class of objects. A BANK wouldn't be worth considering if it didn't have a number of CUSTOMERS and their ACCOUNTS. If we only wanted to model a single BANK, we could limit our focus to the relevant objects within the BANK (i.e., ACCOUNTS) and just take the BANK for granted. However, if we want to be able to compare BANKS, we could consider each BANK to be a distinct object of type BANK. Figure 8-1 illustrates this starting point.

NOTE: There are various graphical conventions used by different authors to illustrate complex object models. The most popular set of conventions will be briefly introduced later in this chapter. However, at this point our diagrams will be kept simple.

- Classes or potential classes will be illustrated with circles.
- All types of relationships will be illustrated with lines.
  - Broken lines will be used at this time to identify relationships that may need further analysis.

We need to analyze each of these classes to see if there are more classes that we should add to our model.

8.2.4.2 Banks

First, let's consider BANKS. BANKS provide lots of BANKING SERVICES, which compose another potential class of objects. These include:

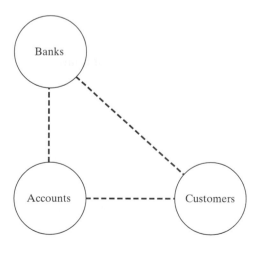

Figure 8-1   The start of a bank account model

- Accounts
- Loans
- Free calendars
- Miscellaneous services

Some day we might want to expand our model to include more BANKING SERVICES. This will be easier to accomplish if we include BANKING SERVICES in our model at this time. However, at this time we will only include one type of BANKING SERVICE, namely ACCOUNTS.

Figure 8-2 illustrates the inclusion of BANKING SERVICES in our model. This is accomplished by adding the new class and its two relationships to existing classes.

8.2.4.3 Accounts

Now let's consider ACCOUNTS. CUSTOMERS have ACCOUNTS. There is a real relationship between these two classes, which can be illustrated in our model but does not require further analysis for now.

We already know that BANKS provide ACCOUNTS, but we need to explore this relationship further. We also know, from the real world, that a particular AC-COUNT is part of a particular BANK that is generally referred to as a BRANCH. Look at the strip of ACCOUNT information on the bottom of a check—it has a BANK code, a branch code, and an ACCOUNT code all to identify your AC-

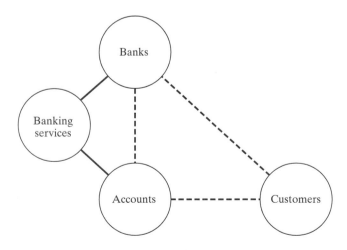

Figure 8-2   Recognizing ACCOUNTS as a type of BANKING SERVICE

COUNT. This might lead us to realize that ACCOUNTS are part of BRANCHES, which are part of BANKS.

We need to do more than say that an ACCOUNT is part of a BRANCH; we need to set up a mechanism for linking them. We can do this by considering what services the BANK via its BRANCH performs on the ACCOUNT. The most obvious is that the BRANCH creates ACCOUNTS for CUSTOMERS. This takes us beyond passive relationships to define at least one interaction between these object classes.

We can summarize our expanded understanding of this system by saying:

- An ACCOUNT is an instance of a BANKING SERVICE
- Provided to a CUSTOMER
- By a BRANCH of a BANK

Figure 8-3 illustrates the inclusion of BRANCHES in our model. Further analysis reveals that the inclusion of BRANCHES fully specifies the previous relationship between BANKS and ACCOUNTS. We can remove our dashed relationship line between these two classes because it is no longer needed. However, we should recognize that BRANCHES provide BANKING SERVICES on behalf of BANKS by an additional relationship between BRANCHES and BANKING SERVICES.

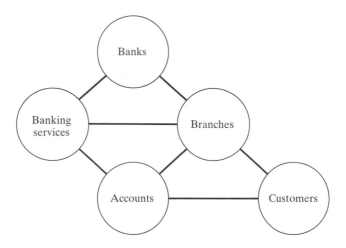

Figure 8-3 Recognizing BRANCHES as instances of BANKS

8.2.4.4   Customers

While we already accepted the relationship between ACCOUNTS and CUS-TOMERS, we still need to consider our model from the perspective of CUS-TOMERS. An ACCOUNT is tied to a single logical CUSTOMER. However, this CUSTOMER can be:

- An individual
- A couple
- An organization
- A business
- A government agency
- Other groups

Also, a CUSTOMER can have and often does have more than one ACCOUNT. This suggests that CUSTOMER is more general than ACCOUNT. By investigating ACCOUNTS and CUSTOMERS further, we can determine that there is a strong relationship between them; in fact, they share some features. For example, if an AC-COUNT has $5, and it is BOB's ACCOUNT, then BOB has $5.

Thus, CUSTOMERS own their ACCOUNTS, and we should consider CUS-TOMERS making their ACCOUNTS in the system. But then, what about our idea of BRANCHES making ACCOUNTS? This requires us to further consider the relationship between CUSTOMERS and BRANCHES.

So let's define CUSTOMERS:

- A CUSTOMER is an INDIVIDUAL who has some business dealing with a BANK.
- However, INDIVIDUALS (a different class of objects, not yet considered) exist independent of any BANK.
- But, CUSTOMERS are only CUSTOMERS (in our system) if they have a BANK ACCOUNT.

Thus we can see that a CUSTOMER can be considered part of a BRANCH, and that it is the BRANCH that makes an INDIVIDUAL into a CUSTOMER. Figure 8-4 illustrates our revised model.

By putting all the above together, we get:

- The BRANCH of the BANK makes INDIVIDUALS into CUSTOMERS that will, in turn, make ACCOUNTS, which are instances of the BANK BRANCH's BANKING SERVICES.
- A CUSTOMER is the BANK's model of an individual (couple, and so on).
- An INDIVIDUAL deals through the BANK (as a CUSTOMER) to access his ACCOUNT.

This example shows that:

- All kinds of things may be objects
- We may miss important layers of object classes (BRANCHES, BANKING SERVICES)
- We may confuse one object class (CUSTOMER) for a different object class (INDIVIDUAL)

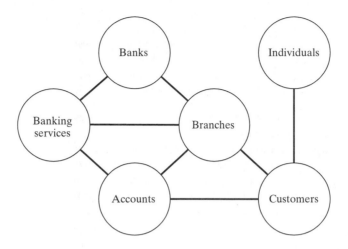

Figure 8-4   An expanded model of the classes related to BANK ACCOUNTS

8.2.4.5   Considering Relationships

While we have now identified a number of classes of objects, we haven't yet considered what to do with them. We need to consider their relationships more formally.

As part of this consideration, it is important for us to remember why we care about these objects. Although the initial example didn't state a purpose explicitly, it was motivated by the desire to develop a system to manage bank accounts. We can start our consideration with the most straightforward relationships and work our way through to the others.

8.2.4.6   Banks and Branches

People typically say, "I'm going to the bank" to mean "I'm going to a particular BRANCH of the BANK." To most people, the BRANCH is the BANK. It offers all the services of the BANK and has all the attributes that they care about. **Thus,** we can consider that a BRANCH is an instance of the BANK.

NOTE: If we were looking at this problem from some other perspective, we might have determined that a BRANCH was part of a BANK. We have to analyze applications from their appropriate perspective!

8.2.4.7   Banks and Banking Services

NOTE: The term BANKING SERVICES sounds quite task oriented. However, remember that we consider them a generalization of ACCOUNTS. BANKING SERVICES is an abstract class that may be useful to allow us to properly position other classes, such as LOANS, at a later time.

Thus, we have already considered that an ACCOUNT is an instance of a BANKING SERVICE.

Rather than dealing with BANKS and BANKING SERVICES, it may be easier to consider BANKS and ACCOUNTS and then to insert BANKING SERVICES.

There is more to a BANK than just ACCOUNTS or even just BANKING SER-VICES. A BANK involves CUSTOMERS (and STAFF and FACILITIES and so on).

Thus, ACCOUNTS (and BANKING SERVICES) can be considered part of BANKS. By inheritance, they also become part of BRANCHES.

8.2.4.8   Individuals and Customers

It is now easier to shift our consideration to INDIVIDUALS and CUSTOMERS than to continue on with the BANK's side of things.

INDIVIDUALS act as CUSTOMERS some of the time. At other times, INDI-VIDUALS act in different ROLES. A ROLE involves only selected aspects of an individual. Thus, a ROLE is part of an INDIVIDUAL, and being a CUSTOMER is an instance of a ROLE. Because we are only concerned about one role of an INDI-VIDUAL in this system, we need not define a class of ROLES. However, based on the relationship between ROLES and INDIVIDUALS, we can see that being a CUSTOMER is only PART of being an INDIVIDUAL.

8.2.4.9   Individuals, Branches, and Customers

Before a CUSTOMER exists, an INDIVIDUAL has to approach a BRANCH and make a formal request to become a customer. This request may take the form of opening an account or establishing some other formal relationship via some other customer service. (For our purposes, getting a free calendar doesn't qualify as be-coming a customer because the bank branch doesn't keep track of you!) It is the BRANCH that makes an INDIVIDUAL a CUSTOMER by creating a customer record for that individual.

Thus, CUSTOMERS are part of both INDIVIDUALS (as previously dis-cussed) and of BRANCHES. If you take either the INDIVIDUAL or the BRANCH from the CUSTOMER, it ceases to exist (even though the BRANCH and the INDIVIDUAL may continue to exist).

8.2.4.10   Branches, Customers, and Accounts

So far we have determined that:

- ACCOUNTS are part of BRANCHES (by inheritance)
- CUSTOMERS are part of BRANCHES (by their creation)

The final relationship involves CUSTOMERS and ACCOUNTS.

In this case, a CUSTOMER can have zero, one, or more ACCOUNTS. (Zero ACCOUNTS would be permissible if the CUSTOMER made formal use of other

BANKING SERVICES, such as LOANS.) An ACCOUNT can only have one CUSTOMER (by definition, even if that CUSTOMER is a couple of individuals or an organization).

In neither of these descriptions have we used any words that can lead us to either a generalization on an aggregation relationship. While both BRANCHES and INDIVIDUALS create CUSTOMERS, only BRANCHES (not CUSTOMERS) can create ACCOUNTS (even though they do so for CUSTOMERS). Thus, ACCOUNTS are not actually parts of CUSTOMERS. Rather, ACCOUNTS are objects with which CUSTOMERS interact. They do this by transferring information and/or money. The relationship between ACCOUNTS and CUSTOMERS is an association, which can be characterized by ACCOUNTS being owned by CUSTOMERS.

Figure 8-5 illustrates our revised model with information about the relationships contained in it. It uses labels and simple arrowheads to specify these relationships, rather than any of the more complicated conventions used by more detailed object-oriented approaches.

NOTE: This still isn't a complete analysis of this system. It only works for INDIVIDUALS who are already CUSTOMERS. It doesn't consider how INDIVIDUALS can become CUSTOMERS. To do so requires that a relationship be added between INDIVIDUALS and BRANCHES that will only be used to create CUSTOMERS.

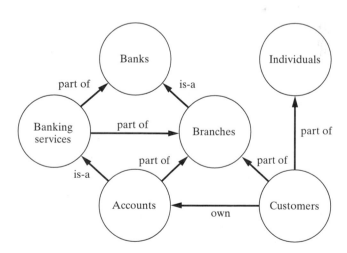

Figure 8-5   An expanded model of the BANK ACCOUNTS classes and relationships

8.2.5 A Procedure for Identifying Object Classes and Their Relationships

The following is a helpful procedure for identifying objects relevant to a given problem. It is not the only procedure and is not guaranteed to work perfectly. But it can help some people, sometimes.

- Look for objects in the problem statement. Remember that objects:
    - Exist in the real world
    - Can be considered on their own
    - Can be named by nouns
    - Have individual attributes
    - Have individual actions (operations)
- If a task analysis was performed, consider that:
    - Users are objects
    - Content chunks are objects
    - Tools are objects
    - Tasks are **Not** objects
- Look for classes of objects in the problem statement (or in your identification of objects). Remember that classes:
    - Include similar objects
    - Share the same types of attributes
    - Share the same operations
- Look for words suggesting relationships in the problem statement (that exist between objects) to find objects related to those already identified, such as:
    - "Has . . ."
    - "Makes . . ."
    - "Is an instance of . . ."
    - "Is part of . . ."
    - "Does something to . . ."
- Look for other relationships in the problem statement (or in your identification of objects) to find relationships already identified. Focus on dividing them into:
    - Generalization/specialization relationships (e.g., "is an instance of . . .")
    - Whole/part relationships (e.g., "is part of . . . .")
    - Association relationships (e.g., all other relations)
- Look for other objects beyond those identified by the problem statement, including:
    - Objects that are external but that might interact with the objects already identified
    - Instances/generalizations of objects
    - Parts of/assemblies of objects
- Look for other related classes beyond those identified. Consider if they enrich the problem statement without making it unnecessarily complex or general.
- Draw a diagram that includes the object classes and their relationships, then use the diagram to verify the completeness and correctness of your set of object classes. Verify the diagram in discussions with representatives of the different groups of stakeholders. Focus on what the diagram contains rather than how pretty it is.

Find further information about relationships in the Chapter 8 Cyber Supplement.

8.2.6 Attributes

All objects of a given class have the same attributes, but each instance of an object has its own values for each of these attributes. Attributes may be defined for a particular object class or inherited from a generalized object class of which the particular object class is an instance.

Norman[12] states, "Each object knows things about itself, called attributes. . . Attribute names (e.g., name, shoe size, eye color, and so on) become the template or pattern that can be applied to all object instances within a class that has attributes associated with it. . . each object instance has its own personal data values for each attribute that makes the attribute template."

Booch[13] refers to attributes as properties of an object "A property is an inherent or distinctive characteristic, trait, quality, or feature that contributes to making an object uniquely that object. . . . All properties have some value. This value might be a simple quantity, or it might denote another object."

Since there are an infinite number of ways of describing most objects, there may be an infinite number of attributes of an object. However, for practical purposes, we usually limit ourselves to considering the attributes of an object that are relevant to the current problem/task/application/etc. Some attributes of a person include name, address, phone number, age, sex, and religion. However, for purposes of delivering a pizza to a person, only the address is really essential. Additional useful attributes may include: name, if a number of people may be found at the same address, and phone number, in case the delivery person gets lost. The other potential attributes are not likely to be relevant and can safely be ignored.

Attributes describe properties of an object. These properties include:

- Characteristics of the whole object.
  - Characteristics usually have a simple value, i.e., a number or a name or some relatively simple combination of numbers and names.
  - We generally don't care any further about characteristics than knowing their value. For example, even though the name of a manufacturer of an object can be used as a reference to another object (the manufacturer), in most cases merely knowing the name is sufficient.
  - However, sometimes we might wish to follow up such a reference.
- Parts of the whole object.
- Parts always refer to other objects, which can be described on their own.
- Often we will find it easier to deal with parts as separate objects to keep each of our object descriptions as simple and focused as possible.
- However, if we don't need a part beyond stating that it is part of an object, then dealing with it simply as a value rather than as a reference will be sufficient.

Because both characteristics and parts can be either simple values or references to other objects, we generally do not distinguish between them. What is important is that we identify as many of each as are relevant to our application.

Consider a chair. Some of it's characteristics include:

- Name: secretarial chair, kitchen chair, rocking chair, Queen Anne chair
- Age: when manufactured or when acquired

- Manufacturer's name
- Value

Some of its parts include:

- Seat (required)
- Back (required)
- Elevation mechanism, or "what keeps it off the floor" (required):
  - Four legs
  - A post
  - A box
- Arms (optional)

8.2.7 An Example of Identifying Attributes

Now that we've identified the classes and relationships we can investigate the classes of objects in further detail, starting with important attributes.

NOTE:

- In this example, lowercase letters are used for the names of attributes that have simple values, and uppercase letters are used for names of attributes that are satisfied by references to other objects.
- It is helpful to provide comments, starting with a dash after the attribute names, to briefly explain each of the attributes. In a complete analysis, each attribute would be analyzed much further before proceeding to design. This further analysis would include identifying permissible values, formats, and uses of the attribute.

8.2.7.1 Object Class = Banks

ATTRIBUTES =
    name—we need to distinguish between banks
    BANKING SERVICES—these objects are part of the BANKS
    BRANCHES—these objects are part of BANKS

NOTE:

- We only need this class if we want to consider multiple banks. Otherwise we could treat BANKING SERVICES & ACCOUNTS only as parts of BRANCHES.
- These are all the attributes we need for this object class given our current purpose.

8.2.7.2 Object Class = Banking Services

ATTRIBUTES =
    service-type—used to distinguish between different types of services.
    account-number—used to identify each individual banking service provided to a customer. Different banking services will use different numbers.
    prime-rate—defined by the bank for use in calculating interest rates for all banking services.
    rate-difference—an amount subtracted from prime-rate to determine the actual interest paid on a particular account.

Balance—current balance of the account, loan, or other banking service.
TRANSACTIONS—records of each transaction that changes the individual banking service of a customer (e.g., payments and withdrawals).
CUSTOMER—even though we only identified ACCOUNTS as being owned by CUSTOMERS, it is useful to generalize a link to the CUSTOMER for each individual BANKING SERVICE.

NOTE:

- BANKING SERVICES is considered an "abstract class" because it doesn't have any direct instances in this problem. Customers don't go to banks for BANKING SERVICES, they go for ACCOUNTS, LOANS, and so on. However, it is useful to gather the common features of all BANKING SERVICES in this (abstract) class so that we only have to define them once and so that they can be reused for any new banking services that we develop or add later.
- This analysis of attributes has identified the need for a new class of objects, TRANSACTIONS, that needs to be added to our model.

8.2.7.3   Object Class = Transactions

ATTRIBUTES =
    dACCOUNT—the ACCOUNT to debit the transaction against
    cACCOUNT—the ACCOUNT to credit the transaction against
    date-received—when the transaction was received
    date-processed—which may be a different date
    transaction-type—e.g., debit or credit
    amount—only a numeric value is allowed here
    currency—allows foreign exchange transactions
    initiator—the source of the transaction, which could be a CUSTOMER, a bank employee or some other source

NOTE:

- Considerable analysis of TRANSACTIONS was done to identify all the necessary attributes.
- Two ACCOUNT numbers are needed to allow transactions to include transfers between accounts. Both attributes, if used for an object, would point at ACCOUNTS.
- Two dates are needed because not all transactions are processed on the day when they are received.
- Dealing with different possible initiators will require additional analysis.

8.2.7.4   Object Class = Branches

TYPE = BANKS
ATTRIBUTES =
    branch-number
    branch-name
    branch-address
    branch-phone
    branch-fax

8.2.7.5 Object Class = Individuals

ATTRIBUTES =
    name
    address
    phone
    age
    CUSTOMER—a possible role of an individual

NOTE:

- Name, address, and phone are used for both BRANCHES and CUSTOMERS. In object-oriented design, it is likely that a new class IDENTIFICATION would be created to deal with these common attributes. However, we will not introduce such a class at this time other than in this note.

8.2.7.6 Object Class = Customers

TYPE = INDIVIDUALS
ATTRIBUTES =
    ACCOUNTS—points to particular accounts owned by this customer.

8.2.7.7 Object Class = Accounts

TYPE = BANKING SERVICES
ATTRIBUTES = ???

NOTE:

- This "type" of identification links ACCOUNTS to BANKING SERVICES in order to inherit all the features (ATTRIBUTES and SERVICES) from it.
- We only need to identify attributes that are specific to ACCOUNTS, because the other attributes of BANKING SERVICES, including their linkage to a CUSTOMER, will automatically be inherited.
- Since we have not identified any attributes unique to ACCOUNTS, the need for ACCOUNTS as a separate class should be questioned. However, this class will be retained until after the analysis of the operations for each of these classes.

8.2.8 A Procedure for Identifying Attributes

The following is a helpful procedure for identifying attributes relevant to objects in a given problem. It is not the only procedure and is not guaranteed to work perfectly. But it can help some people, sometimes.

1. Look for data values in the problem statement. Remember that attributes:
- Are applied to all objects in a given class where the attribute is defined
- Can have values that differ between objects
- Can be constant values for a given object (such as a person's name)
- Can be variable values for a given object (such as a person's age)
- Can be numeric values, alphanumeric expressions, or other objects

2. Look for any other data features that might be needed by the objects you have identified for the relevant content, tasks, or tools.

3. Consider whether attributes should be defined as variables for a given object class or whether they should come from another object that is defined separately. If the attribute logically belongs to another object then consider whether or not to establish that object and identify its relationship with the current object.

- If the newly identified object may be relevant in some further way beyond providing a value for this attribute, then it should be added to the analysis
- If the only part of a newly identified object is it's data value, then it may be appropriate to treat the value as an attribute of the first object (e.g., although an address more properly is an attribute of a house, it is often the only features of a house that is relevant to describing many people and thus the address is often dealt with as an attribute of a person and the house is ignored)

4. Add your attributers to your object diagram, then use the diagram to verify the completeness and correctness of your set of attributes. Verify the diagram in discussions with representatives of the different groups of stakeholders. Focus on what the diagram contains rather than how pretty it is.

 Find further information about attributes in the Chapter 8 Cyber Supplement.

8.2.9 Operations

All objects of a given class have the same operations, which can be modified by the attributes of the object (e.g., the drive operation of a vehicle may be modified by a speed attribute). Operations may be defined for a particular object class or inherited from a generalized object class, of which the particular object class is an instance.

Functions include:

- The actions that users perform to accomplish parts of a task
- The actions that a system performs in response to user initiated actions

While an individual operation may occasionally accomplish a task, often a sequence of operations (referred to as a scenario or a use case) is required to completely accomplish a task. Operations are also called **functions, methods, processes,** or **services** in various object-oriented methodologies. Some approaches further differentiate by considering:

- Functions as operations that return a value
- Processes as operations that change something

Norman[14] refers to operations as functions, "A function is a transformation or action taken by the information system. Information systems usually have many functions. Functions carry out and enforce business policies, rules, and procedures. Other synonyms for function are process, service, and method, the last two becoming more familiar with the popularization of object-oriented technologies."

Booch[15] states, "The terms operation, method, and member function evolved from three different programming cultures (Ada, Smalltalk, and C++, respectively). They all mean virtually the same thing."

Operations define what an object can do. Like attributes, an object may perform an infinite number of operations, only some of which are relevant to the current problem/task/application.

Operations are the actions of an object. These actions can be:

- High-level actions of the object, which may result in the accomplishment of one or more tasks
- Lower level actions of the object, which may result in the accomplishment of one step in the accomplishment of a task

Regardless of the level of the action, actions are more closely related to the use of specific tools than the actual accomplishment of tasks. Actions can happen independent of identifiable tasks. They only accomplish tasks if the task needs to be accomplished. For example, telling someone something what they already know does not accomplish the task of educating them or informing them about that thing.

While a consideration of the tasks an object is to accomplish is a useful starting point for identifying the operations of an object, it is equally important to consider each of the interactions of the object. These inter-"actions" define the need for actions that are performed by the object. These actions may be based on any of the four basic types of data processing, either individually or in combination:

- Input of content to the object
- Processing of content by the object (e.g., modification, formatting, calculation, comparison, sorting)
- Storage of content by the object
- Output of content by the object

Operations can be discovered by asking:

- What content does the object receive/input/accept?
- What content does the object process?
- What content does the object store/save/remember/recall?
- What content does the object output?

Operations also involve control. However, control can be exercised via actions involving content:

- Inputs can request an object to take some additional action (e.g., to analyze some other content and to make a decision).
- Processing can cause an object to take some additional action (e.g., a decision may result in the object taking an action that produces some output).
- The output from one object can request an action by some other object that produces further output (e.g., my brain sent a number of messages to type (and to correct the typing) of this sentence).

Many objects have similar operations. Thus, most objects of type "form" have some or all of the following operations:

- Create an instance of the form
- Add content to the instance of the form (e.g., fill out information on it)
- Change content on the instance of the form
- Save the instance of the form
- Output an instance of the form
- Print an instance of the form
- Duplicate an instance of the form

- Sort instances of the form
- Find the first form
- Find a specific instance of the form
- Find the last form
- Find the previous form
- Find the next form
- Select a set of instances of the form based on some selection criteria
- Compare content on multiple forms
- Summarize content from multiple forms

8.2.10   An Example of Identifying Operations

Now that we've identified the classes, relationships, and attributes we can investigate the operations performed by objects in these classes, based on these relationships and using these attributes.

NOTE: This example is careful to define operations in the class where they best belong.

- Some objects, such as BANKS and INDIVIDUALS, exist on their own, and some objects, such as the remainder of objects in this example, only exist because other objects have created them.
- Once created, objects are responsible for their own operations, which they may initiate on their own or in response to a request from another object.
- Where an object is an instance of a more general class of object, it may inherit its operations from that more general class.

8.2.10.1   Object Class = Banks
OPERATIONS =
   Create BRANCHES—branches only exist because they have been created by banks.
   Create BANKING SERVICES—banking services only exist as services of a bank.

NOTE:

- In this situation, the only role of the BANK is to perform various creation operations that are necessary to enable the BANK ACCOUNT system.
- Once BRANCHES and BANKING SERVICES are created, there are no further interactions needed with BANKS.
- While BANKS can also (merge and/or delete) (BRANCHES and/or SERVICES) these operations go beyond the simple model we have been considering so far. Further analysis might identify a need for these additional operations.

8.2.10.2   Object Class = Banking Services
OPERATIONS =
   Set prime-rate—recognizes the potential to change the prime-rate in the future. This will require an analysis of which object will be authorized to request such a rate change.

Set rate-difference—recognizes the potential to change the rate-difference in the future. This will require an analysis of which object will be authorized to request such a rate change.

Find balance—based on requests of CUSTOMERS when dealing with their ACCOUNTS (which are instances of BANKING SERVICES).

Create TRANSACTIONS—based on requests of CUSTOMERS when dealing with their ACCOUNTS (which are instances of BANKING SERVICES) or based on requests by the BANKING SERVICE when it calculates adjustments.

NOTE: These operations could be used by various banking services, including ACCOUNTS, loans, and so on. They have been defined at this generalized class level rather than being defined for each specific class where they could be used.

8.2.10.3 Object Class = Transactions

OPERATIONS =

Find transaction—only allows transaction information to be presented based on a valid account number. If the system is automated, a password or personal identification number (PIN) may be added to increase security.

Edit transaction—only allows transaction information to be edited by authorized requests.

Submit transaction for processing—sends the transaction to ACCOUNTS for processing.

NOTE: Once a transaction is created, it is an independent entity, responsible for controlling its own processing.

8.2.10.4 Object Class = Branches

OPERATIONS =

Create CUSTOMERS.

Create ACCOUNTS.

NOTE: Although the BRANCH creates CUSTOMERS and ACCOUNTS for INDIVIDUALS, it does so for different specializations of INDIVIDUALS. ACCOUNTS can only be created for CUSTOMERS.

8.2.10.5 Object Class = Individuals

OPERATIONS =

Send request to BRANCH to create a CUSTOMER—this is necessary to initiate the creation of any new CUSTOMERS.

NOTE: Once a CUSTOMER has been created, the CUSTOMER will perform all further interactions of the INDIVIDUAL with the BANK.

8.2.10.6 Object Class = Customers

OPERATIONS =

Send request to BRANCH to create an ACCOUNT.

Send request to ACCOUNT to create a TRANSACTION.
Send requests to TRANSACTION to find/edit/submit itself.

NOTE: Although the CUSTOMER is always dealing with the BANK, different requests for servicing are handled at different levels within the BANK.

8.2.10.7   Object Class = Accounts

OPERATIONS =

Calculate account adjustments—this will calculate the service charges and interest payments that are unique to ACCOUNTS and create TRANSACTIONS to post these charges to the ACCOUNT.

NOTE:

- There will need to be conditions that trigger the calculation of account adjustments. Identifying these conditions will require further analysis and modifications to our model.
- ACCOUNTS will have different adjustments from loans or other types of BANKING SERVICES. Thus there is a purpose to keeping this class in our analysis.

8.2.11   A Procedure for Identifying Operations

The following is a helpful procedure for identifying operations relevant to objects in a given problem. It is not the only procedure and is not guaranteed to work perfectly. But it can help some people, sometimes.

1. Identify the user's tasks mentioned in the problem. Consider interactions between users and other objects.
2. Identify internal processing mentioned in the problem. Consider interactions between other objects.
3. Consider what transformations may need to be applied to attributes of the objects already identified.
4. Add your operations to your object diagram, then use the diagram to verify the completeness and correctness of your set of attributes. Verify the diagram in discussions with representatives of the different groups of stakeholders. Focus on what the diagram contains rather than how pretty it is.

   Find further information about operations in the Chapter 8 Cyber Supplement.

8.2.12   Diagrams to Visualize Object-Oriented Systems

Diagrams can often help us visualize how a system works and if it is complete or not. (Isn't a picture worth a thousand words?) Diagrams can illustrate various levels of detail, including:

- A complete system or subsystem involving a number of classes (with or without their contents) and their relationships
- Certain relationship(s) of certain classes (with or without their contents)
- A single class and its contents

Remember, the purpose of a diagram is to help illustrate and communicate its contents. When a diagram no longer helps, then it is a waste of time. Diagrams illustrating classes and their relationships can get very complicated as they try to illustrate the many relationships that may exist between a number of object classes. Developers often use a computer-assisted software engineering (CASE) tool to help manage class descriptions and to generate class relationship diagrams of selected portions of a system.

This section discusses only the most common types of object-oriented analysis and design diagrams. Many more advanced diagramming techniques are presented in advanced software engineering books.[16–18]

8.2.12.1 Illustrating Relationships

The most common object-oriented diagram is one that illustrates the relationships between classes of objects.

- Classes are usually diagrammed as rectangles, rather than the circles previously used in this chapter. These class rectangles can easily be expanded to include various pieces of information within the class symbol (as discussed below).
- Relationships are usually diagrammed as lines with annotations to indicate different types of relationships.
  - Generalizations are illustrated with a line connecting the related objects with an open triangle next to and pointing at the generalized object.
  - Associations are illustrated with lines connecting the associated objects.
  - Aggregations are illustrated by adding an open diamond to the end of the line next to the aggregate object.
  - Composites are illustrated by adding a filled-in diamond to the end of the line next to the composite object.
- Since associations may be based on a wide variety of relationships, it is common to label associations in class diagrams. Association relationships are bidirectional, but can be referred to by specifying the semantics of the relationship and indicating the direction of this relationship with an arrowhead as part of this label (e.g., is an instance of, is a part of, owns, etc.); or by the roles of the related objects (e.g., generalization, specialization); whole, part; owner, owned item; and so on.

The expanded model of the BANK ACCOUNTS system can be revised according to these diagramming conventions as illustrated in Figure 8-6.

8.2.12.2 There Are Subsystems and There Are Subsystems

It has been found that the human mind can only consider approximately seven (plus or minus two) different chunks of information at a time.[19] Thus, diagrams with more than seven distinct objects can never be considered fully at one time. This does not mean that diagrams (or other visual media, such as Web pages) should never have more than seven objects on them. Rather, it suggests that objects should be organized in a manner that helps the user to focus on those that need to be used together. Various techniques for organizing large amounts of content are discussed in Chapter 11.

Complex diagrams may be replaced by a series of simpler diagrams, which focus on subsystems rather than illustrating all of the system components at one time. Of-

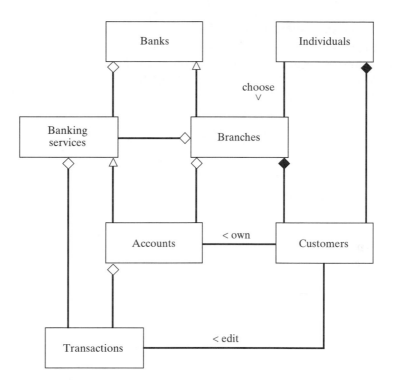

Figure 8-6   A formal class diagram of the bank accounts system

ten a system can be decomposed into a number of subsystems in order to reduce the number of classes that are considered at one time.

Traditionally, the concept of a subsystem was that of one of a number of distinct parts into which a system could be taken apart. In that concept, items (objects) that were part of one subset would not be part of any other subsystem. If a system can be divided into meaningful, nonoverlapping subsets, then each subsystem could be analyzed and designed largely on its own, with only a minimum of effort being allocated to interfacing the various subsystems together. This traditional concept of subsystems is very useful in dividing large development projects into smaller projects that are (hopefully) easier to manage.

However, the traditional way is not the only way of considering subsystems. A subsystem is just a part of a system that is useful to consider by itself. It docs not have to be exclusive of other subsystems. People often localize their attention to a grouping of objects small enough to be considered at one time. An object, and all the objects it directly interacts with, can also be considered a subsystem, even if each of the objects in that subsystem (including the main object at the center) also belongs to a number of other overlapping subsystems.

8.2.12.3 Illustrating a Single Class

The rectangles used to illustrate classes can be expanded to provide more than just the name of a class. This usually involves dividing them into three or four horizontally stacked sections, containing some or all of the class's name, type (where applicable), attributes, and operations. Only a class name is required. Other information may be added as it is discovered and as it is needed. Figure 8-7 illustrates the general format for and some examples of diagrams for object classes.

Find further information about object and class diagrams in the Chapter 8 Cyber Supplement.

| Name: of object class |
| Type: of generalized class |
| Attributes: |
| *attribute 1* |
| *attribute 2* |
| ... |
| ... |
| *attribute n* |
| Operations: |
| *operation 1* |
| *operation 2* |
| ... |
| ... |
| *operation n* |

| BANK |
| name |
| BANKING-SERVICES |
| create BRANCHES |
| create BANKING SERVICES |

| BANKING-SERVICES |
| service-type |
| acccount-number |
| prime rate |
| balance |
| TRANSACTIONS |
| CUSTOMER |
| set prime-rate |
| set rate difference |
| find balance |
| create TRANSACTIONS |

| ACCOUNTS |
| Type: BANKING SERVICE |
| |
| calculate account adjustments |

Figure 8-7 Class diagrams

8.2.13 Analyzing the Dynamics of Systems

So far our model is a static one, describing related objects that have the potential to interact. Static models do not go into sufficient detail to understand potential sequences of interactions. Dynamic models can be built by combining a number of scenarios that describe how a system is or could be used.

Scenarios are step-by-step descriptions of one possible way to accomplish a task with a certain set of operations and attributes. Scenarios may encompass a whole series of events leading to the accomplishment of some purpose. Since tasks can often be accomplished in a number of ways, there may be a number of possible scenarios that could involve different sets of operations/attributes for a given task. Scenarios are the most natural way for users to discuss the details of what happens, why it happens, and how it happens.

Rumbaugh[20] states, "A scenario describes the sequence of events that occurs during one particular execution of a system."

Many authors refer to (some aspects of) scenarios as "use cases."

Larman[21] states, "A use case is a narrative, textual description of the sequence of events and actions that occur when a user participates in a dialog with a system during a meaningful process."

Jacobson[22] states, "A use case is a specific way of using the system by using some part of the functionality. Each use case constitutes a complete course of events initiated by an actor and it specifies the interaction that takes place between an actor and the system. A use case is thus a special sequence of related transactions performed by an actor and the system in a dialogue. The collected use cases specify all the existing ways of using the system."

Scenarios describe a series of interactions between objects (such as would occur in a conversation). Scenarios can be given distinctive names and can be described as a dialogue between the objects. Scenarios can illustrate:

- What happens in normal or usual cases
- What happens in exceptional cases

Scenarios can be the starting point for analysis. The developer can identify scenarios by asking the user to describe "what goes on to accomplish this application" and then asking for elaborations on how it currently happens. The developer should identify both what the users currently do and what they would like to do. Scenarios can be further elaborated to identify pertinent objects, tasks, content chunks, tools, and related requirements.

NOTE: The purpose of analysis is to identify primarily what happens, but users may be more comfortable describing how it happens and leaving the developer to generalize the what from the how. While analysis should de-emphasize the how, it is still necessary to recognize how things are currently done in order to design improvements at a later time.

Scenarios are even more important in design where they can focus on how the user will use the system being designed to accomplish the necessary tasks. (We will discuss more about this later.)

Scenarios also can be used to confirm an analysis or design. In such a case, users try to determine whether a model (developed in a top-down manner) will specify or meet all of their needs. Scenarios can also be used as scripts for user tests. Scenarios can be described with:

- A meaningful and distinctive name
- A brief description that focuses on how they are unique from other scenarios
- The sequence of steps involved, including identification of which object performs which step

Various forms of sequence, activity, or state transition diagrams (each of which is beyond the scope of this book) can be used to illustrate scenarios, depending on the aspect of the scenario being illustrated and the level of understanding of the intended audience.

 Find further information about scenarios and analyzing the dynamics of systems in the Chapter 8 Cyber Supplement.

8.2.14   The Complexities of Analysis

The discussions above and the example following give a glimpse of just how involved a good analysis can become. It is very important that developers spend the necessary time and effort on analysis because it will be the foundation of the system that is being developed.

This foundation is not only important in the immediate development but throughout the life of the system being developed. It has often been estimated that 80% to 90% of development expenditures on traditional systems are spent on maintenance. It can be expected, due to their need to evolve continually, that this figure will be even greater for e-Commerce systems.

Once a task-based analysis, like the one discussed in Chapter 7, is transformed into an object-oriented analysis, as discussed in this chapter, it should not be discarded or ignored. It is important to maintain both types of analysis information.

- An object-oriented analysis tells the developer what to do.
- A task-based analysis tells the developer how it should be done.

Both types of information are important in future modifications and enhancements as well as in the initial development of a system.

8.3   APPLYING OBJECT-ORIENTED ANALYSIS

8.3.1   Conducting Object-Oriented Analyses in Organizations

Analysis is generally an iterative process. That is, the developer does some analysis, evaluates the results, and usually determines that further analysis needs to be done and added to what was there. Iteration continues until the analysis appears to be complete. A CASE tool can help in collecting analysis information, developing class and other useful diagrams, and in analyzing areas where further information is definitely required.

The question then arises, "How do you know your analysis is complete?" There are a number of incorrect answers, including:

- When your analysis is as detailed as possible—since you may have missed more general information
- When you've analyzed all the main concepts—since you may have missed how they relate to one another
- When you can't find anything new to add—since you might not have looked hard enough
- When you've expended all your analysis budget (While this is a really bad criterion, it is invoked all too often, usually leading to some really ugly system failures.)

A better rule of thumb is this:

- When all the analysis information you gather keeps turning out to be the same as what you've already got, (often just in different words)

Looking at an application from a variety of perspectives can help in identifying different requirements. So far we have primarily been developing our ideas about our applications in a top-down manner (from general to specific):

- In Chapter 4, we went from generally identifying an application to developing a more detailed application description
- In Chapter 6, we went from our application description to identifying a number of different potential general approaches to serving it
- In Chapter 7, we went from the application description, which included the identification of tasks, users, content, and tools, to develop more detailed descriptions of tasks, users, content, and tools
- In this chapter, we are going from identifying (laterally) a set of objects (from our users, content, and tools) to identifying relationships, attributes, and operations for these objects

However, there are other methods that developers use to understand and develop applications. They can be categorized based on their direction of increasing detail or generalization. Development (and especially analysis) can proceed:

- Top-down—considering/finding the most general information first, then elaborating on it in a series of increasing detail
- Bottom-up—considering examples first, then trying to build a series of generalizations that work for increasing numbers of examples
- Lateral—shifting approaches or paradigms to consider or find additional information at the same level of detail

While the top-down approach is the traditional one used for teaching systems development, developers often follow an opportunistic approach, proceeding in whichever direction works best in the current situation. Thus, in practice a lot of development takes some bottom-up directions.

8.3.2 Student Assignment—Object-Oriented Analysis

1. Identifying Object Classes

Based on your increased understanding of your application, reevaluate again what is really important for a good basic system. You don't have to redo your formal feasibility study, but you do have to consider the various types of feasibility when deciding what to include as a basic system. As an extension to the technical feasibility, you should consider that all the components of your basic system should work together in some organized manner. Remember to make sure that your current idea of a basic system:

- Is feasible
- Contains significant competitive advantages that will support your e-Commerce entry and provide a basis for your basic system to grow from towards a deluxe system in the future

Briefly explain the rationale for your (redefined) concept of a basic system.

NOTE: From here on you will be focusing on this basic system. Make sure that it is an interesting one with significant potential for complex series of interactions between at least some of the users and the e-Commerce application. Identify and briefly describe the relevant classes of objects for your team's project (from your previous analysis). Classify them in terms of their importance:

- Essential to the success of a basic system
- Required for the success of a deluxe system
- Useful to consider but not essential or required

NOTE: You are expected to identify at least 15 classes and no more than 35 classes.

2. Developing Class Descriptions

For each of the classes of objects in your basic system (if less than ten classes, add the next most important object classes that will work with these object classes to get at least ten object classes), identify the relevant attributes and operations for each class. The information can be presented as:

Class: xxx descriptive sentence
Type: (if applicable)
Attributes:
      123 descriptive sentence
      456 descriptive sentence
      789 descriptive sentence
Operations:
      abc descriptive sentence
      def descriptive sentence
      ghi descriptive sentence
Class: yyy descriptive sentence
Attributes:

Be careful to name your classes, attributes and/or operations in an easy-to-understand manner. You should include a short sentence of description of each to the right of the name to help other people to understand what you mean by each name.

NOTE: In a professional analysis, each object, attribute, and operation would require much further analysis and much more description than this.

8.4 AN EXAMPLE OF APPLYING OBJECT-ORIENTED ANALYSIS

The example of *Savor the Cup* grows increasingly complex, as most real systems do throughout development. Already in the last chapter it was impossible to provide a complete example. The example in this chapter will continue to highlight certain aspects of this application rather than trying to completely document it.

8.4.1 Identifying Classes and Their Relationships

8.4.1.1 Identifying User-Based Classes

A start at identifying object classes can be made by considering the different user groups already identified. There were six major groups who interact: customers, sales, accounting, logistics, purchasing, and suppliers.

However, from the perspective of both customers and suppliers, they interact with *Savor the Cup,* which employs a variety of people. This interaction between customers and suppliers and *Savor the Cup* could be described in various different manners:

- Customers and suppliers interact with various parts of *Savor the Cup.* Each part of *Savor the Cup* performs a specialized set of business functions.
- Customers and suppliers interact with various *Savor the Cup* employees.
- Customers and suppliers interact with *Savor the Cup,* which is composed of *Savor the Cup* employees with various specializations.

Since each of these observations is correct, we need to choose the one that will be most useful in developing our application.

- We don't know anything significant about *Savor the Cup* employees in general that would be useful in defining them as a new class. There doesn't seem to be anything of importance in common between these different people other than that they work for the same company.
- The *Savor the Cup* employees are only important to the system because of the business functions they perform. While employees may change, the functions need to continue.
  - It may be possible for one individual to perform the work of multiple *Savor the Cup* employees.
  - The new system may replace some of the roles of different *Savor the Cup* employees.
- The focus of the system is to provide an organizational Web site for *Savor the Cup.*

Based on these reasons, the first alternative for considering relationships has been chosen. This involves adding a new class for *Savor the Cup* and considering sales, accounting, logistics, and purchasing as parts of *Savor the Cup.*

There are specialized groups within each of customers, sales, and suppliers. While there are differences between specialized groups, each member of a specialized group is an instance of the more general group to which it belongs. These involve generalization-specialization relationships. Various groups interact with one another via communicating important pieces of content.

Figure 8-8 is an initial class diagram that was constructed from this analysis. This diagram does not contain all the classes involved, but it does provide a starting point for further object-oriented analysis.

NOTE: This diagram was getting too complex to fully illustrate all the specialized classes involved. In order to capture all the information discussed above, specialized classes were listed rather than being pictured within their own class boxes.

8.4.1.2   Including Content-Based Classes

Each of the relationships in Figure 8-8 are expressed in terms of content that flows between objects. This makes Figure 8-8 resemble the data flow diagrams that were popular in the 1980s. It also suggests that Figure 8-8 is not a proper object class diagram. Further analysis is required to recognize content-based classes that are important to the system.

The task analysis in the example in Chapter 7 identified a large number of chunks of content that were related to different users. Further object-oriented

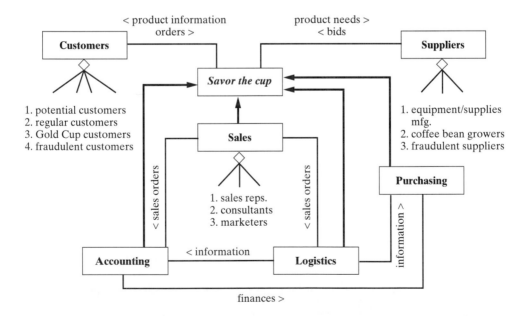

Figure 8-8   A class diagram based on the users of the *Savor the Cup* system

analysis has identified four main classes to which these content chunks and the content flows identified in Figure 8-8 belong:

- **Public information** (on products and services), which is created by *Savor the Cup* sales and/or purchasing departments and can be used by customers, suppliers, and the sales department
- **Sales orders,** which can be created by customers or the sales department and are used by various parts of *Savor the Cup*
- **(Supplier) bids,** which can be created by suppliers and are used by purchasing
- **Internal information,** which is created by various parts of *Savor the Cup* and is used by various parts of *Savor the Cup*

Figure 8-9 is a class diagram that was constructed from this analysis.

NOTE: This diagram only contains the main user-based and content-based classes. Sales and purchasing were included because of their specific roles in creating sales orders for customers and in receiving supplier bids. However, their role in creating and obtaining public information is not shown explicitly. Instead, for the time being, the creation and obtaining of public information is associated with the entire *Savor the Cup* organization. This relationship will require further analysis.

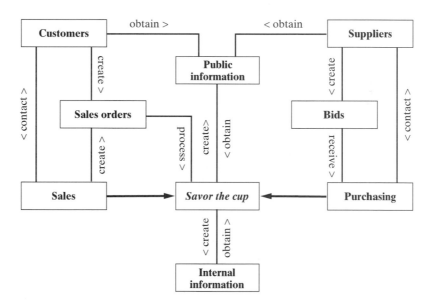

Figure 8-9   A class diagram based on the main users and content in the *Savor the Cup* system

8.4.1.3 Including Tool-Based Classes

Let's focus further on the problem of creating and obtaining public information. People require tools to create or obtain information, and one tool may not fit all needs.

The tool used to obtain information often depends on what's available as well as what kind of information is desired. However, we can identify two basic types of tools:

- Tools for general information, including advertisements, brochures, conference presentations, magazine articles, and other formats intended to present information to a wide variety of users in hopes that some of them make use of it. These tools are used when the people creating the information do not know the specific needs of individual users and/or when the people obtaining the information are not sure what they need.
- Tools for specific information, including questions or conversations that can occur in face-to-face meetings, in telephone calls, or in mail. They can also include tools that help a person search through general information to find the specific information needed.

Tools used to create information depend on meeting the needs of the tools that will be used to obtain the information. Tools for creating general information often involve writing, editing, composing, and organizing the information. Tools for creating specific information often work directly with the tools used to obtain it and may work with existing general information.

Despite the quality of public information provided by *Savor the Cup*, there are likely to be items of information that customers and/or suppliers cannot find and which they can only obtain by direct contacts with selected *Savor the Cup* employees. Figure 8-10 is a class diagram that was constructed from this analysis.

NOTE: Since this diagram is very cluttered both with overlapping lines and with considerably more than seven objects, the labels on various associations have been omitted. Ideally, it should be broken into a number of more detailed diagrams, each focusing on selected aspects of the system.

Additional tools that need to be considered include:

- Order forms—used by customers and sales representatives to enter orders and used by various users to process orders
- Bid forms—used by suppliers to enter bids, and used by purchasing to receive bids
- Tools for creating, obtaining, and processing internal information used by various parts of *Savor the Cup*

8.4.2 Describing Classes

Each of the identified object classes will need to be modeled in the system. The following is an example of the description of one of the classes of objects in the *Savor the Cup* system.

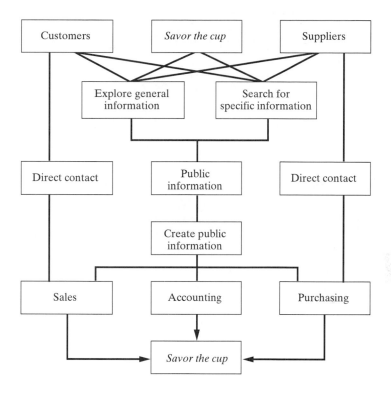

Figure 8-10 A class diagram focused on the creation and obtaining of public information in the *Savor the Cup* system

Class: **Customers**
Attributes:
- Customer number
- Identification information (name, address, phone, fax, e-mail)
- Customer type (potential, regular, Gold Cup)
- Customer account information (cash, COD, credit card, *Savor the Cup* credit limit)
- Outstanding charges (links to accounting information)
- Customer profile (business/individual characteristics)
- Purchasing profile (analysis of previous purchases)
- Previous purchases (links to previous sales orders)
- Current purchases (links to current sales orders)
- Assigned sales representative (link to sales representative)

Operations:
- Get general information
- Get specific information
- Make purchases
- Make inquiries about purchases
- Pay account
- Contact sales representative
- Identify oneself to *Savor the Cup* (necessary to allow access to selected attributes and operations)
- Change information that *Savor the Cup* has about a customer

NOTE:

- This description works for all customers.
  - A customer type attribute is sufficient to distinguish between different types of customers. Separate class descriptions will not be required.
  - Potential customers do not have customer accounts. Therefore there is no information about them. However, once a potential customer wishes to make a purchase, the potential customer will be required to become a regular customer.
  - Fraudulent customers may be difficult to identify. Likewise, labeling a customer as a fraudulent customer in an organization's system might lead to libel suits. However, factors leading to the assumption that a customer is a fraudulent customer could be contained within the customer profile attribute.
- There is a difference between the attributes that describe an object and the content with which it performs its operations. Further analysis was necessary to identify the information that *Savor the Cup* uses in dealing with its customers.
- Further analysis will be needed to determine which attributes will be made available to which users.
- Operations dealing with establishing a person's identity and changing a customer's information are recognized in this description. While their need is most evident in a computerized system, they actually also exist in manual systems, even if they are often done as part of other operations.

8.4.3 Scenarios

There are many possible ways of accomplishing the task of "searching for information about the industry." The following high-level scenarios identify just some of these.

Name: Regular monitoring of trends.
  Description: Users constantly monitor general information for trends.
  Steps:
    1. User explores general information about the industry once a week.
Name: Looking for answers in general information.
  Description: Users who are familiar with general information may choose to look at it first to find specific information.
  Steps:
    1. User explores general information trying to find a specific answer.
Name: Searching for specific information.
  Description: Users may search for specific information.

Steps:
1. User searches to finds desired specific information about the industry.
Name: Asking marketing representatives.
Description: Users may choose to ask their marketing representative for information about the industry.
Steps:
1. User contacts sales representative and asks for desired information about the industry.
Name: Going from general to specific information.
Description: Users who are familiar with general information may choose to look at it first to find specific information rather than using a search tool with which they are less familiar.
Steps:
1. User explores general information trying to find a specific answer, but is unsuccessful.
2. User then uses a search tool to find desired specific information and is successful.
Name: Going from general to specific information to marketing representative.
Description: Users choose to look at general information first to find specific information and to use other operations if not successful.
Steps:
1. User explores general information trying to find a specific answer but is unsuccessful.
2. User then uses a search tool to find desired specific information but is unsuccessful.
3. User then contacts sales representative and asks for desired information about the industry.

NOTE:

- These are just some of the many possible scenarios that could be used to accomplish the task. Additional scenarios could deal with getting parts of the answer at a time via different operations and then putting a complete answer together.
- These scenarios are only described at a high (operational) level. They could be elaborated by describing specific interactions between the customer and the other objects involved. There could be various possible elaborations of each of them, which would involve various detailed scenarios. These detailed scenarios will be considered in Chapter 11.

8.5   CHALLENGES AND OPPORTUNITIES IN APPLYING OBJECT-ORIENTED ANALYSIS

The following are the most frequent problems encountered with object-oriented analysis. They only apply to some developments and are listed here to help you to avoid them.

Challenges with the Selection of Classes

- Classes may be difficult to identify if an object-analysis is done without a preceding analysis of users, content, and tools.
- Some classes as originally identified may be too complex (they may be able to be divided into two separate classes with or without a common parent class).
- Where additional objects are identified, beyond the original set of users, content, and tools, further task analysis may be required to identify how these objects interact with the application.
- If developers do not give classes names that were simple and concise, considerable confusion may result.

Challenges with Detailed Analysis

- Some developers focus their attention on easy-to-understand classes rather than ones that are most important to their application.
- Some developers do not provide sufficient descriptions for their classes, attributes, and/or operations to make it clear what each is supposed to be or do.
- Attributes and operations listed in a class should be limited to those operations relevant to the application.
- The "Type" section of a class description may be used incorrectly. Instead of a class being of "Type: another class," some developers may use type as being either: "user," "tool," or "content."

Challenges with Attributes

- Some classes may not have an obvious attribute that distinguishes between instances of some classes. For example, people's names may be poor identifiers because some people might have the same name as others—in such cases a user number or some other identifying attribute may be necessary to distinguish between people.
- Where attributes are identified prior to operations, some important attributes may be missed. The identification of attributes and operations needs to be iterative and to take into account interdependencies between attributes and operations.

Challenges with Operations

- Operations need to describe actions that a class of objects performs rather than actions that are performed on the class of objects.
- Operations may need to be more specific than the tasks that they are used to accomplish.
- Some operations may be used for part or all of a number of different tasks.

8.6   CYBER SUPPLEMENTS FOR CHAPTER 8

Look at the Chapter 8 Cyber Supplements on the Web to find:

- Further information regarding objects and their relationships, attributes, and operations
- Further information regarding object and class diagrams

- Further information regarding scenarios and analyzing the dynamics of systems
- Practice activities for conducting an object-oriented analysis

REFERENCES

[1] R.J. Norman, *Object-Oriented Systems Analysis and Design* (Upper Saddle River, NJ, Prentice-Hall, 1996).

[2] M. Smith and S. Tockey, *An Integrated Approach to Software Requirements Definition Using Objects* (Boeing Commercial Airplane Support Division, 1988).

[3] J. Rumbaugh, M. Blaha, W. Premerlani, F. Eddy, W. Lorensen, *Object-Oriented Modeling and Design* (Englewood Cliffs, NJ, Prentice-Hall, 1991).

[4] I. Jacobson, M. Christerson, P. Jonsson, G. Overgaard, *Object-Oriented Software Engineering* (Wokinghan, England, Addison-Wesley, 1992).

[5] G. Booch, *Object Oriented Design with Applications* (Redwood City, CA, Benjamin/ Cummings, 1991).

[6] Ibid.

[7] Ibid.

[8] Ibid.

[9] Ibid.

[10] Ibid.

[11] Ibid.

[12] Ibid.

[13] Ibid.

[14] Ibid.

[15] Ibid.

[16] G. Booch, J. Rumbaugh, I Jacobson, *The Unified Modeling Language User Guide* (Reading MA, Addison-Wesley, 1999).

[17] Ibid.

[18] R. Pooley and P. Stevens, *Using UML: Software Engineering with Objects and Components* (Reading MA, Addison-Wesley, 1999).

[19] G.A. Miller, The magical number seven, plus or minus two: some limits on our capacity for processing information, *The Psychological Review* (1956, 63:81–97).

[20] Ibid.

[21] C. Larman, *Applying UML and Patterns: An Introduction to Object-Oriented Analysis and Design* (Upper Saddle River, NJ, Prentice-Hall, 1998).

[22] Ibid.

Some Important e-Commerce Issues

Outline

9.1 INTRODUCTION TO IMPORTANT E-COMMERCE ISSUES

It is important that an analysis is focused on and is limited to identifying only those requirements that need to be satisfied. Traditional systems analyses focus on specific needs that fall within some concept of an application's boundaries. Even where these boundaries are well specified, an analysis can get quite complex, as noted in Chapter 8. However, the nature of e-Commerce requires that developers also consider various additional issues and requirements that are imposed upon e-Commerce by the environment in which it will operate.

9.2   UNDERSTANDING IMPORTANT E-COMMERCE ISSUES

9.2.1   Identifying e-Commerce Issues

The ubiquitous nature of e-Commerce is increasingly leading to the recognition of a number of important e-Commerce issues that need to be resolved. In some cases the resolution is up to individual e-Commerce sites, and in some cases governments are starting to get involved. The White House's Framework for Global Electronic Commerce[1] provides a good overview of a variety of legal and social challenges facing the future of e-Commerce. It is based of the following principles:

- "The private sector should lead.
- "Governments should avoid undue restrictions on electronic commerce.
- "Where governmental involvement is needed, its aim should be to support and enforce a predictable, minimalist, consistent and simple legal environment for commerce.
- "Governments should recognize the unique qualities of the Internet.
- "Electronic Commerce over the Internet should be facilitated on a global basis."

It identified the following issues:

- Customs and taxation
- Electronic payment systems
- "Uniform commercial code" for electronic commerce
- Intellectual property protection
- Privacy
- Security
- Telecommunications infrastructure and information technology
- Content
- Technical standards

The Sacher Report[2] of the Organization for Economic Cooperation and Development (OECD) identified the following sets of e-Commerce issues:

- Commercial issues
  - Consumer protection
  - Ensuring market diversity and competition
  - Financial and payment systems
  - Taxation
  - Intellectual property rights
- Security issues
  - How secure is "secure"?
  - The institutional aspects of security

- Authentication/nonrepudiation/data integrity
- Certification
- Data protection
- Infrastructure issues
  - Network capacity
  - Network access
  - Network development
  - Standards
- Social and cultural issues

The World Wide Web Consortium (W3C) is engaged in developing technical solutions to a number of e-Commerce–related issues.[3] Some of these efforts include:

- Providing guidelines for designing accessible Web pages[4] and user agents[5]
- Encoding "Metadata" that describes the contents and uses of Web pages[6] so that they can be automatically evaluated
- Providing and verifying "Digital Signatures"[7]
- Specifying Web site privacy policies and negotiating with users on privacy related issues[8]
- Standardizing the negotiation of payments between browsers and servers on the Web[9]
- Facilitating the licensing of intellectual property[10] and enabling "micropayments" for accessing documents on the Web[11]

The report on Work on Electronic Commerce Standardization to be Initiated[12] by the ISO/IEC JTC1 Information Technology Business Team on Electronic Commerce identifies a combination of business and technical issues related to the development of e-Commerce and especially related to enabling automatic e-Commerce between organizations.

Many additional issues can be identified from the growing literature on e-Commerce that is available on the Web. However, many of these issues, especially the more technical ones, are beyond the scope of this book.

The following sections introduce some of the most important e-Commerce issues that need to be included in the analysis of requirements of e-Commerce systems. They also provide references to further information on each of these topics. For the latest developments in important e-Commerce issues, please consult the Web site that supports this book.

 Find reviews of and links to further surveys of important e-Commerce issues in the Chapter 9 Cyber Supplement.

9.2.2   Accessibility

While consideration of accessibility originated with concerns for overcoming limitations presented to people with disabilities, it has evolved into a concern that all potential users be readily facilitated in the use of computing systems when and where they need them.

ISO DTS 16071[13] defines **accessibility** as, "The usability of a product, service, environment or facility by people with the widest range of capabilities." It further notes that, "Although 'accessibility' typically addresses users who have a disability, the concept is not limited to disability issues."

This wider concept of accessibility includes:

- **Universal accessibility,** which refers to the issues involved in providing accessibility that encompass all potential users in all situations.
- **Ubiquitous computing,** which refers to the potential that computing can be integrated into a variety of devices beyond the traditional concept of a personal computer.
- **Mobile computing** involves a range of devices with wireless access to the Internet. Mobile computing devices include specially equipped notebook and handheld computers.

It is obvious that e-Commerce systems will fail if their intended users cannot use them. What is less obvious are some of the barriers that prevent some people from being able to effectively use systems. They include:

- Many people still do not have any access to the Internet due to geographic or financial reasons. If they can only interact with an organization via the Web, then they cannot and will not interact.
- Some people with access to the Internet are not willing to use it voluntarily to conduct business. They may be willing to gather information via the Web provided that they can then conduct their business in a more traditional manner.
- Some people's access to the Internet is limited by various technical constraints, including access speeds, access times, etc. Fancy Web pages with graphics and client side programs (such as Java scripts) that take a long time to load may discourage or even prevent these people from doing business with a Web site. Traditional Web pages may be difficult to use on the limited screens of many mobile computing devices.
- Some people with full access to the Internet may be unable to make full use of this access due to personal disabilities. While they can generally interact with textual information via assistive technologies, they may encounter difficulties with graphics or sounds that are not available alternatively as text. **Assistive technologies** take information intended for presentation via one medium (e.g., displayed text) and present in another media (e.g., voice output).

Organizations should analyze the effect each of these barriers has on the success of their applications. This can lead to developing systems that meet the different needs of all possible users.[14] This may require developing multiple systems or multiple versions of a system in order to accommodate different needs.

NOTE: It is essential that the needs of different users are analyzed before attempting to develop any particular designs.

An increasing proportion of the population is aging and developing disabilities associated with this aging. Along with this increase has come an increasing demand for services that are accessible to the disabled.

- Title III of the Americans with Disabilities Act[15] "prohibits discrimination on the basis of disability by public accommodations and requires places of public accommodation and commercial facilities to be designed, constructed, and altered in compliance with accessibility standards established by this part." While this act was originally focused on physical facilities, such as buildings, its intent can be readily transferred to virtual businesses.

- In addition to the W3C guidelines referred to above, ISO has developed guidelines[16] that deal with providing accessibility to people with disabilities.
- The HUSAT Research Institute has developed a handbook on user-centered design for assistive technology.[17]
- The Trace Center of the College of Engineering at the University of Wisconsin–Madison[18] monitors and publicizes various activities related to improving accessibility.

 Find reviews of and links to further discussions about accessibility issues in the Chapter 9 Cyber Supplement.

9.2.3   Individual Privacy

Privacy refers to various aspects of the protection of personal information. The protection of personal information is gaining increasing importance in many countries around the world. Germany, France, and Sweden all passed comprehensive privacy legislation in the 1970s. This influenced the Council of Europe to adopt, in 1980, a Convention binding member countries to create legislation establishing fair information practices. The Organization for Economic Cooperation and Development (OECD) adopted a set of privacy principles in 1980.[19]

In 1995, the European Union (EU) passed a Data Protection Directive[20] protecting personal information and harmonizing privacy laws among its member states. The directive, which was to be implemented in national legislation by October 1998, forced all member countries to adopt privacy legislation or revise existing laws to comply with the EU Directive. The EU Directive requires that the laws of member states protect personal information in both the private and public sectors. These laws must contain provisions to block transfers of information to nonmember states (such as Canada and the United States) that do not provide an "adequate" level of protection. Actual privacy protection measures differ considerably between countries.

The United States has developed a "Safe Harbor" policy[21] that organizations may voluntarily implement and that the European Union accepted as meeting its directive on privacy. These principles involve:

1. "NOTICE: An organization must inform individuals about the purposes for which it collects information about them, how to contact the organization with any inquiries or complaints, the types of third parties to which it discloses the information, and the choices and means the organization offers individuals for limiting its use and disclosure.

2. "CHOICE: An organization must offer individuals the opportunity to choose (opt out) whether and how personal information they provide is used or disclosed to third parties (where such use is incompatible with the purpose for which it was originally collected or with any other purpose disclosed to the individual in a notice).

3. "ONWARD TRANSFER: An organization may only disclose personal information to third parties consistent with the principles of notice and choice. Where an organization has not provided choice because a use is compatible with the purpose for which the data was originally collected or which was disclosed in a notice and the organization wishes to transfer the data to a third party, it may do so if it first either ascertains that the third party subscribes to the safe harbor principles or enters into a written agreement with such third party requiring that the third party provide at least the same level of privacy protection as is required by the relevant safe harbor principles.

4. "SECURITY: Organizations creating, maintaining, using or disseminating personal information must take reasonable measures to assure its reliability for its intended use and reasonable precautions to protect it from loss, misuse and unauthorized access, disclosure, alteration and destruction.

5. "DATA INTEGRITY: Consistent with these principles, an organization may only process personal information relevant to the purposes for which it has been gathered. To the extent necessary for those purposes, an organization should take reasonable steps to ensure that data is accurate, complete, and current.

6. "ACCESS: Individuals must have [reasonable] access to personal information about them that an organization holds and be able to correct or amend that information where it is inaccurate.

7. "ENFORCEMENT: Effective privacy protection must include mechanisms for assuring compliance with the safe harbor principles, recourse for individuals to whom the data relate and are affected by noncompliance with the principles, and consequences for the organization when the principles are not followed."

Because the Safe Harbor policy is considered "voluntary" there is no legal means of enforcing it. The Canadian Personal Information Protection and Electronic Documents Act,[22] based on the Canadian Standards Association's Model Code for the Protection of Personal Information,[23] addresses the ways in which organizations collect, use, and disclose personal information. It also addresses the rights of individuals to have access to their personal information and to have it corrected if necessary. It is based on ten principles:

1. "Accountability: An organization is responsible for personal information under its control and shall designate an individual or individuals who are accountable for the organization's compliance with the following principles.

2. "Identifying Purposes: The purposes for which personal information is collected shall be identified by the organization at or before the time the information is collected.

3. "Consent: The knowledge and consent of the individual are required for the collection, use, or disclosure of personal information, except when inappropriate.

4. "Limiting Collection: The collection of personal information shall be limited to that which is necessary for the purposes identified by the organization. Information shall be collected by fair and lawful means.

5. "Limiting Use, Disclosure, and Retention: Personal information shall not be used or disclosed for purposes other than those for which it was collected,

except with the consent of the individual or as required by the law. Personal information shall be retained only as long as necessary for fulfillment of those purposes.

6. "Accuracy: Personal information shall be as accurate, complete, and up-to-date as is necessary for the purposes for which it is to be used.

7. "Safeguards: Personal information shall be protected by security safeguards appropriate to the sensitivity of the information.

8. "Openness: An organization shall make readily available to individuals specific information about its policies and practices relating to the management of personal information.

9. "Individual Access: Upon request, an individual shall be informed of the existence, use, and disclosure of his or her personal information and shall be given access to that information. An individual shall be able to challenge the accuracy and completeness of the information and have it amended as appropriate.

10. "Challenging Compliance: An individual shall be able to address a challenge concerning compliance with the above principles to the designated individual or individuals accountable for the organization's compliance."

The law proposes that unresolved disputes can be taken to Federal Court, which may order an organization to correct its practices and award damages, including punitive damages up to $20,000, to the complainant.

The United Kingdom has a Data Protection Act[24] that is based on the following principles:

1. Conditions for processing data fairly and legally must be met.
2. Personal data must be used for the lawful purpose for which it was obtained.
3. Personal data must be appropriate to their purposes.
4. Personal data must be accurate and kept up-to-date.
5. Personal data can only be retained while justified by its purpose.
6. Personal data processing must be in accordance with the rights of data subjects.
7. Appropriate safeguards must be implemented for processing, storing, and transmitting personal data.
8. Personal data must not be transferred to a country that does not conform to the EU directive on Data Protection.

It establishes a Data Protection Commissioner, an office of Data Protection Registrar, and a multilevel procedure for dealing with violations of the act.

The result of each of these, and similar, laws is to restrict the types and uses of information that e-Commerce sites can collect and use relating to their customers and suppliers. It is no longer acceptable for an organization to assume that it can collect and use any personal information that it wishes.

- The selling or trading of personal information, which has become a common business practice, is increasingly being recognized as an unwarranted invasion of personal privacy.
- Even where the collection of personal information is warranted, organizations are increasingly being made responsible for protecting this information from unwarranted uses.

Find reviews of and links to further information about privacy issues and regulations in the Chapter 9 Cyber Supplement.

9.2.4 Intellectual Property Ownership

Intellectual property encompasses those types of data whose ownership is protected by national and international laws and treaties. The creator of specific types of data, which involve certain unique characteristics, is granted the right to claim ownership and to sell or otherwise financially benefit from this ownership of it in recognition of the effort that went into creating it. Intellectual property rights vary between different types of data and between different countries.

An organization can and should protect various types of intellectual property from being copied by competitors. There are a variety of different methods of protecting an individual's or an organization's rights to intellectual property. There are an increasing number of instances where content is a commodity that is bought and sold. In these instances the "owners" of the content may attempt to restrict access to and use of it by both technical and legal means.

There are a number of international treaties dealing with intellectual property protection that can be applied to e-Commerce. Treaties are between governments and do not directly deal with individuals or organizations. They do not protect the rights of individuals or organizations in countries without legislation based on the treaty or in countries that are not a member of the treaty. Complaints regarding violations of treaties can only be dealt with by negotiations between governments. Treaties require each government, which is part of a treaty, to enact its own legislation to implement the treaty.

There may be considerable differences in the actual intellectual property legislation of different counties (such as the differences between American, British, and Canadian copyright laws). These differences may include:

- The specific criteria for different types of intellectual property protection
- Application procedures for intellectual property protection
- The duration of protection
- The ability to renew or extend protection
- The rights of the public or the government to make copies without compensation

Since e-Commerce crosses international boundaries, care must be taken to ensure that intellectual property will be protected appropriately in all jurisdictions where it will be used. Details of national intellectual property protection laws are beyond the scope of this book.

Find links to further information about intellectual property protection in the Chapter 9 Cyber Supplement.

Current legal protection of "intellectual property" includes the provisions described below.

Copyright protects ownership and copying of the artistic composition of a work. In most countries copyright can automatically be claimed without the need for formal applications to government authorities. Copyright protects the original features of a work in all media that may be used for the storage, transmission, and presentation of the work. Copyright does not prohibit significantly different compositions dealing with the same content. According to the World Intellectual

Property Organization Copyright Treaty,[25] "Copyright protection extends to expressions and not to ideas, procedures, methods of operation or mathematical concepts as such." Performances and recordings of performances are protected by an extension to copyright provisions.[26]

Patent protects ownership of technical works and prohibits a wide range of similar works, including those produced by deliberate "reverse engineering." Patents require formal application and proof of uniqueness of systems and processes and must be approved by national patent authorities.

Trademark protects ownership of words and images associated with an organization and its products and/or services. Trademarks require formal application and proof of uniqueness of some name or artistic composition being used on a regular basis in conjunction with carrying out a business. Trademarks also provide protections against variations of the trademark that are intended to mislead the public. However, the extent of protection from variation is often unclear and may differ from case to case.

License agreements can grant various restricted rights of copying and/or use by particular contacts between the provider of the content and the user of the content. By entering into a license agreement, the user of the content agrees to abide by the terms, whatever they are, of the license. Licenses may also include specified penalties for violation of these terms.

Internet domain names are used to establish logical connections to individual computers, including those hosting Web sites. They are assigned by central registration authorities to allow symbolic rather than physical accessing of sites on the Internet.

The United States is actively pursuing the development of further forms of intellectual property protections. An attempt, led by the United States, to extending intellectual property rights to the ownership of facts was rejected by the World Intellectual Property Organization.[27]

While the Web sites may make information highly accessible, this does not mean that people have a right to misappropriate what is available there. Making unauthorized copies can cheat the owner of rights (including the right to proper financial compensation) and may have the user relying on unreliable content (such as content that is not up-to-date).

Where users desire greater access to or control over content than is currently provided to them, they may attempt to circumvent access controls, whether by legal means or otherwise.

It is important that developers consider the ownership, access, and protection needs of both the owners and the users of content.

9.2.5 Enabling International e-Commerce

Enabling international e-Commerce involves specifying transactions in a precise manner that allows for automated processing, including necessary localization, to occur. The ISO/IEC Information Technology Business Team on Electronic Commerce (BT-EC)[28] identified a variety of issues that are especially important in standardizing transactions for international e-Commerce.

Localization involves modifying transactions to meet a range of specific needs of a user, including jurisdictional, linguistic and cultural, sectorial, human rights, and consumer rights. These modifications can be facilitated by standardized codes used to represent currencies, countries, languages, and commodities involved in the transactions.

According to the BT-EC a **jurisdiction** is "a distinct legal and/or regulatory framework which places constraints on the global marketplace and in doing so often defines/establishes a local market." e-Commerce systems need to handle the unique regulatory demands of various different jurisdictions within which they operate. ISO 18038[29] deals with the coding of jurisdictional domains.

An e-Commerce system can considerably expand its potential market if it is able to provide linguistic adaptation to serve:

- Various different natural languages
- Variations in the usage and dialects of a single natural language
- Variations in a natural language due to specific cultures or economic/technical sectors.

Providing linguistic adaptation to an e-Commerce system when it is first developed costs less than developing separate systems to meet the needs of each linguistic, cultural, or sectorial group.

Various economic/technical sectors often assign unique interpretations to select terms from a natural language. For example, the distinction between data and information, which was discussed in Chapter 3 and which applies within the computing sector, is not universally recognized by people proficient with the English language. When an e-Commerce system crosses sectorial boundaries it is important that they are able to resolve any ambiguities that may be created by a particular sectorial interpretation of the content that it provides. Different jurisdictions often have different regulations regarding human rights and consumer rights that may affect an e-Commerce system.

 Find links and references to further information about enabling international e-Commerce in the Chapter 9 Cyber Supplement.

9.2.6 Contractual Relations

For commerce to exist, each party of a business transaction must be able to trust that each other party will fulfill their obligations.

- In transactions between friends this trust can result from friendship.
- As business is conducted at increasing distances between parties who often do not know each other, there is greater reliance on governments (or other intermediaries) ensuring that the other parties are accountable for their obligations.

The United Nations Commission on International Trade Law (UNICTRAL) has developed a model law for regulating electronic commerce.[30] The OECD has also developed guidelines for consumer protection in e-Commerce.[31]

Since various electronic payment systems are still developing, it is more important to focus on the concept of electronic payments than to focus on a particular technology for achieving them.

According to UNICTRAL, there is a need for "both a domestic and a global uniform commercial legal framework that recognizes, facilitates, and enforces electronic transactions worldwide." This need may be met by financial institutions, which guarantee these transactions, or by government legislation, which recognizes and allows enforcement of these transactions. In specific, there is a need to recognize the legitimacy of electronic contracts, electronic signatures and certifications, and electronic payments and to develop safeguards for each of their use.

Find links to further information about electronic contracts, signatures, certifications, and payments in the Chapter 9 Cyber Supplement.

9.2.7 Security

In addition to the trust required for contractual relations, there are a number of additional security-related issues that should be considered, including:

- Protecting information from unauthorized use
- Protecting information senders and recipients
- Protecting individuals from malicious acts such as unauthorized accesses and viruses

While there are a number of technical solutions to each of these issues, the development of appropriate technical solutions will only be done in response to requirements that have been identified within the analysis.

Find links to further information about Internet security issues in the Chapter 9 Cyber Supplement.

9.2.8 Customs and Taxation

Customs and taxation can still be applied in the conventional manner to physical goods and services delivered in traditional manners, even if they are contracted for via e-Commerce. However, it may be very difficult to track the delivery of information-related goods and services delivered over the Internet to be able to assess the appropriate taxes.

Since additional taxes could inhibit the growth of e-Commerce, the Framework for Global Electronic Commerce[32] recommended that "no new taxes should be imposed on Internet commerce" and that any changes made to deal with information-based products and services should be made to "existing taxation concepts and principles."

9.3 DEALING WITH IMPORTANT E-COMMERCE ISSUES

9.3.1 Dealing with Important e-Commerce Issues in Organizations

The e-Commerce issues, discussed above, are related to various feasibility considerations, which where discussed in Chapter 6. However, they may be far more complicated than was first envisioned. Because of the complexity of analyzing these various issues, many organizations may not have sufficient expertise to deal with these issues on their own. An organization may need to consult one or more expert(s) in international business.

Organizations need to conduct a thorough analysis of each of these issues to identify:

- Issues that should be dealt with by the establishment of general organizational policies
- Specific requirements, related to these issues, that need to be included in the development

Wherever appropriate, it is useful to establish policies that can be used throughout the organization and for all systems being developed. Where relevant policies exist, developers should refer to these policies within the list of project requirements to ensure that these policies will be followed in the development.

The existence of policies related to an issue does not mean that all requirements related to the issue have been identified. There may be various situations, which need to be accommodated, that are too specific to be dealt with by organizational policies.

Where new policy establishment is justified, it will often require the involvement of senior management who may not be directly involved with the development of a particular system. Such policy making may take longer than is available within a particular development. Where delays in establishing policies may occur, developers should identify both the requirements that are expected to be part of the policy and any other application-specific requirements.

9.3.2   Student Assignment—Important e-Commerce Issues

Students are encouraged to investigate each of these issues in further detail by following up on the references cited in this chapter and on the Web site supporting this book.

Students should then analyze their chosen application in terms of each of the six groups of issues discussed in sections 9.3.2—9.3.7 to determine for each issue:

- How the issues should be dealt with in terms of existing and/or new organizational policies
- Which specific requirements the issue creates for the development

9.4   AN EXAMPLE OF DEALING WITH IMPORTANT E-COMMERCE ISSUES

Because *Savor the Cup* is already an international organization, it already deals with a number of these issues to some extent. However, its development of e-Commerce will add new challenges relating to many of these issues that need to be met.

9.4.1   Accessibility Example

Organizational Policies

Accessibility is already related to *Savor the Cup's* goal of "being responsive to customer needs." It is further reinforced by the decision to retain local branches to serve customers, which can be viewed as a policy decision.

However, a new policy could be established that requires that "All information and e-Commerce systems of *Savor the Cup* should comply with the recommendations of ISO Technical Specification 16071."[33]

Specific Requirements

The identification of ISO TS 16071 provides a sufficient set of specific requirements for this application.

9.4.2 Individual Privacy Example

Organizational Policies

An analysis of *Savor the Cup* found that while information on individuals was generally kept confidential, largely to keep it from competitors, there are no policies that deal with individual privacy in the way it is discussed above.

This has led to identifying the need to establish both a privacy policy and to implement measures to ensure that it is followed by *Savor the Cup*.

Specific Requirements

Until an organizational privacy policy is established, it will be necessary to develop a suitable privacy policy to be used with and posted as part of the e-Commerce system.

9.4.3 Intellectual Property Ownership Example

Organizational Policies

The main exposure that *Savor the Cup* has had with intellectual property ownership is to trademark its name and the names of some of its products and services. A further analysis of this issue has revealed that individuals within the organization are not sufficiently aware of or in compliance with the various implications of copyright on what they do.

This has led to identifying the need to establish both a copyright policy and to implement measures to ensure that it is followed by *Savor the Cup*.

Specific Requirements

Care needs to be taken to ensure that the system being developed is in compliance with various intellectual property protections.

Savor the Cup needs to apply for a suitable Internet domain name, such as "*SavortheCup.com*," as soon as possible to ensure its rights to a recognizable address.

9.4.4 Contractual Relations Example

Organizational Policies

Currently, *Savor the Cup* researches and follows up on the national contractual regulations of each country where it has an office. It employs legal experts to ensure that it is in compliance with local laws and that it can enforce its contracts. This approach has worked quite well, despite the difficulties of maintaining different sets of similar contracts.

When doing business in countries where it does not have an office, *Savor the Cup* enters in contracts that are based out of one of its branch offices and stipulates that the laws of the country where the branch office is situated will govern the contract. Again, this works quite well.

Specific Requirements

The system being developed will need to handle these existing contractual relations. Further analysis should be conducted to identify any countries where these policies may be insufficient.

9.4.5 Security Example

Organizational Policies

Savor the Cup has existing organizational and computing policies that handle various security concerns in a satisfactory manner. The policies balance the need to share information effectively throughout the company with the need to protect it from being accessed in unauthorized manners. These policies are currently implemented by a combination of employee training and organizational information audits.

Specific Requirements

Further analysis should be conducted to identify additional security concerns, especially those related to using the Internet for e-Commerce activities.

9.4.6 Customs and Taxation Example

Organizational Policies

Currently, *Savor the Cup* researches and follows up on the national customs and taxation of each country where it has an office and/or where it conducts business. It employs legal and financial experts to ensure that it is in compliance with local customs and taxation requirements. This approach has worked quite well, despite the difficulties of dealing with different sets of similar customs and taxation requirements.

Specific Requirements

Customs and taxation information for each country that it does business with should be included in the system being developed. The system should also include a means of easily updating this information as needed.

9.5 CHALLENGES AND OPPORTUNITIES IN DEALING WITH IMPORTANT E-COMMERCE ISSUES

The following are the most frequent problems encountered when dealing with important e-Commerce issues.

Challenges Due to a Lack of Understanding

- Some developers may assume that the users will identify all the important issues, and if they are not mentioned, then they are not important.
- Some users may assume that e-Commerce developers should recognize and understand the relevant important issues.
- Some people may assume that these issues will be handled the way they always have and that nothing needs to be done about them.
- Some people may assume that these issues have been sufficiently investigated in the feasibility study and may fail to investigate them further.
- Some of these issues are difficult to research, which may lead to a failure to properly understand and handle them.

9.6 CYBER SUPPLEMENTS FOR CHAPTER 9

 Look at the Chapter 9 Cyber Supplements on the Web to find:

- Reviews of and links to further surveys of important e-Commerce issues

- Reviews of and links to further information about privacy issues and regulations

- Links to further information about intellectual property protection

- Links to further information about electronic contracts, signatures, certifications, and payments

- Links to further information about Internet security issues

- Practice activities dealing with various e-Commerce issues

REFERENCES

[1] The White House, A Framework for Global Electronic Commerce, 1997, http://www.ecommerce.gov/framewrk.htm

[2] Organization for Economic Cooperation and Development (OECD), *Electronic Commerce: Opportunities and Challenges for Government* (The "Sacher Report", 1997) (downloadable from http://www.oecd.org/dsti/sti/it/ec/index.htm).

[3] W3C and Electronic Commerce, http://www.w3.org/TR/EC-related-activities

[4] W3C, Web Content Accessibility Guidelines, http://www.w3.org/WAI/GL/WCAG10

[5] W3C, User Agent Accessibility Guidelines, http://www.w3.org/TR/UAAG10

[6] W3C, Metadata Activity Statement, http://www.w3.org/Metadata/Activity.html

[7] W3C, Digital Signature Initiative, http://www.w3.org/DSig/

[8] W3C, Platform for Privacy Preferences (P3P) Project, http://www.w3.org/P3P/

[9] W3C, White Paper: Joint Electronic Payment Initiative, http://www.w3.org/TR/NOTE-jepi

[10] W3C, Intellectual Property Rights Overview, http://www.w3.org/IPR/

[11] W3C, Micropayments Overview, http://www.w3.org/ECommerce/Micropayments/

[12] ISO/IEC Information Technology Business Team on Electronic Commerce, Work on Electronic Commerce Standardization to be Initiated, 1998.

[13] "International Organization for Standardization," ISO Draft Technical Specification 16071, Ergonomics of Human System Interaction—Guidance on Accessibility for Human-Computer Interfaces, 2000.

[14] C. Stephanidis and G. Salvendy, "Towards an Information Society for All: HCI Challenges and R&D Recommendations." *International Journal of Human-Computer Interaction*, 11(1), 1-28, 1999.

[15] U.S. Government, Americans with Disabilities Act, Part 36 – Nondiscrimination on the basis of Disability by Public Accommodations and in Commercial Facilities, http://www.usdoj.gov/crt/ada/reg3a.html

[16] Ibid.

[17] TIDE (Technology Initiative for Disabled and Elderly People_ 1062 USER (User Requirements Elaboration in Rehabilitation and Assistive Technology) Project, USERfit Handbook, (Brussels-Luxembourg, ECSC-EC-EAEC, 1996).

[18] The Trace Center of the College of Engineering at the University of Wisconsin–Madison, http://www.trace.wisc.edu/

[19] OECD, Guidelines on the Protection of Privacy and Transborder Flows of Personal Data, Sept. 23, 1980, http://www.oecd.org/dsti/sti/it/secur/index.htm

[20] Directive 95/46/EC of the European Parliament and of the Council of 24 October 1995 on the protection of individuals with regard to the processing of personal data and on the free movement of such data, http://europa.eu.int/eur-lex/en/lif/dat/1995/en_395L0046.html

[21] International Safe Harbor Privacy Principles, http://www.ita.doc.gov/td/ecom/Principles 1199.htm

[22] Canada, Personal Information Protection and Electronic Documents Act, http://www.parl.gc.ca/36/1/parlbus/chambus/house/bills/government/C-54/C-54_2/90052bE.html

[23] Canadian Standards Association, CAN/CSA-Q830-96, Model Code for the Protection of Personal Information.

[24] The United Kingdom, Data Protection Act 1998, http://www.hmso.gov.uk/acts/acts1998 /19980029.htm

[25] World Intellectual Property Organization, WIPO Copyright Treaty, 1996, http://www.wipo.int/eng/diplconf/distrib/94dc.htm

[26] World Intellectual Property Organization, WIPO Performances and Phonograms Treaty, 1996, http://www.wipo.int/eng/diplconf/distrib/95dc.htm

[27] James Love, Government Proposes New Regulations of Sports Statistics and Other "Facts," Consumer Project on Technology, 1996, http://www.cptech.org/ip/wipo-sports.html

[28] Ibid.

[29] "International Organization for Standardization," ISO/IEC Working Draft of International Standard 18038, Identification and Mapping of Various Categories of Jurisdictional Domains, 2000.

[30] The United Nations Commission on International Trade Law (UNICTRAL), UNICTRAL Model Law on Electronic Commerce with Guide to Enactment, 1998, http://www.uncitral.org/english/texts/electcom/ml-ec.htm

[31] OECD, Recommendation of the OECD Council Concerning Guidelines for Consumer Protection in the Context of Electronic Commerce, http://www.ftc.gov/opa/1999/9912/oecdguide.htm

[32] Ibid.

[33] Ibid.

10

High-Level Design

Outline

10.1 INTRODUCTION TO HIGH-LEVEL DESIGN

At this point in a development, it is expected that most requirements, especially the most significant ones, have been identified. While general solutions will have been analyzed in terms of feasibility, the developer should not have made a firm decision on a particular solution yet. Arriving at a suitable solution involves careful design. It is the role of the design phase to consider various possible solutions and variations on each and to develop a particular solution that **works well for all** of the requirements.

NOTE: This does **not** say that the role of design is to come up with **the best possible** solution.

- Since at this point there are still an infinite number of potential solutions, it would be impossible to determine which solution would truly be best.
- Often some requirements may conflict with others; thus solutions may have to compromise in how they fit the overall set of requirements.
- Different people and organizations will have different ideas of what constitutes the best solution.

This chapter deals with high-level design. A **high-level design** is like a plan for a design. It identifies what will have to be designed in detail later in the development. It does this by identifying the major components that need to be designed and any overall design approaches and guidelines that will be used throughout the design.

Whereas analysis focused on identifying and separating out different requirements and the relationships between each, high-level design focuses on combining these requirements and relationships in a manner that optimizes the synergy produced by their combination.

10.2 UNDERSTANDING HIGH-LEVEL DESIGN

10.2.1 Designing a Credible e-World

While there are many e-Worlds being developed on the Web as fantasy worlds, an e-Commerce application must be successful in achieving real world objectives for its real world users. e-Commerce applications, while being part of cyberspace, rely on being credible e-Worlds in order to convince their users to accept them as an alternate to the "real world."

e-Commerce applications (and most other Web sites) need to avoid being online ego trips for their owners/developers. They need to avoid the "Field of Dreams Syndrome" in which the developers and owners assume that "If you build it, they will come." Even if they do come, it is important to ensure that they will stay long enough to meet your objectives (such as generating sales and/or increasing customer satisfaction, loyalty, and/or service), which may include coming back to further meet your objectives in the future.

Whereas the analysis should have identified the most important needs for the system to meet, the design should ensure that these needs can be met. This involves ensuring that each of the groups of stakeholders involved will be satisfied. ISO 14915-1[1] recognizes the need for multimedia systems, including e-Commerce systems, to meet the needs of "information providers" and "information recipients" as well as the needs of the sponsors of the system. For example:

- An organization may sponsor an e-Commerce system to make current sales, to encourage future sales, and to develop customer loyalty
- A marketing manager may provide information to be used in the system primarily in order to make current sales
- A customer may try to receive information from the system in order to figure out how to use a product that was already purchased from the organization

An **information provider** is a person who creates content that will be used publicly in an application, whether or not the content was created expressly for the application. This concept does not include individuals, such as customers, who enter orders or other types of private content into a system. **Information recipients** are any people who may make use of the content of a system as information consumers. Some users may act as both information providers and information recipients.

There may be multiple groups of information providers and multiple groups of information recipients involved with a single system. These groups are not necessarily independent from one another because the information from the providers is destined for the recipients. This information, however, does not flow directly between groups, but is mediated by the multimedia system produced by the developer. It may also require the services of a human mediator in order to remove unwanted biases and/or to insert sponsor-desired biases.

Each of these major groups of stakeholders can have their own distinct set of objectives for the multimedia system, which may even be in conflict with one another. Often meeting one particular need of one group will necessitate meeting certain needs of one or more other groups. For example, in order to convince customers to buy products and/or services an organization may need to meet the customers' need for after-sales support.

There is often a challenge to developers to find sufficient, suitable information providers from which to obtain the required content of a system. Not all information that is provided to developers is equally good. Much of it needs to be analyzed and designed before it can be used successfully. While many people may be able to provide content/information from their own perspective, it may not meet the needs of other people.

Information providers can be divided into primary information providers and secondary information providers. A **primary information provider** may have some control over the content and/or design of the system and/or have particular tasks they want the system to accomplish. **Secondary information providers** are not able to control how information they have created is used. They may not even know where or how it is being used.

Information providers within a sponsoring organization may often act as primary information providers. However, developers should be careful to distinguish between those who have authority to control the content from those who would like this authority but who do not have it. Information provided from sources outside the sponsoring organization may be used "as is" or may be reformulated for its particular use within the organization's systems. However, in most cases, external sources of information are treated as secondary information providers.

Both primary and secondary information providers may have a variety of motivations and biases, which can influence the selection and presentation of information content that they provide.

It is generally expected that information is obtained from people who are suitably knowledgeable and who thus can claim to be "experts" regarding that information. However, there is a large range of "experts" with very differing motivations, including:

- True experts—with expertise, information, and understanding to share with all and who recognize the different needs of different groups of people (this type of information provider is relatively rare)
- True experts—with expertise and information to share with other "experts" but who are unable to explain information to nonexperts
- True experts—with strong personal biases that may limit the usefulness of the information they provide
- "Wannabe" experts—trying to be accepted as experts, who may make up information for anyone who is interested enough to listen to them

Information providers generally bias the information they provide based on:

- Past experiences (both with the content and with the intended recipients)
- Current agendas or interests (even if they are not strongly biased)
- The organizational culture (regardless of whether or not they accept it)

Allowing specific information providers to have an extensive say in the development of a system may result in various difficulties, including:

- The tendency to reuse existing media clips and other content design, whether it is appropriate or not
- The tendency to use only selected sources of information
- The application being biased toward the needs of the information providers while ignoring the needs of the information recipients

Some information providers may use the system to regularly update some content items, such as product and/or service information. Design must include the provision of suitable organizational controls, such as updating of content to ensure accuracy to auditability and checking for intentional and unintentional biases.

In some cases information providers also may be members of one or more groups of information recipients. In general, however, the needs and characteristics of information recipients are likely to be different from those of the information providers and even different from those expected of them by the information providers. Some of the most important characteristics of users, which can lead to particular design implications, include the user's:

- Background knowledge—if some users do not have sufficient background knowledge they may require access to optional tutorial material
- Attitudes and experiences—which may help or hinder developing a suitable business relationship

- Style preferences—which may help or hinder their acceptance of a system
- Openness to change—which may influence the effectiveness of various strategies
- Relationships with information providers—which may involve trust/distrust and/or dependence/independence

e-Commerce applications need to be designed for their users, while serving their sponsors. They need to provide immediate relevance to attract and retain their intended users. To be successful they often need to provide additional entertainment (subjective content) and education (objective content) to users, beyond the application content previously identified in our analysis. The developer needs to balance the objective and subjective contents of e-Commerce applications and to design in a manner that will motivate the users. This requires developers to not only know the characteristics of their users but also to understand and predict how the users will react to attempts to engage them with the system and its objectives.

The developer has to determine the following:

- Where a single design is sufficiently acceptable to all groups of users
- Where multiple versions of a single design would better suit the different needs of different groups of users
- Where different designs may be needed to meet the needs of different groups of users

10.2.2   The Transition from Analysis to Design

Analysis is concerned with identifying requirements. Ideally it should identify all potential requirements. However, in practice, additional requirements may be identified throughout the life cycle. As discussed above, additional design-related requirements may be introduced to provide a credible e-World for users. Although analysis should evaluate the feasibility of satisfying each of the requirements, it should avoid specific decisions about how the requirements will be met in the future system.

We have examined two types of analysis:

- Task analysis (which identified users, tasks, tools, and content) focuses on analyzing the real world. It identifies the users' requirements in a manner that the user can understand so that the user can be sure that we have identified all the right ones.
- Object-oriented analysis (which transformed users, content, and tools into objects) focuses on identifying a means of modeling the real world in terms of object classes and relationships. It provides developers a basis for design and for the evaluation of that design.

Design involves creating plans for an application program to meet some of these requirements. Design is a creative process, and like other creative processes it may lead to a number of different possible outcomes. Developers should not start design with preconceived notions, prejudices, or plans. Rather, the design process should allow the developers and the users to explore and evaluate potential designs and to come up with a suitable design.

NOTE: It is impossible to come up with the definitive "best" design because only a limited number of possible designs can ever be considered. However, it is important to consider various possibilities at each stage of the design process.

Application programs are models of the real world. We should remember that models are intentionally incomplete representations of the real world. Each type of model focuses on some aspects of the real world and ignores others. Thus, an object-oriented analysis model focuses on requirements that may or may not be met by an object-oriented design model.

Like analysis, the design process can be subdivided for our consideration into various subprocesses:

- High-level design—involves identifying the main components of our model and creating a structure for their overall interaction. High-level design will be discussed in this chapter.
- Detailed design—involves a detailed plan of each of the components of our model and of all interactions with the model. Detailed design will be discussed in Chapter 11.
- Technical design—involves planning how each of these components can be implemented. Technical design will be discussed in Chapter 12.

10.2.3   Development Methodologies

Various methodologies have been developed in an attempt to help developers both with individual technical processes of the development life cycle and in the transition between processes. Norman[2] states that a **methodology** is "the packaging of methods and techniques together. The way something gets done. The purpose of a methodology is to promote a certain problem-solving strategy by preselecting the methods and techniques to be used."

Each development methodology can be analyzed in object-oriented terms:

- The attributes of a methodology are different types of documentation
- The operations of a methodology are different methods designed to use the documentation to develop a software system

Booch, Rumbaugh, and Jacobson[3] joined together in developing the Unified Modeling Language, which "is a graphical language for visualizing, specifying, constructing, and documenting the artifacts of a software intensive system" and which supports various popular object-oriented methodologies.

Most methodologies demand that developers follow their methods accurately and completely in return for the promise of a successful systems development. The implication is that if you had followed the methodology correctly, then you wouldn't have had any difficulties. However, developers often have difficulties in following the methodologies accurately and completely. In a study by Rosson[4] of professional software developers, it was found that:

- Only half of these developers choose to follow a given methodology
- Only half (of the half who claim to be following a methodology) follow it correctly (so don't feel bad if you've had some difficulties up to now)

At this point we have enough experience to consider the nature of the purposes of a methodology and its attributes and operations. These purposes are different, depending on the individual's perspective.

- All stakeholders expect the methodology to lead to the development of a good system.
- End users would like the methodology to produce easy-to-understand documentation throughout the life cycle so that they can be sure that the developers are developing the best possible system for them.
- Developers want a methodology that doesn't impinge on their freedom but that does help them both in developing the desired system and in dealing with the other stakeholders (end users and managers). This help generally should include minimizing the amount of documentation that the developers have to create.
- Managers want a methodology that ensures that the development is on schedule and on budget. Thus, it must produce documentation that proves that the developers are progressing throughout the life cycle.

Often these different purposes are in conflict. When forced to use a given methodology and to produce given documents, developers may go through the motions just to satisfy managers and end users, without making much use of required documentation in the actual development.

Rather than blindly accepting all that goes along with a methodology, it is important that the various stakeholders determine what they really want and need out of the methodology and how to ensure that they get it.

- If some parts of a methodology aren't useful to any of the stakeholders, then perhaps they are not needed.
- If parts of a different methodology could be useful, then perhaps they should be included in the development.

Blindly following all the potential recommendations of all the authors could yield a documentation nightmare that could lead to spending lifetimes on developing documentation and never getting the desired system delivered to the users.

People often wonder why the U.S. military has been known to pay $10,000 for a hammer. The answer is in the overly cumbersome procurement process that requires standard sets of documentation, known as MIL-SPEC, no matter how complex or simple the desired system is. For most organizations it is best to allow the complexity of the methodology and its associated documentation to be tailored to meet the needs and complexities of the application.

 Find a discussion of and links to further information about development methodologies in the Chapter 10 Cyber Supplement.

10.2.4 The Complexities of Design

Design is a complex activity that is influenced by a number of factors. The fact that the majority of the requirements have been established in an analysis does not mean that all designs that meet these requirements are equally satisfactory nor that the cheapest and/or fastest design will be sufficient. There is an ongoing need for informed user involvement, despite technical complexities that may be considered within the design process. While the users may not understand all of the technical details, they do not need to do so in order to contribute significantly to the design.

Users can be involved in design by various user centered development processes[5] and methods,[6] such as:

- Asking them for suggestions of what they would like or how something should be done
- Asking their opinion of proposed designs, including prototypes of designs
  - Asking them to suggest how to improve proposed designs
  - Asking them to select between alternative designs

 Find a discussion of and links to further information about user-centered design in the Chapter 10 Cyber Supplement.

In addition to involving the main developers and users, design can benefit from the services of a variety of specialists, including user interface developers, graphic designers, marketing professionals, and industrial psychologists.

 Find a discussion of and links to further information about how various types of professionals can aid in design in the Chapter 10 Cyber Supplement.

10.2.4.1 Trade-offs Between Quality, Speed, and Cost of Development

Norman identifies the problem of trying to optimize quality, speed, and cost in development. Attempts to improve one will negatively affect one or both of the others. To consider these trade-offs, think of the following:

- A limited length of string with ends tied
- A surface where the center point represents the minimal acceptable quantities of quality, speed, and cost
- Three distant points, in opposite directions, that represent the ideal values of quality, speed, and cost

You can stretch the string in any shape, as illustrated in Figure 10-1, but it cannot be stretched any longer than it already is. By stretching it in different shapes, you can:

- Maximize efforts in one direction, which may or may not achieve the ideal value of one of the three
- Divide efforts in two directions (although any one direction will be somewhat smaller than if maximized on its own); however, the central point may distract somewhat from making a straight line between these two dimensions
- Maximize all three directions by stretching the string in a triangle (with a corresponding decrease in each dimension from its maximum potential size)
- Take into account compromises between competing needs by adjusting each of the three dimensions accordingly

10.2.4.2 Integrating Different Components

For a system to work, all of its components must work together. An e-Commerce system requires that software, people, hardware, data, and procedures all work together successfully. Often developers focus on designing software that, if used correctly (with assumed procedures) by the right users on suitable hardware and with correct data, will accomplish the desired application. However, that's too much to assume if

Best quality

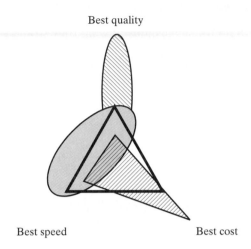

Best speed   Best cost

Figure 10-1   Selecting tradeoffs between quality, speed, and cost

you want an e-Commerce system that will be used. As a result, developers need to consider:

- The range of differences among potential users (which should have been identified in the analysis)
- The range of different types of hardware, including special accessibility devices (such as page readers) and older models of computers that might be used by the intended users
- The range of valid data and methods for helping to identify erroneous data
- The minimum set of procedures that users need to know to use the system

The overall design of complete systems is often separated from and conducted before a high-level design of the required software.

10.2.4.3 Ongoing Feasibility Determinations

As discussed in Chapter 6, there is a need for ongoing and increasingly accurate feasibility and profitability determinations.

- An initial feasibility study, conducted before the analysis, should not be used to establish a design. Rather it should have verified that there are a range of possible designs that are feasible.
- Throughout the analysis, as more requirements were identified, various decisions needed to be made as to which requirements to keep for the time being and

which to save for later development. While this should have established an ideal set of requirements for the design, it may not be possible for the design to satisfy all requirements in a manner that is technically and financially possible and that is on schedule. As the understanding of these requirements changes throughout design, so does their feasibility.

10.3 PERFORMING HIGH-LEVEL DESIGN

The simplest approach to object-oriented design is to develop a set of design objects, where each design object directly represents a different analysis object. In this way the design can easily be shown to model the requirements, and with them to also model the "real world." However, such a model typically is very difficult to use. If people don't understand the model it is based on, they may not know where to look for the functionality and information that they need.

It is important to maximize the usability of our system and the objects in it. To accomplish this, we need to design our application in terms of a set of objects that meet the functional (task) and information (content) needs of each of the users.

Arriving at a good set of objects often takes a number of iterations and may be significantly assisted by using a prototyping approach.

 Find a discussion of the use of prototyping in high-level design in the Chapter 10 Cyber Supplement.

10.3.1 Some Approaches to Object-Oriented Design

There are many different approaches to object-oriented design, each of which can provide helpful insights into design.

Rumbaugh[7] suggested three types of models:

- Object models—which describe objects that "promote understanding of the real world and provide a practical basis for computer implementation."
- Dynamic models—which describe "changes to objects and their relationships over time."
- Functional models—which specify "the results of a computation without specifying how or when they are computed."

Jacobson[8] suggested three different types of objects:

- Interface objects—to model "bi-directional communication between the system and its users." These interface objects represent the tools with which the user interacts.
- Entity objects—"usually correspond to some concept in real life, outside the system." They are used "to model information that the system will handle over a longer time." These entity objects represent content with which the user interacts.
- Control objects—"typically work as glue or cushions to unite the remaining objects so that they form one use case." These control objects represent the tasks that the user tries to accomplish.

Norman[9] identified "four components that make up the entire object-oriented model of the proposed information system":

- Problem domain (PD)—this component is developed in the analysis phase and is the basis for all other components.
- Human interaction (HI)—this component concentrates on how the user interacts with the system.
- Data management (DM)—this component concentrates on how the system interacts with and stores the data.
- System interaction (SI)—this component concentrates on how the hardware is used as part of the system.

It is interesting to note the potential relationship of the main focus of these four components on our initial foci of analysis:

- The problem domain primarily focuses on TASKS
- Human interaction primarily focuses on USERS
- Data management primarily focuses on CONTENT
- System interaction primarily focuses on TOOLS

This book will focus on a part of the design process (the design of human/user interactions) that is generally of greatest impact on the development of e-Commerce systems. Further details of the technical aspects of design belong more in a book on Software Engineering.

10.3.2 Refining System Boundaries

High-level design starts with refining system boundaries, which involves deciding which objects and/or requirements are to be served by the application software being developed (this is similar to revising the initial identification of the application). Whereas analysis boundaries limited what was considered part of the problem, design boundaries limit what will be part of the solution.

With most modern applications, and especially with e-Commerce applications, the complexity of the application makes it infeasible to meet all the possible requirements at one time. (There is a long history of complex projects never being finished.) It is best to pick some reasonable subset of the requirements to design a first version of the system and to defer the other requirements to later evolutionary developments.

In establishing design boundaries the developer needs to consider how essential the requirement is to the success of the system and to the success of other requirements that were already selected for the system. The developer needs to go beyond any original ideas of a basic and a deluxe system and to get the users, and especially the sponsor, to identify the actual system that will be designed. This may involve:

- Reevaluating the idea of what is truly important for a basic system
- Identifying whether or not the required resources (time, people, and so on) are available
  - Developing at least a basic system

- Developing additions to the basic system (Considering what else is most desirable to develop. This involves deciding between alternative sets of needs that could be added within existing resource constraints.)
- Identifying other requirements that may be met at no additional expenditure of resources

System boundaries for purposes of design are then set at the basic system plus any additional needs that can be accommodated within budget, because they are worth the extra expenditures that will be required for them or because they won't require extra expenditures.

Rather than throw away the rest of the analysis or totally ignore those requirements that can't be met at this time, the developer should:

- Keep these requirements as a source of information about possible future enhancements
- Consider (later during detailed design) the effects of specific detailed designs on facilitating or inhibiting possible enhancements that could meet these needs in the future

Refining system boundaries will:

- Limit the objects that will be modeled within the application program
- Limit the attributes and operations of each of the objects modeled
- Limit the other related requirements that need to be considered in the design

10.3.3 Designing the Main Components and the Application Structure

The main objective of high-level design is the design of the main application components and an application structure for these components. These two activities generally are conducted together in a highly iterative manner.

Designing the main components of a system involves choosing a set of high-level presentation segments that can represent the objects (within our refined system boundaries) in the application program.

According to ISO 14915-2,[10] **a presentation segment** "provides the physical implementation of one or more content chunks as part of an application." Typical examples of presentation segments include pages, panels, windows, and boxes.

e-Commerce applications serve the needs of complex collections of tasks, users, and content. Design transforms these needs into an organized series of interactions that can occur in a series of "windows," "pages," "screens," "views," or other types of high-level "presentation segments." Each presentation segment should meet the needs of both the organization responsible for it and the various intended users of it. These needs may be substantially different or even in conflict with one another, as discussed earlier in this chapter in the section on "Designing a Credible e-World."

The most common high-level presentation segment in an e-Commerce application program is a Web page. Web pages present content (attributes of objects) to the user and allow the user to interact with the object's operations. Web pages may be divided into panels when two or more major chunks of content may be used together and may also be used on their own. Web pages and panels use scrolling to allow the user to access more content and interactions than fit within the hardware limitations of a physical screen. Each presentation segment can be designed as an object within a network of interconnected objects. The challenge is to relate these objects to all the other objects we have already identified.

Developers should also consider the more limited capabilities of various hand-held mobile computing devices that may also be used to access an e-Commerce site. Defining presentation segments in terms of the content chunks they serve provides a consistent high-level design that can be implemented with alternate detailed designs to meet the specific needs of different types of computing technology.

NOTE: The set of presentation segments generally requires the inclusion of extra objects (beyond those identified in the analysis) to allow the user to use and/or customize the use of the application software. These objects may provide introductions, overviews, and maps of the application structure, security/log-on processing, and application customization.

Whereas content chunks are semantic and typically have only logical boundaries, presentation segments have physical implementations, including physical boundaries, that can be readily accessed by navigation controls. Presentation segments contain both information content and the navigation controls and links to allow users to access this information content. Ideally they include complete content chunks along with the structure that relates these content chunks to one another.

At this stage, requirements need to be allocated to presentation segments without designing how specifically the presentation segments meet the requirements. These presentation segments should:

- Meet the content and task needs of all groups of users (within the refined system boundaries)
- Represent all objects with which the users will need to interact at a given point in the application

Designing the application structure involves specifying how the main components within the application program will interact with each other. This structure needs to work for all the tasks, users, and content chunks that are within our design boundaries.

Many application programs, and especially most e-Commerce programs, may be so complex that most users/tasks only use parts of the complete application structure. Thus, the application structure is actually a composite of the structures used by each of the users and tasks that it serves. Additional structuring may relate to the "natural" or "traditional" structure(s) of the content, regardless of the users and/or tasks.

It is desirable that an application's structure should correspond to the real world as much as possible. However, a number of constraints may limit the extent of this correspondence, including:

- Differences in the needs/wants of different groups of users
- Differences in the needs of different tasks
- Differences in various potential structures of the content
- Different traditional designs of tools used within the application
- Technological limitations
- The resulting complexity that would be involved in trying to be all things to all people and all other of the above needs

Attempts at using a single hierarchical organizing principle are likely to fail to produce a satisfactory design.

- Structures based on the needs of one particular group of users may not suit the needs of other user groups.
- Structures based on the needs of one organization of tasks may not suit the needs of other tasks.
- Structures based on the needs of one approach to the content may not suit the needs of various groups of users, the needs of various tasks, or the needs of other approaches to the content.

10.3.3.1 Using Content as a Basis for Presentation Segments

ISO 14915-2[11] provides a basis for the structuring of e-Commerce (and other multimedia) systems based on content chunks that can be used to meet one or more needs. It recommends combining these content chunks into a structure of presentation segments that is made accessible with a suitable navigation structure. It provides guidance both in selecting suitable content chunks and suitable navigation structures that meet the needs of different tasks and different users.

Applications can be built up from suitably sized chunks of content. Content chunking produces:

- A content structure that specifies the relationship between individual chunks of the content and identifies navigational needs between them
- Chunks that are parts of the content and correspond to important concepts within the content

The size of individual content chunks is determined by the various needs that must be met, rather than just keeping content chunks sized as they were in the analysis. In addition to structuring content to meet the need of the tasks and the users (as identified in the analysis), various other semantic approaches to structuring content might be useful in the structuring of e-Commerce systems in order to facilitate learning and/or exploration.

Developers can identify all applicable semantic approaches to structuring content by first asking "Which approaches are needed by the tasks of the application?" and then asking "Which approaches would any users of this application need or want to use to explore the multimedia?" Different information providers might structure the content they provide differently, based on different approaches.

There are a number of potential semantic approaches to structuring content, including, but not limited to:

- **Task-based structuring**—in which the content structure is determined by the structure of the tasks of the application. As discussed above, different users might require different task structures based on different subsets of the complete set of available tasks and/or other user differences.
- **Conventional structuring**—in which the content is structured in the "traditional" way that it is taught to students or the "traditional" way it is organized by researchers in the field. This "traditional" structure might include one or more other structuring approaches or could be just a random order that's been used for as long as anyone can remember.

- **Historical order structuring**—where the content is structured in the order of its development or discovery. This need not be a totally linear order because various developments and/or discoveries can build on a number of others, which they could choose to reference.
- **Order of use structuring**—in which the structure is arranged in the order in which users are expected to apply the content. Different groups of users might require different structures, involving different chunks of content, to correspond to differing orders of use.
- **Importance-based structuring**—in which the structure is arranged in the estimated order of relative importance to the user of different chunks of content. Different users might require different structures, involving different chunks of content, to correspond to differences in the importance of use.
- **Frequency of use structuring**—in which the structure is arranged in the estimated order of relative importance of different chunks of content to the user. Different users might require different structures, involving different chunks of content, to correspond to differing frequencies of use.
- **Alphabetical order structuring**—in which the content is alphabetically structured based on an index of meaningful descriptors. This structure need not be linear, because various chunks can refer the user to other descriptors, where the desired information and/or where related information can be found.
- **Logical group structuring**—where the content is structured in clusters based on some set of major logical concepts. Individual chunks of content may appear in multiple locations in such a structure.
- **Generalization granularity structuring**—where content is organized from general to specific (or from specific to general), like the structuring of classes of objects. While similar to the software engineering structuring of object classes, this form of structuring is also often used in pedagogy to assist people in developing an understanding of various types of content.

NOTE: It may be useful to allow users easy access to switching between different approaches. This often is done using a panel located at one of the sides of a Web page.

Once all the applicable approaches are identified, the content can be divided into individual "content chunks" which correspond to the individual components of the content that are required by each of the particular structuring approaches. These content chunks usually will be smaller than or equal to those previously identified. These chunks can contain:

- Detailed content
- Structuring content that provides an introduction to, a summary of, a comparison of, or that otherwise helps structure a number of other content chunks
- Both detailed content that is not located elsewhere and structuring content

A combined structure can be designed to meet the needs of differing individual approaches to structuring content. This involves determining the overlap between chunks of content identified by each of the individual structuring approaches and further dividing them into smaller chunks, where necessary.

A single content chunk that completely meets one or more of the needs of one or more groups of users to accomplish one or more tasks should be contained in its own high-level presentation segment, as illustrated in Figure 10-2. Where this chunk meets the needs of various user groups/tasks, this presentation segment can be linked into various structures for ease of access.

A content chunk that is used on its own for one presentation segment may also be presented in a different presentation segment if it is needed to be used in combination with another content chunk for some users and/or tasks, as illustrated in Figure 10-3. In this way both presentation segments are tailored to meet the specific needs of their users and/or tasks, without providing too little or too much content. While this content may be presented in a number of ways to meet differing needs, it should be stored in a single place within the application to ensure that any changes that are made to the content apply to all locations where the content is presented.

A chunk can be divided into separate content chunks if only a part of a chunk is used to completely satisfy the needs of one or more different sets of needs. A content chunk may be divided into two chunks if there are no overlapping needs for content, as illustrated in Figure 10-4, or into three if there are some overlapping needs and some nonoverlapping needs for parts of the content, as illustrated in Figure 10-5.

NOTE: It is not unusual that, during the design, further requirements will be discovered that have been missed in analysis. In the course of identifying presentation segments, requirements for content chunks (or user groups, tasks, or tools) may be identified that were overlooked in the analysis. Where new requirements are identified in high-level design, they require a proper analysis prior to developing descriptions for the related presentation segments. This should lead to a revision of the requirements analysis of users, tasks, content, and tools (as discussed in Chapter 7) and a revision of the formal analysis (as discussed in Chapter 8).

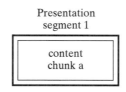

Figure 10-2 A one-to-one relationship between a content chunk and a presentation segment

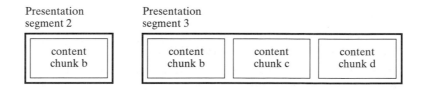

Figure 10-3 A content chunk used in two presentation segments

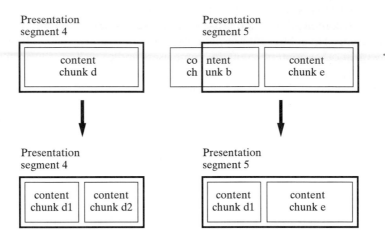

Figure 10-4   Dividing a content chunk into two non-overlapping chunks

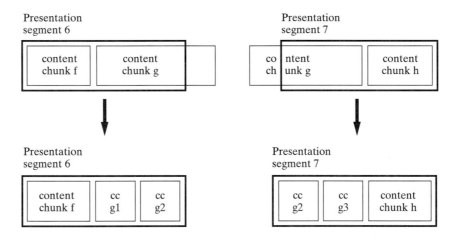

Figure 10-5   Dividing a content chunk with overlapping uses

10.3.3.2   Making the Content Accessible

The above-identified presentation segments need to be structured so that they can be used to meet various content-related needs.

The developer needs to identify links that are needed to allow access between presentation segments and that meet the needs of the different semantic structural approaches identified for the system. Because links in Web pages only go in one direction, pairs of links are often required. Each presentation segment should be considered individually to ensure that all required links originating with it are identified.

Additional content-related presentation segments should be identified that summarize or organize the detailed content already identified and that will help users to identify and use different semantic approaches. Examples of such presentation segments include tables of contents for each semantic approach and a home page or set of home pages for the Web site.

Appropriate structuring of presentation segments can provide users with the ability to use any applicable structural approach (or combination of applicable approaches) to explore the content of the multimedia application.

Users might need or wish to be able to access individual content chunks regardless of how these chunks are physically implemented and presented. Meeting these needs involves designing links that can take the user both to presentation segments (that are part of the application design) and to particular content chunks (within presentation segments) and often involves providing a search capability in addition to providing specific links.

Guidance on designing navigation structures to facilitate user access is provided in ISO 14915-2.[12]

The developer should evaluate the structure of content-based presentation segments and links to determine whether it meets all the intended needs:

- Providing content required by tasks, including:
  - Tasks identified by the information providers
  - Tasks needed by the information recipients
  - Additional system-related tasks that support exploring and navigating the content
- Providing content related to users, including:
  - Customer/vendor account information
  - Special user accessing and security information
  - Content related to individual users, such as orders, invoices, and so on.

NOTE: User-related content is included rather than user objects, since the system is only modeling the users who are their own objects.

If any required content presentation segments or links are missing, they should be added at this point.

10.3.3.3 Adding Tools to Use the Content

Up to this point the focus has been on designing content to meet various needs. e-Commerce involves more than just presenting users with content. Tools allow users to interact with content and to process business transactions. Tools are used to get the computer to implement or to assist in implementing tasks.

Some, but not all, tools may require a separate presentation segment:

- Tools that are specific to a single content chunk that occurs on a single presentation segment can be incorporated onto that presentation segment
- Tools that are used with more than one presentation segment often require their own presentation segment (regardless of whether it is implemented as a separate

screen or panel or just as a pop-up window or dialog box) that is linked to from all the presentation segments requiring the tool

Additional presentation segments may be required to provide users an index of various tools.

10.3.3.4   Limiting Access

Access limitations can be implemented to control access to portions of the Web site and/or selected content and to provide security to data that is transmitted between the user and the Web site.

It is seldom appropriate for all users to have access to all presentation segments in an e-Commerce application.

- Access to presentation segments with personal information should be limited to:
  - Those individuals or organizations whose personal information they contain
  - Those persons in the organization owning the e-Commerce system who have a legitimate need to access this information
- Access to presentation segments with accounting information should be limited to:
  - Accountants and managers in the organization owning the e-Commerce system who have a legitimate need to access this information
- Access to presentation segments with pricing and sales information should be limited to:
  - Marketing people and their managers in the organization owning the e-Commerce system who have a legitimate need to access this information
- Additional access restrictions may be identified based on organizational policies and/or to restrict access to content where it is part of a product or service of the organization

Users are typically required to identify themselves using a user name and password to gain access to restricted presentation segments.

Privacy concerns may require greater levels of security to protect data that is transferred between the user's computer and the organization's computer. This type of security is typically provided by the use of secure server technologies.

High-level design should consider the need for access restrictions on each presentation segment. Where some users may require access to only some of the content planned for a presentation segment, the developer may need to either split the presentation segment or to create alternate presentation segments in order to control and to provide access appropriately. Technologies for limiting access are discussed further in Chapter 12.

10.3.3.5   Presentation Segments as Web Objects

Once a set of presentation segments and links has been established, each of these presentation segments will need to be implemented as specific Web objects (such as pages, panels, pop-up windows, dialog boxes, and so on). While the particular design of each object involves detailed design, high-level design should determine those circumstances in which a user may wish to have simultaneous access to more than one presentation segment at a time. The recognition of such circumstances should lead to the development of a general strategy that can be applied consistently throughout the detailed design of the system. Such a strategy may involve the use of multiple panels or other general design styles.

10.3.4 Describing Presentation Segments

High-level designs can be documented as a set of presentation segment descriptions. Table 10-1 provides a format recommended for high-level descriptions of presentation segments.

The first section of this description identifies and justifies the presentation segment. Care should be taken to distinguish between multiple presentation segments that may be related to similar content. This justification can include descriptions of unique methods or circumstances of the presentation segment's intended use.

The second section of this description links the presentation segment to the requirements it is intended to serve. It links to the task analysis components of users, tasks, content, and tools. (Formal requirements are directly translated into design in the third section of the description.)

- Relationships to content are listed first, to recognize the relationship between presentation segments and content structures.
- The listing of users and tasks should include all users and tasks that might make use of this presentation segment, not just the most obvious ones.

Table 10-1 A format for high-level presentation segment descriptions

PS name	Each presentation segment (PS) should be given a unique, meaningful name that could act as a title when the segment is presented.
Justification	Provide a brief justification (1 to 3 lines) of the reason that each PS is unique from the others.
Requirements Served	
Content that the PS contains	Content chunk name, Content chunk name, ...
Users that the PS serves	User group name, User group name, ...
Tasks that the PS serves	Task name, Task name, ...
Tools that the PS replaces	Tool name, Tool name, ...
Design	
Links to tools/other PSs	Name of PS to link to, Name of PS to link to, ...
Attributes/specific content contained in the PS	Object name.attribute name, Object name.attribute name, ...
Operations performed via interactions with the PS	Object name.operation name, Object name.operation name, ...
Access restrictions	None/limited to identified users/other
Concurrency or other style requirements	None/specify any that apply
Additional Notes	

- The listing of tools focuses on those tools that are replaced (or duplicated) by the content chunk itself. It need not list those tools that are replaced (or duplicated) by other presentation segments linked to this one.

The third section of this description provides high-level design information about the presentation segment. Analysis attributes and operations are either incorporated as parts of the given presentation segment directly or as links to additional presentation segments.

- Links to other presentation segments are identified first and need not also be specified as attributes and operations.
- The attributes and operations can be named in the form of {object name.attribute name} and {object name.operation name}. This allows the developer to recognize that presentation segments may combine the attributes and/or operations of a number of objects (identified in the analysis) in a single presentation sequence.
- Access restrictions and concurrency or other style requirements can provide further information about high-level design requirements.

Further information, useful to explain the high-level design, can be added as notes to the descriptions. The types and quantity of such notes may vary considerably between designs.

While graphical representations can be used to illustrate the relationship of various presentations segments, it is best to illustrate parts of a system rather than to try to illustrate all of the presentation segments and links in a single diagram.

10.4   HIGH-LEVEL DESIGN OF BUSINESS TRANSACTIONS

Optimizing the business activities involved in a business transaction involves ensuring that the design for each activity supports moving the user toward actualization of the transaction and/or actualization of future transactions. Good design often involves combining portions of different business activities within a single presentation segment. This section considers examples of the processing of a typical business sales transaction by traditional and e-Commerce systems.

10.4.1   Computer Support of Transactions by Traditional Systems

Traditional systems (pre-e-Commerce systems as discussed in Chapter 3) tend to use computer support late within the set of business activities involved in a business transaction. This involves using computers to record the details of sales- and processing-related invoices and payments (business transaction actualization) and analyzing the results of these activities (business transaction post-actualization). Where traditional systems provide assistance in identifying products (business transaction identification) this capability is often very limited in its capabilities and only available to employees of the organization owning the system. Often computer support for each of these specific business activities is provided by a separate software system.

High-level design within traditional systems often focuses on the design of a single activity and a single user. For example, the high-level design of a sales entry system focuses on getting the user (often sales representative) to fill in a sales order. The design of traditional systems is often based on precomputing artifacts, such as precomputer sales slips. In order to simplify their design, they often require the user to follow a sequence of steps based on the format of those artifacts. While this sequence may serve the needs of accessing completed sales orders, it may not suit the needs of filling out sales orders. For example, the details of the products being purchased are generally established before considering the address where the products are to be shipped. The flexibility that a sales representative would have in filling out any portion of a written sales order first is often taken away by many traditional systems. However, as long as the system is only used within the organization, the organization's employees may be forced to put up with the limitations its design imposes upon them. The traditional sequential design of a sales order entry system is illustrated in Figure 10-6 within the context of the traditional handling of a complete business transaction.

In this example, the "Computerized Sales Entry System" could consist of a single presentation segment that would be used exclusively by sales representatives. In many instances a computerized sales entry system would be constructed separate from the accounting system, which would process invoices and payments and would require a number of additional presentation segments. The analysis of sales and processing of inventory would involve additional systems for specialized users.

Generally, an accounting system is computerized in an organization prior to the development of the sales entry system. Developing the sales entry system involves generating data that can be input by the accounting system. Where packaged software is purchased for these applications, it is advisable to purchase both packages from the same supplier to ensure that they will work properly together. However, both types of packages have been readily available for a number of years.

10.4.2   Adding e-Commerce to a Legacy System

Problems may occur when an organization tries to use a legacy system as the basis for developing an e-Commerce system. An organization wishing to interface e-Commerce with a legacy system needs to be able to ensure that the data can be transferred accurately and efficiently between the two systems and that the sequence of processing meets the needs of the users.

Interfacing with packaged accounting and other types of related legacy systems may be a significant problem. Many developers of packaged software make use of proprietary file systems that are only available to other programs produced by the same developer. Technical concerns related to interfacing with legacy systems are discussed in Chapter 12.

While data transfer needs to work with legacy systems, their user interface design may not be suitable for replicating within an e-Commerce system. This includes both the detail design of individual presentation segments and the ordering and structuring of these segments. High-level design of an e-Commerce system, regardless of whether it interfaces with a legacy system or not, should focus on the needs of the various user groups. This may even include providing multiple presentation segments to deal with the same content in different manners for one or more groups of users.

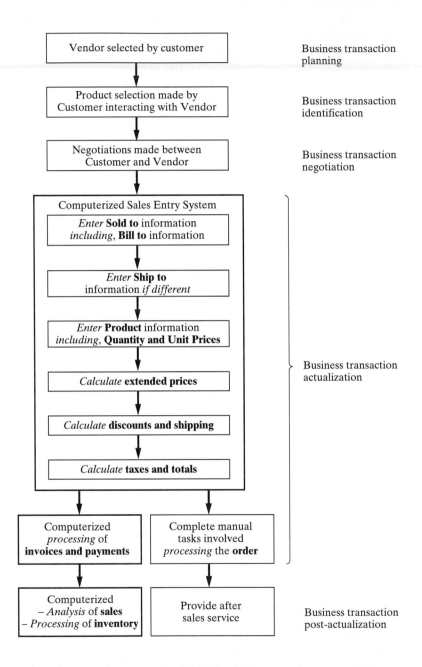

Figure 10-6 Traditional computerized and manual processing of a business transaction

For example, external users expect to be able to select the products they wish to order before having to identify themselves. Then once their decision to order products is made, they expect this information to be automatically entered into the start of a sales order. This involves providing a direct linkage between business transaction identification and business transaction actualization, and even completing part of business transaction actualization before completing the mutual identification that is traditionally part of business transaction planning. e-Commerce systems are likely to chase away many potential customers if they are designed based on traditional computer sales entry systems and require customers to identify themselves before trying to identify desired products.

10.4.3 A Typical e-Business Front-End Design

This section deals with the e-Commerce system design that can lead a customer to making a purchase. The design of the negotiation and actualization of the purchase will be considered in the following section. While discussion is based on the general characteristics of a number of successful e-Business sites, care should be taken that the design of a particular e-Commerce site meets the requirements of a thorough analysis and does not just mimic other sites. Care should especially be taken that the resulting site possesses significant competitive advantages to ensure its success.

Front-end design needs to encourage customers to visit and to buy. This often combines the three business activities of business transaction planning, business transaction identification, and business transaction post-actualization into a number of different interlinked Web pages.

Figure 10-7 illustrates how a typical e-Business might accomplish these goals. Solid boxes are used to represent one or more Web pages. Solid lines are used to represent links between Web pages. Dashed lines associate common features with the various Web pages that contain them. Heavy dashed lines are used to illustrate how as many Web pages as possible should allow and encourage customers to select products to buy with the ability to place a product in a virtual "shopping cart/basket" should be part of each of the pages where they originate.

Encouraging customers to visit a Web site involves more than just having a "home page." It involves making as many pages as possible welcoming and accessible to the user. Each page should satisfy a need and should link to other pages in the site that can satisfy other related needs. In addition to ensuring that the visual design of pages, which is discussed in Chapter 11, is inviting and helpful, each page can have a number of useful keyword descriptors attached to it to help various Web search engines find the page. In this way more search engines will lead more potential customers to a page within the site. These descriptors can be developed from the presentation segment descriptions created as part of a high-level design.

Expecting users, with or without the help of search engines, to find a Web site is not enough. Organizations need to actively promote their Web sites wherever possible. While such promotion is beyond the scope of this book, it is essential to getting users to visit a Web site.

Home pages traditionally are the pages that are easiest to find, because they are located at the simplest addresses on the Web (e.g., *www.savorthecup.com*). They vary considerably. Pages that just name the organization and make the user follow a link

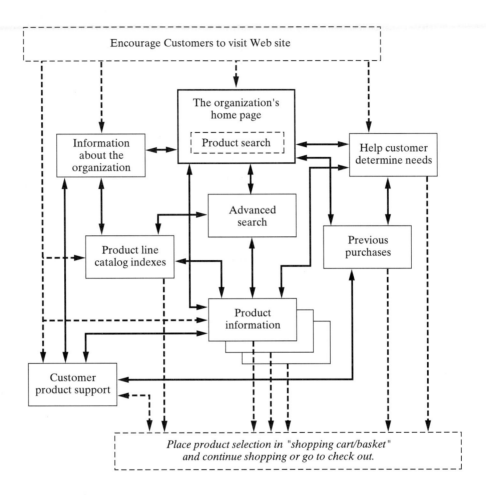

Figure 10-7 The front-end design of a typical e-Business system

to a second page before being able to do anything are a waste of the user's time. They are especially irritating to users if they waste further time with time-consuming graphics/animations before allowing the user to proceed. Home pages should welcome the user and provide easy access to the main components of the Web site. This ease of access can be improved by allowing the user to search the Web site for desired content from the home page.

Information about the organization can assist users in evaluating the organization as a provider of products and/or services. Rather than just being linked to the home page, it should lead the user to information about the product lines of the organization, which may be provided by an on-line catalog.

Information about the organization can make use of product support information, primarily intended for business transaction post-actualization, to help convince potential customers that the organization will provide them with the support they might need. Additionally, product support information can explain how to use products and can encourage the purchase of products.

While the physical structure of printed catalogs discourages the inclusion of a product in multiple locations, on-line catalogs can use a highly interlinked network structure to assist the user in finding a desired product. The structure of an on-line catalog can be developed by combining the different ways users might be expected to look for products. Once the structure has been designed, a database of information can be used to automatically create and update the structure available to its users.

A basic search capability on the home page may help users find products and/or other information they want. However, it is useful to have an advanced product search capability where users can easily use a combination of criteria to find specific products that best meet their needs. The complexities of such a search are best handled on a Web page of their own. Users should be allowed to move easily between searching and using the product line catalog.

Product information may be provided at various levels of technical detail, as indicated in Figure 10-7 by the multiple overlapping boxes. When first accessing product information from some location within the Web site, users typically should be taken to a page that presents the information about the product that is most commonly needed. They should be able to go from there to other pages, where necessary, to find more detailed product information. All pages containing product information should encourage and allow the user to immediately select to purchase the product. It may be useful to allow customers to access their previous purchases to identify items they may wish to reorder. Users should be able to easily select to reorder one, multiple, or all items from a previous order.

Most front-end pages primarily serve business transaction identification. Some e-Commerce systems may choose to provide users with assistance in business transaction planning by helping them to determine their needs. Where such a service is provided, the determination of needs should be performed in a manner that supports purchase of products from the organization and that does not assist customers in selecting products from the competition. (Tools that assist users in evaluating between competitive products could be provided as a product of their own for sale to potential customers.)

10.4.4 A Typical e-Business Back-End Design

Back-end design handles the processing of a decision to buy. This generally combines the business activities of business transaction negotiation and business transaction actualization into a number of different interlinked Web pages. Much of the processing involved in this back-end design is similar to that involved in the sales entry processing of traditional systems. It should be noted that neither traditional nor most e-Business systems involves a very developed amount of business transaction negotiation.

Figure 10-8 illustrates how a typical e-Business might accomplish these goals. Solid boxes are used to represent one or more Web pages. Dashed boxes represent specific activities within a Web page. Solid lines are used to represent links between Web pages or between parts of Web pages. The shaded box contains Web pages that should be processed in a secure server mode to provide privacy for customer information involved in the transaction.

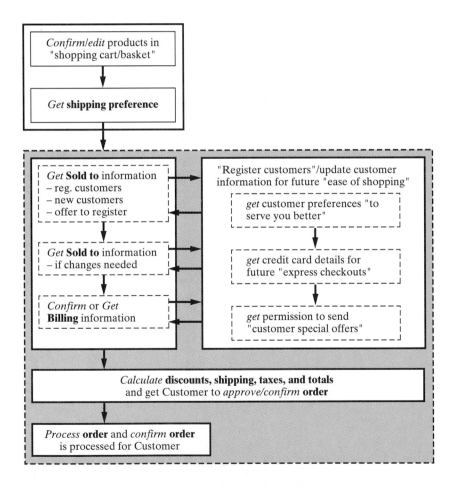

Figure 10-8 The back-end design of a typical e-Business system

The starting point for back-end processing involves confirming the customer's selections, which usually have been stored in a "shopping cart/basket" and establishing the customer's shipping preference. Confirmation can include giving the customer the opportunity to go back to the front-end and make additional selections. At this point the customer is often still anonymous to the system. Because of this anonymity, it is inadvisable to conduct any real negotiations within this page. Publicly offered discounts and promotions can be offered and a number of possible prices can be quoted to the user based on eligibility for different discounts or promotions. However, it is advisable to handle the determination of eligibility within the processing of customer information.

Going beyond this first page involves sensitive information that is best processed by a secure server. Secure processing involves three stages comparable to parts of traditional sales entry, which often have their own Web pages, and an additional (optional to the customer) stage, which should always have its own Web page.

The first stage involves getting customer-related information. It is important to distinguish between information that is essential to processing the transaction and information that the organization might like to collect about the customer. Demanding unnecessary information from a customer may result in the loss of actualizing the transaction. It is appropriate and is increasingly becoming expected for pages requesting any customer information to provide a link to a page outlining the organization's privacy policy. Existing "registered" customers should be able to use their customer account code and a password to load all of their standard information from the organization's database. They should then be allowed to make changes to this information in their permanent customer record or for this transaction only. New customers should be encouraged but not forced to become "registered" customers while completing their information for this transaction.

While organizations need to adhere to any privacy policies they publish as well as to applicable privacy legislation (as discussed in Chapter 9), it is often advantageous for an organization to get additional information about their customers. The acquisition of additional information should be handled by a separate Web page. Customers can be encouraged to provide this information by various incentives including using the information as a basis for receiving discounts or special offers during the current transaction or in future transactions and using the information to provide express check out services in the future. Because of the value of this information the rest of the Web site, and particularly the page getting customer information for the current transaction, should have convenient links to encourage customers to register with the organization. Pages used to register customers should include a link to a page outlining the organization's privacy policy.

Once all the customer and other transaction information is entered, the system can calculate discounts, shipping charges, taxes and totals and produce a completed sales order for the customer's final approval. In addition to approving this order, the customer should be encouraged not to cancel the transaction at this stage by having the alternative of going back to previous steps and make any desired changes.

Once the customer approves the order, it becomes a binding contract. The site should confirm that the order has been accepted by the organization and is being processed for the user. An additional confirmation may be e-mailed or otherwise transmitted to the customer as added confirmation. The customer should be given an opportunity to make a copy (printed or saved to a file) of the completed order. The customer should then be provided a link back to the organization's home page with an invitation to find further information of interest and/or to create further orders. When the customer leaves this page, the system should automatically exit from secure server mode.

 Find further discussions and examples of the high-level design of transactions in the Chapter 10 Cyber Supplement.

10.5 APPLYING HIGH-LEVEL DESIGN

10.5.1 Applying High-Level Design in Organizations

10.5.1.1 Keeping Boundaries Realistic

A successful analysis will have produced a very large wants list (which is good). Based on the typically slow speed of getting changes made to traditional information systems, organizational professionals may try to get all these needs met in the first release of an e-Commerce system. However, this is an inappropriate strategy to take for a number of reasons, including:

- Trying to do too much at once may take too long and the competition may beat you. Remember: there is little or no need for a second e-Commerce site doing the same thing on the Web.
- Trying to do too much may make the development too complicated to readily manage, leading to further delays and cost increases.
- There can't be the long delays that sometimes have accompanied changes to traditional information systems. An e-Commerce site should be constantly evolving. If it doesn't keep evolving it will soon be surpassed by its competition.
- It's good to have somewhere to evolve to, and so it's good to have recognized some good requirements that can be met by the next version of the system.

10.5.1.2 Spending Time on High-Level Design

Once a set of requirements has been identified, there will be considerable pressure to meet those requirements as soon as possible. This pressure can include focusing on detailed designs that can meet individual requirements without spending sufficient time on how these detailed designs will be put together and without sufficient time on how to design an efficient system. While simple systems require little high-level design, e-Commerce systems require careful high-level design before proceeding to detailed design.

10.5.1.3 Designing Consistent Styles

Detailed design of large e-Commerce systems is often conducted by a number of different developers. Future evolutions of the system may involve many others. An e-Commerce system should have a consistent "look and feel" and should convey the appropriate corporate image. Systems without a consistent style present the attitude that their sponsoring organization does not really care about them and create distrust in the minds of their users.

It is not sufficient to expect that a suitable look and feel will evolve. Considerable planning and design is needed before detailed design commences. Designing consistent styles (to be applied in detailed design of each of the individual screens) involves:

- Identifying/designing styles of presentation design (such as color, type face, general screen layout, and so on)
- Identifying/designing consistent methods of interaction (ways of interacting with the application such as menus and direct manipulations) and associated controls (such as common command buttons, e.g., "back" or "print")
- Identifying appropriate standards and guidelines to apply in design (such as those of ISO, the World Wide Web Consortium, and other applicable agencies)

While many of these issues will be dealt with in this book in Chapter 11, Detailed Design, it is important for organizations to include the designing of consistent styles as part of high-level design before proceeding to detailed design.

10.5.2   Student Assignment—Applying High-Level Design

1. Identifying presentation segments
(You do not have to refine your system boundaries for this assignment.) Use the set of objects identified in the Student Assignment of Chapter 8 and design a high-level set of presentation segments to serve these objects. Explain your reasons for each of the presentation segments in your design.
2. Describing presentation segments
Develop descriptions for each of (at least) the ten most important presentation segments.

10.6   AN EXAMPLE OF APPLYING HIGH-LEVEL DESIGN

10.6.1   Identifying Presentation Segments

Table 10-2 summarizes the main object classes identified in the formal analysis of *Savor the Cup.*

A brief reevaluation of system boundaries confirmed that these are the major classes that should be served in the system being designed.

The identification of suitable presentation segments should start by considering the content classes. However, in this case, the content classes were analyzed very generally and were strongly tied to the user classes.

Due to space limitations, the example in Chapter 8, Formalizing Analysis, did not deal with content in the same level of detail as was identified in Chapter 7, e-Commerce Requirements Analysis. The following general design of presentation segments (which are identified by bold italic type) is based on the completed formal analysis, which needed to be conducted prior to high-level design.

Public information (on products and services) needs to be available at a variety of levels, each served by their own presentation segments. Examining the current public information that is provided by *Savor the Cup* can identify different types of public

Table 10-2 The major classes of objects identified for *Savor the Cup*

User-Based Classes	Content-Based Classes	Tool-Based Classes
Customers	Public information (on products and services)	Tools for general information
Suppliers		
Sales	Sales orders	• Creating public information
	Bid (supplier)	• Exploring public information
• Sales reps	Internal information	• Searching for public information
• Consultants		
• Marketers		Tools for specific information
		• Face-to-face meetings
Purchasing		• Telephone calls
Logistics		• Mail
Accounting		
		Order forms
		Bid forms
		Tools for creating, obtaining, and processing internal information

information. Some of the different presentation segments that need to be designed include:

- *General information* about *Savor the Cup*
- A general *overview of the range of products and services* provided by *Savor the Cup*
- *A product listing*
- A catalog of particular products and services that includes:
  - *A table of contents*
  - *General information on individual types of products and/or services*
  - *Specific information on particular products and/or services*
  - *Support information for users of particular products and/or services*
- *General industry-related information*
- *Information on special offers from Savor the Cup*
- *Information on products being sought* by *Savor the Cup's* purchasing department
- *Information to assist in contacting Savor the Cup*

Access to some of this "public information" may be limited to Gold Cup customers and employees of Savor the Cup and will require a *tool for users to identify themselves.*

Only one type of *sales order* presentation segment is needed, however, a variety of different types of access and processing need to be considered.

- Blank sales orders should be available to everybody
- Once sales orders are filled in, they should only be available to the customer and employees of *Savor the Cup*
- Filling in sales orders will involve customer information that should be kept in a separate *customer record* presentation segment that was not identified previously as a content object

- Calculating prices may depend on the type of customer (based on information from a customer record) as well as on other factors

Only one type of *supplier bid* presentation segment is needed. The different types of access and processing are similar to those for sales orders.

There are many types of internal information, each of which require their own presentation segments. Some of the different presentation segments that need to be designed include:

- Internal information on products
  - *Internal product/service specifications*
  - *Internal product/service availability*
  - *Internal product/service pricing information*
  - *Internal product/service sales techniques*
  - *Internal product/service consulting techniques*
- Internal information on customers
  - *Basic customer information*
  - *Customer profiles*
  - *Customer account information*
- Internal information on suppliers
  - *Basic supplier information*
  - *Supplier profiles*
  - *Purchase orders*
- Internal logistics information
  - *Outstanding order status*
  - *Manufacturing schedules*
  - *Schedule of required shipping dates*
- Financial-related information
  - *Sales orders*
  - *Basic customer information*
  - *Customer account balances*
  - *Purchase orders*
  - *Basic supplier information*
- Performance-related information
  - *Information on accessing individual Web pages*
  - *Information on requests processed by the system*
  - *Audit trails of transactions processed by the system*

The identification of presentation segments could continue with a consideration of the user classes. However, in this example, the needs of user classes were considered at the same time as the needs of content. Further consideration failed to identify additional needs for different presentation segments.

Consideration of the tool classes found that the presentation segments, identified above, all tend to focus on exploring information and interacting with it. A number of other tools need to be included on their own presentation segments. These include:

- General use tools
  - *A tool for users to identify themselves*

- *A tool for searching the site for specific information*
- *Tools for communicating directly between individuals/organizations,* which facilitate
    - Meetings
    - Individual conversations
    - Mail
- Tools to assist customers
    - *A tool to help customers identify and evaluate their own needs*
    - *A tool to assist customers in comparing products and services*
    - *A tool to assist customers in developing custom blends*
- Tools to assist sales
    - *A tool for creating and/or modifying product and/or service information*
    - *A tool for sales tracking*
    - *A tool for scheduling future contacts with customers*
    - *A tool for sales analysis*

The various presentation segments, identified above, can be grouped in a variety of semantic manners. One example of a logical grouping is based on:

- Products/services, which are the main focus of the system, given their own logical category
- Other presentation segments grouped into categories based on who can access the content of these segments

General presentation segments available to everybody

- *General information* about *Savor the Cup*
- *General industry-related information*
- *A tool for searching the site for specific information*
- *A tool for users to identify themselves*
- *Tools for communicating directly between individuals/organizations,* including *information to assist in contacting* Savor the Cup

System-related presentation segments only available within *Savor the Cup*

- *Information on accessing of individual Web pages*
- *Information on requests processed by the system*
- *Audit trails of transactions processed by the system*

Product and/or service-related presentation segments

- A general *overview of the range of products and services* provided by *Savor the Cup*
- *A product listing*
- A catalog of particular products and services that includes:
    - *A table of contents*
    - *General information on individual types of products and/or services*
    - *Specific information on particular products and/or services*
    - *Support information for users of particular products and/or services*
- *Information on special offers* from *Savor the Cup*
- *Information on products being sought* by *Savor the Cup's* purchasing department
- *Internal product and/or service information*

- *Tools for creating/modifying product and/or service information*
  - *Specifications*
  - *Availability*
  - *Pricing information*
  - *Sales techniques*
  - *Consulting techniques*

Customer-related presentation segments

- All product and/or service presentation segments that are publicly available
- *Sales orders*
- *Basic customer information*
- *Customer account information*
- *A tool to help customers identify and evaluate their own needs*
- *A tool to assist customers in comparing products and services*
- *A tool to assist customers in developing custom blends*

Supplier-related presentation segments

- All product and/or service presentation segments that are publicly available
- *Supplier bids*
- *Basic supplier information*
- *Purchase orders*

Sales-related presentation segments

- All product and/or service presentation segments
- All customer-related presentation segments
- *Customer profiles—not available to customers*
- *A tool for sales tracking*
- *A tool for scheduling future contacts with customers*
- *A tool for sales analysis*

Purchasing-related presentation segments

- All product and/or service presentation segments
- All supplier-related presentation segments
- *Supplier profiles—not available to suppliers*

Logistics-related presentation segments

- *Internal product/service availability*
- *Sales orders*
- *Purchase orders*
- *Outstanding order status*
- *Manufacturing schedules*
- *Schedule of required shipping dates*

Accounting-related presentation segments

- Financial-related information
  - *Sales orders*
  - *Basic customer information*
  - *Customer account balances*

> - *Purchase orders*
> - *Basic supplier information*
> - Performance-related information
>   - *Information on accessing individual Web pages*
>   - *Information on requests processed by the system*
>   - *Audit trails of transactions processed by the system*
>
> A variety of other semantic structures may be more appropriate. However, this structure provides a starting point for developing descriptions of individual presentation segments. Once these descriptions have been developed, further semantic approaches can be considered and links to facilitate them can be added.
>
> ### 10.6.2   Describing Presentation Segments
>
> For this example (Table 10-3), it was decided to describe some of the presentation segments that are closely related to customers selecting and ordering products and services, starting with sales orders.

Table 10-3   A presentation segment description for sales orders

PS Name	*Sales order*
Justification	Sales orders are central to most forms of e-Commerce. They bring together buyers, sellers, and products and/or services in a contractual format

Requirements served

Content that the PS contains	Customer information
	Product/service information
	Sales information
	Accounting information
Users that the PS serves	Customers
	Sales
	Accounting
	Logistics
Tasks that the PS serves	Placing an order (customers/sales)
	Modifying an order (customers/sales)
	Accounting for an order (accounting)
	Manufacturing/shipping an order (logistics)
	Sales tracking (sales, accounting, logistics)
	Sales analysis (sales, accounting)
Tools that the PS replaces	Paper form of sales order

Design

Links to tools/other PSs	Basic customer information
	Tool for users to identify themselves
	Other sales orders of that customer
	Tool for searching the site for specific information

	A table of contents
	Specific information on particular products/services
	Tool to help customers identify/evaluate their own needs
	Tool to assist customers in comparing products/services
	Tool to assist customers in developing custom blends
Attributes/specific content contained in the PS	Sales order. number
	Sales order. date
	Sales order. customer (which is composed of)

- Customer. number
- Customer. name
- Customer. billing address
- Customer. contact person

Sales order. ship to

- Customer. ship address

Sales order. payment

- Customer. credit information
- Sales order. customer purchase order reference

Sales order. item ordered (which is composed of)

- Product. number
- Product. name
- Product. unit price
- Sales order. item ordered. quantity

Sales order. discount

- Customer. discount

Sales order. shipping charges

Sales order. taxes

Sales order. status

Operations performed via interactions with the PS	Sales order. create
	Sales order. find
	Sales order. modify
	Sales order.copy
Access restrictions	Limited to the order's customer and *Savor the Cup* employees
Concurrency or other style requirements	none

Additional Notes

This design allows users to create new sales orders with a minimum amount of work. Wherever possible, users may be given the option either to use existing information or to enter the information directly.

- Sales orders make use of data (attributes) from other objects including customers and products.
- Repeat customers may wish to copy and modify a previous sales order rather than creating a new one from the start.

Sales orders need to identify the customer. Often customer identification is the first section of a sales order; however, there is no need to force users to do this first (Table 10-4).

A tool for users to identify themselves needs to be used by existing customers to verify who they are and to automatically load basic customer information (Table 10-5). Because of its simplicity and because it is only used with other presentation segments, this tool may be implemented by a pop-up window or similar mechanism. However, that determination will be left to the detailed design. Selecting the products may be done by customers who know what they want or as customers decide.

- If customers know what they want they can type their wants directly into the sales order.
- Sales orders could be started for users who find items they would like to order while browsing through other parts of the e-Commerce site.

Customers often refer to specific information on particular products and/or services in order to make their purchasing decisions (Table 10-6).

Table 10-4   A presentation segment description for basic customer information

PS Name	***Basic customer information***
Justification	Basic customer information is used to identify customers on e-Commerce sales orders for billing and shipping purposes.
	NOTE: A ***privacy policy*** should be provided by the system to explain the need for and the uses of this information to customers. This is a new requirement for an additional presentation segment that was overlooked in the previous analysis and design.
	Where customers do not have existing accounts, they need to enter the relevant customer information and choose between setting up an account or using a credit card as a one-time customer.

Requirements served

Content that the PS contains	Customer information
Users that the PS serves	Customers
	Sales
	Accounting
	Logistics
Tasks that the PS serves	Placing an order (customers/sales)
	Modifying an order (customers/sales)
	Accounting for an order (accounting)
	Shipping an order (logistics)
	Scheduling future contacts with customers (sales)
	Sales tracking (sales, accounting, logistics)
	Sales analysis (sales, accounting)
Tools that the PS replaces	Various customer records kept by different employees of *Savor the Cup*

Design

Links to tools/other PSs	Tool for users to identify themselves, other sales orders of that customer
Attributes/specific content contained in the PS	Customer. number
	Customer. name
	Customer. billing address
	Customer. ship address
	Customer. contact person
	Customer. phone
	Customer. fax
	Customer. e-mail
	Customer. credit information
	Customer. discount
Operations performed via interactions with the PS	Customer. create
	Customer. find
	Customer. modify
Access restrictions	Limited to the customer and *Savor the Cup* employees
Concurrency or other style requirements	None

Additional Notes

While basic information will lead to customer accounts for most customers, some customers, using a general purpose credit card, may not wish to establish regular "accounts." Customers should be allowed the choice of establishing accounts as regular customers or identifying themselves for purposes of this sales order. Customers not wishing accounts need not enter as much information.

Customers may find what they are looking for via a number of ways, including:

- A tool for searching the site for specific information (Table 10-7)
- A table of contents (Table 10-8)

Grouping these two into a single presentation segment was considered but rejected because:

- They are conceptually very different actions to a user
- Combining them would present unwanted and unneeded content each time the combined presentation segment was accessed
- Users generally know which of these two actions they want
- Both presentation segments can have links to the other to assist users in changing their minds

Customers may wish to compare alternatives before making a purchasing choice. They can use a tool to assist customers in comparing products and services (Table 10-9).

Table 10-5   A presentation segment description for customer identification

PS Name	*User identification*
Justification	This PS is needed to allow certain users to access other PSs that are restricted, and/or to access information on certain PS that is restricted.
	It is handled via a single PS that other PSs link to rather than being handled in multiple different locations.

Requirements served

Content that the PS contains	User identification
Users that the PS serves	All user groups
Tasks that the PS serves	User authorization
Tools that the PS replaces	Typically performed personally by sales representatives

Design

Links to tools/other PSs	None, when finished, it automatically returns to PS that accessed it
Attributes/specific content contained in the PS	User. name
	User. password (not displayed)
	User. authorization levels (not displayed for most users)
Operations performed via interactions with the PS	User. enter name
	User. enter password
	User. change password
	User. allow or disallow access
	User. change authorization levels
Access restrictions	Only accessed by other PSs, when needed
Concurrency or other style requirements	None

Additional Notes

This user identification can authorize the use of various other parts of the system by a variety of different users. It does not just serve to authorize access to customer information or sales orders.

Customer will be sent to this presentation segment to create a personal password, during user identification of new customers, in order to provide and protect access to their sales orders, whether or not these customers wish to establish permanent customer accounts.

Only the system administrator is allowed to use this presentation segment to allow different levels of access to different users.

Table 10-6 A presentation segment description for specifications of particular products/services

PS Name	***Specifications of particular products/services***
Justification	While a **product listing** can contain product names, numbers and prices of a number of products, it is only useful if customers (or other users) know exactly what they want. Often they require further information before making the decision to purchase a product or service.

Requirements served

Content that the PS contains	Detailed description of a product and/or service
Users that the PS serves	Customers, sales, purchasing, logistics
Tasks that the PS serves	Determine characteristics of product and/or service
	Select appropriate product and/or service
Tools that the PS replaces	Product listing in a catalog

Design

Links to tools/other PSs	Support information for particular products/services
	Specifications for similar products/services
	Overview of the range of products and services
	Product listing
	A table of contents
	General information on types of products/services
	Information on special offers from *Savor the Cup*
	Tool to assist customers in comparing products/services
Attributes/specific content contained in the PS	Product. number
	Product. name
	Product. description
	Product. illustration
	Product. uses
	Product. quantities
	Product. prices
	Product. availability
Operations performed via interactions with the PS	Product. find
	Product. order
Access restrictions	None for reading
	Can only be created/updated by ***tools for creating/modifying product/service information***
Concurrency or other style requirements	May be used concurrently with specifications of other products/services

Additional Notes

Customers may wish to compare specifications from multiple products at one time. This can be facilitated by either viewing multiple specifications concurrently or by using the tool to assist customers in comparing products and/or services.

Table 10-7 A presentation segment description for a search tool

PS Name	***A search tool***
Justification	Allows users to search public information based on key words and link to all pages containing the key words. This allows users to quickly access the information they want. Without this tool, users would have to search through the entire system on their own.

Requirements served

Content that the PS contains	Key words
	Descriptions with links to pages that meet the key word criteria
Users that the PS serves	All users
Tasks that the PS serves	Finding information about the company
	Finding information about the industry
	Finding information about products and/or services
Tools that the PS replaces	Without this tool, users would have to search through the entire system on their own.

Design

Links to tools/other PSs	This page would include fixed links to the main pages for
	• General information about *Savor the Cup*
	• General industry-related information
	• The list of products/services
	• The table of contents of products/services
	The page would create additional temporary links to access the pages containing results of the search.
Attributes/specific content contained in the PS	Search. keywords
	Search. results
Operations performed via interactions with the PS	Search. find
Access restrictions	None
Concurrency or other style requirements	The search results should remain available while the user still needs to link to pages found in the search.

Additional Notes

The results of a search are only available temporarily, as long as the user can return to them via regular Web browser tools (such as: forward/back or go). They can only be used during the user's current session until the user performs another search.

Table 10-8 A presentation segment description for a table of contents of products and/or services

PS Name	*A **table of contents of products/services***
Justification	This table of contents provides a structured summary of the different products and services available from *Savor the Cup*.
	This structuring helps users to recognize the variety of different products and/or services provided by *Savor the Cup*.
	It provides links to a variety of different levels of information about *Savor the Cup*'s products and/or services.

Requirements served

Content that the PS contains	Information about other presentation segments
Users that the PS serves	All users
Tasks that the PS serves	Finding information about products and/or services
Tools that the PS replaces	Without this tool or the search tool, users would have to search through the entire system on their own.

Design

Links to tools/other PSs	There are two main types of links to information:

- General information on types of products and/or services
- Specifications of particular products and/or services

There are a number of additional links that should be available at all times, when users scroll through the main types of information:

- Product listing
- Tool to help customers identify/evaluate their needs
- Tool to assist customers in comparing products and/or services
- Tool to assist customers in developing custom blends
- Search tool

Attributes/specific content contained in the PS	This presentation segment primarily contains links to other presentation segments.
Operations performed via interactions with the PS	Users primarily follow links
Access restrictions	None
Concurrency or other style requirements	None

Additional Notes

This is a relatively simple presentation segment with very minimal interaction.

Table 10-9 A presentation segment description for a product/service comparison tool

PS Name	***A product and/or service comparison tool***
Justification	This tool is designed to assist in the comparison of similar *Savor the Cup* products and/or services.
	• It is not currently planned to assist in comparisons with other brands of products and/or services.
	• It does not suggest which product or service the user should choose, since that would require considerable understanding of the user's needs, which is dealt with by a different tool that helps customers identify and evaluate their own needs. The two tools may be integrated in some future version.
	It works by:
	• Allowing users to display the specifications of two or three similar products and/or services side by side.
	• Allowing users to highlight those parts of each specification that they choose to highlight.
	• Allowing users to print the set of specifications with their highlighting.

Requirements served

Content that the PS contains	Specifications of particular products/services
Users that the PS serves	Customers
	Sales
Tasks that the PS serves	Comparing alternatives
Tools that the PS replaces	Without this tool or the search tool, users would have to perform these comparisons on their own.

Design

Links to tools/other PSs	Specifications of particular products and/or services
	Sales orders
	Search tool
	A table of contents of products and/or services
	Tool to help customers identify/evaluate their needs
Attributes/specific content contained in the PS	Compare. number of products/services
	Compare. product/service specifications
	Compare. similar products/services
Operations performed via interactions with the PS	Compare. select product/service to display
	Compare. suggest similar products/services
	Compare. highlight/remove highlight
	Compare. order product/service
Access restrictions	None
Concurrency or other style requirements	Concurrency handled internally

Additional Notes

This design involves a relatively simple implementation intended to act as a competitive advantage. It has potential to be improved upon in future designs.

10.7   CHALLENGES AND OPPORTUNITIES IN APPLYING HIGH-LEVEL DESIGN

The following are the most frequent problems encountered with high-level design:

Challenges with Revising Boundaries

- Some developers base their designs on all the classes, attributes, and operations that were identified in the analysis, without considering those that are most important to implement first. This results in complicated initial designs with little direction for future enhancements.
- Some developers only consider the requirements of customers, without considering the needs of employees who are responsible for revising and/or processing the content of an e-Commerce system.

Challenges with Segmentation

- Some developers use a one-to-one correspondence between analysis objects and high-level design objects, without examining:
  - Where objects need to be used together (multiple objects in a single presentation segment)
  - Where an object needs to be used in multiple different presentation segments
- Some developers focus on a single type of object (e.g., only on user objects) rather than identifying a complete (but limited) set of presentation segments that could provide the basis of a reasonable design.
- Some presentation segments are too complex and should be separated into linked sets of simpler presentation segments.
- Some presentation segments serve the logical needs of the computer more than the real needs of the users. Users should be able to recognize the purpose of each presentation segment that they will use and to recognize when to use it.

Challenges with Justifications

- Justifications may only redescribe an object (or a refined object) and fail to explain why the presentation segment is unique within an application.

Challenges with Additions

- Presentation segments, attributes, and operations may be introduced in the development of descriptions that were not previously identified. While this is good, the analysis needs to be revised to properly identify the full range of requirements for these new additions.

10.8   CYBER SUPPLEMENTS FOR CHAPTER 10

Look at the Chapter 10 Cyber Supplements on the Web to find:

- A discussion of the use of prototyping in high-level design

- A discussion of and links to further information about development methodologies

- A discussion of and links to further information about user-centered design

- A discussion of and links to further information about how various types of professionals can aid in design

- Further discussions and examples of the high-level design of transactions

- Practice activities dealing with the high-level design of e-Commerce systems

REFERENCES

[1] "International Organization for Standardization," ISO Draft International Standard 14915-1, Software Ergonomics for Multimedia User Interfaces: Design Principles and Framework, 2000.

[2] R. J. Norman, *Object-Oriented Systems Analysis and Design* (Upper Saddle River, NJ, Prentice-Hall, 1996).

[3] G. Booch, J. Rumbaugh, I. Jacobson, *The Unified Modeling Language User Guide:* (Reading MA, Addison-Wesley, 1999).

[4] M. B. Rosson, S. Maas, and W. A. Kellogg, "The Designer as User: Building Requirements for the Design Tools from Design Practice," *Communications of the ACM,* (31:11, Nov. 1988): 1288–1298.

[5] "International Organization for Standardization," ISO International Standard 13407, Human Centered Design Processes for Interactive Systems, 1997.

[6] "International Organization for Standardization," ISO Committee Draft 16982, Usability Methods Supporting Human Centered Design, 2000.

[7] J. Rumbaugh, M. Blaha, W. Premerlani, F. Eddy, W. Lorensen, *Object-Oriented Modeling and Design* (Englewood Cliffs, NJ, Prentice-Hall, 1991).

[8] I. Jacobson, M. Christerson, P. Jonsson, G. Overgaard, *Object-Oriented Software Engineering* (Wokinghan, England, Addison-Wesley, 1992).

[9] R. J. Norman, *Object-Oriented Systems Analysis and Design* (Upper Saddle River, NJ, Prentice-Hall, 1996).

[10] "International Organization for Standardization," ISO Committee Draft 14915-2, Software Ergonomics for Multimedia User Interfaces: Multimedia Control and Navigation, 2000.

[11] Ibid.

[12] Ibid.

Detailed Design

11.1 INTRODUCTION TO DETAILED DESIGN

A **detailed design** identifies how to present content and to accomplish tasks for the users of individual presentation segments. It involves identifying media for presenting specific pieces of content and identifying interactions that lead to the accomplishments of tasks.

Each of these presentation segments will be a tool for one or more groups of users to use in accomplishing one or more tasks. Like all tools they should integrate with other tools, both computerized and noncomputerized, which are or will be used by these same users. They should also meet identified usability requirements and standards.

An overall concern in detailed design is to ensure that the resulting structure of design elements will meet the expectations and capabilities of the user. This involves designing the user's experience with the presentation segments as well as the presentation segments themselves.

This chapter will consider detailed design in terms of:

- General design guidelines
- Presentation design, which involves:
  - Designing the physical implementation of presentation segments as an interacting set of media objects that implement attributes, links, and controls
  - Arranging the various media objects at appropriate locations within the presentation segment (in terms of space and time)
- Interaction design, which involves:
  - Considering that the operations of objects are composed of a series of basic operations
  - Developing scenarios for each object level operation
- Prototype design, which involves:
  - Identifying series of screens and links that can be used to prototype the interactions of users with a screen and interaction design

While each of these design activities are discussed separately, they are multiple aspects of detailed design that are often performed simultaneously (and could be performed in any convenient order). It is useful to iterate through a design, since decisions affecting one aspect of design may also influence other aspects of design.

Technical design, to be discussed in Chapter 12, involves:

- Designing processing
- Designing databases
- Designing networking

11.2 GENERAL DESIGN PRINCIPLES

Ensuring that all of the analysis requirements are met by a detailed design may result in a correct and complete system within the bounds of the application. However, it will not guarantee that the design is usable or that the intended users will want to use it. Developers require additional guidance to help them design usable systems.

There are many sources of very detailed guidance about user interface design. However, some of these sources of guidance are so detailed as to create considerable problems in their own use.[1] This section will present some general guidelines that can be readily understood by most people and that apply to most e-Commerce systems. The following guidelines are based on the "Dialogue Principles" of ISO 9241-10:[2]

- The design should be **suitable for the tasks** being performed.
  - It should contain only those elements related to performing the user's tasks.
  - Where a request is not available, such as due to requiring another request to precede it, then it should either be removed from the screen or presented on the screen in a distinctly lighter manner (e.g., gray instead of black).
- The design should be **self-descriptive.**
  - The user should not need to refer to any external documentation in order to use the system.
  - Feedback should be provided to acknowledge user requests. This can be accomplished either by:
    - Making requested changes in data that is displayed.
    - Where displayed data is not involved, specifically acknowledging that the request has been successfully completed.
  - Feedback should also be provided to explain the occurrence of errors and to suggest possible actions to avoid the errors.
- The design should **allow the user to control** the processing.
  - The user should be able to select the request needed to perform the currently desired task.
  - The user should be able to interrupt the dialog at any time and to return to the start of the dialog.
  - The user should be able to end using the system at any time.
  - The system should not unnecessarily limit the amount of time a user has to take actions.
- The design should **conform to the user's expectations.**
  - The type of input and output involved should be clear to the user (this can be accomplished with appropriate units or other descriptors if necessary).
  - The actions of requests should be clear to the user (this can be accomplished by providing instructions or other descriptions where necessary).
  - The system should use the user's vocabulary and avoid confusing terms.
  - Dialogs should be consistent across similar tasks.
- The design should be **error tolerant.**
  - Designs should avoid as many occasions for errors as possible.
  - Where feasible, the user should be able to undo the effects of a previous set of processing actions (both requests and data inputs).
  - In critical situations where undoing is not possible, the user should be asked to confirm potentially destructive requests before they are performed.
  - The user should be able to correct information before processing it (this means that data input should generally be separated from requests for processing).

- The design should be **suitable for individualization.**
  - Users should be able to use those parts of a system that they need without having to use parts they do not need.
  - The design should be able to present content in different manners to meet the needs of different users.
  - The user should be allowed to use alternate methods of interaction to increase accessibility.
- The design should be **suitable for learning.**
  - The design should reduce complexity and maintain consistency.
  - Users with varying levels of understanding should be able to use the system.
  - The user's memory load involved in using the system should be kept to a minimum.
  - The user should be kept informed about the current location within the system and the current status of any interactions.
  - Increased usage of the system should lead to increased learning about the range of possibilities of the system.

The following guidelines are based on the design principles for multimedia user interfaces of ISO 14915-1:[3]

- The design should be **suitable for its communication goals.**
  - It should meet the needs of both information providers and information recipients.
  - It should facilitate communication between:
    - The e-Commerce system and users.
    - Users and the e-Commerce system.
- The design should be **suitable for perception and understanding.** This principle refers to the "attributes of presented information" that ISO 9241-12[4] identified that should be considered in designing screens of information. These attributes can be reworded to apply to all kinds of information presentation (including audio as well as visual and even other potential modalities):
  - Clarity—the content is conveyed quickly and accurately.
  - Discriminability—the different chunks of content presented can be distinguished accurately.
  - Conciseness—users are not overloaded with extraneous content.
  - Consistency—combines unique design with conformity to users expectations.
  - Detectability—the users can find and/or identify the required content.
  - Legibility—information is easy to read or to hear.
  - Comprehensibility—the meaning is clear, understandable, unambiguous, interpretable, and recognizable.
- The design should be **suitable for exploration.** Exploration makes use of various navigation paths between individual presentations.
  - The complexity of most e-Commerce systems makes it impossible to explicitly plan all the possible ways that users may use to explore them.
  - The design of e-Commerce systems should support, rather than inhibit, different methods of exploration.
  - Exploration may involve:
    - Following individual links.

- Following paths provided by sets of links.
- Jumping to new topics identified by searches.
- Returning to locations previously visited.
- Saving a location for future revisiting.
- The design should provide **suitable engagement.**
  - Engagement involves:
    - Attracting the user's interest.
    - Keeping the user's interest.
    - Developing user loyalty.
    - Encouraging the user's future return.
  - Engagement can be increased by:
    - Building mutual commitments/co-dependencies.
    - Encouraging user interaction.
    - Maintaining a high degree or realism.
    - Attention-generating gimmicks.

11.3   PRESENTATION SEGMENT DESIGN

11.3.1   Media Design

e-Commerce applications are generally implemented as multimedia systems on the World Wide Web. Designing presentation segments for e-Commerce systems involves designing an attractive and usable set of Web pages. It needs to consider the appropriate types of media to use for each presentation segment. The various unique technologies that are used for input and/or output between a user and a computer are referred to as **media.** Some examples of different types of media include:

- Visually displayed text
- Audio presented text
- Tactilely presented text (e.g., Braille output)
- Visually displayed graphics
- Visually displayed pictures
- Animations
- Movies
- Audio presented music

Media design involves planning the physical implementation of presentation segments by one or more media objects. A **media object** is a component of a presentation segment that is implemented by an object that is implemented by a single media type. Media can be combined and are used as a composite media object. According to ISO 14915-2,[5] a **composite media object** is "either a single media object that is used on its own or a combination of media objects which are used together and presented synchronized with one another and/or automatically linked to one another." Different media objects may be used to implement the attributes, operations, and links of a presentation segment.

Attributes of presentation segments contain content that can be input or output. Input content is always variable. Output content may be fixed (unchanging) or variable (based on changes in the system and/or the user). The variable nature of content is readily handled by considering each attribute as a separate media object, with its own attribute(s) and with operations that allow the user and/or the system to vary the contents.

Operations initiate some action. Some typical actions include:

- Linking to another screen
- Creating a new record (a new instance of an object)
- Getting data from a database
- Processing data
- Saving data

Media objects act as controls that have attributes (which a user can see and interact with) and operations that perform the intended operations for the presentation segment. By recognizing links as being implemented as objects, we recognize that they provide information to the user to aid in selecting them and then, when selected, they perform the operation of taking the user to another location within the system.

Additional objects may be inserted in the design in order to help the user of a particular presentation segment. Some examples of such enhancements include:

- Text objects used as a title, heading, or instruction
- Picture objects used as a logo or to make the screen attractive
- Music objects used to set a mood

Media design involves the selection and positioning of media objects within presentation segments. Content can be presented by one or more media objects either sequentially, in parallel, or in a combination of manners. Media objects can range in size from presenting a structure of content chunks to presenting only a portion of a content chunk, as illustrated in Figure 11-1.

While ISO 14915-3[6] discusses the uses of a number of types of media, it does not provide a definitive taxonomy of these different types. Attempts at predefining a set of different media types may run into difficulties. Rather, it is useful to define media types based on a number of the properties that they exhibit in a given media object. There are many properties of media that need to be considered in their selection, including:

- Audio, visual, or tactile (each with a range of associated properties)
- Fixed (changing only with state changes) or temporal (changing/moving over time)
- Language-based, rule-based, or random
- Realistic, symbolic, or abstract nature

While many media objects are composed of a single choice from each of the above sets of properties, additional types of media objects may be composed of multiple choices from some of the above sets of properties.

A recognizable media "type" may be used in a number of different ways. For example:

- Text, which is language-based, is usually displayed visually, in a fixed location on a screen. However, it may range considerably in its realistic, symbolic, or abstract nature.

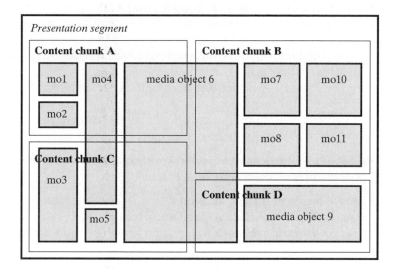

Figure 11-1   An example of the correspondence between media objects, content chunks, and presentation segments

- Text may be presented temporally by moving across a screen or being presented via audio or even via a tactile Braille output device.
- Recorded or synthesized audio text may be combined with a movie or animation or be played to describe some fixed object displayed as a picture or illustration on the screen.

ISO 14915-3[7] provides guidance on the selection of media properties for presenting different types of content, including:

- **Content representing objects:**
  - Physical content—represents physical objects in the real world
  - Conceptual content—represents facts or opinions that do not have a corresponding physical presence
- **Content describing objects/groups of objects:**
  - Descriptive content—attributes relating to some object
  - Value content—quantitative information describing properties of an object
  - Spatial content—information about the spatial dimensions of objects or groups of objects

- State content—properties that remain constant for an object or group of objects during some period of time
- Relationship content—information about relationships between objects
- **Content describing actions of objects/groups of objects:**
  - Discrete/continuous action content—descriptions of movements or other activities
  - Procedural information—information about a sequence of actions organized to achieve some task
  - Event content—descriptions of the effects of an action that results in state changes
  - Causation information—descriptions of the cause/effect of an event or sequence of events involving one or more objects

ISO 14915-3[8] provides guidance on using combinations of selected types of media in a single presentation segment, including:

- Types of media that work well together
- Combinations of media that should be avoided
- The use of contact points for referencing from one medium to another

 Find further information about media selection and combination in the Chapter 11 Cyber Supplement.

Once the preferred media are designed, consideration should be given to meeting the accessibility needs of users who cannot use those media types. For example, it is possible to provide a text description of pictures/illustrations that would not normally be presented but that can be accessed by "screen reader" software for people with visual difficulties. Alternate presentation possibilities meet the needs of a variety of users, including:

- People with visual impairments
- People who are using the Web page in a visually limiting environment
- People using devices with limited display capabilities (such as on various mobile computing devices)

ISO 16017[9] provides detailed guidance on accessibility issues related to the use of different types of media.

 Find further information about designing for accessibility in the Chapter 11 Cyber Supplement.

11.3.2   The Use of Illustrations in Presentation Segments

Illustrations are important in providing the user with a sense of reality regarding both the organization and its products. Illustrations can be very powerful marketing and support aids. However, care needs to be taken that illustrations are used appropriately within e-Commerce sites.

Corporate logos have long been recognized as important symbols projecting an organization's identity. Where an organization has a suitable logo, it can be used on each of the pages in a Web site to provide continuity and a reminder of with whom the user is dealing. It is often better to use a single corporate logo on the corner of a page than to use it repeatedly as a tiled background under the entire page. Color schemes from a corporate logo may help to provide further continuity, if they can be incorporated within the design of the Web site without providing a visual distraction.

There is a wide range of media that can be used to illustrate a product, including:

- Graphics/sketches
- Fully rendered, realistic artist's drawings
- Photographs

While photographs or artist's drawings may provide the most realism and are useful in marketing products, sketches focusing on particular details can be more useful in explaining the components and/or workings of a product.

The size of illustrations should be appropriate to the purpose of the illustration. Since larger illustrations take longer to load, delaying their use, illustrations should be no larger than required to serve the purpose for which they are being used. Often various sizes of the same illustration will support different uses within the same Web site.

When many illustrations of a number of different products are used on a single page (such as in a catalog), it is often advisable to present them as thumbnails. A **thumbnail** is a small picture, often comparable in size to a typical control icon, which is intended to provide recognition of some object or concept. Thumbnail size is also appropriate for presenting corporate logos.

Thumbnails are often used as links to further information, either to a page of information about the item pictured by the thumbnail or to a larger (often full-screen size) version of the illustration. Care should be taken to use links associated with thumbnails in a consistent manner throughout an application and to make their use understood to the user.

When illustrations are presented on a page describing a specific product, they should be large enough for users to recognize the main features within the illustration. Illustrations on product information pages should not be so large as to detract from accompanying written product information. If a larger version of an illustration would be useful, it should be made available via a link to this illustration, and users should be made aware they can access the illustration via this link.

Animations can help to demonstrate products. However, animations may be very time consuming and distracting if not desired by the user. It is best that animations not be forced on users, but be made available to users via special controls. Users should have the ability to pause and to end animations. Users should be made aware of audio explanations that accompany animations.

11.3.3 Some Principles for the Design of Presentation Segments

The design of presentation segments needs to involve both static and dynamic considerations:

- Static—all elements on the presentation segment should be clearly recognizable and understandable both on their own and in their combinations with other screen elements.

- Dynamic—all elements of the presentation segment should be easily usable for the various users to perform their various intended operations.

The following are just a few of the many human-computer guidelines that should be taken into account in designing presentation segments:

- **Composition**
  - Each presentation segment is composed of a number of media objects.
  - The type of media object should be selected based on the purpose it fulfills and in relation to the other media objects with which it will be used.
- **Layout**
  - Presentation segments can be divided into a number of sections.
    - These sections should each have some logical purpose.
    - Sections can be presented together either concurrently or in some temporal sequence.
    - Sections may overlay other sections, temporarily or permanently.
    - Each presentation segment should have a descriptive title:
      - Fixed visual presentation segments usually will have their title at their top
      - Temporal presentation segments usually will have their title at their start
  - The most important parts of the presentation sequence should be the most obvious.
  - It is important to separate sections of a presentation segment either by lines or by use of blank space.
  - Additional graphical elements may be used to clarify the layout and to make it attractive to the user.
- **Sections of a layout**
  - Control objects (implementing operations):
    - Should be arranged in separate sections apart from sections of content objects (often around the outside edges of the presentation segment) if they relate to operations that effect the entire presentation segment
    - Should be arranged within sections with content objects if they perform operations that only relate to that single section of the presentation segment
  - Content objects (implementing attributes) should be arranged in sections of similar content objects that:
    - Have similar purposes
    - Are used together
    - The user may choose between
  - Sections of a presentation segment should be small enough to be analyzed successfully at one time (i.e., they should contain a maximum of 7 ± 2 distinct media objects along with an optional heading).
  - Individual links are placed in locations where they are most likely to be used.
- **Ordering within sections**
  - Objects within a section should be ordered in a logical manner. Examples of these manners include:
    - Based on the conventional order users expect
    - Based on the order in which users are likely to use them
    - Based on their frequency of use, from highest to lowest
    - Based on alphabetical order

- **Dividing sections**
  - Larger sections can be divided into smaller sections that work together.
  - The distance between sections should be proportional to their importance to one another.

Mullet and Sano discuss further considerations relevant to the design of presentation segments in *Designing Visual Interfaces*.[10]

11.3.4   Controls and Links

Both controls and links provide the functionality of an e-Commerce system by allowing users to interact with systems composed of groups of Web pages. A **control** is "an object, often analogous to physical controls, which allows a user to take some action which manipulates data, other objects, or their attributes" according to ISO 14915-2.[11] A **link** is a control that allows the user to navigate a connection among or within media. Links may be activated by an action of the system or the user. There are a number of types of links defined by ISO 14915-2,[12] which include fixed links, temporal links, computed links, and user-defined links.

- A **fixed link** is a permanent link between two locations in the system that can be activated at any time (most links in current systems are fixed links).
- A **temporal link** is a permanent link between two locations in the system that is only available at certain times (e.g., a link used to access information that is only relevant during a portion of a movie).
- A **computed link** is a temporary link that is created on demand between two locations in the system and where the location that is linked to is dynamically determined based on the state and/or history of the system and where the link remains available only while needed (e.g., the links created in the results of a search).
- A **user-defined link** can be a fixed or temporal link created by a user during the use of an application that is intended to supplement the links created by the system's developers (e.g., bookmarks are user-defined fixed links).

Controls and links need to be designed to meet the various needs identified in the analysis and to be obvious to their users by meeting the general design principles discussed above.

Users require the capability to interact with and to navigate between content that is presented via specific media objects. **Navigation** involves the user's movement between media objects. There is a range of navigation techniques defined by ISO 14915-2,[13] including automatic navigation, predetermined navigation, user-determined navigation, and adaptive navigation.

- **Automatic navigation** occurs where content is presented by the system without the user's input.
- **Predetermined navigation** occurs where the user has only one choice as to where to go next but has control over when to go to this next content.
- **User-determined navigation** occurs where the user can choose which content to go to by selecting from a number of options.

- **Adaptive-determined navigation** occurs where the navigation choices available are determined by the system based on the content and some combination of an individual's history, an individual's personal characteristics, a group's social history, and/or a group's characteristics.

It is important to consider scope of controls in their design.

- The physical nature of presentation segments and media objects assists users in recognizing the effects of general actions (including navigation actions) that are performed on them. These actions can be initiated using controls that have a consistent look and "feel" throughout an application.
- Specific interactions with content chunks generally require specific controls. The conceptual nature of content chunks (identified in the analysis) makes it important that all navigation actions specific to content chunks be made explicit.
- Users might need to interact with a combination of media objects, implemented as "composite media objects," rather than having to interact with each media object independently. Composite media objects allow controls to act on a number of media objects that are used together in parallel and/or in series.
- Moving between presentation segments can have a greater impact on the user's future options than moving between media objects within a particular presentation segment, because it typically involves loading a new Web page or frame to replace an existing one. This can create special difficulties if the originating page or frame was dynamically created (such as in response to a search). Users might need to understand the differences resulting from these two similar types of navigation.

Graphical controls are often designed to look like their real world counterparts or to be otherwise recognizable. It is important that users can distinguish controls from other presented content and that they can recognize the purpose of these controls. The use of controls often involves two steps:

- Selecting the control (e.g., placing the cursor over the control)
- Activating the control (e.g., pressing a mouse button while the control is selected)

In some cases, selecting a control may automatically activate it. Automatic activation should be used with care and only where it will not initiate actions that may be destructive or that cannot be undone. Entering content into a field typically becomes important only once a control causes the content to be processed. For example, a sales order is only submitted for processing once it has been completed.

In some cases the entry or selection of content can be linked to automatically activate a control. For example:

- Rather than typing in a state code into a form, the user is allowed to select one from a list, and then the selected code is automatically entered where it is required in a form.
- Once the last field on a form is entered, the form may automatically be processed. NOTE: This type of linkage doesn't allow users to review what they have done and should generally be avoided.

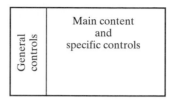

Figure 11-2   Using frames to separate general controls from other application content

ISO 14915-2[14] provides further guidance on the design and use of controls and links. Horton discusses further considerations relevant to the design of icons that can be used to implement controls and links in *The Icon Book*.[15]

11.3.5   Presentation Segment Combinations

While presentation segments are the main high level unit of design, there are varieties of situations in which combining multiple presentation segments may improve design. **Frames** are a programming technique that allows the combination of multiple presentation segments (implemented as separate Web pages) to be presented to a user as a single, composite Web page. Care needs to be taken that such combinations do not decrease the resulting usability.

Where frames are used in an e-Commerce system, an alternate version that does not use fames should be available to those users may not be capable of or agreeable to using frames. This is especially important in supporting handheld and other mobile computing devices, which may have the display capabilities of personal computers. Thus, high-level designs are initially developed on the basis of single presentation segments, as discussed in Chapter 10. These single presentation segments need to include all the content and control that may be required when using the presentation segment. Where frames are added to a design, they may involve new presentation segments that need to be added to the high-level design and that need to receive their own detailed design.

Where it is intended that a set of controls should always be available to users throughout a Web site, a separate frame may be used to provide them, as shown in Figure 11-2. This is often used to provide a set of links to the major sections of a Web site. The particular controls and links presented in this frame may change to reflect changes in the main frame used to provide content and specific controls. A typical e-Commerce use it to provide users with easy access to different product lines and/or different methods of finding products they might wish to buy.

Designs should consider those users who may have minimized the display of the general controls frame as well as those users who cannot or will not use frames on

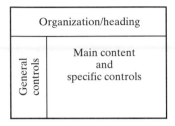

Figure 11-3   A typical arrangement of three frames

their systems. When controls that are relevant to the main content a user is currently accessing are presented via a separate frame, they should also be available at the bottom of the page in the content frame and/or wherever appropriate within the content frame. Controls that are not important enough to be included in a single-frame design also may be a waste of display space in a multiframe system.

Another use of a frame is to standardize the presentation of the organization's name and logo and/or heading information to identify the Web site and major areas within the Web site to the user. Designing for both systems with and without frames is more difficult when considering a frame for organization/heading purposes than when considering a frame for general controls. Communicating the name of an organization is important to all pages within an e-Commerce system. If separate frames are not used, then the organization/heading content should be presented at the top of the page. But if separate frames are used, presenting it at the top would present a redundancy and an annoyance. However, it may be useful to include organization/heading content at the bottom of a frame for those situations in which a user prints the frame. This alternate positioning can be accomplished by available programming capabilities, provided the need for such alternatives has been established in the design.

A frame for organization/heading purposes can be used to accompany the various main pages of a Web site, with or without a frame for general controls. The combination of three frames is illustrated in Figure 11-3. As can be seen in this illustration, the use of multiple frames may significantly reduce the space available on the display for presenting the main content and specific controls that the user needs to accomplish the immediate task. Where frames are used to present supporting content/controls they should be kept relatively small and should not be allowed to interfere with the user's ability to accomplish specific tasks in the frame, or frames containing the main content.

In addition to providing general content/controls, frames can be used to present multiple content items in a manner where they can be used both separately and together. The alternative to this use of frames is to include these different presentation segments together as one large presentation segment. This also can be accomplished

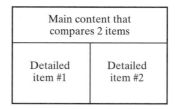

Figure 11-4   Using three frames to compare two items

via Web programming if identified in the design. Figure 11-4 illustrates the use of three frames being used to compare two items. The frame containing the main content in this example should include the name of the organization and any general controls.

There are many other potential uses for frames to help combine and arrange presentation segments. Each design involving frames should be evaluated in order to ensure that it improves the functionality and usability of the system and that it does not create unnecessary difficulties for its user.

11.4   INTERACTION DESIGN

11.4.1   Detailed Interaction Design

Each of the operations identified in our object-oriented analysis (which we will refer to as object-level operations) generally involves a series of basic operations. These basic operations include ones that both the user and the computer perform (on their own) and the various interactions between the user and the computer.

11.4.1.1   Basic Operations

The computer is capable of performing four basic operations:

- Input content (e.g., data)
- Process content
- Store content
- Output content

All other (more complex) operations are a combination of some or all of these main operations.

People can also perform these four basic operations. These basic operations can provide a basis for describing various types of interactions with users. Each of these eight basic operations is composed of an actor (either the computer or the user) and

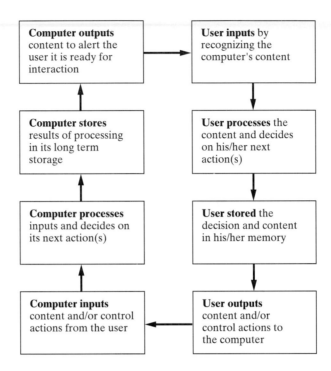

Figure 11-5   The cycle of basic operations involved in human-computer interactions

an action performed by that actor (input, process, store, output). Interactions involve a continuing cycle of these basic operations, as illustrated in Figure 11-5.

NOTE: A similar cycle, starting with computer output and ending with computer storage, was recognized in the early days of computing and has been featured as the basis for the design of various commercial software systems, including IBM's Report Program Generator II (RPG II).

A **computer output (CO)** is generally considered the start of the cycle because it is generally necessary to let the user know that the application (or this part of it) is ready to start doing things for the user and to prompt the user to take some action. The output of a computer can include a number of individual components that serve a variety of purposes, including:

- Information on the status of the application
- Information on the current location within the application
- Information about what user actions will be permitted at this time
- Displaying, inputting, and/or editing content
- Providing control objects with which to interact

Most outputs are arranged on a screen so that the user can look at them as long as they apply. In most applications there is no urgency that users immediately act on computer outputs. In multi-application systems, users may even obscure one application's screen while dealing with a second application before coming back to deal with the first application. Thus, at any point within an application the current screen should provide the user with sufficient information to aid in deciding what to do next. When moving between screens within an application, some information may need to be kept available on the new screen.

In order to simplify things for the user, it is desirable that object-level operations use as few different screen designs as possible. It is preferable if an object-level operation can be performed using only a single-screen design, where only parts of the screen change between different basic operations.

NOTE: It is important to recognize that, in this discussion, *user input* (UI) refers to the action of users getting inputs. This is opposed to the action of "a user inputting content to the computer," which will be referred to as a *user output* (UO) because it involves "a user outputting content that is input to the computer." This usage allows considering the user independently without having to also consider the computer.

Successful **user inputs (UI)** require that the user is able to recognize and understand what the computer has output. Thus, if a user misses part of the output (due to poor design), the user may fail to take an appropriate action. It isn't enough to just produce correct output; rather the output must be usable by all its intended users.

While they are working, users will also input additional information from their environment and from their memory. This additional information may distract them (e.g., noises may obscure audio outputs, and personal worries may cause one's attention to wander) or help them (e.g., additional information from a hand-written note or from one's memory may be useful in selecting one product from a group of similar products). The designer cannot eliminate the potential for additional inputs nor guarantee their availability. However, the designer should consider how they might affect the performance of the application.

A range of **user processing (UP)** may be done with or without the assistance of the computer. All user processing of content focuses on the decisions which this processing involves. This processing includes:

- Deciding what to do next
- Deciding how to do it
- Deciding to actually do it
- Deciding when it is done

While users may perform additional processes (such as calculating an average cost) these processes can be described as the results of specific versions of these four types of decisions. In each case the decision may be formulated to consider whether or not to proceed with a single option or formulated as a choice between a number of alternatives.

It is important to consider whether or not the user will have all the ingredients necessary to make the appropriate choice. Decisions require both sufficient information and sufficient decision-making skills (processing capabilities).

NOTE: Lack of sufficient decision-making skills can be due to a variety of reasons, which include:

- Lack of general intelligence/abilities
- Lack of training in making this or similar decisions
- Lack of practice in making this or similar decisions
- Lack of recognition of this decision being similar to previous decisions that the person made or for which the person was trained

In many cases the decisions involved in user processing may be trivial and thus can be assumed to take place without the need of explicit design. However, this dispensation does not apply to all types of user processing.

An important aspect of design is the allocation of processing between users and systems. While it may seem natural to get the computer to do as much processing as possible, relieving the users of unnecessary work, it is also important to allow the user as much control as possible over this processing. Allowing the user control involves allowing the user to make decisions.

Interactive systems typically involve numerous important occasions for user processing. Wherever significant user processing is required it needs to be considered in the design.

Users are often expected to remember, via **user storage (US),** some data, information, and knowledge. However, the more that users are required to remember, the more that they can forget. User storage involves both memory recall and memory storing.

- Memory recall—users may need to remember both content relevant to decisions and information about the context of the decision, including the sequence of actions that led to the current decisions.
- Memory storing—users may need to recognize what it is important for them to remember for potential future use.

Displaying important content (including relevant history information) as part of a computer output can assist user memory recall. User memory recall can further be helped by allowing the user to obtain additional, optional computer outputs (e.g., of help information) by making specific requests for such outputs.

User memory storage can be assisted by various techniques, which make important content memorable. These techniques include:

- Appealing to the user's interests
- Situating the content within an easy-to-remember context
- Suggesting memory aids

In many cases the need for user storage may be trivial and thus can be assumed to take place without the need of explicit design. However, this dispensation does not apply to all types of user processing.

NOTE: It is important to recognize that, in this discussion, *user output* (UO) refers to the action of users producing outputs. This is opposed to the action of "a user getting content from the computer," which will be referred to as a *user input* (UI) because it involves "a user imputing content that was output by the computer." This usage allows considering the user independently without having to also consider the computer.

User outputs (UO) involve presenting content and/or activating a control (as inputs to the computer).

The design of both the computer outputs and the computer inputs will have an effect on the accuracy and efficiency of user outputs. Likewise, where a user will output content or control information, the method required of the user may have an effect on both the accuracy and efficiency of this output. For example:

- Where content is already known to the system it is often preferable to allow users to select from available content rather than requiring it to be rekeyed into the system to avoid making typing mistakes
- Some frequent users may prefer to be able to use "quick keys" to having to go through long menu selections to find computer functions that they use frequently, while occasional users may prefer menus that don't require user storage of quick keys
- Controls should be separated sufficiently to ensure ease of the user selecting the desired one and to ensure against accidental slips, which could result in selecting a control not intended by the user

In most cases user outputs are paired with **computer inputs (CI).** However, the computer has to be prepared to receive the input before it will accept it. If it is not prepared for the input, the input may result in an error or may be ignored. Design of computer inputs may involve:

- Identifying the inputs relevant to a given screen
- Identifying when the inputs should be available to the user
- Identifying one or more dialog techniques (including menus, command languages, direct manipulation, form filling, natural language, specialty I/O) to use for the inputting
- Identifying a specific design of the technique(s)
- Identifying and designing appropriate input edits

Once an input is received it is often subjected to a series of "edit checks" to determine if the input is valid and should be processed or whether it should be rejected. Some typical edit checks include:

- Checking numeric fields for valid numbers
- Checking province/state abbreviations with a table of postal abbreviations
- Checking that a customer number is valid and that the customer is in good standing

While input editing could be considered a type of computer processing, it generally is considered along with the inputting because it is necessary to insure that all inputs are valid before they are handled by the intended processing of the application. Where problems are uncovered by input edits, they should lead to understandable computer outputs that identify the problem and help the user to rectify the situation.

Computer processing (CP) focuses on what the computer does internally to the various inputs it receives. Design issues relating to computer processing will be discussed in Chapter 12 as part of the discussion of technical design.

Computer storage (CS) focuses on what the computer stores internally. Design issues relating to computer storage will be discussed in Chapter 12 as part of the discussion of technical design.

11.4.1.2   Approaches to Considering Basic Operations

Each of these basic operations exists in most object-level operations, whether or not they have been specifically identified and designed. However, some developers may fail to consider many of them.

- "Software engineering" often focuses on computer processing and computer storage (which will be discussed as part of technical design in Chapter 12).
- Many approaches to "human-computer interaction" focus more on the design of computer interactions (computer output and computer input) than they do on the human side of interactions.
- However, if the developers ignore the users or take them for granted, a number of problems may occur once these users are expected to use the resulting system.

It is important for users, especially those users involved with procuring systems and/or managing the development of systems, to ensure that their involvement in interactions is considered properly in the design phase.

Object-level operations can be described by a sequence of all, or at least the main, basic operations required to complete the object-level operation. Some of the basic operations in this sequence (especially those involving storing) may be omitted in various situations where they can be assumed to be trivial or unnecessary.

- Outputs by either the user or the computer result in inputs by the other, provided that the other is prepared to receive them.
- Actions by users are often immediately input and output by the computer, providing further feedback inputs to the user. Such feedback is important in ensuring the user that the computer has input and recognized the user's actions correctly.

The consideration of basic operations can be simplified by focusing on what the user and the computer do to each other, which is contained in their outputs.

- The **computer** primarily **outputs** content to the user. The user's success in dealing with this content will depend on both the skills of the user and the quality of the output.
  - If computer outputs are designed appropriately, the user can be expected to be able to recognize (user input) them. Where the user may miss recognizing significant computer outputs (such as with warning messages), the computer can ask the user to confirm recognition of its outputs.
  - If user processing and/or decisions are kept simple and are appropriate to the user's capabilities, the user can be expected to be able to make them correctly. The system can analyze user actions and ask the user to confirm actions that may appear to be questionable or unclear.

- Although users should remember what has gone on, it is useful to make records of major interactions available, upon request, to assist their memory.
- We should recognize that these expectations may exceed reality; thus we need to question their validity each time they are used and to test that the resulting system works in accordance with these expectations. If they are found to exceed reality, additional design of both computer outputs and user operations will be necessary.
- The **user** primarily **outputs** information that is entered into the computer.
  - Computer inputs are the main source of determining what the needs of users are at any point in time.
  - Consideration of computer processing and storage details can be deferred until after the interface is designed and will be dealt with in Chapter 12.
- The design of computer input (from **user output** actions) is usually highly connected with the design of **computer output.** Computer output should meet the needs of users.

11.4.2 Defaults

Defaults are values that are assumed to be reasonable and are provided by the system to assist a user in making requests of the system, but which are subject to confirmation or change by a user. When defaults are used, the system should present the most likely value as the default. Defaults can be used for the values of both attributes and controls. Some examples of defaults include:

- Once a customer number is entered, the system can retrieve other content associated with that customer number (such as name and address) and present it as a set of default values in an order form that the customer is completing. The customer, however, may wish to use a different address or phone number for this order than the one stored in the system's customer file.
- When a user requests the system to delete a record from the system, the system may respond with a request for the user to confirm the deletion before processing it.
  - If the default action associated with pressing the return key is to delete, users will not have to stop and think about what they are doing, and the confirmation request is of little value. It will cause delays without accomplishing its purpose of making sure that a destructive action is really intended.
  - If the default action associated with pressing the return key is to cancel the delete request, then the user will have to make a second decision about whether or not the record should really be deleted before the system takes this action.

11.4.3 Scenarios

Scenarios provide a compact way of describing how object-level operations can be accomplished. Scenarios specify what each actor (either the computer system or the user) does to the other. A scenario can describe a step-by-step dialog between the user and the computer. In this dialog, one actor says (outputs) something, the other

Table 11-1 Examples of good and poor scenario steps

Example of Good Scenario Steps (focusing on what the screen is to be used for)	Example of Poor Scenario Steps (focusing on how the screen is to be used)
user: enters the customer's name	Type the customer's name into the name field on the customer record screen
user: requests the record to be created	Click on the create button on the customer record screen
computer: displays the customer's record	

responds (outputs), and then the first responds, and so on until the reason for the interaction is completed. In some cases an actor may say or do a number of things before the other actor responds. Scenarios often focus on the major events in an interaction without listing steps that can be safely assumed. Where an input, decision, or storage operation is important to recognize, it should be included in the scenario.

Scenarios should focus on what the user does (e.g., what the user or computer outputs) and not on how it is done (output). By focusing on what the user or computer outputs, it is possible to use the scenario to evaluate a number of potential designs. Table 11-1 provides examples of well worded and poorly worded scenario steps.

An example of a customer using an order form and a catalog to order a single item illustrates the attributes of a scenario:

- A scenario is more compact than a corresponding description of all the object-level operations
- A scenario focuses on a single set of steps that describe only one of the many possible ways of accomplishing an object-level operation

The following example illustrates a scenario involving one of many possible ways of placing an order:

- The user chooses to place an order from some other location in the application
- The computer presents the user with an order form
- The user enters "Jim" as the "first name"
- The user enters "Carter" as the "last name"
- The user enters "1C115 Engineering" as the "address"
- The user enters "4893" as the "phone"
- The user requests the product catalog
- The computer presents the main page of the catalog
- The user requests to search for "Web-authoring software"
- The computer presents a list of Web-authoring software packages in the catalog, along with their prices and links to further information about them
- The user (who knows what package is wanted and recognizes it in the list) selects "Tapestry 4.0"
- The computer asks how many copies are wanted
- The user replies "1" copy
- The computer asks if further items are wanted from the catalog
- The user replies "no"

- The computer returns to the sales order form and awaits further inputs from the customer
- The user (decides that the order is complete and) requests that the order be processed
- The computer checks the order for all required information
- The computer (recognizing that the order is complete and acceptable) confirms the order to the user

Alternate scenarios could start with the user identifying an item while browsing through the catalog (or while searching for a particular item in the catalog) and, once it is found, deciding to order it. Additional scenarios could consider the ordering of multiple items.

11.4.4 Dialog Design

Series of interactions meeting the needs of a range of scenarios are implemented as dialogs between the computer and the user. Amendment 1 of ISO 9241-1[16] provides guidance for selecting between and combining four major dialog techniques, each of which has additional design guidance that is provided by their own part of the ISO 9241 standard:

- Menus (ISO 9241-14)[17]
- Commands (ISO 9241-15)[18]
- Direct manipulation (ISO 9241-16)[19]
- Form filling (ISO 9241-17)[20]

A **menu** is any set of options presented by the system from which the user can make a selection to be used as input to the system. Menus may be used for a wide variety of input tasks and may select values and/or initiate control actions. Menus are easily implemented across a wide range of technologies and media. Menus may be output by a system using a variety of visual and/or audio media and allow the user to use a variety of media to make a selection that is input to the computer. A wide range of users can use menus with relatively high accuracy when selecting between a limited number of choices.

Commands include words, abbreviations, or strings of words that a user can use to make a request of the system. A **prompt** is an indication output by a system that the system is ready to accept the entry of a command from the user. Commands are organized into **command languages** that involve specifically defined syntactic structures and semantic meanings. Command languages require greater user skills and experience but may provide a greater flexibility in combining choices, provided the application can process these combinations. This flexibility also involves the greatest potential for inaccuracies in dialogs. Commands can be implemented across a wide range of technologies and media.

Direct manipulation is a technique that gives the user the impression of acting directly on objects within the system. Direct manipulation generally involves graphical media and requires that the user has a variety of spatial mental and spatial skills. It provides a good combination of flexibility and accuracy for those users capable of using direct manipulation. Direct manipulation interactions pose the greatest challenges for being translated via assistive technologies for users with special needs. Direct manipulation also places the greatest demands on the technology being used to implement it.

Form filling is useful for inputting specific data into a highly structured format. According to ISO 9241-17,[21] a **form** is a structured display with labeled fields that the user reads, fills in, selects entries for (e.g., through choice buttons or radio buttons), or modifies."

NOTE: Various programming languages and systems may have alternate definitions of forms. Form filling makes use of the user's knowledge of filling out noncomputerized forms. However, implementing forms on a computer may add additional limitations to the user's flexibility beyond those already imposed by paper forms. Form filling can be implemented across a wide range of technologies but is usually implemented in combination with graphical media.

 Find further information about dialog design in the Chapter 11 Cyber Supplement.

11.4.5 Designing for Success

Although our analysis focused on what was supposed to happen, our design needs to deal with all the different possible scenarios of what might happen. Thus, the set of design scenarios should include ones that deal with the various situations where errors may occur or where users may run into difficulties so that the design will include appropriate error handling and user guidance. It is not enough to just design how things will go if everyone does things correctly. It is essential also to design for situations where things don't go perfectly.

11.4.5.1 Sources of Errors

Errors can result from a variety of stages in the user's interaction with the system.

Errors in Deciding What Is Needed to be Done

A variety of errors can result from problems relating to:

- The system not outputting the required information in a usable manner
- The user inputting information from the system (either due to missing information or to misinterpreted information)
- The user processing this information incorrectly (either due to using incorrect information or due to using faulty decision-making skills)

These situations can result in the user not understanding the situation (required task) or not understanding the **software** (required tool). These situations can result in errors of **omission** (missing doing something that should have been done) or **commission** (doing the wrong thing).

Errors in Doing What was Decided

A variety of errors (which are further errors of commission) can result from problems relating to:

- The user not understanding how to use the system to implement the decision
- The user accidentally making an output error (e.g., a typing mistake or unintentionally activating the wrong system control)

- The system misinterpreting a user's action (e.g., making an error in voice recognition)

Some specific user errors in doing what was decided can be due to:

- Confusion in choosing between various similar functions (specific software tools)
- Confusing the use of a particular function with the use of other, similar functions
- Making typing or selection errors
- Performing the task at an inappropriate time
- Confusion in the order of the parts of a function or in the order of a set of functions (including missing or repeating parts or functions)
- Forgetting what the task's objective was before completing it
- Getting interrupted before completing a task and forgetting to complete it

These situations can result in the user performing an inappropriate task instead of the intended one or failing to perform the appropriate task.

11.4.5.2 Methods for Dealing with Errors

The main methods for dealing with errors are described below.

Avoiding occasions for errors is best! If you can identify what might cause an error, the system can often be designed in a manner that removes the ability for the error to occur. Some examples of error avoidance include:

- If money left out on a bank counter might get stolen, then the money shouldn't be left on the counter; it should be put in a cash drawer that only the bank teller can get at, thus avoiding giving customers an opportunity to steal it.
- If a user might get confused about where the command [control C] means "copy" and where it means "break," the design could be revised so that it always means "copy" and that something else is used to mean "break."
- If a user enters information, various edit checks can be performed before allowing the information to be processed and stored by the system. For example, employees below age 16 years or above age 65 years might be rejected from an employment system.

Facilitating correcting the problem and/or recovering from a loss due to errors is second best! If you can identify a potential cause for an error but can't design the system to avoid the error (since the error is a result of performing a valid operation at the wrong time), then you should provide a suitable mechanism for correcting the error. Some examples of error recovery include:

- If you accept that convenience stores are frequently robbed, you may wish to install security cameras to assist in apprehending the robbers.
- People buy property and car insurance to recover from potential losses (but due to deductibles, you can't recover completely).
- If a user might accidentally delete something that shouldn't be deleted, then:
  - An undo function might help if the problem is noticed immediately.
  - A history file that contains deleted items might help if the problem isn't noticed until later.

Limiting the impact of errors (limiting the amount of a loss) is third best! If you can identify a potential cause for an error but can't design in a manner that prevents the error, you may be able to limit the potential for loss and/or amount of an individual loss when the error does occur. This is useful even in circumstances in which you might be able to recover from/correct the error.

Some examples of limiting the chance of loss/errors include:

- Car and property insurance policies always have a deductible on their payment for losses to discourage clients from being careless—the client must pay the deductible before collecting.
- If a user enters information, various edit checks can provide the user with warnings before allowing the information to be processed and stored by the system. For example, employees younger than 16 years or older than 65 years could be allowed only after the user confirms that an exception has been made to the standard employment policy.

Some examples of limiting the amount of loss include:

- If a convenience store has lots of cash on hand, it might lose lots of money in a robbery. Most convenience stores limit the amount of cash accessible at night by having the clerks deposit excess amounts in a safe that they can't open, thus limiting the amount that can be stolen in a given robbery.
- Cash machines limit the amount a person can withdraw at a time to protect them from robberies.
- Software programs can limit the impact of errors in a number of ways, including:
  - Limiting access to a system (or a part of a system) to those trusted and trained employees who need access.
  - Limiting the power of various functions, such as allowing a delete command to only delete one record at a time.
  - Limiting the amount of change to the system (such as the amount of expenditures the employee can authorize) that an employee can make without obtaining additional authorization.

Informing the user that an error has occurred isn't enough! If the system can identify that an error has occurred, then it should be able to do something about it. This does not mean that the system should take control away from the user. If the error cannot be avoided, the system should at least help the user to recognize the error and identify what can be done to handle it. This should include providing the user with a means of correcting detectible errors.

NOTES:

- The basic risk management techniques discussed above are nothing unique to computers.
- Computerization is no excuse to avoid following proper business practices. Computerization requires that good business practices are included in the analysis and design of all systems.
- If risk management techniques limit the ability of the organization to function, they become a major risk to its success. Risk management techniques need to be usable.

11.4.5.3 Some Guidance on Helping Users

User guidance is additional information beyond the regular user–computer dialog that is provided to the user on request or automatically provided by the system.

- User guidance to help users in accomplishing their tasks is appropriate to all styles of interaction.
- User guidance should be readily distinguishable from other displayed information.
- User guidance should not disrupt the user's task.

ISO 9241-13–User Guidance[22] identifies a number of special types of user guidance, including the following:

- **Prompts** are system outputs requesting input from the user. Prompts should indicate implicitly (generic prompt) or explicitly (specific prompt) the types of input that will be accepted by the dialogue system.
- **Feedback** is output presented to the user by the system in reaction to the user's input or a system event. Every input by the user should produce timely and perceptive feedback from the system. Feedback associated with normal task performance should be nonintrusive and should not distract the user from the task.
- **Status** is user guidance information that indicates the current state of components in the system hardware and/or software. The level of status information should be appropriate to the user's current task.
- **On-line help** provides additional user guidance and support for the user when interacting with the dialog and user interface. It explains what can be done, where, when, and how it can be done. On-line help can also give support to complete user goals. On-line help can provide different levels of information for users with different levels of skills.
- **Error messages** provide specific information where the system detects an error. If system failures can be anticipated, an indication of the potential problem should be provided before the failure occurs. If brief error messages are displayed, users should be able to request more detailed on-line information or should be referred to additional off-line information. Error messages should convey:
  - What is wrong
  - What corrective actions can be taken
  - The cause of the error

 Find further information about designing e-Commerce systems to promote the success of their users in the Chapter 11 Cyber Supplement.

11.5   USING INTERFACE PROTOTYPES IN DESIGN

A picture is often "worth a thousand words." Verbal descriptions of how a user and a system interact with each other are often difficult to visualize. An alternative method of communicating an interaction design is to develop a prototype of the interface.

A prototype is an intentionally incomplete model. Prototypes can be useful tools to assist designers and users to communicate and evaluate possible designs. User interface prototypes can be developed to demonstrate combinations of content and dialog designs. They can demonstrate what the user would see (in the real system) if one or more scenario(s) were followed.

A prototype of the interface can demonstrate how the interface will look and act to the user without requiring the cost (in time, money, and other resources) of developing a complete working system. This allows the user to determine whether or not the design is suitable and to suggest the need for changes before large investments are made in developing a complete system, which may need to be changed. The use of prototypes to obtain development information from users has already been discussed in Chapter 5. This section focuses on developing prototypes.

Simple but effective prototypes can be constructed based on a set of Web pages that are linked together in various ways.

- Each page represents what the user would see at some point within a scenario.
- The only action that can be performed on any page is to follow a link to another page.
- Each link represents an action that the user could take at that time within a scenario.
  - A link from an empty field (or unselected control) can take the user to an almost identical page that differs only by having some sample data filled in the field that was used for the link (or the control highlighted to indicate its selection), as it would appear on the original page in a fully functioning system
  - A link from a control can take the user to a page that represents a sample set of the results that would be produced by activating the control in a fully functioning system. This could include the requesting of data/information from the computer
  - Navigational links can take the user to another page, the same as they do in a fully functional system

Table 11-2 identifies variations between pages that may occur in a prototype. These variations are based on whether or not a user action will be followed by another user action and gives examples of each.

Table 11-2 Prototype variations based on sequences of actions

Types of Action	Example of Scenario Steps (the What)	Example of Design Variation Produced (the How)
1. A user action will be followed by another user action (that will produce its own variation).	The user enters the customer's name. (This will be followed either by more data entry or by the user activating a control, either of which is a separate action.)	The user clicks on a blank name field in a customer record page, which links to (a *variation* that is) a similar page with a sample customer name in the name field.
2. A user action will be followed by one or more system actions (that together produce a set of variations).	The user wants to submit an order.	(After a set of previous transitions where the fields in the order were filled in), the user clicks on a "place this order" control, which links to (a *variation* that is) a similar page, which includes information that the order has been placed and includes a unique order number for the user to use for future reference.

Table 11-3 contains an example of a scenario that involves one of many possible ways of placing an order that illustrates the development of a script of instructions given to the user of the prototype and the design of a set of pages (and links) for the prototype.

Table 11-3   Designing a prototype to fit a scenario

Instructions to User of the Prototype	Expected Action of the User in the Scenario	Prototype Page and Link Design
1. You are to place an order using this order form. To use it, you should click on fields where you wish to enter information or on controls that you wish to activate.	The user will consider the page and then move on to the next instruction in the prototype scenario.	1. Scenario starts with the initial order form page that the user would have seen upon arriving from the other location.
2. Enter "Jim" as the "first name."	The user wishing to enter "Jim" as the "first name" clicks on the "first name" field.	2. A link is followed to a page that appears identical to page 1, except that it has "Jim" filled in the "first name" field.
3. Enter "Carter" as the "last name."	The user wishing to enter "Carter" as the "last name" clicks on the "last name" field.	3. A link is followed to a page that appears identical to page 2 except that it has "Carter" filled in the "last name" field.
4. Enter "1C115 Engineering" as the "address."	The user wishing to enter "1C115 Engineering" as the "address" clicks on the "address" field.	4. A link is followed to a page that appears identical to page 3 except that it has "1C115 Engineering" filled in the "address" field.
5. Enter "4893" as the "phone."	The user wishing to enter "4893" as the "phone" clicks on the "phone" field.	5. A link is followed to a page that appears identical to page 4 except that it has "4893" filled in the "phone" field.
6. Consult the catalog to find a particular product to order.	The user wishing to request the product catalog clicks on a "consult catalog" control.	6. A link is followed to the main page of the catalog (an entirely different page), which contains both a field for entering a product description and a control to search for the product. It may also contain a list of different product categories.
7. Search for "Web-authoring software"	The user wishing to search for "Web-authoring software" clicks on the data entry field associated with the "look for product" control. (If the user chooses to select a product category rather than use the search function, this would lead to a different scenario that should be discussed separately).	7. A link is followed to a page that appears identical to page 6 except that it has "Web-authoring software" filled in the "search" field.
8. (Although this is a two-step process, the user should be left to determine "how" to accomplish it with any further instructions.)	The user then has to click on the "look for product" control.	8. A link is followed to another different page that is designed to present various "Web-authoring" packages in the catalog along with their prices and links to further information about them.

Table 11-3 Continued.

Instructions to User of the Prototype	Expected Action of the User in the Scenario	Prototype Page and Link Design
9. Select "Tapestry 4.0" to order.	The user wishing to order "Tapestry 4.0" clicks on it.	9. A link is followed to a page that appears identical to page 8 except that it has "Tapestry 4.0" displayed in boldface text (to indicate it has been selected) and has a new question, "How many copies would you like to order?" added along with a field for entering the number of copies (that may have a default value of 1 already in it).
10. Order 1 copy.	The user wishing to order 1 copy clicks on the field for entering the number of copies.	10. A link is followed to a page that appears identical to page 5, except that it has "Tapestry 4.0," the quantity of 1 copy, and the price filled in the appropriate fields.
11. That's all you wish to order.	The user clicks the "process order" control.	11. A link is followed to a page that appears identical to page 10, except that it has "order processed" and a confirmation number on it. It, like all pages of the order form type, should also have a "start a new order" control to take the user back to page 1.

NOTES:

- Although this prototype involves eleven separate Web pages, it actually involves variations of only three different presentation segments.
- While this design specifies which designs are required and how variations differ from one another, it does not specify the rest of the detailed design that will be involved in designing each of these three different presentation segments. (As such, it may be considered a high-level prototype design.) Further detail design of each of these presentation segments is needed before constructing the prototype.
- Alternate prototypes could be developed that include the same first six steps but that illustrate different uses of the catalog and/or ordering multiple products.

11.6 APPLYING DETAILED DESIGN

11.6.1 Applying Detailed Design in Organizations

The detailed design of an e-Commerce application involves more than just the design of computer software. It is the design of a business as customers and/or suppliers will experience it. This text concentrates on how these experiences can be translated into an e-Commerce system. There are a number of additional organizational design factors to consider. In addition to the benefit of computer professionals, good design can benefit from the input of:

- Marketing and corporate image experts
- Graphic designers
- Organizational design and management experts
- Industrial psychologists
- Senior management

Timing is important in getting input for design. Involving each of these types of people along with various types of computer professionals in all aspects of design could lead to delays that would prevent the intended system from being developed in a timely manner. Major delays could also result from these experts objecting to designs that have already been completed.

Organization-specific design guidance can be collected ahead of time and incorporated into an organizational "style guide." Style guides are much more specific than typical sets of standards or guidelines. Style guides specify preferred design options from among a wide variety of acceptable options. A style guide can specify a variety of design choices, including:

- Criteria to use in choosing appropriate types of media that can be used in certain situations (e.g., a style guide may specify when to use movies, animations, music, and other specialty types of media)
- A standard layout or a small set of standard layouts for Web pages
- A standard set of controls that should be accessible from all or most Web pages
- A standard color and/or pattern to be used as the background of all Web pages or at least of all pages in this e-Commerce system
- A standard version and size of a corporate logo and a standard placement of it on all Web pages

Developing a style guide involves deciding how the e-Commerce site should look and act, regardless of what it should do.

11.6.2   Student Assignment—Applying Detailed Design

Select one of the presentation segments from your high-level design with a number of design possibilities to use as the basis for your detailed design. The presentation segment that you select should:

- Contain multiple attributes (individual fields of variable content used for input and/or output)
- Involve multiple operations (actions that can be used [individually or in sequences] to accomplish multiple tasks)
- Serve multiple different user groups

NOTES:

- Multiple means at least two and preferably more.
- It is preferable if multiple tasks can be performed using only variations of this one presentation segment; otherwise multiple detail designs may be needed in order to complete this assignment.
- A presentation segment used only for initiating searches or obtaining reports is not acceptable for this assignment.

- You may wish to develop all parts of this assignment in an iterative manner to ensure that the screen chosen for this part actually works well for the other parts.

1. Perform a detailed design of the selected presentation segment. This design should contain all the necessary content and control objects required to successfully implement the high-level design of the selected presentation segment. This design should make good use of the design principles discussed above.

This design should be illustrated by a Web page that could form the basis for prototyping the design.

NOTES:

- This page should illustrate your design but should not contain any of the programming necessary to actually function. Since this is only an initial prototype, both content and controls can be represented by text. What is important is that all objects are located on the screen where they are intended to be according to your detailed design.
- This page may, but need not, include sample content.

Supplement the design with a brief description of why you designed your page in the manner that you did.

2. Develop scenarios that focus on using the page. Develop at least five scenarios of specific ways in which the page could be used to perform some (more than one) of the tasks that it is intended to serve. These scenarios should ideally make use of different sets of content and controls. Each of these scenarios should involve four or more steps.

NOTES:

- It is expected that many more scenarios could be developed, so try to pick ones that are both interesting and illustrative of a range of uses of the page.
- If any of your chosen scenarios require the use of additional pages of a different design, then you must include their design as part of what is required by Part 1 of this assignment.

Each scenario should be written up in the manner illustrated in Table 11-3 above.

11.7   AN EXAMPLE OF APPLYING DETAILED DESIGN

Remember, it is intended that the design allow users to create new sales orders with a minimum amount of work. Wherever possible, users may be given the option either to use existing information or to enter the information directly.

- Sales orders make use of data (attributes) from other objects, including customers and products.
- Repeat customers may wish to copy and modify a previous sales order rather than creating a new one from the start.

11.7.1   Applying Some Detail Design Considerations

Sales orders are generally composed of a combination of textual, numeric, and graphical visual media objects. The graphical media objects are used:

- To provide identification of the sales order with a particular organization
- To help structure the components of the sales order
- To represent controls
- To make the sales order attractive

Each of the other media objects (other than those used solely to make the sales order attractive) have a purpose, which needs to be accessible even where graphical media may be replaced by other media. Accessibility support of these purposes can be met by providing a text-based alternative that can be used by people unable to use graphics.

The attributes and operations (and links, which are treated as controls below) identified in the high-level design can be allocated to identifiable sections of design and commented on in order to provide a basis for an initial consideration of composition and layout.

Sales orders are created in a number of ways, including:

- A user, accessing the sales order page, creates a blank sales order, which can then be edited and submitted
- A user selecting items to order from the catalog or product list and then accessing a sales order that has been created that lists those items and can then be edited and submitted

Where and when information is available, it may be automatically inserted into the appropriate attributes as a default. Where no information is currently available, the initial values of these attributes should have an initial default value of "blank."

Sales orders are not fully created until they have been submitted as an order to *Savor the Cup.*

- Sales orders created, but not submitted, during a user on-line session will be lost.
- If technically possible, the user should be warned about the possible loss of a sales order before shutting down a Web browser session.
- It should be easy for a user to delete a nonsubmitted sales order to avoid being warned about the potential loss of a sales order that was not wanted.

Likewise, modifications of sales orders require multiple steps:

- Finding the sales order
- Making the modifications to it
- Submitting the intended modifications

Processing of modifications are not complete until submitted and should be subject to the same warnings as the creation of sales orders.

A general content section is used to identify the e-Commerce site.

Attribute: organization. identification	**Fixed Graphic:** logo, including company name (not previously identified)
Control: link to organization's e-Commerce home page	**Fixed:** based on organization. identification (not previously identified)

A general sales order content section is used to identify sales orders.

Attribute: sales order. number	**Default:** blank Automatically assigned by system upon submission of an order Can be entered by a user on a blank sales order and used with sales order. find
Control: sales order. find	**Fixed graphic:** (can be used to access existing orders, with appropriate authorization)
Control: sales order. copy	**Fixed graphic:** (can be used to access existing orders, with appropriate authorization) Leaves sales order. number blank in new copy
Attribute: sales order. date	**Default:** today's date or date based on existing order

A general customer-related content section is used to access customer information.

Attribute: customer. number	**Default:** blank
Attribute: customer. name	**Default:** blank
Control: find. customer	**Fixed graphic:** (can be used to access existing customers, with appropriate authorization)
Control: link to tool for customers to create a permanent account	**Fixed graphic:** (*previously identified as* tool for users to identify themselves)
Control: link to tool to find other sales orders of that customer	**Fixed graphic:** only available for use once customer has been authorized
Attribute: sales order. customer purchase order reference	**Default:** blank (optional, if user wishes to fill in)

A section of order-specific customer attributes can be automatically filled in for existing customers, if a customer record has been accessed.

Attribute: customer. contact person	**Default:** blank or based on existing order or based on value from customer record
Attribute: customer. ship address	**Default:** blank or based on existing order or based on value from customer record
Attribute: customer. billing address	**Default:** blank or based on existing order or based on value from customer record
Attribute: customer. credit information	**A complex object** including three "radio bullet" options (of which only one can be selected at a time):

- **Default:** bill to *Savor the Cup* account if one exists and credit has been established
- Bill to *VISA* with an account number, name, and expiration date which both **default:** blank
- Bill to *Master Card* with an account number, name, and expiration date which both **default:** blank

(not previously analyzed below this general level)

Multiple sales item lines are needed for most sales orders. The number of items per order can be expected to vary considerably. The design needs to take this into account in the most effective way.

- Initially the number of lines will be set to five, which is one more than the current average number of items per order.
- There should always be at least one blank line available to encourage adding further items to the order. As soon as all available sales item lines are filled, an additional blank line should be added automatically.

Each **sales item line** will contain:

Attribute: product. number	**Default:** blank Entered either directly by user or based on selection of a product from the catalog or product list
Attribute: product. name	**Default:** blank Entered automatically based on the entry of a valid product number
Control: link to specific information on particular products and/or services	Link based on product. name
Attribute: product. unit price	**Default:** blank Entered automatically based on the entry of a valid product number
Attribute: sales order. item ordered. quantity	**Default:** 1 if product. number is entered, else blank User may change it
Attribute: sales order. item ordered. total price	Calculated automatically (not previously identified)
Control: sales order. item ordered. delete/cancel	**Fixed graphic:** If an order. number is present, it sets sales order. item ordered. quantity equal 0 or else it deletes the line from the sales order (previously identified as part of sales order. modify)

A **section of sales assistance functions** group a number of tools together. When a product or service is found that the user wants to add to the order, the user can use a control on the page where it is found to automatically add a **sales item line** for the product or service.

Control: link to tool for searching the site for specific products or services	(previously identified as tool for searching the site for specific information)
Control: link to table of contents of the catalog	
Control: link to tool to help customers identify and evaluate their own needs	
Control: link to tool to assist customers in comparing products and/or services	
Control: link to tool to assist customers in developing custom blends	

As items are added or modified within the **sales item lines,** a number of summary attributes need to be updated in a **sales order summary section.**

Attribute: sales order. discount	This attribute cannot be added or modified by customers. **Default:** blank or based on existing order or based on value from customer record Sales representatives may be authorized by the system to modify it NOTE: at this time discounts are only available on entire orders and not on individual items
Attribute: sales order. shipping charges	Calculated automatically by the system based on the items selected and the location of the customer NOTE: various shipping options are not available at this time
Attribute: sales order. taxes	Calculated automatically by the system NOTE: depending on the location of the customer, this may involve a number of different taxes, including: • State/provincial sales tax • Federal sales tax/value added tax • Import duties
Attribute: sales order. status	This identifies the current stage of processing for an order. Currently there are only two stages identified: • Submitted • Shipped NOTE: this does not take into account orders where only part of the order has been shipped

A brief consideration of how this design fits the needs of different users can identify possible deficiencies.

- The design can work well for customers or for sales representatives submitting or modifying orders.
- The design can work well for accounting.
- The design does not meet all of the needs for sales and shipping-related information of *Savor the Cup* employees.
  - Sales representatives are not allowed to provide differing discounts on individual line items.
  - Sales representatives would like to know the profit margins on each of the items and on the order as a whole in order to adjust customer discounts.
  - Logistics personnel would like to be able to track the shipping of partial orders.

The further requirements of sales and logistics were not identified in the analysis. Some requirements are relatively easy to meet within the current design. However, meeting other requirements would be too difficult at this point in the development to be worth attempting for now.

- Displaying the profit margins (on individual line items and the overall order) to sales representatives (only) can be accommodated relatively easily. Profit margins will be expressed in terms of percentage (%) to be on par with the percentage used to represent discounts. The requirement can be met by adding:
  - An **attribute** (visible only with the appropriate authorization) to each **sales item line** that is entered automatically, based on the entry of a valid product number
  - An **attribute** to the **sales order summary section** that calculates the overall profit margin of the order
- The other two requirements will be retained for consideration in future enhancements to this system.

Further considerations include:

- This design example has missed identifying the need for a title on this page. A title, **attribute,** should be added to the **general sales order content section.**
- This design example has identified a number of "graphics" without specifying their appearance. These graphics can be implemented in a number of ways, including:
  - Being just an area around another object that the user can select and activate
  - Being button-shaped objects containing words
  - Being icons, which convey all their meaning via pictures

There are many ways that these sections could be combined into a suitable layout.

- The easiest, though not necessarily the best, is as a number of sections vertically below one another in the order discussed above.
- There are many possible two-dimensional layouts.
- Some designs may choose to open and close windows on individual sections while leaving certain "important" objects visible at all times within the two-dimensional space of a typical browser window.

This example will leave it up to the reader to decide which layout you would prefer to use given the guidance available above and via other sources.

Find and experience various design possibilities for this example in the Chapter 11 Cyber Supplement.

 ### 11.7.2   Considering Some Scenarios

There is an infinite number of possible scenarios that could be performed using *Savor the Cup's* sales order. Consideration of the tasks associated with this order form can help to identify the major scenarios.

The following factors can be combined in a number of different ways to identify different scenarios of customers/sales representatives using it to **place an order:**

- Whether or not the order is based on a copy of a previous order
- Whether or not there is existing information on the customer
  - If there is, whether or not any of it should be changed for this order or permanently
  - If there isn't, whether or not the customer wants to save this for future use
- Whether or not the customer knows **each** of the specific products he or she wants or only has a general idea
  - For those known products, whether or not the customer knows the product number of each of the desired products
  - For those products with known product numbers, whether or not the customer is willing to pay the prices that appear on the order
  - For those products with unknown product numbers, how the user uses the system to find the appropriate product can vary
  - For those unknown products, how the user decides on the products to order can vary

While it would be impossible to consider each of the possible scenarios generated from these factors, it is desirable that each of these factors be explored in at least one scenario. Selected scenarios and prototypes to evaluate the design can be developed similar to the example presented in Table 11-3.

It is easier to consider different scenarios of customers/sales representatives using it to **modify an order:**

- The order has to be found by an authorized user
- Each attribute (that needs to be modified) needs to be identified
- **Each** attribute (to be modified) can be:
  - Changed
  - Added
  - Deleted
- The changed sales order needs to be submitted

Accounting needs to be able to access all submitted versions of an order along with records of who made changes when. This would involve another tool to assist in accessing these records. This tool could be implemented as one or more additional controls for navigating between records. While these controls might only be available to accounting users, further analysis should be conducted to see if they could also be of use to other users.

Other parts of *Savor the Cup* could likewise use the sales order design to access specific orders identified in tools designed to serve their needs. In each of these cases, further design is necessary before scenarios of their uses can be considered.

11.8   CHALLENGES AND OPPORTUNITIES IN APPLYING DETAILED DESIGN

The following are some of the many problems encountered with detailed design.

Challenges with Media
- Some designs make use of inappropriate media and distract users with unnecessary "bells and whistles."
- Some designs make use of very sophisticated media that require "helper applications" that typical Web browsers may not have installed on their computers. Rather than loading and installing these helper applications, users may try to use the Web pages without these media.
- Some designs make use of annoying blinking graphics.
- Some controls may not be obvious to the users and may appear just as content.
- Combining controls with content may cause users to accidentally activate the control while attempting to change the content, whether or not that is the intended action of the control.

Challenges with Layout
- Some designs do not consider that different users may access Web pages with different size browser windows.
- Some designs use excessively wide, fixed-width Web pages, which require most users to do considerable scrolling in two dimensions.
- To compensate for potentially small browser windows, some designs put all or most media objects on the left, requiring users to scroll down to get to other components that could have been laid out on unused space above.
- Some designs are too crowded. Visual objects require sufficient visual separation for ease of recognition and discrimination.

Challenges with Content Design
- Some designs do not provide user guide that would be necessary to help users make proper use of the design.
- Some designs use inappropriate language, despite warnings to say "user requests to save data" rather than "person clicks button."

Challenges with Scenarios
- Some scenarios just consider the user's actions and ignore actions by the computer.

- Some scenarios just consider overall variations rather than identifying step-by-step variations that resulted from particular actions.
- Some organization-wide scenarios fail to consider how different individual users in the scenario interact with each other.
- Some scenarios don't consider major decisions or other processing actions that needed to occur.
- Some designs require too many different presentation segments to accomplish a scenario.
- Some scenarios may be too long and should be separated into multiple scenarios.
- Some important scenarios may be missed.

11.9 CYBER SUPPLEMENTS FOR CHAPTER 11

 Look at the Chapter 11 Cyber Supplements on the Web to find:

- Additional information about media selection and combination

- Additional information about designing for accessibility

- Additional information about dialog design

- Additional information about designing e-Commerce systems to promote the success of their users

- Examples of various design possibilities for *Savor the Cup's* sales order processing

- Practice activities dealing with the detailed design of e-Commerce systems

REFERENCES

[1] S. Stanners, "Usability of ISO 9241, Part 14, Menu Dialogues" (Boca Raton, FL, Office Ergonomics Center Technical Report, IBM PC Company, 1993).

[2] "International Organization for Standardization," ISO International Standard 9241-10, Ergonomic Requirements for Office Work with Visual Display Terminals (VDTs): Dialogue Principles, 1996.

[3] Ibid.

[4] "International Organization for Standardization," ISO International Standard 9241-12, Ergonomic Requirements for Office Work with Visual Display Terminals (VDTs): Presentation of Information, 1998.

[5] "International Organization for Standardization," ISO Committee Draft 14915-2, Software Ergonomics for Multimedia User Interfaces: Multimedia Control and Navigation, 2000.

[6] "International Organization for Standardization," ISO Draft International Standard 14915-3, Software Ergonomics for Multimedia User Interfaces: Media Selection and Combination, 2000.

[7] Ibid.

[8] Ibid.

[9] "International Organization for Standardization," ISO Draft Technical Specification 16071, Ergonomics of Human System Interaction—Guidance on Accessibility for Human-Computer Interfaces, 2000.

[10] K. Mullet and D. Sano, *Designing Visual Interfaces* (Englewood Cliffs, NJ, Prentice Hall, 1995).

[11] Ibid.

[12] Ibid.

[13] Ibid.

[14] Ibid.

[15] W. Horton, *The Icon Book* (New York: John Wiley & Sons, 1994).

[16] "International Organization for Standardization," ISO Final Draft International Standard 9241-1:1997/FDAM1 Ergonomic Requirements for Office Work with Visual Display Terminals (VDTs): General introduction Amendment, 2000.

[17] "International Organization for Standardization," ISO International Standard 9241-14, Ergonomic Requirements for Office Work with Visual Display Terminals (VDTs): Menu Dialogues, 1997.

[18] "International Organization for Standardization," ISO International Standard 9241-15, Ergonomic Requirements for Office Work with Visual Display Terminals (VDTs): Command Dialogues, 1997.

[19] "International Organization for Standardization," ISO International Standard 9241-16, Ergonomic Requirements for Office Work with Visual Display Terminals (VDTs): Direct Manipulation Dialogues, 1999.

[20] "International Organization for Standardization," ISO International Standard 9241-17, Ergonomic Requirements for Office Work with Visual Display Terminals (VDTs): Form Fill Dialogues, 1998.

[21] Ibid.

[22] "International Organization for Standardization," ISO International Standard 9241-13, Ergonomic Requirements for Office Work with Visual Display Terminals (VDTs): User Guidance, 1998.

Technical Design and Construction

Outline

12.1   INTRODUCTION TO TECHNICAL DESIGN AND CONSTRUCTION

While the concepts introduced in this chapter are essential to the development of e-Commerce systems, they require far deeper coverage than can be provided in this text or even in a single text on its own. People typically require a complete program in computer science to achieve a sufficient level of understanding and experience in order to be able to apply them successfully.

NOTE: People wishing to develop e-Commerce systems who do not have sufficient technical skills are strongly advised to have the technical design and construction performed by qualified and experienced e-Commerce development professionals.

This chapter introduces these concepts in order to provide the reader with an overview of the range of technical issues that must be addressed to successfully develop an e-Commerce system. It does so, however, without the usual depth of coverage found in other chapters of this book.

12.2   A CLIENT SERVER MODEL OF E-COMMERCE

e-Commerce applications are generally performed by a number of interconnected computers, which work together based on the client server model of distributed computing. In this model:

- A **server** is a system that provides services to a number of client systems. An **e-Commerce server** is a system that is used by organizations to make e-Commerce services available to a number of clients.
- A **client** is a system that is used directly by users to accomplish some application. An **e-Commerce client** is a system that is used to conduct e-Commerce for a user with one or more e-Commerce servers.
- Clients are connected to servers via the Internet. This may be done via a permanent connection, via a dial-up connection, or via a wireless connection.
- A computer system may perform both as a server and as a client to other servers.
- The software used by a server or a client involves multiple components that must work together.

12.2.1   Platform Considerations

A **platform** is some combination of hardware and software that is used to allow the running of an application program. **Platform dependencies** result from differences in the operation or lack thereof of an application program that are caused by attempting to run it on different platforms.

- If users cannot run an e-Commerce system on the platform available to them, they may find it easier to deal with a competitor rather than to acquire a new platform.

- If users experience differences in the use of the e-Commerce system when moving between platforms, they may make mistakes and/or find it easier to deal with a competitor.

Platform independence is created when the user does not experience differences that may exist due to platform dependencies. Separate versions of e-Commerce software, developed to run on different platforms, should minimize platform dependencies experienced by the user. The Web can help minimize the effects of platform dependencies on users by helping software to recognize the particular platform that is being used by a client and allowing the server to send the appropriate version of its Web pages and associated software to that client.

The use of standard operating systems helps limit (or at least shift) the effects of differences in computer hardware. The main hardware dependency affecting an e-Commerce system is the difference in general components and their capabilities between different hardware systems that will be used as clients.

There are an increasing variety of operating systems that provide software platforms for running e-Commerce application programs for servers and clients. Operating systems used as platforms for e-Commerce include:

- Windows
- Macintosh OS
- Unix
- Linux
- A variety of specialized operating systems that are used for mobile and handheld computing

There are a number of variations of most of these operating systems. For example, varieties of the Windows operating system include: Windows 3.0, Windows 95, Windows 98, Windows ME, (which are all similar with increasing levels of functionality) and Windows NT (which is substantially different from a technical perspective).

The World Wide Web is based on a number of standards that are intended to help users to avoid problems caused by platform dependence. It accomplishes this by handling platform dependencies within various platform dependent versions of standard Internet client programs. An **Internet client program** is one that provides general Internet accessing capabilities to support the running of client programs that interact across the Internet with one or more server programs. Web browsers were the first type of Internet client programs to provide users with platform independence. Despite the goal of platform independence, major problems in accessibility still remain.

- For a Web-based application to be platform independent, a version of the Web browser must exist for each specific platform. Currently, the main Web browsers have versions for each of the main platforms. However, there are often slight differences between each of the versions of a given browser.
- The two most widely used Web browsers (Netscape and Internet Explorer) have a slightly different set of Web features that they support and are likely to continue to support slightly different Web features in an attempt to be unique. This has led to two slightly different platforms for Web-based programs.
- Some e-Commerce applications, such as Real Player, are now being developed as Internet clients that operate on their own without the assistance of a Web

browser. For a user to be able to use such a system there needs to be a version that will run on the user's operating system.

- The introduction of new hardware, such as handheld mobile devices, has introduced new differences, including smaller display areas, which provide new platform dependencies. These platform dependencies are reflected in the operating systems and Internet clients that are run on these types of hardware.

Although platform independence is a useful goal, it is not likely to be fully achieved given the evolutionary trends in the computing industry. With the increasing number of platforms, it is becoming increasingly difficult to develop e-Commerce systems that will be platform independent. A decision has to be made about which platforms need to be targeted for development. Factors that may be taken into account include:

- The traditional platform(s) used by the organization
- The traditional platform(s) used by the majority of proposed external users
- The trade-off between cost and universality
- The desire to be backward compatible (to run on old systems)
- The desire to include the latest features (which may only be supported on a limited range of current platforms)
- The features and costs of any new systems being purchased to be used with the software

Decisions need to be made to determine which platforms must be capable of running the e-Commerce software being developed. It is generally reasonable to expect that the software should run on client systems that are two years old. Platforms may differ based on:

- The computer hardware used
  - Not everyone has the latest or most powerful hardware
  - Unless other criteria have been established, a **default** is to expect that the software should run on computers that would have been considered to be "average" in terms of their capabilities two years before now
- The operating system used
  - Unless other criteria have been established, a **default** is to expect that the software should run on versions of the main operating systems that were available two years before now
- The browser or other Internet client used
  - Unless other criteria have been established, a **default** is to expect that the software should run on versions of the main browsers and Internet clients that were available two years before now

Once software is constructed, it then should be tested on each of the intended platforms to ensure that it meets its platform independent goals.

12.2.2   e-Commerce Clients

The software involved in an e-Commerce client system is illustrated in Figure 12-1. In most cases, the user has a choice of operating systems and may be running a number of other programs, besides one or more Internet client programs that are used to

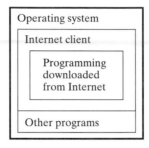

Figure 12-1 The typical software architecture and environment of an Internet client

perform e-Commerce. Web browsers and most other Internet client programs download additional programming (such as Web pages) that allow them to perform a variety of applications.

The programming involved in a Web page or other downloaded program is generally developed to be as platform independent as possible. The World Wide Web consortium (W3C) was established to promote the ongoing development of other standards related to supporting platform independence on the Web. Client side programs consist of Web pages that make use of markup languages and applets.

Markup languages are composed of various tags that are used to identify treatments that an Internet client is intended to perform on selected portions of a Web page. A **tag** is a unique sequence of characters that is placed at the beginning and end of a selected portion of a Web page that is used to specify a particular treatment it is intended to receive. Markup languages allow client systems to present content to and receive content from users in a platform-independent manner. Markup languages also facilitate the loading and running of **applets,** which are small application programs downloaded from a server and run by a client.

The HyperText Markup Language (HTML) is the original markup language that made the Web possible. HTML provides platform independence, as long as the Internet client is willing to, and capable of, interpreting the HTML in a platform-independent manner as defined in the current HTML standard. The current standard for HTML[1] is located at: *www.w3.org/MarkUp.* The standard for HTML is constantly evolving, thus different versions of Internet clients may be using different versions of HTML. HTML is designed so that browsers or Internet clients will process all the HTML features that they are capable of handling and will ignore any features that they do not support.

Developers of competing Web browsers and other Internet client programs often provide extensions to the current version of HTML in order to provide their products with a competitive advantage. If these extensions are incorporated within an e-Commerce system, they may introduce platform dependencies, which will encourage the use of the particular browser or Internet client in order to be able to use the system fully. New versions of the HTML standard have typically evolved to include some of the more popular extensions first introduced by various browsers, while rejecting others, which were not found to be compatible with the objectives of HTML.

Some programming developed in HTML provides difficulties when implemented on "small information appliances" such as handheld computers. To meet the need of providing a markup language with greater platform independence, W3C developed XHTML, the intent of which is "to provide an XHTML document type that can be shared across communities (e.g., desktop, TV, and mobile phones), and that is rich enough to be used for simple content authoring." The current standard for XHTML[2] is located at: *www.w3.org/TR/xhtml-basic.*

Extensible Markup Language(XML), also developed by W3C, provides additional capabilities that can be combined with HTML to provide greater programming power in client applications. The current standard for XML[3] is located at: *www.w3.org/XML. XML* Base is version of XML intended to support a wide range of computing devices. The current standard for XML Base[4] is located at: *www.w3.org/XML.*

Scripting languages, such as Visual Basic Script (VBScript) and Java Script (JScript), provide advanced programming capabilities for applets that are downloaded to and run in client systems. Some uses of applets include:

- Preprocessing/validating information in the client before submitting it to a server
- Providing interactive functionality for the client without the need for ongoing access to the server
- Accessing functions within the Internet client program

12.2.3   e-Commerce Servers

The software involved in an e-Commerce server system is illustrated in Figure 12-2. An organization can choose the platform that best serves its needs for its e-Commerce Web server independent from the platforms used by the client servers that various users use to access it. An optimal of flexibility is achieved by separating various components.

- The use of separate interfaces allows new interfaces to be built quickly to serve the needs of interfacing the e-Commerce application with different types of client systems.
- In addition to facilitating the development of new interfaces, separating the logic from the interface, it is possible to integrate existing legacy system logic without needing to completely redevelop it.
- Separating the content from the application logic by placing it in a database makes it easier to modify content without having to also modify the interfaces and/or the processing logic. The use of separate databases also facilitates the integration of e-Commerce data with other organizational systems.

There is a variety of programming languages and server systems available to assist in the development of e-Commerce servers.

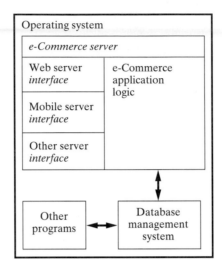

Figure 12-2   The typical software architecture and environment of an e-Commerce server

   Find references to further sources of information about client server models of e-Commerce applications in the Chapter 12 Cyber Supplement.

12.3   UNDERSTANDING TECHNICAL DESIGN

Technical design focuses on designing how to program or how to acquire e-Commerce and related software to create an e-Commerce system. Because of its combination of internal and technical natures, users are seldom consulted about most technical design issues and are seldom able to verify that it has been conducted correctly. However, this does not mean that users should not and cannot provide meaningful input into and expect meaningful output out of this process. Where user involvement is precluded, the design may:

- Contain errors based on developer assumptions
- Fail to deal with some existing situations
- Be difficult to modify in the future to accommodate additional needs

Technical design should proceed from a detailed design of the basic objects required by the system. When developers go directly from high-level design to technical design, errors of omission and commission are likely to occur. Various software objects are responsible for:

- Interactions with users
- Handling communications with clients
- Processing application logic
- Saving data in the organizational database

Technical design should include:

- Designing how each medium and other object is to be implemented
- Designing computer processing (including input edits)
- Designing a well-organized database or set of databases
- Designing data communications

12.3.1   Designing the Implementation of Media and Other Objects

Designing media objects needs to go beyond user interface concerns (as identified in Chapter 11, Detailed Design) to consider how each of these objects can be fully implemented. In designing media objects, it is useful to consider the various recommendations of applicable international standards, including:

ISO 9241-12 Presentation of Information
ISO 9241-13 User Guidance
ISO 9241-14 Menu Dialogues
ISO 9241-15 Command Dialogues
ISO 9241-16 Direct Manipulation Dialogues
ISO 9241-17 Form Fill Dialogues
ISO 11581-1 Icons—General
ISO 11581-2 Object Icons
ISO 11581-2 Pointer Icons
ISO 11581-4 Control Icons
ISO 11581-5 Tool Icons
ISO 11581-6 Action Icons
ISO 14915-2 Multimedia Navigation and Controls
ISO 14915-3 Media Selection and Combination

Technical design needs to go into sufficient detail so that there are no remaining questions about the programming required to fully implement each object. This design should specify how:

- To achieve the agreed-upon "look and feel" with particular types of media objects
- Components of the design (media objects) interact with
  - Each other
  - Other objects in the system
  - The user

Different types of media objects can use different approaches to achieve a "look and feel."

- Some media objects (such as fixed text that is presented on a display) can be easily implemented directly via simple HTML code.
- Some media objects (such as text that is obtained from a database and that then is presented on a display) require interfacing with other software (such as database systems).
- Some media objects (such as movies) require the use of sophisticated software to be installed in the Internet client in order to handle their presentation to the user.

Media objects typically are responsible for handling only input-related and output-related processing involving interactions with users:

- Input processing involves validating input requests and then sending these requests to other programming objects (internal to the system) for further processing
- Output processing involves receiving output requests from other programming objects (including objects internal to the system), formatting the contents of the request, and outputting the formatted content to the user

 Find references to further sources of information about e-Commerce uses of different types of media in the Chapter 12 Cyber Supplement.

12.3.2   Designing Computer Processing

Computer processing design involves identifying all the objects (whether media objects or internal objects) that need to be programmed and describing them in sufficient detail so that this design can be directly translated into program code, either by a programmer or by a CASE tool.

Technical design needs to go beyond just identifying approaches that can be used to specify a particular approach to be used. Designers need to specify basic requirements for programming to ensure that the code for each object is developed in an object-oriented manner that will facilitate future modifications to the system. The programming interfaces to each object in the system are designed to accommodate the set of allowable interactions between objects.

Each programming language may have different capabilities and features that need to be understood in designing a set of objects for an application. Regardless of the programming language chosen, care should be taken that the design of all objects supports the future evolution of e-Commerce systems.

There are three main processes within the design of computer processing:

- **Hierarchical decomposition.** This involves various strategies to divide and further subdivide complex operations to the level of very simple processing routines, each of which performs only a single procedure or function. The results of hierarchical decomposition are often illustrated using a structure chart. While some development approaches have suggested additions to structure charts to take them beyond illustrating just the hierarchical decomposition, attempts to use them for multiple purposes can lead to considerable confusion.

- **Control flow design.** This involves designing the decision logic that leads from one operation or processing routine to another. There are a number of different diagrams that can be used in the design of control flow, each with their own emphasis.
  - A **decision tree** (which looks like a structure chart turned on its side) can illustrate the different possible results from different sets of answers to a series of questions or decision points. Decision trees can help to ensure that all possible combinations of a set of decisions have been considered and that they have been included in the design.
  - A **state transition diagram** can illustrate the various potential outcomes of an event or sequence of events where the outcomes of an event are dependent on the state in which the event occurs. These outcomes include changes to the system and actions by the system in response to various combinations of inputs. **States** exist where different combinations of attributes can lead the same input to be processed in different manners.
- **Processing routine logic design.** This involves the actual design of the routines that will perform the processing. This detailed logic is often described in "structured English," which is also known as "pseudocode." Structured English reads like English but is structured for easy translation into real programming code.

Object-oriented methods make use of generalization and inheritance in order to develop routines that can be reusable software components. In object-oriented terms, there are two different types of simple routines into which all operations should be decomposed:

- A **procedure** changes data value(s) in some data structure as the result of its processing
- A **function** acts as a data value as the result of its processing

NOTE: It is possible to design and code programs without such detailed decomposition. However, failure to go to such detail will make it much more difficult and costly to make future modifications (which should be expected in e-Commerce systems).

12.3.3 Database Design

Each object has its own set of attributes, many of which must be stored in the system. A well-organized database management system (DBMS) is essential to e-Commerce systems. The DBMS will store records of all transactions conducted via the system and make these records available when and where they are required.

12.3.3.1 Accessing Records

Records can be stored either in some sequential order or randomly. How they are stored is less important to most users than how they can be accessed. Records can be accessed in a number of ways, including:

- Sequentially, where the first record in a group is accessed, and then the next, and so on. Sequential access can be used where either:
  - All records need to be accessed and the order of their access doesn't matter
  - All records need to be accessed and they are stored in the order in which they are needed

- Directly, where a unique "record key" is used to find a particular record
- In a logical group, where various criteria are used to search for (and group) all records whose attributes match these criteria

There may be a number of different types of needs of accessing the same information within a given application. Database design needs to identify the best way of meeting these potentially conflicting needs.

12.3.3.2 Database Objectives

Databases should meet the following objectives:

- **Data integrity,** which involves ensuring the correctness, protection, and security of a piece of data or of a database.
- **Data sharability,** which involves the ability to share data between applications and between users on a need-to-know basis.
- **Data availability,** which involves the ability to access data when it is needed by a user or by a system.
- **Database evolvability,** which involves the potential to make changes to the database to meet changing needs.
- Avoiding **redundancy,** which occurs where multiple copies of a set of data can lead to incompatibilities when updates are made to only some of these copies.

Relational database technology has been developed which can help meet these objectives. While relational database management systems make the construction and use of simple databases relatively easy, there is considerable technical expertise required to design more complicated databases.

12.3.3.3 Attributes

Attributes provide the building blocks for records, files (sets of records), and databases. While many attributes come from our analysis and design of our objects, additional attributes may need to be added to assist with the technical implementation of our application.

Attributes can be distinguished as to whether they:

- Are part of a record key
- Describe the object
- Help the system to manage the records

Key attributes are attributes that can be used individually or in combination to provide a unique record key that can be used to identify a record. Where a number of attributes are used together to act as a record key, they are each part of a composite record key.

Historically, numbers (such as customer numbers, social security/social insurance numbers, driver's license numbers, employee numbers, credit card numbers, and so on) have been assigned as unique identifiers of people by various organizations in order to avoid the possibility of two people's common identifier (their name) being the same.

Meaningful values of key attributes are often preferable to the use of arbitrary identification numbers. Combinations of attributes (such as a person's name and address or name and phone number) may work well in many cases. While it is recognized that two people with the same first and last name may live at the same address, these two attributes may be sufficient for the needs of most systems. Where further information is needed to distinguish between a parent and a child, then adding the date of birth generally is sufficient. Few systems need to worry about what to do with twins with the same name living at the same address.

Care needs to be taken with using meaningful attributes based on personal information to avoid designs that violate the privacy of people whose records are stored in the system. For example:

- If I entered my name "Jim Carter" into a system that had multiple Jim Carter's in it, it would be a violation of the privacy of the other Jim Carter if the system asked me to choose which "Jim Carter" I was by presenting the addresses of each "Jim Carter" it knows.
- If an individual with a very unusual name finds out that a system has more than one person with that name, it might be very easy to figure out who the other person is even without further information.

Many e-Commerce systems have taken the approach of allowing customers (and other users) to select their own unique identification key (user name) rather than to assign them automatically. Users can choose any identification key they want as long as another user has not chosen it. In this way they can control their privacy while still having a key that is meaningful to them.

The purpose of most attributes is just to describe the various properties of an object. **Descriptive attributes** are attributes that contain the object content, which is relevant to the application. Where key attributes contained information that had uses beyond just identifying a given record or user, those attributes can be considered both key and descriptive attributes. The design of descriptive attributes should consider:

- The design of how the attributes will be input and output
- The range of possible values of the attributes
- The potential need for reformatting the attributes to handle different needs for their input, output, processing, and storage

Developers create a variety of attributes for internal uses. The users may never see or recognize these attributes. These attributes help the developer to construct a robust system that works effectively for the user. Norman[5] identifies three different types of these developer-added attributes:

Audit attributes are attributes that are automatically added to a record to provide an audit trail of interactions with the record. They may include names, dates, and other summary information relating to the creating, modifying, and/or accessing of a record. Where large amounts of audit data are required, it may require the use of separate records that are linked to the record it is auditing. Examples of audit attributes include:

- Systems can be made to record the time/date when a piece of information was changed and even the user's identity of the person who made the change
- Web sites often record the "Number of visitors" they have had

Care needs to be taken in the design of audit attributes to ensure that they provide valid audit information. For example, even if a "Number of visitors" counter is properly implemented, it doesn't account for multiple visits by the same person. Individuals can easily access a Web site multiple times just to increase such a counter.

Control attributes are attributes that are used to store the current state of processing of a record or the current ability to perform certain types of processing to the record. Examples of control attributes are found in most word processors, which remember whether or not you have saved a document since the last change made to it or whether you have made changes since you last saved it.

- If a document was saved since the last change, you can "SAVE AS," but you don't need to "SAVE."
- If a document was changed since the last save, you need to "SAVE."
- If you choose to quit before performing a SAVE, the system should ask you if you want to SAVE before EXITing.

Security attributes are a particular type of control attribute used to control access to the record. An example of the use of a security attribute is that passwords may be used to protect chunks of data.

12.3.3.4   Records Storage Within Databases

Attributes are arranged into records, files, and databases. A **record** is some collection of attributes that describes some entity or event. The concept of a record is based on the various paper documents that provide a basis for various types of business records. Business records are generally identified as content in a requirements analysis. In order to use records effectively within a computerized database, "computer records" need to be developed to facilitate processing rather than just as the electronic storage of traditional paper records.

Records are often distinguished based on the permanence or transience of their importance.

- Records describing an entity that may be permanently relevant through a considerable portion of the life of a system (such as a customer record or a product record) are often referred to as **master records.** While the value of different attributes in a master record may change, the record is likely to be kept in the system.
- Records describing an event in the life of one or more entities (such as a sales record or a payment record) that are most relevant to users of a system only during a short period of time are often referred to as **transaction records.** While these records may need to be retained in some form to meet legal retention requirements, they are unlikely to be actually referred to after a short time (such as a day, week, or month) from their creation.

A **file** is a collection of similar records that may be used individually or together. The concept of a file is based on file folders that are dedicated to storing records of a single type (such as only customer records or only sales slips). There are two main purposes of files from a user's point of view:

- **Master files** generally store the most important and most general data about objects. Master files often contain records that are relevant throughout the life of a system. Records in a master file generally use the name of an object and/or an object's identification code as a record key.

- **Secondary files** generally store data that relate to one or more master records. These data may involve optional or multiple descriptions about an object, information about events the object participated in, and/or relationships between objects. Records in a secondary file generally use additional information about the record in addition to the name of an object and/or an object's identification code as a composite record key. Records in a secondary file usually require corresponding records in a master file.

Computer files generally store records sharing a single format in a file structure that best serves the various needs of accessing these records. Some computer files (often referred to as **index files**) exist to assist in accessing records in one file that have some relationship with records in another file.

A **database** is a collection of files used to support one or more applications. Computerized databases differ from sets of file cabinets in that they can support the easy access of records that are related to one another in a variety of ways (rather than being limited to sequential, physical access).

Normalization is a technique for designing an optimal structure of internal data files and records to meet the processing needs of an application. It generally involves the logical restructuring of records into efficient sets of records that are flexible enough to meet both current and future input and processing requirements. Normalization is based on two main principles:

- Simplicity
  - Sets of simple records can be combined in different ways to meet different needs
  - There should only be a single record key, which can be a compound key, within each record. Where alternate references or keys are to be used, these should be contained in different records that refer to this record.
  - There should be no repeating groups of data within a record. Where repeating groups of records occur, they should be in separate, secondary records.
- Avoiding redundancy
  - Data stored in descriptive attributes should only occur once within a database. Data should be referenced from (rather than duplicated in) other locations where they may be relevant
  - Data should be stored in a single format that can be converted for various uses rather than stored in multiple descriptive attributes, the values of which could conflict with each other

Normalization is a multistep process for the logical transformation of data structures to an idealized design for implementing relational databases. The first three steps are the most important and are what we will consider.

In order to illustrate the process of normalization, consider the example of an existing Textbook Order form. Examination of such a form results in identifying the following attributes, where key attributes are presented in italics:

- *Class identification* (e.g., "CMPT 275 Section 01 Fall 1999") made up of
  - *Class code*
  - *Section number*

- *Term*
- *Year*
- Order date (in year, month, day format)
- Multiple lines for each book, each consisting of:
  - ISBN (International Standard Book Number—a unique book identifier)
  - Title
  - Author
  - Quantity
  - Price
- Total value of the order

NOTES:

- The order form does not have an order number because the class identification (which acts as a composite record key) is sufficient to identify an order.
- This composite key will be referred to as class identification unless there is a need to deal with its various parts separately.
- If there could be multiple orders for a single class section, the order date could also be used as part of the composite record key.

First (1st) Normal Form eliminates repeating groups within a record by placing them in separate records with composite record keys that include the record key of the original record. In this example, the textbook order record will be divided into two records (each record will be given a descriptive name that will be in all capital letters). The initial record can be transformed into 1st normal form:

ORDER–CLASS	Will be composed of the attributes (class identification, order date, total value of order)
ORDER–BOOK	Will be composed of (class identification, ISBN, title, author, quantity, price)

Second (2nd) Normal Form separates data that is fully functionally dependent on a record key from additional data that may depend on only part of the record key. In this example, ORDER–BOOK contains some data related to the order and some data that are related only to the book being ordered. The 1st normal records can be transformed into the following 2nd normal form:

ORDER–CLASS	Will be composed of the attributes (class identification, order date, total value of order)
ORDER–BOOK	Will be composed of (class identification, ISBN, quantity)
BOOK	Will be composed of (ISBN, title, author, price)

Third (3rd) Normal Form removes (redundant) nonkey attributes, which are based on other nonkey attributes. In this example, the total value of order can be calculated by multiplying the quantity by the price of each of the books ordered. The 2nd normal records can be simplified into the following 3rd normal form:

ORDER–CLASS	Will be composed of the attributes (class identification, order date)
ORDER–BOOK	Will be composed of (class identification, ISBN, quantity)
BOOK	Will be composed of (ISBN, title, author, price)

Textbook orders in the database should be structured into these three files rather than a single file based on the physical order form.

12.3.4   Communication Design

The advent of the World Wide Web and its increasing importance, have helped to standardize basic forms of data communications. Communications design involves selecting the hardware devices, communications software, and communications services to use to support an e-Commerce system.

An e-Commerce system may physically involve a number of individual hardware servers and communication services. A **hardware server** is an individual hardware device that performs a specific function or a set of functions within a client-server environment. Both client systems and server systems may be composed of a number of hardware servers. Hardware devices may fulfill the role of one or more of the following types of serving:

- A **file server** provides storage of, and access to, central databases and program files for one or more computers to which it is attached either directly or via a network.
- A **print server** provides printing for one or more computers to which it is attached either directly or via a network.
- A **processing server** runs one or more application programs for one or more terminal servers to which it is attached either directly or via a network.
- A **terminal server** provides a physical system with which a user interacts directly via a variety of input and output devices such as displays, keyboards, mice, etc. Terminal servers can include personal computers, laptop computers, mobile computers, and a variety of other computing devices.
- A **communication server** provides a gateway between various networks of computers.

Distinct types of servers are often used for implementing major organizational systems, such as e-Commerce server systems and e-Commerce clients that are used in organization-to-organization e-Commerce. It is common for an individual user to use a personal computer with an attached printer to fulfill all the needs of an e-Commerce client system.

Clients and servers can be connected together via different types of physical and logical networks. The two main types of physical networks are local area networks and wide area networks. The two main types of logical networks, in addition to the standard Internet, are intranets and extranets.

A **local area network (LAN)** can be used to connect hardware servers within a corporate building or a campus of closely related buildings. Most local area networks are implemented via dedicated wiring between devices. It is possible to implement part or all of a local area network via wireless technology; however, that may introduce additional security risks. A local area network requires the use of a communications server to connect it with external computers and/or networks.

A **wide area network (WAN)** connects systems and or local area networks with each other over any distance. The Internet, which is the most famous wide area network, has the advantage of being readily available in most locations around the world and therefore being available to most potential users. However, it has the disadvantage of its public availability, making it an insecure means of communicating. This requires that e-Commerce applications provide their own security, where necessary. Organizations may use dedicated communication lines to obtain a higher level of security as the basis of their own wide area network.

An **intranet** (an internal portion of the Internet) is a local area network that is designed for the exclusive use by its members and that is connected to the Internet via a firewall.

A **firewall** is a system that is used as a separate part of a network, which is within the firewall, (such as a local area network or an individual computer) from the remainder of the network, which is outside the firewall. A firewall can control who has access to systems on the other side of the firewall and what requests and data can be sent across the firewall.

An **extranet** (an extended intranet) makes use of encryption and similar security techniques to act similar to an intranet for members who have to communicate with each other over the Internet.

In addition to programming interfaces to accommodate different types of clients, additional communication software may need to be developed to provide firewalls, encryption, and other security for various e-Commerce interactions, as identified above. It should be noted that the needs of and the technologies for Internet security are continually evolving just as the expectations of and technologies of e-Commerce are evolving. Providing and maintaining security needs to be an ongoing activity of organizations with e-Commerce systems. Assessing security needs and developing suitable security designs requires expert knowledge in the field of computer security. Many organizations may choose to hire specialist consultants to assist them in this area.

While there are a wide variety of communication services available to be used with e-Commerce, the two main design considerations involve connecting the e-Commerce server to the Internet and ensuring that the e-Commerce system will operate properly over the range of communication services that various users may choose to use.

An e-Commerce server needs to be connected to the Internet via a connection with sufficient speed and capacity to handle its anticipated communications load. Very popular Web sites may require multiple servers and/or multiple connections to handle their communications load. The design of communications needs to consider providing:

- Sufficient server capacity to meet normal and peak demands
- Sufficient communication capacity to meet normal and peak demands
- Suitable connection capacity to meet normal and peak loads
- Security and user authentication to protect the system and its individual users

Once e-Commerce systems have been developed, they need to be made available on the Internet. This involves more than just acquiring a physical connection to the Internet. Users need to be able to readily find and communicate with an e-Commerce server.

Users access an e-Commerce server via a unique domain name (such as *SavorTheCup.com*). A **domain name** is a logical name that is used on the Internet to identify a computer. Once an organization chooses a suitable domain name for an e-Commerce site, it needs to register it with the appropriate Internet registration authority (such as Network Solutions for .com names). Each domain has its own registration authority. If an organization wishes to have one or more national domain names (such as: *SavorTheCup.ca* for Canada, *SavorTheCup.uk* for the United Kingdom, *SavorTheCup.fr* for France, *SavorTheCup.de* for Germany,) each name will have to be registered with the appropriate registration authority. It may be useful to register a number of similar domain names in order to prevent the competition from registering them and using them to divert users from an organization's site. Multiple Web sites (such as for the various national domains) can be hosted on the same Web server. Each additional site can contain a single page that can be used to send potential users to the organization's main site.

Registering only gives an organization permission to use a domain name. The Internet still needs to be able to use the domain name to provide users with access to the computer that is to host it. Domain names are logical names that are easy for users to remember. However, the Internet uses an actual system of addresses that are easier for computers to handle. Although the Internet is a true network, which may have multiple connections between the computers it connects, it uses a hierarchical addressing technique to identify the individual computers it connects. This addressing technique ensures that each computer has a unique identity, so that messages transferred over the Internet arrive at their intended destination regardless of the path they take. The unique address used internally by the Internet to identify computers that are connected to it is referred to as an **Internet protocol (IP) address.**

An **Internet service provider (ISP)** is an organization that possess IP addresses and rents them along with Internet connection services to individuals and organizations that wish to connect to the Internet. IP addresses can either be fixed or dynamically allocated by an ISP. Fixed IP addresses cost more but are important in ensuring accessibility to an e-Commerce site.

To assist in message transfer between computers, the Internet contains a network of domain name servers. A **domain name server (DNS)** is a special system on the Internet that provides cross-referencing between logical (domain name) Internet addresses and physical (Internet Protocol/IP) Internet addresses. At least two Domain Name Server (DNS) hostcomputers (each with their own fixed IP address) need to make the linkage between a logical domain name and the fixed IP address of a Web server. If sites for multiple domain names are contained on a single computer, each site requires its own two DNS host references.

Each of these steps has costs associated with them.

- Large organizations can accomplish everything in-house, except the actual registration, which must be processed by Network Solutions (whether you deal directly or through an organization that acts as a domain name registrar).
- Small organizations may wish to contract for all these services to be provided by a single Web services organization.
- Organizations should be wary of accepting free services, since they generally come at hidden cost. The most typical cost of "free services" (such as free DNS hosting) is the requirement to allow advertisements to be added to each of your Web pages. Web sites with such ads have very little credibility. This could lead to

having your competitor's ads over your pages. Free services should only be considered for Web sites that do not involve e-Commerce.

It is important to design to ensure operability of an e-Commerce application for users of various communications technologies. This involves identifying constraints that might be placed on them via slow speed, dial-up, and/or wireless communications and then either designing the regular e-Commerce interface(s) or designing an alternate interface version of the e-Commerce system to accommodate these constraints.

Find references to further sources of information about communication design for e-Commerce systems in the Chapter 12 Cyber Supplement.

12.4   UNDERSTANDING CONSTRUCTION

Construction refers to the actual processes of building software systems. While it is possible for most people to create small software systems, technically trained specialists primarily perform these processes for major systems (such as e-Commerce systems), often with little input from the intended users.

Regardless of who performs the construction, there are a variety of major technical decisions that should be decided by the users, since they will have to live with the results of these decisions. This section focuses on important construction decisions involving:

- Migrating and/or connecting to legacy systems
- Using programming languages
- Using computer-aided software engineering tools or tool sets
- Contracting for services that cannot efficiently be performed in-house

12.4.1   Migrating and/or Connecting to Legacy Systems

Many organizations have existing legacy systems that they wish to either migrate to the Web or to connect with modern e-Commerce systems. The client server model of e-Commerce, discussed earlier in this chapter, can provide a basis for migrating to or connecting with an e-Commerce system.

Prior to the development of the Web, **electronic data interchange (edi) systems** were developed by various organizations to handle what is now e-Commerce. Edi systems typically involve two components:

- A server program, which provides the main e-Commerce functionality
- A client program, which is used to interact via telecommunications with the server program

Migration of legacy edi systems involves:

- Allowing users on the Web to access the e-Commerce server without needing to have their own special program
- Modifying (or replacing) the server program to support Web access

Legacy server programs involve combinations of application processing and user interfacing functions. It is often desirable to keep well-established and well-tested application processing functions while replacing the user interfacing functions.

- A first attempt at migration could develop a separate program that provides a Web-based interface to users and that interfaces, in turn, with the user interface of the existing legacy system.
- Once the new user interface is proved to be acceptable, further steps may be taken to directly replace the user interface of the legacy system with the user interface from the e-Commerce system.
- Additional interfaces may then be developed, as required, to support alternate technologies.

When connecting with existing legacy systems, a key objective is the sharing of data between systems.

- The shared use of an organizational database can provide the first stage of connecting systems.
- Once data sharing is proved successful, further steps may be taken to introduce direct interactions between legacy system(s) and the e-Commerce system.

 Find references to further sources of information about migrating and/or connecting with legacy systems in the Chapter 12 Cyber Supplement.

12.4.2 Programming Languages

All programming languages are not created equal. Each was created with its own set of biases and its own sets of advantages and disadvantages.

- Developers often choose languages they are familiar with. However, the languages they are familiar with may not be the languages best suited to the system needing to be designed.
- Organizations often prefer the language that was used for their other systems, in the hope that its choice will provide compatibility between systems and to make it easier to maintain all the organization's programs. However, this approach has often led to the prolonged use of inefficient languages.
- New technology, such as the latest advances in the Web, may only be fully supported by a relatively small number of (high-level) languages.

The selection of programming language(s) to be used for construction should take into account:

- The nature of the system being built
- The potential for future upgrades to the system
- The skills of the developers
- The ability to reuse portions of existing systems

This decision may include dividing the system construction into parts that can best be constructed using different languages.

- HTML and Java are popular for programming Web software that is intended to run on the client's server.
- A larger variety of languages (including PHP3, JavaScript, Visual Basic Script, and PerlScript) can be used to program software that is intended to run on the Web server.

NOTE: The evolution of programming languages can create platform dependencies. Specific versions of programming languages are generally included with versions of Web browsers. Testing different versions of Web browsers for platform dependencies may uncover dependencies related to programming language versions.

12.4.3   Computer-Aided Software Engineering

Computer-aided software engineering (CASE) is used to describe a wide variety of analysis, design, and development tools that are intended to help software developers develop good systems. CASE tools are intended to provide a number of benefits that will help improve the quality of resulting software, including:

- Providing (and enforcing the use of) standard development methods and tools
- Providing project management support to developers and their managers
- Improving the reuse of developed software
- Reducing the costs of future maintenance to the software

There are many front-end (analysis or analysis and design only) or back-end (construction or construction and testing) tools but few complete life cycle tools. There is a considerable need for better CASE tools than are currently available. This need has been widely recognized for almost a decade, with few major advances.

In the absence of such advances, marketing people have creatively decided to apply the label "CASE tools" to all kinds of computerized tools that can be applied to some aspect of software engineering. Thus, some companies have even marketed crude text editors that could be used to edit program code as CASE tools. **Beware** of marketing hype about CASE tools.

As with the selection of any type of software, you must first determine what your requirements are before making design decisions involving what to buy. The best way to evaluate a CASE tool or a high-level development tool is to try it out on a real application. This can be a small application, but beware of applications that are too small, since what works easily for small amounts of data may not readily scale up to work as well for large amounts of data. Major features to expect in CASE tools include:

- CASE tools rely on sophisticated databases, referred to as **repositories,** to store and retrieve various types of software system development information. Some CASE tools allow the developer to add or change the types of development information stored in the repository.
- CASE tools rely on sophisticated graphics to be able to zoom into a particular part of the entire analysis or design to allow the developer to consider different views of the development information at the appropriate level of detail. This allows the developer to avoid information overload.
- CASE tools should support the developer throughout the complete development life cycle, from analysis and design through code generation and mainte-

nance. Some CASE tools allow the developer to modify the code produced by the tool. Some CASE tools contain additional features that allow them to optimize the execution of the resulting code.

- CASE tools should also contain suitable project management support to assist developers and their managers throughout the complete life cycle. While CASE tools should be highly interactive to make it easy for developers to change specifications, they should also include version control, so that the developer can refer to a previous version and identify the history of changes within a system's development.
- CASE tools should allow the developers the freedom to concentrate on developing the desired system by freeing them from related administrative duties. CASE tools should assist developers to generate reports and documentation required by their managers with a minimum of effort. The use of CASE tools should not add additional burdens to the software development process.
- CASE tools should allow the developer to choose between alternate styles of diagrams, methods, and reports rather than forcing the use of certain styles. CASE tools should facilitate the incorporation of additional tools to support new diagrams, methods, and reports.
- CASE tools should provide at least a basic level of consistency and completeness checking and be able to alert developers to areas that have not yet been fully analyzed. It would be nice if CASE tools provided active guidance to developers regarding the design process. This seldom occurs.

Limitations of some CASE tools include:

- CASE tools are usually developed to serve particular methodologies. To be able to use the tool, you must understand the methodology. There is generally a significant lag time between the acceptance of an improved methodology and the availability of CASE tools to support that methodology.
- CASE tools should serve developers, managers, and users. They seldom serve all three equally well. Since the managers are the ones who buy them, CASE tools often serve the managers better than they serve the developers or users.

The trend in CASE tools is to use graphical programming, where the developer selects and modifies standard high-level analysis components from a "warehouse" of available items. Through further analysis and design these high-level components are transformed into a design that contains sufficient information for the CASE tool to modify standard code modules and to put them together into a working program. Care needs to be taken that the graphical design of a program is not confused with performing a suitable analysis.

 Find references to further sources of information about CASE tools for developing e-Commerce systems in the Chapter 12 Cyber Supplement.

12.4.4   Tool Sets

Because of the complexity of CASE tools, it takes a considerable time to develop new CASE tools to support new construction techniques. However, this does not mean that modern systems must always be programmed entirely from scratch. Software reuse (the reuse of parts of existing programs) is widely practiced and advocated as a way of improving programming efficiency. It allows programmers to focus on what's needed that's new while reusing existing programming wherever possible.

Tool sets (also known as toolkits or object libraries) are collections of reusable programming parts (referred to by various names such as: routines, fragments, objects). Tool sets may be developed within an organization or purchased from developers who specialize in their creation. Tool sets should:

- Provide programming for the common operations required to develop a range of applications
- Promote ease of interaction between individual tools
- Allow the easy addition of new tools as they become needed

Tool sets can and should allow developers to customize individual tools in terms of how they look and the type of data that they process. The use of tool sets can shift the focus of construction from custom building the entire system to customizing a basic system to meet the specific needs of an organization. The use of tool sets may result in considerable resource savings for both the construction and testing of a system.

 Find references to further sources of information about tool sets for developing e-Commerce systems in the Chapter 12 Cyber Supplement.

12.4.5   Construction Considerations

Chapter 6 identified a range of "Options for Acquiring Software" and counseled against a premature decision to purchase. This section presents a revised set of options for constructing and hosting an e-Commerce system that should be considered at this point in the development.

There are many opportunities for obtaining assistance in developing systems that are more specialized than the all-or-nothing approaches considered in Chapter 6. It is especially useful to separate the actual construction of a system from the analysis and design when considering contracting out some of the development work.

- Analysis and design focuses on what an organization needs and wants. Both analysis and design identify requirements for the system to be constructed:
  - Analysis focuses on what it should accomplish.
  - Design focuses on how it should accomplish that.
  - By developing a design before making a final determination of how the construction will be accomplished, an organization focuses on what's best for its needs rather than settling for what's easiest to obtain.
  - Consultants can be hired to help evaluate an organization's needs and alternatives. They can provide experience and impartiality that may be lacking within your organization. However, in order to ensure their impartiality, they should be hired with the understanding that they (and their companies) should not be eligible to bid on developing or supplying the system to meet these needs.

- Construction attempts to meet these needs and wants within a fixed budget (involving a variety of resources, including money, time, and people).
  - Hiring an e-Commerce development organization to construct a system that meets the needs of a specific design may reduce resource costs. e-Commerce development organizations have specialized staff and can often meet a design quicker and cheaper by adapting a turnkey solution of theirs than by developing a completely custom system from the start.
  - Obtaining specialized tool sets or CASE tools to help with the construction may reduce resource costs. These tool sets or CASE tools may be used in-house by the organization's own computing professionals or by consultants (who could be hired from an e-Commerce development organization).

All e-Commerce systems, regardless how they are constructed, require considerable content to be input. This includes content on the organization, products, services, and organizational procedures. In all cases, the organization is responsible for ensuring that its content is correct and complete regardless of who gathers and physically inputs it. The costs of developing content for an e-Commerce system can be considerable.

12.4.5.1   Selecting Between Turnkey, Customized, and Custom Solutions

Once requirements have been established and even potentially a design developed for meeting these requirements, the organization needs to reevaluate the feasibility of constructing/acquiring a system to meet these requirements or this design. This reevaluation should consider a range of options for constructing or acquiring a system.

Custom systems have very high costs but can exactly meet requirements or designs. A **custom (built) system** is a unique system that has been constructed from basic tools and components to meet a specific analysis and design. Programmers develop custom (built) software systems by translating design requirements into original software programs. If an organization is able to commit the required resources, including skilled computer professionals, then a custom system may be developed in-house. Some considerations of this alternative include:

- This is a costly alternative.
- The time needed for this alternative depends on the availability of experienced computer professionals.
- This alternative is most attractive to organizations with experienced computer professionals.
- This can ensure a good fit between the system developed and the organization's needs.
- Developers may go down the wrong path before arriving at what is needed, incurring unprofitable expenditures as part of their cost of learning.
- This can provide a high level of protection of a competitive advantage.
- This can ensure that the programs are well structured and well documented in order to facilitate making future modifications to the system.

Large organizations often choose to run and maintain their e-Commerce applications on their own systems, especially where:

- They have sufficient computing needs to afford them suitable economies of scale
- They have security/privacy concerns that cannot be guaranteed by an e-Commerce development organization

An external e-Commerce development organization can be hired to develop a custom system that fits an organization's design. Some considerations of this alternative include:

- This is a relatively high-cost alternative but may be attractive to organizations with insufficient experienced computer professionals.
- This alternative may be faster than getting existing computer professionals trained and experienced in e-Commerce development or finding experienced computer professionals to hire. Contracts must be sure to guarantee that a development organization will use only experienced developers on the project, or the organization contracting for services may wind up paying to train employees for the e-Commerce development organization.
- This can ensure a good fit between the system developed and the organization's needs.
- Developers may go down the wrong path before arriving at what is needed, incurring unprofitable expenditures as part of their cost of learning.
- This can protect an organization's competitive advantages as long as the contract forbids the e-Commerce development organization from reusing the software for other customers of theirs.
- Making future modifications to the system may be expensive and/or difficult if the programs are not well structured and well documented. Contracts may create further difficulties by requiring that the original developer be hired to make any future modifications.

Turnkey systems can often be modified (usually by their developers) to be close to meeting requirements and even portions of a design at moderate costs. Commercially available software packages are often referred to as **turnkey systems** based on the metaphor of a person just needing to know how to turn a key to start driving a car. They are intended to be used with little or no basic changes to their operations. Turnkey systems are also referred to as **package (or packaged) software.**

Turnkey systems may allow users a large number of alternatives to customize them to appear unique while actually functioning in a relatively standard manner. They generally facilitate an organization's customization of particular content and presentation details such as:

- Names of:
  - The organization
  - Functions (e.g., change vs. modify)
  - Objects containing content (e.g., customer name vs. client name)
  - Other specific content (e.g., the details of specific products)
- Appearances of:
  - Color schemes used by the system
  - Controls that activate functions (e.g., a set of buttons vs. a pull-down menu)
  - Shape, size, and/or positioning of content objects

Despite the range of customization available in turnkey systems, all possible versions of a turnkey system generally perform the same set of functions in the same manner. This makes it very easy for competitors to acquire the same technology and to use it to copy, thus neutralizing, most competitive advantages.

It is not unusual for custom systems to cost at least ten times the cost of a similar turnkey system. Given this base difference, it may be very cost effective, especially for small- to medium-size organizations, to consider having a turnkey system modified to meet their needs.

To avoid piracy of their software, most e-Commerce development organizations that provide turnkey systems will only allow their software to be run on their own Web servers or servers to which they have privileged access. Thus, lower costs come in exchange for restrictions on your freedom. This may also apply with some developers of tool sets.

An analysis and design can be used as the basis for selecting an existing turnkey system that can be leased or purchased from an e-Commerce development organization. The organization's products and/or services and related content can be added and the system either used **as is** or modified to better fit the requirements. Some considerations of this alternative include:

- This is a relatively low cost and quick alternative.
- This is attractive to start-up organizations and/or organizations with insufficient experienced computer professionals.
- There may or may not be a good fit between available systems and the organization's needs.
- This alternative is readily available to an organization's competition, limiting the competitive advantages if the organization does not include significant modifications beyond the basic turnkey system.
- Making modifications to someone else's system may be expensive and/or difficult and may be restricted by contract to being performed by the e-Commerce development organization that provided the system.

Even though many organizations may choose turnkey systems, it is essential that organizations not commit to such a choice prior to conducting a proper analysis and design. Failure to do a proper analysis and design often leads to the acquisition of a system that does not sufficiently meet the needs of the organization. It is especially important to avoid the tendency to use the specifications of an available system in place of a properly analyzed set of requirements.

Tool sets can provide a middle option that can reduce costs over custom systems while coming closer to meeting an organization's needs than turnkey systems. A **customized system** is one that has been constructed by selecting, arranging, and modifying a set of reusable objects (or other program parts) often provided by a tool set or that has been constructed by significantly modifying the functioning of an existing system. Customized systems can often meet most the needs that custom systems can meet with considerably lower development costs.

An organization may wish to keep control of the development of a unique system but to minimize the amount of effort actually expended on technical aspects of construction. Acquiring a tool set can allow the organization to focus its e-Commerce construction efforts on meeting business, rather than technical, needs. Some considerations of this alternative include:

- This is a moderate cost alternative.
- This can help organizations to develop experienced computer professionals. This focuses their experience on the organization's business practices rather than on programming details.
- There may or may not be a good fit between available tool sets and the organization's needs.
- This alternative can provide better flexibility in changing directions via the future mixing and matching of individual components from the tool set.
- The capital investment in a tool set keeps returning benefits, even as the system it is used for changes.
- This alternative is readily available to an organization's competition, limiting the competitive advantages if the organization does not include significant modifications beyond the basic components in the tool set.
- Making modifications to tools produced by someone else may be expensive and/or difficult and may be restricted by contract to being performed by the e-Commerce development organization that provided the tool set.
- This alternative balances:
  - Flexibility of modifications and additions with control of construction and construction risks.
  - Speed of construction with costs involved.

The choice of an alternative for constructing or acquiring an e-Commerce system should take into account the need for e-Commerce systems to be continually evolving. Custom systems provide the greatest potential for future evolution. Reputable developers of turnkey systems and tool sets are continually enhancing their systems to keep up with evolving expectations on the Web. However, access to some of these enhancements will come at an additional cost.

Regardless of which construction/acquisition option is chosen, the resulting system can be run either on servers owned and maintained by:

- The organization
- An e-Commerce development organization
- An Internet Service Provider (ISP)

e-Commerce development organizations and ISPs often provide Web server services to a number of their clients. These services go beyond just providing disk space and Internet connections and generally include:

- Providing security/protection for the software and data involved
- Ensuring priority repairs to any servers involved
- Providing higher access speeds than most smaller organizations could afford to provide on their own

12.4.5.2 Selecting the Type of Technology

Although simple e-Commerce systems can be developed without using database technology, such systems generally have a low ability to evolve and a low level of effectiveness. Nondatabase systems can provide an organization an opportunity to:

Table 12-1   A basic informational Web site

Main Considerations	Description
Complexity	Low
Cost	$, $$$ custom
Technology	HTML (used to develop linked Web pages)
Developer skills required	Anyone who can use a word processor can create Web pages
Uses	Advertising, information publishing
Interaction	None—users can only browse pages and links
Ability to evolve	Low and expensive, since all information is part of individual Web pages
Effectiveness	Low
Competitive advantages	May be negative when customers see how little such a site does for them, only useful to inform potential customers of your existence

- Get an introductory experience with the Web
- Test some concepts before committing to major developments

The simplest type of Web site is one that just presents information to people. While such a site can be used for some advertising purposes it is generally at a competitive disadvantage in almost all situations. People have grown to expect and to demand more from any e-Commerce site. In many cases potential customers may be less impressed with a non-interactive Web site than with an organization not having a Web site. Table 12-1 identifies some of the main construction considerations regarding a basic information Web site.

It is very expensive to provide any sophisticated functionality to a non-database system because that functionality would need to be programmed for each component (Web page, frame, or object) in the system where it is to be used. As soon as advanced levels of functionality are required, any non-database system will have to be thrown away and replaced with a database system. While data may be salvaged and reused, any functionality developed for a non-database system will be of negligible salvage value. Thus, it is best to limit the amount of development effort put into non-database systems.

The one generally justifiable use of adding functionality to a non-database system is to provide customers (or other visitors to the Site) with an easy means of contacting the organization to request further information. However, it is best to then provide this information by other means rather than by using a non-database system. Table 12-2 identifies some of the main construction considerations regarding a basic information Web site that allows users to submit requests.

Database technology, in and of itself, in not sufficient to achieve major competitive advantages. Many traditional information systems (including DPS, MIS, and SIS systems) make use of databases. Some may even support distributed processing via forms of directed data interchange. However, traditional systems often emphasize protecting the data by hiding it and limiting access to it. While some data should be protected and hidden, this can be like hiding your money under your bed—it's safe but it's not doing anything for you. e-Commerce and other organization-wide systems

Table 12-2 A basic informational Web site allowing users to submit requests

Main Considerations	Description
Complexity	Medium
Cost	$, $$$ turnkey or $$, $$$ custom
Technology	HTML and a scripting language forms for users to make requests/submit orders; information on forms is then processed by organization separately
Developer skills required	Requires basic programming skills
Uses	Allows simple requests to be submitted by users
Interaction	Low; users only interact with the programs added to the Web pages, users do not interact with data
Ability to evolve	Low and expensive, since all information is part of individual Web pages
Effectiveness	Medium-low
Competitive advantages	Primarily useful to inform potential customers of your existence, depends largely on products/service remaining unique

Table 12-3 An e-Commerce system with database supported interactions

Main Considerations	Descriptions
Complexity	Moderate
Cost	$$, $$$ turnkey or $$$, $$$ custom
Technology	HTML and a scripting language and a database
Developer skills required	Requires professional programming skills
Uses	Can operate as a department or a branch of an existing organization, may form the basis of a start-up organization
Interaction	High external, users interact with the information within the application, low internal, application cannot interact with other systems in the organization
Ability to evolve	High, since all information is part of the database
Effectiveness	High on an application level
Competitive advantages	Most possible competitive advantages can be implemented in a modified turnkey or custom system of this type

maximize the usefulness of data by promoting its interchange and reuse. They do this while still providing the security, privacy, and authentication services where they are needed.

The value produced by a traditional information system is generally equal to the sum of the values of its parts (both processing components and data content). Successful e-Commerce systems create additional benefits and opportunities by recognizing that a system can be worth more than the sum of its parts.

Table 12-3 identifies some of the main construction considerations regarding an e-Commerce system that uses databases specifically created for it.

While it is ideal for all new systems to integrate with old systems, this is not always possible. Integration may involve making changes to existing systems as well as

Table 12-4 A fully integrated e-Commerce system

Main Considerations	Description
Complexity	High
Cost	$$$, $$$ turnkey or $, $$$, $$$ custom
Technology	HTML and a scripting language and a database plus additional interfacing
	NOTE: It may be cheaper to replace existing systems by enhancing an e-Commerce system than to interface with some existing systems, especially with purchased/leased systems involving proprietary technologies.
Developer skills required	Integration (rather than replacement) requires very high-level programming skills and knowledge of existing systems involved; replacement may require high-level programming skills
Uses	Fully integrated within an existing organization
Interaction	High external, users interact with the information within the application, high internal, application interacts with or replaces other systems in the organization
Ability to evolve	Very high, since all information is part of the database
Effectiveness	High on an organization level

to the new system being developed. Integration often requires that a new system is able to access and use data stored in existing systems.

- Turnkey systems may be specifically developed in a manner that precludes the integration of other systems with them, either by the use of exclusionary technologies or by the use of "proprietary rights" clauses in the leasing or purchase contract, which prohibit additional uses of the leased or purchased software.
- Where a turnkey system cannot be modified and/or its database directly accessed by the developers of an e-Commerce application, there are only two choices for pursuing integration without replacing the turnkey system involved:
  - The developers of the turnkey system may be willing, for a considerable price, to provide a program that allows you to interface with the turnkey system
  - A complicated program can be developed that simulates a user interacting with the turnkey system and using its regular user interface to access its data
- Legacy systems (systems built long ago with old technologies) may be very difficult to modify due to:
  - Poor design/documentation of the legacy system
  - A lack of current skills in the technologies involved with the legacy system
  - The legacy system already operating to its maximum capacity

In some cases it may be easier and less expensive:

- To have people provide ongoing integration rather than to construct programming to automatically provide this integration
- To completely replace an existing system rather than to integrate with it

Where integration is feasible, it needs to consider which user(s) using which system(s) is/are allowed to do what type(s) of processing on commonly used data/content. Table 12-4 identifies some of the main construction considerations regarding an e-Commerce system that integrates with other existing systems.

Systems serving multiple countries can be created as modifications of a single system, with different country specific information (prices, currency, availability, support, and so on). However, various nations may expect local branches to have their own local systems to keep detailed sales information within the country's borders. Where local systems are used, there may be additional concerns over the capability and reliability of data communications and data transfers between local branch offices, other branch offices in other countries, and the organization's head office.

 Find references to further sources of information about construction considerations for developing e-Commerce systems in the Chapter 12 Cyber Supplement.

12.5 APPLYING TECHNICAL DESIGN AND CONSTRUCTION

12.5.1 Applying Technical Design and Construction in Organizations

The ability to apply technical design and construction in-house varies considerably between organizations. The need for good technical design and construction does not vary. Using an e-Commerce development organization does not guarantee the quality of technical design and construction. Organizations need to evaluate the capabilities of whoever is chosen to perform technical design and construction, since these people are likely to do most of their work largely on their own. Some factors to use in making such a selection include:

- Experience with e-Commerce development as demonstrated by successful systems
- Experience with Web site development as demonstrated by successful systems
- Amount of training on/learning of the latest techniques
- Experience/training in object-oriented development

NOTE: General programming experience is insufficient preparation for the technical design and construction of e-Commerce systems.

12.5.2 Student Assignment—Constructing a Prototype

This week's assignment involves creating an initial prototype that demonstrates the use of the presentation segments and scenarios designed in the assignment in Chapter 11.

NOTE: The construction of your initial prototype does not require any advanced Web programming skills. You should have all the skills necessary to complete this assignment. To go beyond this prototype would usually require the considerable skills of a trained Web programmer. To obtain such skills would require a number of courses in:

- Web programming
- Database development
- Human-computer interaction

1. For each of your scenarios (from the assignment in Chapter 11), identify the variations in your basic presentation segment(s) that correspond to each of the steps in the scenario, that a user of your prototype should observe.

2. Create copies of your presentation segments (as designed in Chapter 11) and modify them to represent examples of each of the variations identified in step 1 above. Save each copy as a separate Web page. Although this involves a number of copies, this should actually involve a minimal effort per copy.

3. Create links between the different copies to produce an example of what the user would see going through the scenarios. Links should go from the location of the appropriate media object. All scenarios should start from a common, initial Web page. The last Web page of each scenario should also contain a link back to the initial Web page.

 Find an example of applying technical design and construction in the development of an e-Commerce system in the Chapter 12 Cyber Supplement.

12.6 CYBER SUPPLEMENTS FOR CHAPTER 12

 Look at the Chapter 12 Cyber Supplements on the Web to find:

- References to additional sources of information about client server models of e-Commerce applications
- References to additional sources of information about e-Commerce uses of different types of media
- References to additional sources of information about communication design for e-Commerce systems
- References to additional sources of information about migrating and/or connecting with legacy systems
- References to additional sources of information about CASE tools for developing e-Commerce systems
- References to additional sources of information about tool sets for developing e-Commerce systems
- References to additional sources of information about construction considerations for developing e-Commerce systems
- An example of applying technical design and construction in the development of an e-Commerce system
- Practice activities dealing with the technical design and construction of e-Commerce systems

REFERENCES

[1] W3C, HyperText Markup Language Home Page, *www.w3.org/MarkUp*

[2] W3C, XHTML Basic, *www.w3.org/TR/xhtml-basic*

[3] W3C, Extensible Markup Language (XML), *www.w3.org/XML*

[4] W3C, XML Base, *www.w3.org/XML*

[5] R. J. Norman, *Object-Oriented Systems Analysis and Design* (Upper Saddle River, NJ, Prentice-Hall, 1996).

13

Testing

Outline

13.1 INTRODUCTION TO TESTING

The purpose of testing is to ensure that a system will be successful at doing the job it was created to do. If the system is the result of good development processes, it is hoped that it will be successful. What an organization actually needs is not always what they get, even in high-profile and carefully performed developments. It is often essential that systems be thoroughly tested prior to being put into actual use. While the success of a system can only truly be evaluated once it is in use, waiting until then may prove disastrous.

The use of the infamous "butterfly ballot" by Palm Beach, Florida in the 2000 U.S. presidential election provides a good example of the importance of testing. Although the ballot was designed "to make it easier for senior citizens to read," it was found very difficult for these same senior citizens to use when it was actually used in the election. Errors in their use of the ballot may have changed the result of the election. If usability tests had been conducted with representative users, these problems could have been identified and corrected before the election.

Usability testing, which was discussed in Chapter 5, is only one of a variety of types of testing that are important in the development of e-Commerce systems. A variety of different tests relating to usability and other concerns may be used in an attempt to predict the success of a system. This chapter will focus on these additional types of testing.

Within traditional software development, testing has generally referred to the testing of programs to ensure that they operate according to their design. Like usability testing, which should be conducted throughout development, some other tests can and should be used throughout development. Although this chapter comes late in this text, it will discuss how various types of testing should be conducted throughout the development life cycle of an e-Commerce system.

13.2 UNDERSTANDING TESTING

13.2.1 Validation

Validation tests the accuracy and completeness of the specifications of a system as a model of what is needed. Pressman[1] states that "Validation refers to a different set of activities that ensure that the software has been built to a traceable set of customer requirements." He also refers to Boehm's[2] statement that validation involves answering the question, "Are we building the right product?"

Validation focuses on determining that a set of specifications or a program does what it is intended to do and identifying and fixing situations where it currently does not. It compares:

- The constructed program/system to the design
- The design to the requirements
- The requirements to the application that will be served by the system

Validation, because of its focus on what is believed to be true, is assumed to be a subjective form of evaluation. However, careful validation can yield highly accurate results.

Proper e-Commerce system validation must go beyond just the checking that a system meets, in some manner or other, a set of "traceable set of customer requirements." The real validation of an e-Commerce system is its ability to generate and handle business. Unfortunately, such validation cannot be determined until after the system has been implemented. This limitation creates two situations:

- Other approaches to validation are required, which can be performed prior to implementation.
- Organizations are often too busy using their new systems and developing even newer ones to properly evaluate the successes and failures of a newly installed system.

13.2.1.1 Acceptance Testing

Acceptance testing is a basic form of validation that involves getting the users to accept that the current phase of development meets their requirements and thus is acceptable.

One of the uses of the traditional waterfall life cycle is to define points, at the end of each phase, where the development work completed in that phase is subjected to the acceptance of the user. Similar points can be identified within other development methods for users to evaluate and accept completed development work. However, the user often is not able to properly understand and evaluate the development information that is presented for acceptance.

Traditional development documentation seldom documents the trail of user requirements that have led to the current phase of development. The lack of such a trail may have serious effects on the success of current and future development. Conklin[3] stressed the need to capture design rationale as a basis for future maintenance. The formal documentation of trails of requirements and other development decisions may be especially useful in support of the ongoing evolution of e-Commerce systems.

13.2.1.2 Competitive Testing

While it is difficult to develop absolute requirements for application quality, the basic criterion for quality of an e-Commerce application is that it be significantly better than its competition. Competitive testing involves:

- **Feature testing** competitive systems to determine what they can do and what you might wish to incorporate into your system
- **Comparative testing** of your proposed system with competitive systems to determine if it will be suitably successful in its competitive environment

Although it is nice if you determine that your system is better than its competition, what really counts are opinions of the various people who can choose between using your system or its competition. There are a number of issues to consider in getting outside users to compare your developing system with its competition.

It is important that you recruit people who can provide the quantity and quality of testing responses that you require. If testers are only committed because you are paying them for their time, you might not receive valuable help for your money. Testing takes time, and the best people are often the busiest doing their own work. To get the right type of testers you will need to be able to convince them of the benefits of being involved in your testing. These benefits may include ensuring that their needs are considered in the development. However, you need to avoid giving testers the impression that they have a special right to make demands on your design that you later may not wish to or be able to fulfill.

While you have to trust your testers, you should consider having them sign a nondisclosure agreement before testing begins. Although you might not mind highlighting the faults of your competitors, you don't want either your faults or your strengths made public, especially before your system is ready for use. Such knowledge could help your competitors to duplicate your competitive advantages and use them even before you have a chance to do so. While nondisclosure agreements may limit what they say about your application, you need to consider how best to maintain the loyalty of your testers.

There are various problems that can arise from getting your customers to test your competition's systems. You don't want to publicize the strengths of your competition. If your testers see that competitive applications are better for them or that your competitors are providing services that you are only thinking about providing, they may be among the first of your customers to leave you.

Your testers will be most effective as long as they see themselves as independent from your development efforts. If they grow too familiar with the development team, they may lose their sense of objectivity and need to be replaced with new testers.

Your testers need to recognize any differences between your developing system and competitive systems. However, not all differences should be treated the same.

- Testing should recognize that you are not trying to duplicate the competition but rather to develop something significantly different and/or better. To do so does not require that your system have all the same features as other systems.
- Where comparing different versions or approaches to a common task, it is important to identify which is preferred or better.
- Where comparing the presence or absence of certain functions, it is important to consider whether or not the functions are essential to the user, not just to the application.

Competitive testing can start even before you start developing a system. It can tell you:

- What your competition is doing right (which you may or may not wish to emulate)
- What it is doing wrong (which you may wish to correct)
- What it isn't doing (which may be an opportunity for you to grab)

Competitive testing during requirements analysis can keep you informed of the current state of the art in the application area. Changes noted at this time may significantly affect your application and any resulting systems. Competitive testing during design can help ensure that your system will be successful in its competitive market. Competitive testing after design can identify new features that may be required in future updates to the system.

13.2.2 Verification

Verification tests the accuracy and completeness of the system and its operations. Pressman[4] states that "**Verification** refers to the set of activities that ensure that software correctly implements a specific function." He also refers to Boehm's[5] statement that verification involves answering the question, "Are we building the product right?"

Verification focuses on determining that the program works correctly and identifying and fixing situations where it currently does not. It compares the constructed program/system with design. Verification, because of its focus on correctness, is assumed to be an objective form of evaluation. However, the choice of testing conditions and of testing procedures can introduce subjectivity into the process.

It is recommended that verification be performed in a bottom-up manner through a number of levels. Verification needs to be performed both on the programs and on the complete system.

13.2.2.1 Program Testing

Computer professionals generally conduct program testing. Care needs to be exercised in the conducting of program testing, to avoid missing problems due to accidental omissions or due to developers not wanting to admit that there may be any problems with their work. It is preferable for the people conducting the program testing to be independent from the people who developed the program.

Program testing usually starts with the smallest units of code (**unit testing**) and works its way through increasingly larger collections of units (**integration testing**) of code up to testing the complete system (**system testing**).

At the systems level, as well as testing correct operation of the code, additional testing is performed to evaluate the operating characteristics of the program. This testing includes:

- **Performance testing** of the system within the range of expected operating conditions
- **Stress testing** of system performance under unusual operating conditions
- **Recovery testing** of the system's response to failures and of the ability to recover from the results of these failures
- **Security testing** of the system's ability to detect and prevent attempts at breaching the system's security

Standard approaches[6] to verification, available for computer professionals, can be used to verify the operations of e-Commerce systems.

Suitable test data must be developed for each of these tests. Test data not only should ensure that expected values of the data can be properly accommodated but also must test what happens to unexpected and/or invalid values of the data. In some cases additional programming may need to be developed in order to provide these test data to units of code or collections of units, to simulate transferring of data from other units of code not currently included in the test.

Once the complete system has been tested with test data, it should be further tested with sample data from the real world. If a system is replacing an existing system, it can be helpful to run both systems in parallel in order to compare their results.

While users may be enlisted to help with program testing, they do not actually use the system to accomplish real tasks. Rather, they use the system to accomplish specially prepared testing scenarios.

13.2.2.2 Live Testing

Live testing is generally managed by computer professionals but also involves users testing the system while performing their regular work-related tasks. Live testing of systems intended for internal use only within an organization is often incorporated within acceptance testing. Live testing of software, such as e-Commerce systems, which are intended for a variety of external users, is generally divided into two phases:

- **Alpha testing** commences once system testing is completed. It involves a limited number of fairly experienced users. They gain early access to a system in return for their:
  - Keeping the details of the system confidential (which may involve signing a nondisclosure agreement)

- Toleration of errors
- Active reporting of difficulties to the developers
- **Beta testing** is conducted when the difficulties identified in alpha testing have been resolved and when the system is thought by the developers to be fully working. It is still likely that additional problems remain undetected at this time. Beta testing involves larger numbers of users but is still limited to those users who:
  - Accept the potential of errors occurring
  - Are willing to report difficulties to the developers

In some situations, live testing is performed as part of the implementation process (as discussed in Chapter 14). However, where possible, it is preferable for systems to be verified via live testing before they are implemented. Performing it prior to implementation may uncover and correct a number of problems that would otherwise add to the stress of the implementation.

13.2.3   Usability Testing

Usability testing has already been discussed in Chapter 5.

13.2.4   Different Approaches to Quality

Unfortunately, *quality* is a word that has many meanings, depending on a person's perspective.

- When *quality* is used as a noun it refers to some attribute or feature of a thing without regard to any evaluation of whether that attribute is good or bad. Systems may be described in terms of an infinite number of noun qualities.
- When *quality* is used as an adjective it refers to a favorable evaluation of the thing to which it refers. There are an infinite number of bases for evaluating adjectival qualities. Despite all being favorable, some of the types of adjectival quality do not have an objective basis. The quality of a given object may not be quantifiable without relating it to the quality of some other object.

While it would be nice for a system to have all kinds of (both noun and adjectival) qualities, achieving these qualities could become very expensive. This may suggest a need to study the feasibility of each type of quality, but there are some specific concerns that we should recognize as being associated with expectations of quality, which will be discussed in this chapter.

There are probably as many approaches to quality as there are people who would care to comment on it; in fact, probably more, because many of these people have multiple notions of quality. Whereas each of these approaches to quality can be argued to be highly desirable, achieving the ultimate in quality is clearly beyond possibility in the real world. As a result of budget limitations and the limitations of people involved in development, compromises must be made. Certain types of quality may be sacrificed in order to divert essential resources to improving quality. Regardless of the approaches taken, the results are always less than perfect. This lack of perfection can be very disconcerting to inexperienced people who are used to school assignments where it is possible to achieve 100%. This affects developers and end users alike and can lead to many project delays as attempts are made to make the system work just a little bit better.

The following are just some of the main categories that can describe qualities related to tools (such as computer software); however, within each category there are a multitude of different opinions.

13.2.4.1   Results Quality

Results quality is another way of describing verification rather than a form of validation. While it is very important, it should not be claimed as meeting the needs for validation.

Results quality focuses on the accuracy and completeness of the results of using the tool. This is often interpreted as guaranteeing "zero defects," which, due to the complexity of most software, is impossible to achieve, despite what anyone may claim. Despite the impossibility of guaranteeing zero defects, varying levels of integrity can be certified.[7] Good testing methods can often reduce the risk of a defect affecting the performance of a system to an almost negligible amount. Researchers in testing and measurement continue to search for a perfect metric that will ensure that software has no defects.

13.2.4.2   Task Fulfillment Quality

Task fulfillment quality provides the most basic level of validation by concentrating on the tasks a system is designed to facilitate. Task fulfillment quality focuses on the ability of the tool to meet its goals and objectives within the organization. This type of quality is expected by the procurers—the people who pay for the development or acquisition of tools. A proper systems development methodology should track task-related requirements from their identification and analysis through design to where the design is tested to ensure that it meets the requirements. The measurement of this quality is a matter of negotiation between the procurers and the developers. Although claims can be made that a system fulfills certain tasks, there can be wide variations in how well different systems fulfill any given task.

13.2.4.3   Feature Quality

Feature quality focuses on the system on its own and apart from its context of use. It is often marketing driven rather than user-oriented. Feature quality assesses the presence or absence of specific features of the tool. This type of quality is often incorrectly measured by counting features without sufficient evaluation of the relative importance and/or usability of individual features. (Thus, it is often referred to as "bean counting.") Marketing people often exaggerate the number of "features" of a product in hopes that naïve consumers will accept the apparent superiority of their product, whether or not any of these "features" are really needed. A more useful form of product quality involves comparing the features of a particular product to some reference set of expected features (as established by some specific product standard). However, such an approach is not feasible for use with e-Commerce systems, where each successful system should have competitive advantages beyond those found in "standard" e-Commerce systems.

13.2.4.4 Characteristic Quality

Characteristic quality focuses on common expectations that can be used for evaluating any tool and/or any components of a software system. These characteristics are often considered as general features of a product and are often expected without being added to the documented project requirements. However, they will be easier to achieve if requirements based on them are specified early in the development.

ISO 9126-1[8] "categorizes the attributes of software quality into six characteristics, which are further subdivided":

- **Functionality,** which is "the capability of the software to provide functions which meet stated and implied needs when the software is used under specified conditions." It includes the concepts of:
    - **Suitability,** which evaluates how system functions meet the needs of user tasks
    - **Accuracy,** which evaluates the achievement of the right results
    - **Interoperability,** which evaluates interactions with other systems
    - **Security,** which evaluates the ability of the system to withstand unauthorized accesses and modifications
- **Reliability,** which is "the capability of the software to maintain the level of performance of the system when used under specified conditions." It includes the concepts of:
    - **Maturity,** which evaluates the ability of the system to avoid failures, regardless of any faults it has
    - **Fault tolerance,** which evaluates the capability of the system to maintain a suitable level of performance in spite of faults or other difficulties
    - **Recoverability,** which evaluates the ability of the system to recover its data and performance after a failure
- **Usability,** which is "the capability of the software to be understood, learned, used and liked by the user, when used under specified conditions." It includes the concepts of:
    - **Understandability,** which evaluates the ability of users to understand how, when, and where to use the system
    - **Learnability,** which evaluates the ability (including the effort required) for users to learn how to use the system
    - **Operability,** which evaluates the ability of the product to be used and controlled by the user
    - **Attractiveness,** which evaluates the ability of the product to be "liked" by users
- **Efficiency,** which is "the capability of the software to provide the required performance, relative to the amount of resources used, under stated conditions." It includes the concepts of:
    - **Time behavior,** which evaluates the appropriateness of response and processing times of the system
    - **Resource utilization,** which evaluates the use of resources in performing system functions
- **Maintainability,** which is "the capability of the software to be modified." It includes the concepts of:
    - **Analyzability,** which evaluates the ability to identify problems in the system
    - **Changeability,** which evaluates the ability to implement modifications to the system

- **Stability,** which evaluates the ability to minimize undesired side effects of modifications
- **Testability,** which evaluates the ability to validate modified software
- **Portability,** which is "the capability of software to be transferred from one environment to another." It includes the concepts of:
  - **Adaptability,** which evaluates the ability to modify software via features rather than reprogramming to meet the needs of different environments
  - **Installability,** which evaluates the ability to install software in a given environment
  - **Co-existence,** which evaluates the ability of the software to share common resources with other installed software
  - **Replaceability,** which evaluates the ability of software to replace other software

Metrics, identified in a set of three technical reports, can be used to evaluate each of these characteristics and subcharacteristics.

- ISO 9126-3[9] provides a set of **internal metrics** that "may be applied to a non-executable software product during its development stages."
- ISO 9126-2[10] provides a set of **external metrics** that "may be used to measure the quality of the software product by measuring the behavior of the system of which it is part."
- ISO 9126-4[11] provides a set of **quality in use metrics** that "measure the extent to which a product meets the needs of specified users to achieve specified goals with effectiveness, productivity, safety and satisfaction in a specified context of use."

13.2.4.5 Development Process Quality

Development process quality focuses on how a tool was manufactured. This approach avoids the other types of quality by making the assumption that "quality manufacturing leads to quality products." While quality development may lead to a quality product, there is no guarantee that it does. Rather, the converse is often true; poor development generally leads to poor products.

Many current "Quality Assurance (QA)" approaches (ISO 9000,[12] ISO 15504[13]) focus on documenting processes that are deemed important to the success of the overall development process. This requires the further assumption that "if the processes are documented, then they are being performed correctly" in addition to the assumption that "quality manufacturing leads to quality products." Proponents of this approach justify focusing on "quality manufacturing" by citing the impossibility to properly assess other types of quality.

The general nature of ISO 9000 allows universal application, giving procurers a single standard to use in their procurement process. This standard can be invoked either on its own or along with any additional user-specified standards. The field of quality assurance has grown up largely to protect professional procurers (purchasing agents) who are often required to procure items and systems that they don't actually understand. In order to make up for their lack of experience and understanding of every possible product in the world (which is quite impossible) they have sought out standard approaches to certifying quality. Despite the fuzziness of the required assumptions and comparisons of it to "bean counting," the QA approach continues to spread throughout industry. It is often fueled by marketing concerns either of being the first to be "ISO 9000 Quality certified" or of needing to "keep up with the competition" who are already "ISO 9000 Quality certified."

13.2.5   The Need for Quality and Standards

We can all agree that we need quality, although we might disagree on what we mean by quality. The problem is that quality generally costs money (both to develop and to certify that it has been developed).

Given the difficulties involved in evaluating and comparing quality, many efforts have been made to at least establish basic levels of expected quality. On the international level these have resulted in various International Standards, including those referenced in this book. International Standards for software are developed by ISO, The International Organization for Standardization.[14]

The ISO standards development process involves experts from interested countries around the world in an effort to ensure quality standards that are fair to all. ISO also develops technical reports on topics for which it might be difficult to reach the required level of consensus to make the material an International Standard.

Initially, most International Standards were developed primarily to assist in product procurement and evaluation. The main driving force behind developing and mandating international standards is the regulation of international trade. While countries are forbidden by various trading conventions such as the Global Agreement on Trade and Tariffs (GATT) from discriminating against foreign products, countries can demand that all imported products meet the requirements of International Standards. This can provide a basic level of protection against shoddy foreign products and provide a more "level playing field" for domestic producers. However, because of the vast array of International Standards that might apply, compliance will likely only be forced on a producer either when a competitor complains about non-compliance or in a law suit alleging negligence.

In some countries, such as Germany, failure to comply with applicable International Standards is legal grounds for a finding of negligence. Within the European Community, EC90/270[15] went beyond dealing with software in product terms to its regulation as a health and safety concern by requiring employers "to protect and inform their workers about, and to ensure compliance of systems to applicable software ergonomics." National members of the European Community have implemented this by referring to ISO 9241 Parts 10–17.

Despite their basic commercial role, many standards by necessity go much further into technical detail than the average procurer is able to understand. Rather, procurers typically rely on statements of their suppliers that a product complies to certain named International Standards. Where proof of compliance is necessary, various test houses (such as Underwriters Laboratories, The American Institute for Research, The Fraunhofer Institute, and others) have been developed to provide independent product certification.

Procurers may not have sufficient technical knowledge to identify all the relevant standards and to evaluate the compliance of products to these standards. Their level of understanding of the role of a given standard may be limited to considering the descriptive name of the standard. Procurers may evaluate products by one or more of the following:

- Consulting consumer evaluation services (e.g., *Consumer Reports*) to evaluate general purpose consumer products
- Looking for only familiar standards (e.g., ISO 9000) without recognizing what they involve
- Looking for only those standards specified by the users and/or their managers (who seldom know about the existence of most standards)
- Comparing products based on the number of standards with which each claims to comply
- Comparing products based on the number of standards with which each is certified to comply
- Consulting experts for additional assistance (which is done only rarely) in evaluating products

While they are written more like a reference book than like a textbook, technical standards often provide a wealth of useful guidance for developers who take the effort to understand them.

Standards can help developers:

- To avoid errors
- To provide consistency
- To enhance usability
- To enhance comfort and well-being

Achieving these goals can help developers improve the quality of their developments.

13.3   APPLYING TESTING

13.3.1   Applying Testing in Organizations

It's too late to start thinking about quality once a system has been constructed. Organizations need to establish quality expectations before development projects are commenced.

Likewise, it's often too late to do anything about quality concerns once a system has been constructed. Organizations need to ensure that quality concerns are included as requirements that need to be met throughout the development life cycle. Procedures need to be in place to ensure that these requirements are met in a timely and efficient manner. These procedures should identify when different types of tests should be performed, procedures for performing and evaluating them, and procedures to ensure that their results will be acted upon.

 Find references to further sources of information about particular types of testing that apply to the development of e-Commerce systems in the Chapter 13 Cyber Supplement.

13.3.2   Student Assignment—Usability Testing

Consider this the first set of a series of sets of prototyping sessions intended to get user reactions to your design for a system for your application. This means that you have a limited agenda of what you intend to get out of this session; i.e., you want to evaluate the page design in general and its usefulness for your scenarios in particular. You will need to analyze the information you receive from selected "users" in determining what you will do next.

1. Find at least three people to help you with this assignment. It would be best if they are familiar with browsing the Web. It is not necessary that they are experts in your application area, but some understanding of the application and its intended users could be helpful.
   - It would be preferable if the people you use belong to different groups of users (that you have identified) who might use the page and scenarios that you are evaluating.
   - If they are not typical users, it may be helpful to explain your expectations of who might be typical users (based on your user descriptions from the student assignment from Chapter 7) to them.

NOTE: If any of the three people do not provide suitable insights into how your design could be improved, you should consider using additional people to evaluate your design.

2. Have each of your test subjects (separately) use the set of pages you designed in Chapter 12 to try out your five scenarios. Your test session should proceed as follows:
   - Obtain their consent to participate, promise them that they have the right to cease their participation if they wish, and assure them that you will not be divulging their identity to anyone outside your project team.
   - Provide a brief description of your project and the organization for which you are developing it.
   - Tell the users that you would like them to try to use the pages you have designed to perform five different scenarios. Explain that when they are to enter information, all they have to do is to click on where they would enter it and it will be entered automatically for them in this demonstration.
   - Tell them that you would like to observe them to see if they run into any difficulties and that you would like them to describe what they are doing as they do it. Also tell them that you would prefer that they tried to accomplish the scenarios without asking for any assistance unless they are really stuck.
   - As they go through the scenarios, observe and record your impressions of any difficulties they encounter.
   - After they have completed the scenarios and returned to the main page, ask them to briefly write down their comments to the following questions:
     - What did you think of the design in general?
     - Did you notice anything missing from the page that should have been there?
     - Did you notice anything on the page that seemed out of place?
     - How easy was it to complete the scenarios on a scale of 1 (hard) to 5 (easy)?
     - What improvements would you suggest?

3. Produce a report of your testing, including:
   - Copies of all scenarios and instructions used
   - Descriptions of your test subjects in terms of:
     - The user group they represent
     - Their age
     - Their educational background
     - Their current occupation
     - **Do not** name them or otherwise definitively identify them
   - Your observations of each user's interactions with the prototype
   - Any comments the users made while interacting with the prototype
   - The user's answers to your questions
4. Evaluate the results of your user testing. This evaluation should identify:
   - What worked
   - What didn't work and why it didn't work
   - What additions the users suggested
   - What changes you should make based on this evaluation

 Find an example of applying usability testing in the development of an e-Commerce system in the Chapter 13 Cyber Supplement.

13.4 CHALLENGES AND OPPORTUNITIES IN APPLYING VERIFICATION AND VALIDATION

The following are some of the most frequent problems encountered with verification and validation.

Challenges with Selective Verification and Validation

- Some developers verify or validate only the most common features of a system.
- Some developers only focus on verification and assume that their development process has guaranteed validation.
- Some developers treat validation as a process that only occurs between analysis and design and not as something required after construction.
- Cost and time overruns from previous stages of development often lead to pressure to cut verification and validation short to "catch up."
- Demand to be able to use the system often leads to pressure to cut verification and validation short to "get the system up and running."
- User interactions with prototypes may give users the impression that the system is ready for use.

Challenges with Usability Testing

- Some developers do not select suitable scenarios to test. This is a problem that carries over from the previous development that is not corrected before user testing.

- Some developers do not distinguish between testing functionality (what the system does, which should be prototyped during analysis) and testing usability (how the user responds to a design), which should be prototyped during design.
- Some developers do not give the users sufficient guidance about sticking to the prototype scenarios, leading their test subjects to complain about limitations in the functioning of the prototype based on their expectations that the prototype would be more complete than it was.
- Some developers have all their test subjects identify the same problems. Either the problems were so major as to attract all the attention and thus the prototype was not really ready for testing, or the test subjects were not as different as they should have been to provide a wide section of possible users.
- Some developers do not use a systematic progression of prototypes, but either keep focusing on a single prototype or jump around between screens with no apparent reason to their actions.

13.5 CYBER SUPPLEMENTS FOR CHAPTER 13

Look at the Chapter 13 Cyber Supplements on the Web to find:

- References to further sources of information about particular types of testing that apply to the development of e-Commerce systems

- An example of applying usability testing in the development of an e-Commerce system

- Practice activities dealing with the testing of e-Commerce systems

REFERENCES

[1] R.S. Pressman, *Software Engineering: A Practitioner's Approach,* 4th ed. (New York, NY, McGraw-Hill, 1997).

[2] B. Boehm, *Software Engineering Economics:* (Englewood Cliffs, NJ, Prentice Hall, 1981).

[3] Jeff Conklin, Design Rationale and Maintainability, *Proceedings of the 22nd HICCS* (IEEE Computer Society Press, 1989).

[4] Ibid.

[5] Ibid.

[6] Institute of Electrical and Electronics Engineers, IEEE Standard 1012 Software Verification and Validation, 1998.

[7] "International Organization for Standardization," ISO International Standard 15026, Information technology—System and Software Integrity Levels, 1998.

[8] "International Organization for Standardization," ISO Final Draft International Standard 9126-1, Software Engineering—Software Product Quality—Quality Characteristics and Sub-Characteristics, 2000.

[9] "International Organization for Standardization," ISO Committee Draft Technical Report 9126-3, Software Engineering—Software Product Quality—Internal Metrics, 2000.

[10] "International Organization for Standardization," ISO Committee Draft Technical Report 9126-2, Software Engineering—Software Product Quality—External Metrics, 2000.

[11] "International Organization for Standardization," ISO Committee Draft Technical Report 9126-4, Software Engineering—Software Product Quality—Quality in Use Metrics, 2000.

[12] "International Organization for Standardization," ISO International Standard 9000-3, Quality Management and Quality Assurance Standards—Part 3: Guidelines for the Application of ISO 9001 to the Design, Development, Supply, Installation and Maintenance of Software.

[13] "International Organization for Standardization," ISO/IEC Technical Report 15504 (Parts 1–9) Information Technology—Software Process Assessment, 1998.

[14] ISO The International Organization for Standardization, http://www.iso.ch.

[15] Council of the European Communities, Directive 90/270 on the Minimum Safety and Health Requirements for Work with Display Screen Equipment, 1990.

14

Implementation

Outline

14.1   INTRODUCTION TO IMPLEMENTATION

Implementation involves the overlapping area at the end of the development and the start of the use of a particular system (or version of a system). Because of this overlapping nature, implementation involves some of the most intense challenges for computer professionals, for organizational professionals, and for interactions between professionals.

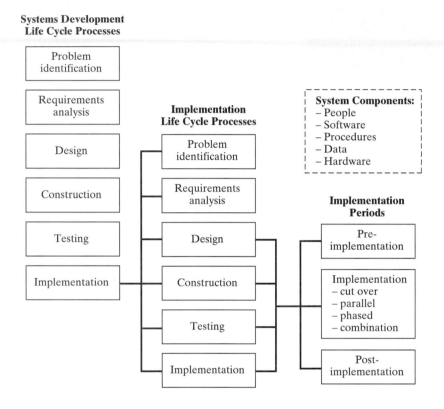

Figure 14-1 An implementation life cycle

Because of the complexities of typical systems implementations, implementation is often dealt with as a major project requiring a life cycle of its own, as illustrated in Figure 14-1. Implementation planning is essential to the success of installing a new system. The product of this life cycle is an implementation plan rather than a system. An implementation plan needs to consider changes to all the components of the organizational system, even if the main changes revolve around implementing e-Commerce software.

Implementation of major systems may have organizational-wide consequences and planning for such implementation often requires senior management involvement. Management involvement should include one or more managers with responsibility for all parts of the organization that will be affected by the implementation.

A plan is similar to a design. While it isn't an end in itself, it is an important step in making something happen. Before developing a plan or a design, we need first to identify what it is that we wish to achieve and then to analyze the specific requirements that need to be met. In other words we can apply the first three major phases of a life cycle to developing an Implementation plan. This plan, like other types of designs, also needs to consider what will go beyond to an eventual successful implementation.

Implementation plans cover a variety of activities, including:

- Converting data from old systems to the new one
- Getting people to convert to the new system
- Helping people use (operate) the new system
- Being prepared to deal with the ongoing need to maintain and upgrade the new system

However, before starting to develop an implementation plan (design) it is important to identify the requirements that it should meet.

14.2   UNDERSTANDING IMPLEMENTATION

14.2.1   Problem Identification for Implementation

The basic problem is that
   "Implementation is Organizational Change."

This leads to a specific problem that
   "Implementing a (insert name here) system is Organizational Change."

Secondary problems include:
   People are threatened by Change.
   People who are threatened may resist Change.

The basic objective is
   To successfully implement the (insert name here) system.

Machiavelli might suggest that
   To successfully implement the system, resistance should be eliminated.

A more enlightened secondary objective is
   To successfully implement the system, people should be reassured that the new system will help and will not threaten them.

This latter objective should suggest that a different kind of expertise is needed for planning implementation from that needed for designing the system, since it focuses on people rather than technology.

However, the design of the "system" should have already considered the needs of these people. If it didn't, it will be a failure. Although this is the first chapter to deal in detail with the need to avoid user resistance (which isn't necessarily related to the actual usability of the system), it deals with this topic much more than most other similar software engineering texts.

The potential for user resistance should have been identified as part of the consideration of operational feasibility; however, nothing that might have created user resistance was considered as development progressed through many decisions in the design and construction. User testing and prototyping can help reduce the potential for user resistance. However, users not directly involved in user testing or prototyping may still feel threatened and feel the need to resist. Increased workloads and stress during implementations can increase resistance. Given this set of concerns, is it any wonder that many implementations fail?

Planning for implementation should not wait until after a system is constructed and tested. Rather, it should begin at least as a part of the design phase, if not earlier.

Implementation involves a combination of technical and organizational change and thus must involve both computer and organizational professionals. Computer professionals are skilled in developing systems. However, the need for considering how people will react to a given system often requires organizational professionals with skills in organizational design and management and/or organizational psychology to be involved.

14.2.2   Requirements Analysis for Implementation

Analysis deals with identifying, "What is needed."

Analysis for implementation should identify, "What needs to be changed?"
    The answer is obviously "the system."

However, such an answer is too simplistic. Each of the main elements of "the complete system" need to be considered. These include five of the seven components identified in Chapter 1:

- People
- Procedures
- Hardware
- Software
- Data

(By this point in a development it is too late to change the goals of the organization and/or the system and it is seldom possible to change government regulations to which a system must adhere.)

Based on the objectives identified above, this list can be reprioritized based on the likelihood of change, putting people first. The nature of the change that is required should also be considered.

14.2.2.1   People

If different groups of users have been identified, each group needs to be considered separately. Their needs in terms of implementation may be just as distinct as their needs for the system.

While the typical focus of implementation is generally on direct users, it should also consider the effects of organizational change on other people in the organization. **Direct users** are those users who use a system by themselves. Direct users may work on their own or in teams and may or may not have access to assistance where necessary. If a manager types his or her own memos with a word processing package, then the manager is a direct user of the word processing system.

Indirect users are those users who have other users directly interact with a system on their behalf. If a manager has a secretary type memos for him or her with a word processing package, then the manager is an indirect user of the word processing system. Indirect users may see little or no difference, depending on whether or not the input they provide or the output they receive changes. However, even if they will not see any changes, they may feel threatened by the fear that they are being left out of being prepared for changes that will inevitably happen. At the very least they may expect implementation of the new system to create problems for others that will ripple over to them.

This fear of a ripple effect of problems may also affect other people not identified as users but who work closely with or otherwise interact with identified users. This fear of a ripple effect also applies to the managers of these various workers. People who may be affected even indirectly by the implementation of a new system or a set of changes to an existing system should be considered as stakeholders, since they have a "stake" in the outcome of the implementation.

People beyond the organization may also be affected or at least threatened by implementations:

- People in organizations with business connections to an organization implementing a new system may be affected by changes in that organization's ability to handle their needs, especially during periods of increased stress in the middle of implementations.
- Family members of users and other organizational employees also may be affected by the needs of these employees to work longer and harder during an implementation period.

Effects of changes to users can include:

- Minor or major changes in the user interface to software
- Minor or major changes in operational procedures
- Additional functionality provided by the software
- Changes to work routine and/or contacts with other workers due to automation and/or additional functionality
- Additions, changes, and/or deletions to job responsibilities due to automation and/or additional functionality
- Additions, changes, and/or deletions of authority relations with others due to changes in access to organizational information
- Elimination of a job (resulting in reassignment or termination) due to automation
- Hiring of additional workers/managers

Additional temporary effects can include:

- Demands for existing employees to work harder or overtime during running of parallel systems
- Employee burn out or illness due to the demands of running parallel systems
- Hiring and training temporary workers to help during the running of parallel systems

The possible effects on other people can range from minor disappointments to major conflicts with users whose increased stress affects their other relationships.

These effects will also add to the stress of the users involved. Care needs to be taken to avoid chain reactions to increased stress.

People may be subject to multiple changes or other effects from an implementation. While each of these might be considered to be minor, a number of minor changes may result in a very major combined effect on some people.

14.2.2.2   Software

Most of the system changes of interest to computer professionals involve software changes. Changes to the application software, as previously discussed, can involve:

- Modifying the existing system
- Adding to the existing system
- Replacing part or all of the existing system
- Developing a substantially new system

These categories identify different types of change to the application software. However, there may be additional software changes to other related software (such as updating or changing operating systems, or other general purpose packages used in conjunction with the application software). These additional changes are more likely when purchasing (rather than custom developing) an application package. The nature of the change depends partly on which other elements of "the complete system" will be affected.

- Modifying the existing system or adding to it will likely have the greatest effect on the users and may have some effect on the set of procedures and/or the data.
- Replacing all or part of an existing system or creating a new system is likely to have effects on most of the other main elements.

Since the software may be the most thoroughly designed and tested part of the complete system, implementation planning can focus more on the other main elements. The main changes that need to be considered regarding software implementation include:

- The ability to fix problems that may occur when the new software is actually implemented
- The ability to avoid confusion and to have sufficient hardware capacity if it is decided to run two sets of software in parallel
- The ability to revert to the old software if major problems occur once the new software is installed, especially where users are cut over to it (without keeping the old system running in parallel)

14.2.2.3   Procedures

Design of the software should deal with changes in how the direct users interact with the software. While this design should attempt to make this interaction intuitive, there is generally a need for support and training of both existing and new users. While the need for training may be recognized (often begrudgingly), the need for additional support is often ignored (because it implies that users may have difficulties with the system). Both support and training involve new procedures outside the basic software system (even if they are implemented via software).

The implementation of a new system will likely require changes in organizational procedures beyond the human-computer interface. The extent of these changes will depend on the design of the system, which, in turn, may ignore the need for these changes because they are outside the boundaries of the "system development."

Changes to procedures involving interactions between people may create greater tension than changes between a person and a machine. This is because people often create greater expectations of each other and are less forgiving of each other than of machines (and associated software). The effect of changes in procedures will be dependent on:

- who is involved
- how major the changes are
- how well accepted the old procedures were
- how entrenched the old procedures were (i.e., were they automatic, or did people have to think about them in order to apply them?)

14.2.2.4   Data

The type and amount of change in data is a major concern in the design of a software system. However, developers may fail to consider the need for possible future data conversions.

Experienced developers often try to avoid changes to existing data and databases, since many database reorganizations become major disasters. They will often go to extreme lengths (similar to a man who shops for a new $500 suit that will go with his one and only $10 tie) to avoid changing existing data. Just think of all the last-minute fuss about the Year 2000 "computer bug"—a situation that had been well known and discussed for most of the decade leading up to 2000. Considering the need for periodic maintenance of software and the average life of state of the art software, there was no justification for any important systems not being prepared to deal with the turn of the century!

Even when software systems are entirely replaced, there may be no need to change existing databases. It is more likely that additional data need to be added (which may often be done by adding new data files rather than by expanding old ones).

- Where databases or their contents need to be changed, these changes may require special programs, extensive conversion processing time, and careful testing to ensure that the data conversion happened correctly. The time involved in conversion processing and testing, where significant, may mean periods of time where regular application processing must be suspended to ensure synchronization of the old and new databases.
- If at all possible, it is desirable to convert databases prior to implementing new software.
- Where a cut over to a new database is to be made, all versions (both old and new) of all systems accessing the database become unavailable during this time.
- Where parallel running of old and new systems is to be done, transactions may be made to a copy of the old data during the conversion process, but will have to be held to apply to the new data once the conversion process is completed.

The complexity of setting up an entirely new database for a new application system varies considerably depending on how much data is expected to be pre-loaded into it. If there is no need for pre-loaded data then it is relatively trivial, compared to where data has to be accumulated or otherwise obtained and then entered.

14.2.2.5 Hardware

While many new software systems are designed to run on existing hardware, this design expectation does not guarantee that no changes will be involved. A new software system may increase usage demands on existing hardware resources beyond available capacity and even beyond initial expectations.

Periods of parallel running of old and new application software and/or old and new databases may cause considerable strains on hardware capacity. Estimates of required hardware capacity should consider peak demands rather than average demands. Where new hardware is required, it generally must be installed and tested before removing any existing hardware that it may be replacing. This can create temporary space overcrowding, leading to a variety of problems, including pressures to cut over to the new hardware without sufficient testing.

14.2.3 High-Level Designs/Plans for Implementation

Design deals with identifying a suitable method of accomplishing
  "What is needed."

Design for implementation should identify "How can the needed changes be accomplished?"
The answer becomes the implementation plan.

The implementation plan should identify how and when to accomplish each of the changes that have been identified. It should plan how to maximize the potential desirable effects and to minimize undesirable ones.

There are many standard treatments (such as user training and database reformatting) that are used in implementations to accomplish changes for each of the main elements of a "complete system." A "**treatment**" is any action that is planned to help people deal with the effects of an implementation. Developers often may tend to select to use the same treatments they have always used rather than evaluating what is really needed. Thus, a general prescription for implementing changes to people is often either to send them a memo (for minor changes) or to send them to training (for major changes). However, despite the long-standing traditional use of these two forms of implementing change, neither is often effective in changing the attitudes of people. The method of accomplishing change needs to be designed to suit the particular needs of the given implementation.

Developers can't and shouldn't expect to accomplish changes instantaneously. Changes don't occur instantly at their proclamation. They take time, which in some cases can be quite significant. They also have to follow a logical order, since some changes are required before others (such as preparing the people for the other parts of an implementation) and some changes need to be done at the last possible minute (such as converting data for a new system).

It is useful to distinguish between those changes that must be made relatively simultaneously and those that can be made at other times.

- Some people may refer to the entire period of time when any implementation-related changes are made as the implementation of a project. However, in this chapter, the implementation period of a project will have a more specific meaning.
- In this chapter, the **implementation period** is the period of time during which the new system is loaded with data and put into regular use and that lasts until any old systems are replaced. This is typically where the majority of changes occur within a relatively short period of time.

14.2.3.1   Pre-Implementation Changes

The **pre-implementation period** is the period of time leading up to the time when a new system is completely implemented. Some changes are prerequisites to the actual implementation of various other changes. For example, developing a readiness for the implementation may help assure people that it does not involve undesirable "surprises." Where there are a number of potentially major negative effects to manage, it may be desirable to spread out the changes, both before and during implementation, in order to be better able to deal with the effects of individual changes.

During the pre-implementation period it is generally desirable:

- To make as many of the changes required by the implementation as possible
- To spread out these changes, as much as possible, to limit the effects of change at any one time

14.2.3.2   Implementation Changes

The actual implementation can be planned as:

- A single cut over
- A parallel implementation
- A phased cut over
- A phased set of parallel implementations

A **"cut over"** occurs when a new system is put in actual use and the old system is removed at the same time. In a single cut over, there is never more than one system in use, and there is often a period where neither system is available. Once cut over has taken place, the new system is the only one that can be used. This forces everyone to use and rely on the new system, which may serve either to stifle employee resistance or to aggravate it. Cut over makes it very difficult to consider going back to the old system regardless of employee resistance or major problems with the new system. If a cut over works well enough, it can cost considerably less than a parallel implementation.

A **"parallel" implementation** occurs where a system is put in actual use for some time before the old system is removed. Parallel implementations allow testing of the new system in action before certifying it to be 100% acceptable. It also allows for discontinuing it if major problems occur and continuing with the old system until the new system can be adjusted and retested via a further parallel implementation. Parallel implementations provide greater security but can strain resources (people, space, equipment, time, budget) in order to achieve this greater security. Because of these strains on resources, parallel implementations are most often used only on mission-critical or organization-critical systems.

A **"phased implementation"** occurs where individual portions of the system, such as certain user groups, are implemented at different times. Phased implementations always involve some aspects of parallel implementations and may involve aspects of cut overs. Phased approaches require that the old system still be run "in parallel" to serve those portions that have not yet been "cut over." Phased implementations require more planning and management but can provide a greater opportunity to address individual needs that occur during the actual implementation by spreading it over various phases. Phased implementations can pose considerable problems where they require data conversion to be phased or where they require different versions of the same databases to be run in parallel.

Despite the best of preparations, there will also be some changes that are fundamental to the implementation period itself, where the intended real people, following the intended real procedures, use the developed/purchased real software with real data on the existing or purchased real hardware.

While the use of real data is often the defining moment, users, procedures, and even software may change up to and even after this actual moment. (Changes to the data after this point would be considered part of using the system, and changes to the hardware after this point would be considered an expansion of the system.)

It is quite likely that a number of unplanned changes will occur in the early use of the system (especially to people and procedures). While these changes can't be planned for directly, it is important that a procedure is planned to help deal with these changes in a usable (accurate, efficient, and satisfactory) manner.

14.2.3.3   Post-Implementation Institutionalization

The **post-implementation period** is the period of time after a new system has been officially implemented and up until the implementation has been fully accepted by all of its users. Implementation doesn't occur instantaneously; rather, it involves a period of turmoil between when the old system was routinely used and accepted and when the new system is generally accepted within the routine of its users and of the organization. While some people may be willing to accept it even before it is installed, it may even take them some time to gain sufficient experience with it to treat it routinely.

Where problems with the new system are found during implementation, they need to be fixed and the fix implemented. Fixes during implementation do not always involve software changes. In many cases fixes during implementation may involve deciding to ignore the problem (live with it) because it does not have significant consequences, or developing a procedure that allows users to "work around" the problem.

It is generally desirable:

- For the post-implementation period to be completed as quickly as possible
- To ensure that users are satisfied with the new system before declaring the post-implementation period completed
- To provide additional assistance in dealing with change and the effects of change throughout the post-implementation period

14.2.4 Detailed Implementation Plan Considerations

Consideration of each of the system components, which implementation can change, can lead to the identification of options for how and when and what can or should be done as part of a successful implementation.

14.2.4.1 People

People aren't just "implemented" like other major system components. They must be prepared to change as required by the implementation. Some people may be already able and motivated to make this change, on their own, without any special help. Other people will require some "treatment" to prepare them for making the necessary changes.

- Suitable treatments should be planned to handle all changes, which on their own or in combination lead to significant effects on people or on the potential success of the implementation.
- Some changes may require a variety of treatments.
- Some treatments may work for a variety of changes.

The most common treatment is training people to use a new system. It is traditional to expect that implementing a new system will involve some need for user training. Software developers generally, and often begrudgingly, accept the assumption that they are expected to design user training materials (even though most of these developers have no formal training in designing education or training). In more ideal situations, developers will enlist the aid of training professionals in this role. However, regardless of who designs and delivers the training, the use of training alone may not be sufficient to support all of the needs users (and any other stakeholders who may have been identified) have for assistance in coping with implementation-related changes.

Training is based on the recognition that:

- Certain skills are required to use a system
- The trainees lack these skills
- The trainees are willing to learn these skills

Without all three of these prerequisites, training will often fail. The most important prerequisite is the willingness of people to learn these skills. Training seldom devotes much time or effort to convincing the people of the importance of learning these skills. While some people enjoy taking training, others may be threatened by it because:

- They must recognize their lack of skills
- Training is usually reserved for major changes, which means that it will likely deal with skills that are hard to learn (this may also have the additional negative effect of prejudicing these people against the new system)
- Failure to learn these new skills may have a negative effect on the person's future employment

Something often needs to be done first to reduce the threat of both training and the new system. What is generally missing with the implementation of new systems (regardless of how good the new systems are) is sufficient motivational marketing of the benefits of the new system (and of any training that will help people to easily achieve these benefits).

Developers of all kinds of systems (not just information systems) that will be imposed upon people (rather than sold to them) generally get so caught up in their good feelings about the new system that they mistakenly expect everyone to share these feelings. They seldom consider the need to motivate (market) the new system to its intended users. Developers intimately familiar with the details of the new system expect that the new system will speak for itself and that everyone will love it. Providing users with skills training often only addresses the users' logical needs. Before users are ready to have their logical needs addressed, they must first have their emotional needs (and fears) satisfied.

Implementation planning for peoples' needs should involve at least three distinct types of treatments:

- **Marketing** (and selling the personal benefits of) the new system to the people
- **Training** the people to use the new system
- Providing ongoing **support** for people in using the system

In planning these treatments, it should be remembered that people may respond best if they are involved in developing and implementing the treatment for themselves.

- People are more likely to resist or ignore what they are told, especially if it includes changes or threats to the way that they are currently doing things.
- People should not be left on their own to deal with change because they may choose to ignore it. When making changes involving external users, it is important to help and encourage them to make the necessary changes.
- If people take part in making changes, they are more likely to take ownership of the change and to work harder to help make it happen. When making changes involving people in an organization, it is best to involve these people in making the change.

Implementation planning should not only focus on the needs of the end users.

- Marketing to and training of end users about the new system, without first marketing to and training of their managers, can lead to unnecessary conflicts between the two. Implementation preparation for new systems should start with the highest levels of management involved and work its way down through the organization. In this way management commitment can be secured early and managers need not be intimidated by the advanced knowledge of their subordinates.
- Stakeholders also need to be considered. In many cases it is infeasible to train them. Thus, implementation planning needs to focus on:
  - Marketing, which can be accomplished by motivating them (e.g., promising certificates for a dinner for two, at a choice of high-quality restaurants, after the implementation period is completed to all affected employees as a minor compensation for inconveniences that the implementation causes to personal and family relationships)

- Support, which can be accomplished by ongoing motivations (e.g., actually providing the dinner certificates and other rewards for other employees that they can share with their families)

NOTE: The evolving nature of e-Commerce systems will have this on-going motivation also act as marketing to prepare stakeholders (e.g., the families of employees) for the implementation of the next version of the system.

14.2.4.2   Software

Often software is developed on hardware different from that on which it will actually run. Implementing software involves installing it and testing it on the intended hardware before actually using it. This installation testing should occur on each separate machine where the software is to be used, since each machine may have its own differences due to its unique history. While these differences generally will have no impact on new software, there are occasions where unexpected problems may arise. Installation testing on a number of similar machines need not be extensive, but should be sufficient to ensure that the software is functioning properly before it is used for real work.

Where software is to be installed by users on their own machines, detailed help needs to be provided to assist both with the installation and with testing the success of the installation. A popular practice is to provide auto-installation software that, when inserted into a computer and activated, will automatically install the new application software. However, since testing recognizes the possibility of failure, provision of similar installation testing assistance is virtually nonexistent.

Developers often take the attitude that if the software doesn't work when installed, it is the user's existing hardware and/or software system's fault, and quickly shift the blame to the user. Such blame shifting doesn't help resolution of such problems. Shifting the onus to the users to solve installation problems doesn't work at all for e-Commerce, where customers may be driven to the competition by difficulties they have with using a particular organization's software.

The promise of the Web is that the average user doesn't have to do anything to install or test the majority of software that it delivers. Developers of e-Commerce systems should avoid requiring users to install "plug-ins" or any specialty software (beyond a recent version of one of the major Web browsers). Where special features such as animations or sound necessitate the use of plug-ins, developers should choose commonly used popular versions, which many users are likely to have already installed, and users should be provided as much assistance as possible in obtaining and installing these plug-ins.

All software requires some form of installation testing prior to being used for significant real work. However, since most e-Commerce users will not perform any testing, it is essential for developers to test e-Commerce software on a wide variety of platforms (see Chapter 12 for a discussion of Considering Platform Dependencies).

14.2.4.3   Procedures

Implementing new procedures can be the cause of the greatest amount of confusion, especially during a parallel implementation. As soon as new procedures are announced, users need to be able to distinguish which procedures apply only to the new system (to be implemented in the future) and which changed procedures can be implemented immediately.

Where new procedures can be implemented with the old system, they should be implemented as soon as possible in the pre-implementation period. It is preferable to limit the number of procedural changes necessitated during the actual implementation of the new system, to avoid unnecessary mental overloading on the users. Only those procedures clearly related to the new system should remain to be implemented during the actual implementation period.

While there are some people who blindly follow whatever procedures they are given, many people will follow them better if the reason for the new or changed procedure is explained to them. This explanation can provide the necessary motivation to change user resistance into user acceptance.

Announcing and explaining changes in procedures to users as soon as possible, can give the users time to identify situations that may have been overlooked in the development of the procedures. These situations may require further changes that can be made before the main implementation of the new system.

14.2.4.4 Data

There is a major difference between implementing systems, which require no previous data, and systems, which will make use of previous data.

Where no previous data are required, there still may be data-related preparations that need to be planned (such as, the ordering of special forms for data collection or the purchasing and testing of various sources of external data/information).

Running systems in parallel creates special requirements for dealing with previous data:

- The old system will have to be stopped while a copy is made and installed into the new system, so that there is one database for each system that can be separately updated.
- A method for comparing the databases at the end of the parallel run should be planned, and any specialty software required for this comparison should be acquired.

Where data conversion is required, the conversion needs to be designed, and special software will often need to be developed. Before converted data can be used, whether in a cut over or in a parallel implementation, it needs to be tested. Often this testing may require the development of additional software.

Considerable time (and processing capacity) may be required for data conversion and conversion testing:

- It is best to schedule conversion and conversion testing for a time when the system is not needed and can be taken out of use.
- A distant second best is to schedule conversion at a time when the need for the system and associated data will be at a minimum. Copies of all transactions processed against the old database during conversion need to be kept so that they can be processed against the new database after conversion.

14.2.4.5 Hardware

As already discussed, implementation may involve problems relating to existing hardware capacity and/or space to house new hardware, especially during parallel implementations. Planning needs to consider not only the hardware itself but also needs relating to furniture, lighting, soundproofing, temperature control, media supply and storage, and electrical and communications connections. Where multiple changes are needed they must be coordinated so that the changes do not interfere with one another and that the changes are done in the optimal order. Again, it is ideal to complete as many of these changes as is practical during the pre-implementation period.

When new hardware is installed, people expect it to do something. An installed computer that is sitting idle can predispose people to thinking that it is useless and that the software must have bugs, which is preventing its immediate use. Thus, it is best to test new hardware away from its intended location and not to install it until close to the main installation date. It is better that hardware that is installed early at least have a game running on it or be used for some other trivial purpose, than allow it to remain turned off in view of its future users until the main installation date.

14.2.5 Some e-Commerce–Related Implementation Concerns

External users require more careful handling than employees.

- Employees generally can be required as part of their job to adapt to new systems.
- In many cases external users have to be found or led to an e-Commerce application. Due to the competitive nature of the Web, loyalty cannot be taken for granted; rather, it has to be continually encouraged in order to retain external users.

Attempts to reach new external users and to retain current external users may require additional software and/or other resources that were not considered in the main analysis and design of an e-Commerce system.

- Many Web sites resort to give-aways, contests, games, and other gimmicks to encourage potential users to visit them. It is still unclear how many of these gimmicks actually result in solid business relationships.
- Likewise, some Web sites provide additional content and/or tasks support only to those users who have established some level of relationship with them.

Additionally, not all desired external users may be Web users. There is still a large portion of the general population without access to (and even without interest in) the Web. If they were part of a targeted group, then alternative methods of conducting business may be required to reach them. This may be especially true for start-up businesses that intend to concentrate on the Web.

Internal users of new systems will be most ready to use them if they participated in the development of these systems. Participation can provide both the necessary motivation and much of the necessary training. However, if an application grows quickly, as many e-Commerce applications have done, then additional internal users, who did not participate in the development and who may have been hired after the development, will need to be motivated and/or trained.

Software will need to run on the hardware that external users choose to use or they won't use it. External users typically will be expected to supply their own hardware and will expect the organization to supply any needed software. The larger the desired external market, the simpler the software must be both in its construction and in its use.

Start-up organizations and/or businesses developing new applications may benefit from the ability to create and test their initial databases relatively leisurely without needing to quickly convert existing ones. Existing organizations that are replacing or enhancing existing applications, may choose to treat new e-Commerce systems as separate "branches" of the organization with their own dedicated data in order to minimize and isolate the need for extensive data conversion. Over time, existing business could be channeled to these "branches" until all data have migrated.

Because competitors may easily gain access (even under the guise of customers) to an e-Commerce site, care needs to be taken to ensure the protection of data both to ensure their privacy (where appropriate) and to avoid corruption of the data.

Procedures need to be simple, easy to use, and as obvious as possible to eliminate the need for external users to have any special training in order to use the application.

14.2.6   How to Construct an Implementation Plan

An implementation plan should be constructed iteratively. Each iteration should take into account the effect of newly scheduled activities on already scheduled ones to avoid scheduling an unreasonable amount of change, work, or other expectations within any given time period.

People-related implementation activities should be inserted into the plan first, since making changes to people will likely take the longest to implement. This initial plan can be used as an adjustable framework for adding additional implementation activities. While a time frame can be established for the various people-related implementation activities, the people implementation schedule should contain only relative dates.

Provisions should be made for dealing with any changes in the people-related implementation schedule. While there is often a tendency to just try and do more in less time, consideration needs to be made to ensure that the people involved will be capable of actually accomplishing any additional work. This may require the extension or postponement of other implementation activities.

Software implementation activities should be added second. Many e-Commerce implementations center around the implementation of new software. (Adding new products and/or services as additional data to an existing system is often more of a marketing event based on routine systems maintenance, rather than a major implementation.)

The date of expected delivery or of the desired implementation of the software can be used to anchor the schedule to the actual calendar. Since software may not always be ready on time, provisions should be made for dealing with any changes in its implementation schedule.

Data implementation may be highly time crucial and should be added third to the implementation schedule. Scheduling data implementation may have a number of effects on already scheduled activities, including:

- Requiring that people are trained and available to conduct the data implementation activities
- Requiring that the software is tested and ready to use once the data are converted and/or implemented
- Requiring that people are trained in using the software and are ready to start using it once the data are converted and/or implemented

Provisions should also be made for dealing with any changes in the implementation schedule, since data implementation is time critical.

Hardware implementation often can be accomplished prior to the main implementation period, and need not be scheduled until more crucial activities are already scheduled. Scheduling hardware too early should be avoided. Dangers in implementing hardware too early can include:

- Spending money before it is needed, which could have been profitably invested until needed
- Getting less hardware for your money, since computer prices are continually declining as computer capabilities continually increase
- Giving users the impression that the new system won't work if the hardware isn't put to some immediate use

A consideration of the general availability of certain pieces of hardware may influence its scheduled implementation. Unusual or highly specialized hardware needs to be ordered and tested earlier than more common hardware, to ensure that it is ready when needed.

Procedure changes should be considered last in the planning for implementation. This is not because procedures should be left to last in order of implementation, but rather because changes may be needed to procedures to accommodate all of the other changes involved in the implementation.

Once necessary changes in procedures have been identified, it is ideal to change them as soon as possible. Often many procedures can be changed or improved prior to the implementation of any new system that may have identified the usefulness of such a change or improvement.

14.2.7   Evaluating an Implementation Plan

Implementation plans, like all designs, should be evaluated before they are actually used. This evaluation should be conducted independently from those people who developed the plan. While this evaluation is likely to be done as a single activity, it should still consider the aspects of validation, verification, and usability. Evaluation should involve answering the following questions:

- Does the implementation plan meet its requirements?
- Will the implementation plan work correctly?
- Is the implementation plan usable by those people who must use it?

14.2.8 Implementing the Implementation Plan

Implementation plans typically involve a diverse collection of activities that are somewhat interdependent of one another. Wherever a large number of activities are involved, there is a likelihood that one or more activities will be delayed or experience other difficulties. Although various individuals may be responsible for individual implementation activities, it is important that the overall implementation be centrally managed as a major aspect of the project. It is important to recognize the potential effect of any difficulties that are encountered on other implementation activities and to make adjustments to the implementation plan wherever necessary.

14.3 APPLYING IMPLEMENTATION PLANNING

14.3.1 Achieving Implementation in Organizations

The majority of this chapter, like most others, has focused on technical processes that, if accomplished successfully, can lead to success. Each chapter, including this one, also identifies a number of challenges and opportunities related to accomplishing these processes.

If organizations are to achieve the implementation of an e-Commerce system or any other major change, they need to do more than do things right. They need to continually avoid the various threats and challenges to achieving success.

- Organizations should understand the various technical and project processes involved in development and allow the best people to perform them without excessively interfering with how they do them. Methodologies, standards, style guides, and procedures can help with developments. However, there is generally a cost involved with using each form of help. Developers need to balance the increased workload of using any form of development help with the potential benefits it can provide to the development.
- Organizations should understand what can go wrong and continually identify and deal with each difficulty as soon as possible. The commitment and involvement of senior management is essential to the success of an e-Commerce development. The project processes, discussed briefly in Chapter 5, are needed to help ensure this success.

14.3.2 Student Assignment—Implementation Planning

1. Reconfirm the Stakeholders.
   Identify the different groups of users and stakeholders who should be considered in your implementation plan. This should be done by:
   - Listing the user groups identified previously in your project
   - Listing any other groups of stakeholders identified previously in your project
   - Identifying and listing any other groups of stakeholders who may be affected by the implementation of your system
2. Plan People-Related Implementation Activities.
   For each of at least the five most important groups identified in step 1:

- Identify the main changes that implementation will make to members of the group
- Identify the effects these changes might have on the group
- Identify a treatment or set of treatments that can be used to accomplish the change successfully
- Identify when these treatments should be performed relative to the main implementation

3. Develop an Implementation Schedule.

   Develop a schedule for the implementation activities (including individual treatments of particular groups of people and other main implementation activities). Provide a brief discussion as an introduction to your schedule to explain the main decisions you made (such as whether to use a cut over implementation, a parallel implementation, or a phased cut over).

14.4   AN EXAMPLE OF APPLYING IMPLEMENTATION PLANNING

14.4.1   Considering the Stakeholders

The main groups of users were identified in the task analysis (discussed in the example in Chapter 7):

- Customers—as a general group
  - Potential customers
  - Regular customers
  - Gold Cup customers
  - Fraudulent customers
- Suppliers—as a general group
  - Coffee equipment/supplies manufacturers
  - Coffee bean growers
  - Fraudulent suppliers
- *Savor the Cup* staff
- Sales—as a general group
  - Sales representatives
  - Consultants
  - Marketers
- Purchasing
- Accounting
- Logistics

Further analysis identified the additional stakeholders, who may be affected by the implementation of *Savor the Cup's* new e-Commerce system. They are listed in order of the magnitude of the expected effects:

- Development staff involved in the implementation
- Families of *Savor the Cup* staff involved in the implementation
- Senior management at *Savor the Cup,* who expect junior managers to deal with most of the implementation on their own

- Shareholders and creditors of *Savor the Cup,* who expect that *Savor the Cup* keeps increasing in its profitability without taking any major risks
- Government regulators, who expect *Savor the Cup* to comply with their regulations in the way that they specify and without causing them any difficulties

Plans need to be made to help the first two of these groups of stakeholders to deal with the effects of the implementation.

- Overworked and under-appreciated development staff may make more mistakes and have more difficulties in their implementation efforts.
- Dissatisfied families of employees may increase the stress on employees, leading to a range of difficulties with the implementation.

Efforts may be needed to reassure the other three groups of stakeholders that the implementation will not cause them to be negatively affected.

14.4.2   Changes to and Treatments for Stakeholders

Tables 14-1 to 14-9 identify some changes and suggested treatments for some of the stakeholders of the *Savor the Cup* e-Commerce system.

Table 14-1   Existing customers being able to buy on-line

Who:	Existing customers (both regular customers and Gold Cup customers).
Changes:	Customers will have the ability to order on-line by themselves whenever they wish.
Effects:	1. They will still have the choice of ordering in person. 2. They now have the opportunity to order their chosen products on-line.
Suggested Treatments:	1. Contact all customers and inform them of their new options and the opportunities as a result of our new application. 2. Have consultants available for on-site Gold Cup customer training regarding use of the application.
When to Perform:	1. Provide Gold Cup customers with advance notice (at least 3 months) to give them time to plan changes in their internal ordering procedures. 2. Inform all customers as soon as system is implemented. 3. Provide help for Gold Cup customers on an ongoing basis. Expect high demands for help in the first two months after implementation.

Table 14-2   Existing customers receiving information on-line

Who:	Existing customers (both regular customers and Gold Cup customers).
Changes:	Useful information will be made available to them on-line and will be regularly updated.
Effects:	They will have easier access to some of the most important information they need.
Suggested Treatments:	1. Contact all customers and inform them of their new options and the opportunities as a result of our new application.
When to Perform:	1. Inform all customers as soon as system is implemented. This can be combined with informing them about the on-line ordering capabilities of the new system.

Table 14-3   Potential customers being attracted to *Savor the Cup*

Who:	Potential customers.
Changes:	The new system will make it easier for potential customers to find out about and order from *Savor the Cup*.
Effects:	Potential customers need to know about the new system and be able to find it in order to take advantage of it.
Suggested Treatments:	1. Heavy on-line advertising as well as advertising in industry magazines.
	2. Have a sales representative go to selected potential Gold Cup customers to explain and demonstrate the use of the system.
When to Perform:	1. Both treatments should start as soon as the system has been implemented and should continue on an ongoing basis. The greatest efforts should be conducted in the first two months after implementation.

Table 14-4   Sales staff providing information on-line

Who:	Sales representatives.
Changes:	Providing basic customer-related information on-line and making other information into a consulting product.
Effects:	1. This narrows the types of services provided by a sales representative.
	2. Some sales representatives will be reassigned as consultants, some won't. Some sales representatives will want to be reassigned, some won't. There may be differences between what the organization wants and what an individual wants.
	3. Some sales representatives may leave the company because they will not be able to accept these changes.
Suggested Treatments:	1. Since these changes are very major, marketing them needs to be done on an individual basis. Managers will need to discuss changes with each sales representative and should conduct their initial discussions within the same week throughout the entire organization in order to head off rumors that may create larger negative effects than necessary.
	2. A procedure should be established that gives individual sales representatives an opportunity to tell their managers, and the organization, how they would like to fit into the new structure.
	3. Training will be needed to help prepare all affected sales staff for changes in their roles.
	4. Getting sales staff to discuss how they are coping with the change and to share strategies for success may provide ongoing support.
When to Perform:	1. New staffing assignments should be established before training begins.
	2. Training sessions need to be conducted during pre-implementation.
	3. A series of meetings should be planned for the post-implementation period. Because these meetings will occur during a period of possible turmoil and because *Savor the Cup* has sales representatives all over the world, it may be best if these meetings are held using teleconferencing. However, the effective use of teleconferencing requires experience with the medium. Thus, it is important to start using sales representative teleconferences in the pre-implementation period to prepare people for their more important use in post-implementation support.

Table 14-5   Changes to selling involving sales representatives

Who:	Sales representatives.
Changes:	1. The new system will allow customers to order directly without having to contact a sales representative. 2. Sales representatives will use the same system for customers who still order through them.
Effects:	1. This will reduce the contact between sales representatives and many existing customers. 2. This will expand the number of customers a sales representative may be responsible for serving. 3. This may involve various changes in the type of services provided by a sales representative.
Suggested Treatments:	These changes will require training and support.
When to Perform:	This can be combined with the training and support for changes in the provision of information to customers.

Table 14-6   Effects on families of *Savor the Cup* employees

Who:	Families of *Savor the Cup* staff.
Changes:	All families may have their usual routines disrupted by various aspects of the implementation.
Effects:	This may be a very stressful period of time for many families. 1. There may be very minor changes for some families. 2. The greatest effects will involve families of sales staff. Some families may have to move based on transfers to sales staff members.
Suggested Treatments:	It is important to prepare and reassure families as well as possible. The greater the anticipated disruption, the greater the preparation that may be needed. Demonstrations of organizational commitment toward families can be useful. 1. A "sales meeting" to discuss possible advantages of adding e-Commerce to the tools available to sales representatives could be held at a family-oriented location (such as Disney World), and the organization could pay for bringing their sales representatives' families. It would be important to keep the meeting short and to provide significant time for sales representatives to spend with their families. 2. Minor preparation may be required for the families of other staff. This could involve promising special rewards to be provided after implementation is accomplished. 3. Special employee assistance may be required for the families of employees who have to work extended periods of time during implementation. 4. Further support can be provided by post-implementation rewards, such as restaurant gift certificates.
When to Perform:	1. It is best to prepare families before any job changes are announced or discussed. This could be done toward the end of the requirements analysis or during the design. It is preferable that such a meeting be held before the design is totally committed, since it may identify further requirements that should be met. 2. Other treatments should be performed as indicated above.

Table 14-7   Vendors receiving information on-line

Who:	Suppliers.
Changes:	Will have greater access to information about the needs and interests of *Savor the Cup* and will be encouraged to contact *Savor the Cup* on-line or otherwise if they can meet these needs.
Effects:	This may increase communication and improve the relationship between *Savor the Cup* and potential suppliers.
Suggested Treatments:	1. Contact all current vendors and inform them of their new options and the opportunities as a result of the new system.
	2. Have a purchasing staff member contact selected potential vendors to explain the use of the system.
	3. Use on-line advertising as well as advertising in industry magazines to attract the attention of other potential vendors.
When to Perform:	1. Provide current vendors with advance notice (at least two months) to give them time to plan changes in their internal bidding procedures.
	2. Contact potential selected vendors as soon as system is implemented.
	3. Advertising should start as soon as the system has been implemented and should continue on an ongoing basis. The greatest efforts should be conducted in the first two months after implementation.

Table 14-8   Changes to dealing with vendors involving purchasing

Who:	Purchasing staff.
Changes:	They will be able to communicate with suppliers in a more efficient manner.
Effects:	1. This should increase the number of suppliers bidding on the needs of *Savor the Cup*. This may have both good and bad effects:
	• It will increase the work required to evaluate suppliers where many suppliers bid on a particular need.
	• It may decrease the work required to find specialty or new products that purchasing does not already know where to obtain.
	2. "Just-in-time" inventory management is now a more feasible objective, considering that purchasing will have instant communication with the suppliers.
Suggested Treatments:	Purchasing staff need to be:
	• Prepared for changes in their relationships with suppliers
	• Prepared to deal with changes to their work
	• Involved in developing new procedures to handle these changes
	• Reassured that future enhancements to the system will focus on needs they identify based on their use of the new system.
	In order to accomplish these treatment goals:
	1. A discussion should be held with purchasing staff to consider the various changes and to get their suggestions for how to handle them.
	NOTE: Holding a discussion rather than a training session may reduce the threatening nature of some of these unknown changes.
	2. A team should be formed of selected purchasing staff with help from other professionals to:
	• Establish procedures for dealing with the changes
	• Train all members of purchasing staff in these new procedures
	• Start to identify purchasing needs that could be incorporated into the next version of the system

(Continued)

Table 14-8 Continued

	NOTE: Involving the purchasing staff in developing their own response to these changes may reduce the threatening nature of some of these unknown changes.
When to Perform:	1. Discussions should start with production staff as soon as the design for the new system has been finalized.
	2. The discussions should lead directly to the formation of a team to deal with changes.

Table 14-9 Changes involving accounting

Who:	Accounting.
Changes:	1. The need to deal with a new type of sales order.
	2. The need to provide accounting and auditing support to a new system.
Effects:	While not changing the general nature of their duties, the new system will change the tools with which they must work.
Suggested Treatments:	1. Becoming more modern is not sufficient motivation for most people. However, the system may be marketed to accountants by presenting suitable projections that demonstrate how it will help *Savor the Cup* to prosper and to grow in the future. This may be most effective if accompanied by stock options, profit sharing, or other suitable incentives.
	2. Training in dealing with the new systems will be required.
	3. Ongoing support will be required to ensure that proper accounting can be performed on and with the new system. Where accounting needs demand, modifications may need to be made to the new system.
When to Perform:	1. It is useful to market the projected advantages of the new system as soon as possible, to encourage the accountants to identify how it can best be developed to integrate with their needs.
	2. Initial training should be started as soon as the design is completed. This training may uncover aspects of the design that need to be changed before construction is completed.
	3. Further training needs to be conducted once the actual system is constructed. This training may be combined with some aspects of testing the system.
	4. Priority needs to be given to ensuring that the new system meets applicable accounting needs to fulfill both financial and regulatory requirements. It may be unacceptable to wait to meet these needs in a future version.

14.5 CHALLENGES AND OPPORTUNITIES IN APPLYING IMPLEMENTATION PLANNING

The following are the most frequent problems encountered with implementation.

Challenges with Assuming the Best

- Some developers do not identify any negative factors that might influence implementation. They assume that everything would run smoothly.

Challenges with the Scope of Time Involved

- Some developers do not consider the overall time frame of implementation. They just focus on cramming all activities into the main implementation period.
- Some developers fail to consider the needs for ongoing treatments in the post-implementation period.

Challenges with Limiting the People or Effects Involved

- Some developers deal with all the changes, effects, and so on for all people together, instead of considering them separately for each group.
- Some developers only consider the effects of implementation on external users or only on internal users and ignore the effects on other users and other stakeholders.
- Some developers only expect one change per group of people instead of identifying all possible changes.

Evolving Ahead

Outline

15.1   SOME MAJOR THEMES OF E-COMMERCE DEVELOPMENT

This book has presented a life cycle approach to dealing with the main processes involved in developing e-Commerce systems. Because of the nature of using a printed medium, it has needed to present these ideas in a linear manner. However, as first discussed in Chapter 3, e-Commerce systems need to go beyond linear and even hierarchical structures to become value-added networks. The same applies for e-Commerce development. There are many relationships that connect the various development processes into a methodology that produces successful e-Commerce systems. This section reviews some of the major themes, discussed throughout the book, that provide this connection.

15.1.1 Iteration

The concept of iteration, introduced in Chapter 1, connects all processes potentially with all other processes. Iteration involves making improvements while moving throughout a systems development life cycle. Developers must make allowances to recognize that no development is ever perfect. They need to make trade-offs between continued work on a single process and advancing to perform other processes. Developers should still follow the traditional development life cycle as long as it helps them to make progress toward developing the desired system. However, they should not wait for perfection, but continue to progress toward a completed system which, while still being imperfect, is an improvement over the current system. Developers also need to be prepared to add or modify existing development information as new information becomes available or required.

15.1.2 Top-Down Development

Top-down development involves continually increasing what is known about an application and the one or more systems that can serve it. It follows an iceberg model, where what is known at any point in time is only the tip of the iceberg.

Development proceeds from answering why some application could be served better than it is currently served, through identifying what could be done about this, to determining how this could be done, and finally to doing something about it.

Once a system is implemented, it becomes the new tip of the iceberg, or starting point, for identifying and developing further improvements. Thus, while the extent of the complete application (or iceberg) may never be known, more knowledge continues to be developed.

15.1.3 Major Components of an e-Commerce System

Applications provide purposes for development. Applications must relate to the goals and objectives of both organizations and individuals. Applications involve users, tasks, and content and are served by systems that involve users, content, and tools. Existing systems and tools provide the environment into which new systems and tools will be implemented. It is essential that the development or an e-Commerce system stays focused on the set of users, tasks, content, and tools that are involved with or affected by it. Successful development will balance the needs of each of these components within each development process.

15.1.4 Competitive Advantages

There is no need for and no glory in reinventing the wheel or any other type of system. If a system exists that meets an organization's or an individual's needs, is it generally more cost effective to purchase, rent, acquire, and/or use it than to develop a new system for the same set of purposes. If a competitor has a system that meets existing needs of various users, they are likely to use it. There needs to be one or more unique reasons why these users would switch to using a newly developed system. Unique reasons for using a system provide it with competitive advantages.

Because of the continuing rapid evolution taking place on the Web, what may have provided an organization with a competitive advantage at the start of a development project may no longer be a competitive advantage when a newly developed system is ready to be implemented. Changes in what is and what no longer is a competitive advantage may necessitate changes in development projects in order to ensure that systems being developed will have some competitive advantages when they are implemented.

The development of new competitive advantages provided by systems on the Web is easily identified and copied. Organizations need to be continually monitoring the effectiveness of their existing competitive advantages and developing new ones to add to their e-Commerce systems.

15.1.5 User-Centered Development

Because e-Commerce exists within the environment known as the World Wide Web, all e-Commerce users are continually being educated to become more demanding of the systems they use. The Web is continually raising the expectations of users, in terms of both functionality and ease of use. External users have the greatest flexibility in choosing whether or not to use a system, especially where various competitive systems are readily available. External competitors are continually looking for opportunities to capture these external users. However, it also is important to meet the needs and expectations of internal users. While an organization may be able to compel its employees to use a system that it provides, their efficiency will be directly related to how well that system meets their needs.

User-centered development recognizes the importance of meeting the needs of different groups of users, as well as the needs of the organization. This is best accomplished by involving representatives of each group of users in each of the technical development processes.

15.1.6 Handling Complexity

e-Commerce involves highly complex networks of users, tasks, content, and tools. It is this complexity that allows e-Commerce to add value to the basic processing of data. e-Commerce applications and systems evolve to become increasingly complex over time. Each development process adds complexity to the knowledge about these applications and systems, as discussed above.

However, there is a limit to how much complexity that any individual (developer or user) can handle at any given time. Development processes that add complexity must also provide methods for dealing with this complexity. This is generally accomplished by focusing on increasingly small parts of an application or system. This focus goes from considering the whole application (as in Chapters 2 to 4) to detailed requirements for the application (as in Chapters 7 to 9) to how to meet these requirements (as in Chapters 10 to 12). However, the parts of an application or a system do not exist on their own. They interact with other parts and must be considered within their interactions. Developers need to consider the environment within which an application, a system, or a part thereof exists in order to ensure that the resulting system will retain its rich complexity, which creates its added value. Development methods, such as those discussed in this book, can help with the management of this complexity.

15.1.7   Evolution

The instantaneous communication provided by the Internet and the Web fuels the rapid evolution of ideas and systems. Organizations and systems that don't keep evolving are rapidly left behind.

In the real world, it is not uncommon for development to be going on simultaneously on multiple versions (just as I started developing a Cyber Supplement Web site to provide further e-Commerce development information before I completed the writing of this book). Where such overlapping development occurs, good communication and coordination between teams is essential for success. Overlapping developments must be coordinated to ensure that:

- The new portions of the system that are being added in a new development will work with all previous developments
- The users will readily accept the evolving system that results from each of these developments being implemented

Table 15-1 illustrates the possible timing of three overlapping development efforts, each conducted by a separate development team. Time periods are used in the table to illustrate the overlap between different developments. However, they are not based on any particular units of time and are not intended to specify the relative

Table 15-1   Possible overlap in the simultaneous development of multiple versions of an e-Commerce system

Time	Team 1	Team 2	Team 3
	Start of Phase 1		
1	Problem Identification 1		
2	Requirements Analysis 1		
3		*Start of Phase 2*	
4	Design 1	Problem Identification 2	
5	Construction 1	Requirements Analysis 2	*Start of Phase 3*
6		Design 2	Problem Identification 3
7	Testing 1	Construction 2	Requirements Analysis 3
8	Implementation 1		Design 3
9	Problem Identification 4	Testing 2	Construction 3
10	Requirements Analysis 4	Implementation 2	
11	Design 4	Problem Identification 5	Testing 3
12	Construction 4	Requirements Analysis 5	Implementation 3
13		Design 5	Problem Identification 6
14	Testing 4	Construction 5	Requirements Analysis 6
15	Implementation 4		Design 6

duration of any particular activity. In this example, the problems identification of a new phase commences once the requirements analysis of a previous phase has been completed and once that previous phase has determined which requirements it will focus on in its design and further development. The new phase can use this information as the basis for identifying a general purpose that it can attempt to address.

Staffing multiple development teams can involve a variety of decisions that often involve balancing what is best for the project with what is best for the organization and what is best for the individuals involved.

It is generally desirable to keep some team members throughout the complete life cycle (e.g., throughout Phase 1) to provide continuity. Remaining with a single project for an extended period of time reduces the amount of time that is spent by an individual getting acquainted with new projects. It is often beneficial to keep a number of people on a project throughout its complete life cycle.

Some individuals (such as requirements analysts, programmers, user interface designers, database designers, and so on) may be specialists in a certain development process. The organization may choose to keep these individuals working on the same development processes, moving from team to team as needed.

Some individuals may need to be added to a project team as it grows larger or to replace individuals who have left the project and/or the organization. Adding individuals during a development requires more than just assigning the individual. It will require acquainting them with the current state of the project. Where suitable development documentation exists, it can be very important in facilitating this activity. Since people may be added throughout a project, all documentation should be kept up-to-date.

15.2 SOME EVOLVING MODELS OF E-COMMERCE

Just as I was packing up the final version of this book to send it off for printing, I discovered some additional content that may help in understanding the evolving directions of e-Commerce. Although the text is the result of numerous iterations, there is always something more that could be added. Books, like e-Commerce systems, are only effective when their intended users have access to them.

Upon the discovery of this new content, a decision had to be made about what to do with it. While this content might be incorporated earlier in the book, it would need to be presented in a very different manner. As you see it here, this discussion refers to a number of topics that have been developed throughout the text. Placing these models earlier would involve making a variety of changes that would provide significant delays in getting the book to the publisher and eventually to you, the reader. While these changes may be made to a future edition, they are not feasible to incorporate at this time, earlier in this edition. This content also could have been presented in the Cyber Supplement (and will be further evolved there as newer content becomes available). However, it was decided that it could best be presented as part of Chapter 15 as an illustration of evolution. The Cyber Supplements of earlier chapters will refer to it, where appropriate.

Figure 15-1   A simple buyer-seller model of e-Commerce

15.2.1   Simple Buyer–Seller Model

Figure 15-1 illustrates the simplest model of the use of an e-Commerce system. This model only handles needs of buyers or sellers directly related to making a sale or purchase of products and/or services. Buyer and/or seller organizations may need to use additional systems in conjunction with this type of e-Commerce system.

e-Commerce using this model can expand an organization's sphere of operations on an international scale. However, it also exposes an organization to an equally wide sphere of competition. Having a Web presence might not increase or improve the conduct of business if the organization is not dealing in unique products and/or services and/or the organization does not have the best prices.

This model concentrates on a single buyer and a single seller. This model does not deal with how the seller obtains or creates the products and/or services and does not deal with how the buyer makes use of them. While a system may handle activities of a business transaction, as discussed in Chapter 8, most systems of this type focus on helping buyers identify products and place an order.

This model may either be a B2C or B2B model, and seldom would involve both. There are a number of possible ways in which systems based on this model can be constructed. In a B2C system, the business or organization typically uses an e-Commerce server, and the consumer typically uses an Internet client program. In a B2B system:

- One or both, the buyer and the seller, might use specialized edi systems
- One or both, the buyer and the seller, might use an e-Commerce server application
- Either the buyer or the seller might use an e-Commerce client

15.2.2   Intermediate Buyer–Seller–Supplier Model

Figure 15-2 illustrates an intermediate model of the use of an e-Commerce system. Simple buyer–seller systems often evolve into intermediate buyer–seller–supplier models. This model involves an organization acting between customers and suppliers of products. This organization in the middle is often referred to as a box mover. The name *box mover* comes from organizations that take orders for items (such as books, music, or electronics), buy them (usually on a just-in-time basis), and then ship them to the buyer, without even opening the box (or packaging used by the supplier) and/or without adding value to the product in any other way. Box movers are the modern evolution of catalogue shopping services. For purposes of this discussion, the organization in the middle is referred to as the seller. The *seller* can operate as an electronic organization, without any physical contact (via stores or sales representatives) with the customers. Sellers may operate an e-Commerce system of this type as

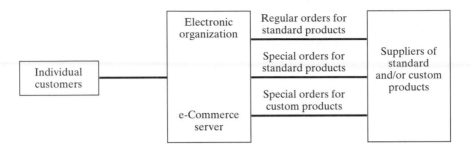

Figure 15-2 An intermediate buyer–seller–supplier model of e-Commerce

a branch of a larger organization that also has local stores. However, where such occurs, the electronic branch is generally treated as a separate organization on its own, which may just happen to be a branch or division of some larger organization.

The main advantages of these types of e-Commerce organizations are their combination of low prices (in return for low services) and potentially wide selection (since they are often not associated with any particular supplier). They perform a similar function to the wholesales of past times and are often vulnerable to being squeezed out of the market by direct sales by suppliers to customers if they do not provide additional value for the customers. This value can often be provided by combining services, not readily available from the suppliers, with products to provide solutions for the customers, instead of just selling them products. The most successful sellers often pioneer unique methods of doing business.

This model recognizes that there are three significantly different types of interactions that may occur with a supplier of a product and/or service. It doesn't limit the seller to just those products and/or services that it currently possesses. By adding special orders for standard products, it may avoid lost sales as long as the customer is willing to wait long enough to receive them. By adding orders for custom products it may further extend its selection of products and services, beyond those readily available from most competitors.

The selling organization requires an e-Commerce server that is available to the customers via the Internet and that can communicate with suppliers either via the Internet or via dedicated edi connections. Customers will interact via Internet clients. Suppliers may interact via a number of technologies, ranging from e-mail to e-Commerce servers to dedicated edi.

15.2.3 The Chain Store Model

Figure 15-3 illustrates an advanced model of the use of an e-Commerce system involving a chain of stores that is controlled from their head office. Intermediate buyer–seller–supplier models often evolve into chain store models when an organization recognizes the benefits of integrating an e-Commerce branch within the over-

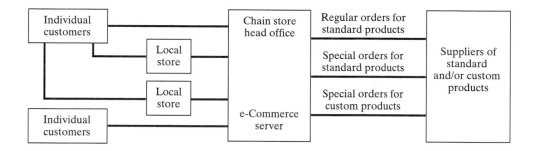

Figure 15-3   An advanced chain store based model of e-Commerce

all operations of the organization. In this model, the head office makes all organizational decisions and controls all e-Commerce activities via its e-Commerce server.

This model adds local presence while providing customers with three options for shopping. Customers can shop on their own at a local store or via the Internet, or via the Web in the store with the assistance of sales clerks. Service can be provided both via the local store and via the Internet.

This model provides significant benefits to customers by making it easier for them to get what they want. The Internet can also help customers by identifying the closest local store that has the desired product, so that the customer could inspect and purchase it in person, if desired. In addition to serving individual customers, the e-Commerce server can provide special services to meet the special needs of organizational customers.

This model provides significant benefits to the overall e-Commerce sales organization by helping to optimize the sales of the products it has distributed across a number of stores while also obtaining additional customers via the Internet.

The importance of maintaining a local presence and providing local service ensures the survival of local stores, even if their role within the organization shifts from that of a traditional local store. This model may increase the sales of individual stores by:

- Directing customers wishing to buy products in person to their location
- Allowing them to sell products that they don't currently have but that the head office can transfer to them from another store or can acquire for them via a special order from a supplier

In addition to requiring an e-Commerce server in the head office, each store needs to have its sales stations connected on-line with this server to keep all inventory records up-to-date.

15.2.4   The Cooperative Model

Figure 15-4 illustrates an advanced model of the use of an e-Commerce system involving a number of cooperating stores making use of some centralized e-Commerce services.

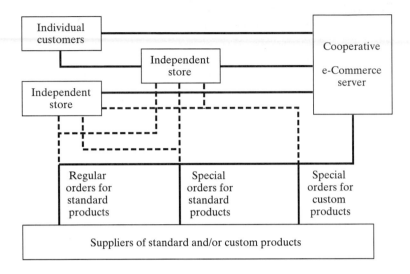

Figure 15-4 An advanced cooperative based model of e-Commerce

This model could be developed by:

- A number of small, independent stores or other organizations that can band together in cooperatives to compete with large chain store type organizations
- A single seller to enlist the assistance of other similar sellers, who are not seen as a competitive threat, in a combined e-Commerce effort
- A chain store organization that recognizes the benefits of providing individual stores with autonomy while supporting them via e-Commerce

This model adds the ability for independent stores to have the option of ordering products directly from suppliers or by using the combined buying power of the cooperative. It focuses on the services that they receive from the e-Commerce server as well as those services they provide to their customers.

The independent stores and the cooperative typically each have their own e-Commerce servers that interact with one another in an organization to organization manner. The particular functions to be performed by each server are subject to negotiation between the independent stores and the cooperative. It is not necessary in this model that all independent stores make use of the same servers or that they each use all the same functions of the cooperative's server.

15.3   CONCLUSIONS AND NEW BEGINNINGS

This book has identified many of the questions and provided examples of a few of the many possible answers relating to developing e-Commerce systems. The Cyber Supplement Web site accompanying the book adds more questions and more answers. However, the supply of interesting questions and answers is limitless and grows constantly with the evolving nature of e-Commerce. This evolution continues to provide new opportunities for all who look for both the questions and the answers. The challenge is to know when to stop. But, of course, if you stop you will eventually lose. Thus, instead of stopping, you must pause just long enough to implement a product (either a new version of a system or, in my case, this book) and then you must start to work on the next version or a supplement to it (such as the Cyber Supplement). I'll be making regular updates to the Cyber Supplement to help you keep up-to-date, until the next version of this book comes out, and then I'll start all over again from wherever I am. To help with this task, I invite you to send in your suggestions of what to add.

In any case, e-Commerce development must evolve. See you at the Web site!

Glossary

acceptance testing A basic form of validation that involves getting the users to accept that the current stage of development meets their requirements.

accessibility According to ISO DTS 16071,[1] "The usability of a product, service, environment or facility by people with the widest range of capabilities." It further notes that, "Although 'accessibility' typically addresses users who have a disability, the concept is not limited to disability issues."

activities

- Are often interchangeable in the achievement of some desired accomplishment
- Tend to be thought of as more specific in nature
- Tend to occur over short and often well-defined periods of time
- Are often discussed in terms of the action they involve
- May be combined to accomplish various processes

adaptive-determined navigation Occurs where the navigation choices available are determined by the system based on the content and some combination of an individual's history, an individual's personal characteristics, a group's social history, and/or a group's characteristics.

adjustments The outputs of an object that are intended to influence the operations of some object. The object to be influenced or controlled can be the same or a different object.

advanced compensation systems Systems that involve the use of information systems to support a variety of compensation schemes that can be customized to individual employees.

aggregations Systems that involve a number of parts of similar and/or different types of objects.

algorithm A set of formal rules for processing data or its derivatives.
- Procedures are verbal algorithms used by people to guide the conduct of operations within an organization.
- Computer programs are formalized algorithms that control the operations of computer systems.

applet A small application program downloaded from a server and run by a client.

application Some purpose or set of purposes that can be fulfilled by using (applying) some system (in some manner).

assistive technologies Technologies that take information intended for presentation via one medium (e.g., displayed text) and present in another media (e.g., voice output).

association Connects two objects based on some linkage between them. It may be referred to by the name of the characteristic that provides the basis for the association (e.g., "parent-child" relation).

attributes These store the data (or other content) that describe an object. The value of some attributes may change from time to time, reflecting the current state of the object. Attributes provide the building blocks for records, files (sets of records), and databases. Various types of attributes include audit attributes, control attributes, descriptive attributes, key attributes, and security attributes.

audit attributes Attributes that are automatically added to a record to provide an audit trail of interactions with the record.

auditing support systems Involve sophisticated tools for in-house and for independent auditing of organizations in a range of areas, including finances, management, and security.

automatic navigation Occurs where content is presented by the system without the user's input.

business modeling Modeling that involves developing and analyzing models of the interactions of significant parts of an organization and potentially of other entities with which parts of the organization interact.

business transaction According to ISO 14662,[2] "A predefined set of activities and/or processes of organizations which is initiated by an organization to accomplish an explicitly shared business goal and terminated upon one of the agreed conclusions by all the involved organizations although some of the recognition may be implicit."

business transaction actualization A transaction in which information is exchanged in order to realize a mutually agreed upon financial transaction. Business transaction actualization includes the exchange of payments for goods and/or services.

business transaction identification A transaction in which information is exchanged about the goods, services, and/or participants in the transaction.

business transaction negotiation An exchange of information in order to achieve an explicit, mutually understood and agreed upon realization of a financial transaction along with any applicable terms and conditions.

business transaction planning Exchange of information between the buyer and seller to help them decide on what actions to take to acquire or sell a good or service.

business transaction post-actualization More commonly known as servicing, is where information is exchanged relating to follow-up activities that take place after a good or service is delivered.

challenges These exist where significant improvements should be made in a development or to a system. Since no development or system is ever perfect, there are always possible improvements.

classes An abstract means of organizing similar objects in order to treat them in a consistent, predetermined manner. Since classes are abstractions of the real world, there is often no readily agreed-on, textbook-like solution to identifying the best set of classes to use.

client A system that is used directly by users to accomplish some application.

command languages Organizations of commands that involve specifically defined syntactic structures and semantic meanings.

commands Words, abbreviations, or strings of words that a user can use to make a request of the system.

communication server A gateway between various networks of computers.

competitive analysis/benchmarking Involves obtaining corporate intelligence (which isn't necessarily readily available) about one's competitors, using this intelligence to predict their likely corporate strategies, and then determining a corporate strategy to match or beat theirs.

composite media object According to ISO 14915-2, "either a single media object that is used on its own or a combination of media objects which are used together and presented synchronized with one another and/or automatically linked to one another."

compositions Aggregations where the parts, once created, exist only because they are part of the whole.

computed link A temporary link that is created on demand between two locations in the system and where the location that it is linked to is dynamically determined based on the state and/or history of the system and where the link remains available only while needed (e.g., the links created in the results of a search).

computer-aided software engineering (CASE) Used to describe a wide variety of analysis, design, and development tools that are intended to help software developers develop good systems.

conformity with user expectations According to ISO 9241-10,[3] a dialogue that "is consistent and corresponds to the user characteristics, such as task knowledge, education and experience, and to commonly accepted conventions."

content All the material that is processed and presented by an e-Commerce system, regardless of how it is processed or presented.

content chunk According to ISO 14915-2,[4] "a unit of content that meets the needs of some specific task. A content chunk can also meet the needs of one or more tasks for one or more users, either by itself or in combination with other content chunks."

control A type of processing that is intended to analyze feedback and to produce adjustments that will influence the operations of an object. A **control** is "an object, often analogous to physical controls, which allows a user to take some action which manipulates data, other objects, or their attributes" according to ISO 14915-2.[5]

control attributes Attributes that are used to store the current state of processing of a record or the current ability to perform certain types of processing to the record.

control flow design Design of the decision logic that leads from one operation or processing routine to another.

controllability According to ISO 9241-10,[6] "Controllability occurs when the user is able to initiate and control the direction and pace of the interaction until the point at which the goal has been met."

copyright Protects ownership and copying of the artistic composition of a work.

critical path method (CPM) A common technique for monitoring progress based on analyzing a networked schedule of activities, linked to their prerequisites (also referred to as PERT/CPM).

cross-elasticity Results from increases in the demand for one product or service causing a corresponding decrease in the demand for other products and/or services.

custom (built) system A unique system that has been constructed from basic tools and components to meet a specific analysis and design.

customized marketing The use of individual customer profiles (refer to customer profiling) in identifying opportunities for customized offers that will be of particular interest to individual consumers, communicating these opportunities to the consumers, and following up on them, as appropriate. Customized marketing is generally implemented as a part of an *e-Business* application.

customized system A system that has been constructed by selecting, arranging and modifying a set of reusable objects (or other program parts) often provided by a tool set or that has been constructed by significantly modifying the functioning of an existing system.

custom manufacturing A type of *just-in-time* activity that involves the optimization allocation and scheduling of various internal and external resources (including people, equipment, materials, and facilities) to efficiently meet rapidly changing needs.

cut over Occurs where a new system is put in actual use and the old system is removed at the same time.

data The raw facts that are the basis for most (and probably all) systems of interest to us. Data can be stored, transmitted, and presented in an infinite variety of forms and formats, including numbers, words, pictures, sounds, and electronic pulses.

data availability The ability to access data when they are needed by a user or by a system.

database A collection of files used to support one or more applications.

database evolvability The potential to make changes to the database to meet changing needs.

data integrity The correctness, protection, and security of data or of a database.

data processing systems (DPS) Systems that process various accounting transactions for an organization. They are designed for operational level workers and concentrate more on the processing of raw data than the production of information.

data sharability The ability to share data between applications and between users on a need to know basis.

data storage Internal area of an object in which it may store information that it has produced. The object can then recall this information at a later time for use in a similar manner to using information that it might be input from some external source.

decision tree An illustration of the different possible results from different sets of answers to a series of questions or decision points.

default A value that is assumed to be reasonable and is provided by the system to assist a user in making requests of the system, but which is subject to confirmation or change by a user.

deliverables The various products of development that are given to the owners and/or users of the system. The format of a deliverable is not as important as the information it contains. While most deliverables are tangible, all deliverables are clearly recognizable by both users and developers.

descriptive attributes Attributes that contain the object content, which is relevant to the application.

dialogue According to ISO 9241-10,[7] a set of interactions "between a user and a system to achieve a particular goal."

direct manipulation A technique that gives the user the impression of acting directly on objects within the system.

direct users Those users who use a system by themselves.

domain name A logical name that is used on the Internet to identify a computer.

domain name server (DNS) A special system on the Internet that provides a cross-reference between logical (domain name) Internet addresses and physical (Internet Protocol/IP) Internet addresses.

dynamic, real-time business performance control Involves tracking the time and costs of production from marketing through scheduling, production, and delivery to the consumer to assist in both the organizational management of these processes and the tactical evaluation and redesign of affected organizational processes and units.

e-Brokerage A specialized type of *e-Business* where the main business function of the organization is to bring buyers and sellers together.

e-Business Any type(s) of business (between an organization and its customers) conducted via the Internet. This typically involves setting up "virtual businesses" or "electronic storefronts" on the World Wide Web.

e-Commerce A generic term that means many things to many people. e-Commerce generally refers to commerce applications that are performed with the assistance of computers and (usually) the Internet.

e-Commerce client A system that is used to conduct e-Commerce for a user with one or more e-Commerce servers.

e-Commerce server A system that is used by an organization to make e-Commerce services available to a number of clients.

economic feasibility Consideration of whether or not an organization should expend the resources necessary to develop a system. Economic feasibility is different from profitability in that some systems might be economically feasible without being profitable (such as systems required by government legislation).

electronic data integration (edi) systems Legacy systems that were developed to handle what is now e-Commerce prior to the use of the Web.

electronic support for non-profit (or "not for profit") organizations Setting up of Web sites that support interfacing between a non-profit organization, its various executives, its general membership, and its potential members.

electronic data interchange (edi) "The automated exchange of any predefined and structured data for business purposes among information systems of two or more organizations."[8]

enterprise-wide systems integration Developing or redeveloping an organization's information infrastructure in a manner that optimizes the benefits to the whole organization rather than to individual parts of the organization.

error tolerance According to ISO 9241-10,[9] "A dialogue is **error-tolerant** if, despite evident errors in input, the intended result may be achieved with either no or minimal corrective action by the user."

external users Users who are not employed by or responsible to (as with members of a nonprofit group) the organization, which controls the e-Commerce system, regardless of whether or not they use the system externally to the organization's facilities.

extranet An extended intranet that makes use of encryption and similar security techniques to act similar to an intranet for members who have to communicate with each other over the Internet.

feasibility The possibility that a system can be acquired or developed and used for some set of purposes within some environment or set of environments.

feedback A specialized type of output that is used as an input to determine how the object producing it is operating.

file A collection of similar records that may be used individually or together.

file server Provides storage of and access to central databases and program files for one or more computers to which it is attached either directly or via a network.

financial transaction A transaction that involves data relating to some exchange of money and/or products or services with some monetary value.

firewall A system that is used to separate part of a network, which is within the firewall, (such as a local area network or an individual computer) from the remainder of the network, which is outside the firewall. A firewall can control who has access to systems on the other side of the firewall and what requests and data can be sent across the firewall.

1st normal form Eliminates repeating groups within a record by placing them in separate records with composite record keys that include the record key of the original record.

fixed link A permanent link between two locations in the system that can be activated at any time (most links in current systems are fixed links).

form According to ISO 9241-17,[10] "a structured display with labelled fields that the user reads, fills in, selects entries for (e.g., through choice buttons or radio buttons), or modifies." NOTE: Various programming languages and systems may have alternate definitions of forms.

frames A programming technique that allows the combination of multiple presentation segments (implemented as separate Web pages) to be presented to a user as a single, composite Web page.

function Within a computer program, acts as a data value as the result of its processing.

generalization-specialization relationships Often referred to just as the generalization or the "IS-A" relationship. **Generalizations** exist where one class of objects also IS-A complete example of another class of objects. For example, a square IS-A rectangle.

hardware server An individual hardware device that performs a specific function or a set of functions within a client-server environment. Hardware servers include communications servers, file servers, printing servers, processing servers, and terminal servers.

hierarchical decomposition Use of various strategies to divide and further subdivide complex operations to the level of very simple processing routines, each of which performs only a single procedure or function.

hierarchical structure Organization of a set of objects or activities in a tree-like manner where each component (object or activity) is associated (at most) with one higher-level component but may be associated with multiple lower-level components.

high-level design Similar to a plan for a design. It identifies what will have to be designed in detail later in the development. It does this by identifying the major components that need to be designed and any overall design approaches and guidelines that will be used throughout the design.

human resource planning and management Optimizing the placement of people within an organization.

implementation period The period of time during which the new system is loaded with data and put into regular use and that lasts until any old systems are replaced.

index file A file that exists to assist in accessing records in one file that have some relationship with records in another file.

indirect users Users who have other users directly interact with a system on their behalf.

information A set of selected or summarized data that is useful for making some decision.

information provider A person who creates content that will be used publicly in an application, whether or not the content was created expressly for the application. This concept does not include individuals, such as customers, who enter orders or other types of private content into a system.

information recipient Any person who may make use of the content of a system. Some users may act as both information providers and information recipients.

information utilities A specialized type of *e-Business* whose main activities include the obtaining, trading, selling, and giving away of information (including advertising).

inputs Defined in terms of the object that receives them and exist regardless of the object that generates them. Data that an object receives can be considered to be an **input** if the object is capable of recognizing and acting upon receiving it. Data that an object does not recognize is not considered to be an input. Data that an object recognizes and refuses may be considered an invalid input. Both users and computer systems receive and process a large variety of inputs. Inputs may contain data and/or requests for the object to take some action.

instances Particular examples of objects that belong to some class.

intellectual property Those types of information whose ownership is protected by national and international laws and treaties.

internal users Those users who are not employed by or responsible to (as with members of a nonprofit group) the organization, which controls the e-Commerce system, regardless of whether or not they use the system externally to the organization's facilities.

internet client program A program that provides general Internet accessing capabilities to support the running of client programs that interact across the Internet with one or more server programs.

internet domain names Used to establish logical connections to individual computers including those hosting Web sites.

Internet protocol (IP) address The unique address used internally by the Internet to identify computers that are connected to it.

Internet service provider (ISP) An organization that possesses IP addresses and rents them along with Internet connection services to individuals and organizations that wish to connect to the Internet.

intranet An internal portion of the Internet that is a local area network designed for the exclusive use by its members and that is connected to the Internet via a firewall.

iteration The revising of the results of any development process when new information makes this revision desirable.

jurisdiction "A distinct legal and regulatory framework which places constraints on the global marketplace and in doing so often defines/establishes a local market."[11]

just-in-time A business strategy involving deferring acquisitions or development of resources (material, product, and people resources) until they are needed.

key attributes Attributes that can be used individually or in combination to provide a unique record key that can be used to identify a record.

knowledge A combination of information and rules for how to use the information. Correct knowledge provides individuals or systems the basis to make "correct" decisions.

learning Occurs when an object stores knowledge that it can use to improve its future processing (including its future controlling). This knowledge may have resulted from processing/control done by the object or from inputs/adjustments into the object.

legacy systems Systems that are already in use by an organization that continue to fulfill an important need within the organization but that include out-dated and/or non-standard technologies that do not readily integrate with current technologies.

license agreements Agreements that grant various restricted rights of copying and/or use by particular contacts between the provider of the content and the user of the content.

life cycle A concept that unifies all the phases of a system's "life" from its start (the identification of a need), through the development of a system, its actual use to solve the problem, up to its end (its eventual replacement). All systems have a life cycle.

linear structure A structure that organizes a set of objects or activities in a sequence where each component (object or activity) is associated (at most) with one previous component and one following component.

link A control that allows the user to navigate a connection among or within media. Links may be activated by an action of the system or the user. There are a number of types of links defined by ISO 14915-2,[12] which include fixed links, temporal links, computed links, and user-defined links.

local area network Used to connect hardware servers within a corporate building or campus of closely related buildings.

localization Modification of transactions to meet a range of specific needs of a user, including jurisdictional, linguistic and cultural, sectorial, human rights, and consumer rights.

logistical management of commodity suppliers A specialized case of *on-line procurement* that involves the development of systems by large consumers to manage the ongoing procurement and delivery scheduling of commodities.

management information systems Systems that analyze data (largely gathered from data processing activities or systems) to provide information that can be used in the ongoing management of an organization.

markup languages Languages composed of various tags that are used to identify treatments that an Internet client is intended to perform on selected portions of a Web page.

master file A file that generally stores the most important and most general data about objects. Master files often contain master records that are relevant throughout the life of a system.

master record A record describing an entity that may be permanently relevant through a considerable portion of the life of a system (such as a customer record or a product record).

matrix management support Management and optimization of the allocation of human and other resources to various projects in matrix-style organizations.

media The various unique technologies that are used to input and/or output between a user and a computer.

media object A component of a presentation segment that is implemented by an object implemented by a single media type.

menu Any set of options presented by the system from which the user can make a selection to be used as input to the system.

method A particular way of accomplishing a process. People may be able to choose between various methods that all could be used for a process. The choice of method often involves consideration of:

- The individual's experience and confidence with each of the methods
- The available tools and support for each of the methods
- The particular advantages and disadvantages of the methods
- The various circumstances in which the method will be used
- Constraints (including time, money, and other resources) on the selection and use of the methods

methodology According to Norman,[13] "the packaging of methods and techniques together. The way something gets done. The purpose of a methodology is to promote a certain problem-solving strategy by preselecting the methods and techniques to be used."

mobile computing Involves a range of devices with wireless access to the Internet. Mobile computing devices include specially equipped notebook and handheld computers.

multi-dimensional profitability tracking and analysis Tracking and managing of the costs of production and of servicing customers to focus on the most profitable mixes of products, product lines, territories, and even individual customers.

navigation The user's movement between media objects. There is a range of navigation techniques defined by ISO 14915-2,[14] which include automatic navigation, predetermined navigation, user-determined navigation, and adaptive navigation.

network structure A structure that organizes a set of objects or activities in an interconnected manner where each component (object or activity) may be associated with multiple other components.

normalization A technique for designing an optimal structure of internal data files and records to meet the processing needs of an application. There are three major stages of normalization: 1st normal form, 2nd normal form, and 3rd normal form.

object A real thing or concept that people deal with in their everyday life. Most people should recognize and agree upon the recognition of most objects.

object library See **tool set.**

on-line procurement Use of the Internet to improve the flexibility in choosing vendors and to reduce the financial and time costs in an organization's procurements of various materials, products, and/or services.

operation An action conducted by an object that causes some change to its attributes or to its environment.

operational feasibility Whether or not the proposed system will meet the needs of its various users and other stakeholders, be accepted by them, and be used.

operational reliability The ability to continue operating satisfactorily under changing conditions, including conditions that may have not been anticipated.

opportunities Exist where significant additions should be made in a development or to a system.

organization A type of system that involves people, information, and other types of resources that work together to achieve a set of organizational goals (purposes).

organizational planning and rationalization Identification of different users of common information and people performing similar tasks and restructuring the organization (using information engineering techniques) to increase the efficiency of the organization.

outputs Whatever an object produces, whether or not they are useful to any other object. Both users and computer systems produce a large variety of outputs. Communication between users and computers is successful only where the output of one object is a valid input of the other object.

overall feasibility Determined by considering the combined operational, technical, and economic feasibilities. It is based on the most pessimistic evaluation from any of its constituents. If a system is infeasible in any manner, then it is overall infeasible. A system is only feasible if it is feasible operationally, technically, and economically.

package (or packaged) software See **turnkey system.**

"parallel" implementation Occurs where a system is put in actual use for some time before the old system is removed.

patent Protects ownership of technical works and prohibits a wide range of similar works, including those produced by deliberate "reverse engineering."

pervasive development processes Processes that need to be performed throughout the systems development life cycle.

pervasive technical processes Processes that are used in the development of a system at various points throughout the systems development life cycle.

"phased implementation" Occurs where individual portions of the system, such as certain user groups, are implemented at different times. Phased implementations always involve some aspects of parallel implementations and may involve aspects of cut overs.

platform Some combination of hardware and software that is used to allow the running of an application program.

platform dependencies These result from differences in the operation or lack thereof of an application program that is caused by attempting to run it on different platforms.

platform independence Created where the user does not experience differences that may exist due to platform dependencies.

post-implementation period The period after a new system has been officially implemented and up until the implementation has been fully accepted by all of its users.

predetermined navigation Occurs where the user has only one choice where to go next, but where the user has control over when to go to this next content.

pre-implementation period The period leading up to the time when a new system is completely implemented.

presentation segment According to ISO 14915-2,[15] "provides the physical implementation of one or more content chunks as part of an application." Typical examples of presentation segments include pages, panels, windows, boxes.

primary information provider A person or group who may have some control over the content and/or design of the system and/or have particular tasks they want the system to accomplish.

print server Provides printing for one or more computers to which it is attached either directly or via a network.

privacy Refers to various aspects of the protection of personal information.

procedure Within a computer program, it changes data value(s) in some data structure as the result of its processing.

processes
- Are required in order to achieve some desired accomplishment
- Tend to be thought of as more general in nature
- Tend to occur over long and often undefined periods of time
- Are often discussed in terms of the accomplishments they are intended to produce
- May be accomplished by various different activities

processing Analysis, manipulation, transformation, use, and/or storage of information. Processing includes validating the contents of inputs, making decisions based on input data and program logic, and taking actions based on these decisions. Many objects (including people, computer systems, and a variety of other machines) are capable of processing information.

processing routine logic design The actual design of the routines that will perform the processing.

processing server A server that runs one or more application programs for one or more terminal servers to which it is attached either directly or via a network.

project processes Those processes necessary to manage a development project.

prompt An indication output by a system that the system is ready to accept the entry of a command from the user.

prototype A mock-up of a system that can be used to identify requirements for a system and to design specific details of a system. Prototypes are intentionally incomplete models of a proposed or an existing system. Prototypes are demonstration vehicles intended to elicit comments from those who look at and/or interact with them.

quality When used as a noun, it refers to some attribute or feature of a thing without regard to any evaluation of whether that attribute is good or bad. Systems may be described in terms of an infinite number of noun qualities. When **quality** is used as an adjective, it refers to a favorable evaluation of the thing to which it refers. There are an infinite number of bases for evaluating adjectival qualities. Despite all being favorable, some of the types of adjectival quality do not have an objective basis. The quality of a given object may not be quantifiable without relating it to the quality of some other object. While it would be nice for a system to have all kinds of qualities, (both noun and adjectival) achieving these qualities could become very expensive. While this may suggest a need to study the feasibility of each type of quality, there are some specific concerns that we should recognize as being associated with expectations of quality, which will be discussed in this chapter.

record Some collection of attributes that describes some entity or event.

redundancy Occurs where multiple copies of a set of data can lead to incompatibilities when updates are made to only some of these copies.

relationships Meaningful connections between objects. There are three main relationships that are central to object-oriented development: generalization-specialization relationships, association relationships, and whole-part relationships.

repository A database that is used to store and retrieve various types of software system development information.

requirements Specifications or descriptions of the needs and wants of users and stakeholders that are intended to be met by the system that is being developed. There are various types of requirements, including:

- Task requirements (also referred to as logical requirements)—which specify what needs to be done
- Usability requirements (also referred to as physical requirements)—which specify how it needs to be done.

scenario A step-by-step description of one possible way of accomplishing a task with a certain set of operations and attributes. Scenarios may encompass a whole series of events leading to the accomplishment of some purpose.

secondary file A file that generally stores data (such as transaction records) that relate to one or more master records.

secondary information providers Providers who are not able to control how information they have created is used. They may not even know where or how it is being used.

2nd normal form Separates data that is fully functionally dependent on a record key from additional data that may depend on only part of the record key.

security attribute A particular type of control attribute used to control access to the record.

self-descriptive According to ISO 9241-10,[16] "A dialogue is self-descriptive when each dialogue step is immediately comprehensible through feedback from

the system or is explained to the user on request."

server A system that provides services to a number of client systems.

stakeholders People who:

- Are affected by the existence of a system, whether or not they are users of the system, (i.e., they have a stake in the outcome of the system)
- The organization cares about, or should care about, regarding how the system might affect them

states Exist where different combinations of attributes can lead the same input to be processed in different manners.

state transition diagram An illustration of the various potential outcomes of an event or sequence of events where the outcomes of an event are dependent on the state in which the event occurs.

strategic information systems Analyze combinations of internal and external information in an attempt to forecast the success of potential future operations of an organization.

suitability for individualization According to ISO 9241-10,[17] "A dialogue is **capable of individualization** when the interface software can be modified to suit the task needs, individual preferences and skills of the user."

suitability for learning According to ISO 9241-10,[18] "A dialogue is **suitable for learning** when it supports and guides the user in learning to use the system."

suitability for the task According to ISO 9241-10,[19] "A dialogue is **suitable for a task** when it supports the user in the effective and efficient completion of the task."

supplier-customer systems integration Generally involves development of complimentary systems to be used by suppliers (*e-Business*) and their customers (*on-line procurement*) to handle automatic ordering and other regular business transactions.

support for distributed workers Involves helping managers and other support personnel to support workers who are located at a variety of different locations other than where the manager or support person is located.

system An organized collection of objects that fulfill some purpose or set of purposes.

tag A unique sequence of characters that is placed at the beginning and end of a selected portion of a Web page that is used to specify a particular treatment it is intended to receive.

task A specific (usually work-related) accomplishment of a person (or group of persons). Tasks accomplish work and/or personal objectives. Applications are typically composed of a number of related tasks that work toward accomplishing major organizational goals. Tasks define what has to be accomplished without dealing with how it will be accomplished. Most tasks can be accomplished in a number of ways, using various tools and/or procedures.

task analysis A process where developers and users (and also other stakeholders, where appropriate) work together to identify possible improvements to a set of *tools* used by different *users* to perform *tasks* on sets of *content.*

technical feasibility Whether or not an e-Commerce application can be constructed in a suitable manner.

temporal link A permanent link between two locations in the system that is only available at certain times (e.g., a link used to access information that is only relevant during a portion of a movie).

terminal server A physical system with which a user interacts directly via a variety of input and output devices such as displays, keyboards, or mice. Terminal servers can include personal computers, laptop computers, handheld computers, and a variety of other computing devices.

3rd normal form Removes (redundant) nonkey attributes, which are based on other nonkey attributes.

thumbnail A small picture, often comparable in size to the size of a typical control icon, which is intended to provide recognition of some object or concept.

tools Any of the many things (computerized or noncomputerized) that help a user accomplish some task (or set of tasks).

tool sets Collections of reusable programming parts (referred to by various names, such as routines, fragments, objects) (also known as toolkits or object libraries).

trademark Protects ownership of words and images associated with an organization and its goods and/or services.

transaction record A record of an event in the life of one or more entities (such as a sales record or a payment record) that is most relevant to users of a system only during a short period of time.

treatment Any action that is planned to help people deal with the effects of an implementation.

turnkey systems Commercially available software packages based on the metaphor of a person just needing to know how to turn a key to start driving a car. They are intended to be used with little or no basic changes to their operations. Turnkey systems are also referred to as package (or packaged) software.

ubiquitous computing The potential for computing to be integrated into a variety of devices beyond the traditional concept of a personal computer.

universal accessibility The issues involved in providing accessibility that encompass all potential users in all situations.

user-defined link A fixed or temporal link created by a user during the use of an application that is intended to supplement the links created by the system's developers (e.g., bookmarks are user-defined fixed links).

user-determined navigation Occurs where the user can choose which content to go to by selecting from a number of options.

users All the people and/or organizations who are involved with accomplishing part or all of an application. Users do something for a system and/or have something done for them by a system, whether they directly interact with the system or interact with it via intermediaries. See also **external users, internal users, stakeholders.**

validation A test of the accuracy and completeness of the specifications of a system as a model what is needed. Pressman[20] states that "validation refers to a different set of activities that ensure that the software has been built to a traceable set of customer requirements." He also refers to Boehm's[21] statement that validation involves answering the question, "Are we building the right product?"

value-added The synergistic effect of a system being of greater value than the sum of the individual values of its components.

verification A test of the accuracy and completeness of the system and its operations. Pressman[22] states that, "**Verification** refers to the set of activities that ensure that software correctly implements a specific function." He also refers to Boehm's statement[23] that verification involves answering the question, "Are we building the product right?"

whole-part relationship A special type of association that connects parts of an object with the whole object. Parts are complete objects on their own as well as parts of larger objects. As separate objects they have their own attributes and operations. Parts are included as attributes of the class that represents the whole.

wide area network A network that connects systems and or local area networks with each other over long distances. The Internet is the most famous wide area network.

wisdom Something we should all strive for; however, it is as yet undefined in information processing. It can be loosely defined as the ability to apply knowledge appropriately. It allows a person or a system to adapt decisions to a particular context.

REFERENCES

[1] "International Organization for Standardization," ISO Draft Technical Specification 16071, Ergonomics of Human System Interaction—Guidance on Accessibility for Human-Computer Interfaces, 2000.

[2] ISO/IEC International Standard 14662, Information Technologies—Open-edi Reference Model, 1997.

[3] Ibid.

[4] "International Organization for Standardization," ISO Committee Draft 14915-2, Software Ergonomics for Multimedia User Interfaces: Multimedia Control and Navigation, 2000.

[5] Ibid.

[6] Ibid.

[7] ISO/IEC International Standard 14662, Information Technologies—Open-edi Reference Model, 1997.

[8] "International Organization for Standardization," ISO International Standard 9241-10, Ergonomic Requirements for Office Work with Visual Display Terminals (VDTs): Dialogue Principles, 1996.

[9] "International Organization for Standardization," ISO International Standard 9241-10, Ergonomic Requirements for Office Work with Visual Display Terminals (VDTs): Dialogue Principles, 1996.

[10] "International Organization for Standardization," ISO International Standard 9241-17, Ergonomic Requirements for Office Work with Visual Display Terminals (VDTs): Form Fill Dialogues, 1998.

[11] ISO/IEC Information Technology Business Team on Electronic Commerce, Work on Electronic Commerce Standardization to be Initiated, 1998.

[12] Ibid.

[13] R. J. Norman, *Object-Oriented Systems Analysis and Design* (Upper Saddle River, NJ, Prentice Hall, 1996).

[14] Ibid.

[15] Ibid.

[16] Ibid.

[17] Ibid.

[18] Ibid.

[19] Ibid.

[20] Ibid.

[21] Ibid.

[22] R.S. Pressman, *Software Engineering: A Practitioner's Approach,* 4th ed. (New York, NY, McGraw-Hill, 1997).

[23] B. Boehm, *Software Engineering Economics* (Englewood Cliffs, NJ, Prentice-Hall, 1981).

Index